THE WAY WE WORK

Getting to Know the Amazing Human Body

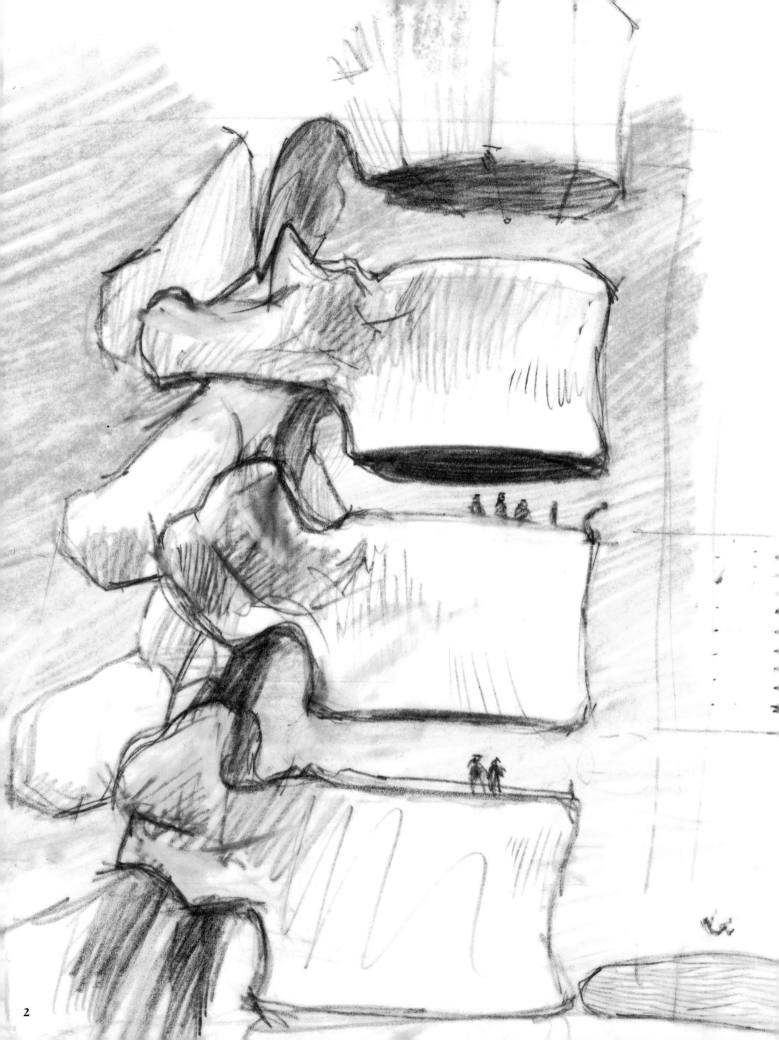

THE
WAY
WE
WORK

Getting to Know the Amazing Human Body

DAVID MACAULAY

WITH RICHARD WALKER

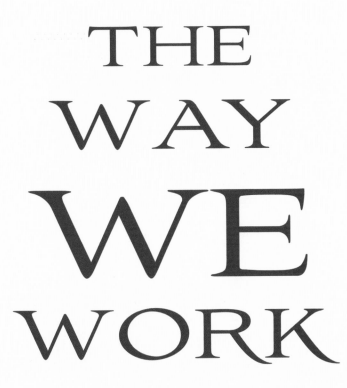

Houghton Mifflin Company Boston 2008

Walter Lorraine Books

A Walter Lorraine Book

www.houghtonmifflinbooks.com

The text of this book is set in Dante.

The illustrations are pencil and watercolor.

Library of Congress Cataloging-in-Publication Data

Macaulay, David.
The way we work : getting to know the amazing human body /
written and illustrated by David Macaulay ; With Richard Walker.
p. cm.
ISBN 978-0-618-23378-6
1. Human physiology—Juvenile literature. 2. Body, Human—Juvenile literature.
I. Walker, Richard, 1951– II. Title.
QP37.M28 2008
612—dc22
2008025109

Manufactured in the United States of America

RRD 10 9 8 7 6 5 4 3 2 1

Acknowledgments

In addition to my friends at HMCo who have once again pulled all the bits and pieces together to produce the book you're holding, and my coauthor Richard Walker, without whose help there would never have been enough bits and pieces, at least in this lifetime, I would like to thank the following:

Anne Gilroy—a clinical anatomist who over four long years did everything in her power to keep me on some kind of track as I bounced, like a kid in a candy store, from one aspect of human physiology to another.

Dr. Lois Smith—professor of ophthalmology, whose kindness is matched only by her astounding knowledge of everything having to do with anything.

John Lewis—for the most exciting and illuminating cellular breakfast conversations I've ever had.

Dr. Eric Walsh—hand man and orthopedic trauma surgeon, whose enthusiasm for this project from the beginning helped keep it rolling.

Dr. Dana Andersen—teacher and surgeon, who by luring me into his operating room gave me a first-hand look inside a living body under attack as he painstakingly worked to win the battle.

Dr. Dan O'Neill—the family gastroenterologist, for his careful and enthusiastic reading of the very first section to be laid out and the last one to be drawn.

Professor Erik Erikson—whose infectious zeal for understanding the way the body works help set me off on this journey in the first place.

My neighbors **Professor Bernard Trumpower** and **Dr. Mary-Margaret Andrews**—who generously read over parts of the book in progress and offered invaluable comments. If any mistakes have crept back in it was in spite of their and everyone else's best efforts.

James and Joan Macaulay—my ever-supportive parents, who willingly took on the reading of each new section as it staggered out of the studio.

Helen Bing—chair of my fan club and ardent supporter of all my efforts from wherever in the world she may happen to be.

The MacArthur Foundation—which during the last year of the project kept food on the table and the lights on as work continued well beyond the limits of any sensible business model.

And **Ruthie**—not only my amazingly objective in-house critic, but also my tolerant and saintly wife—and our children, **Julia** and **Sander,** for their patience, understanding, and faith that all the time we haven't spent together over the past six years might possibly be worth it in the end. We'll see.

CONTENTS

FOR WALTER LORRAINE,
who has always seen the possibilities,

and

DONNA McCARTHY,
who has always given them a beautiful home

INTRODUCTION

Our body may be the first and is certainly the most remarkable thing we learn to take for granted. Because it works twenty-four hours a day, seven days a week, and makes only a few routine demands on our schedules, it's hardly surprising that we're much more familiar with its outside appearance than we are with what's going on inside. That is, of course, until something goes wrong. But why wait for trouble to stimulate curiosity? Each of us owns and inhabits an exceptional example of biological engineering and one that deserves to be understood and celebrated.

Everyone's journey begins as a single cell that contains everything we will need to get the ball rolling. If all goes well, that single cell will multiply into a population reaching tens of trillions. While these cells are invisible to the naked eye, each and every one is alive. And though they may do different work, the fundamental structure and basic operation of every cell is pretty much the same. They all demand and utilize the nutrients that supply energy and building materials, and in the process produce waste that must be eliminated.

Once committed to the building of a multicellular organism, no cell exists in isolation. Each is part of a neighborhood and is in constant communication with its neighbors. Each cell also receives messages from farther afield. We are able to accomplish the huge number of things we do, things that make us human, only because our cells willingly collaborate with each other. This is not a random act of kindness on their part. They are looking out for themselves. If their survival is threatened, so is ours. By arranging themselves into strictly organized groups, each with its own particular functions, they build and operate the systems needed to maintain the steady internal environment upon which they depend, regardless of what's going on outside.

These systems, with familiar names such as *respiratory, circulatory,* and *digestive,* are introduced and explored through the various sections of this book. They are presented one at a time to avoid overwhelming the reader, but it should be kept in mind that just as our cells must work together, one system without the others would undoubtedly fail. What follows is ultimately the story of the superb interdependence of all the systems that make up the human body. This, in essence, is the way we work.

CHAPTER 1

BUILDING LIFE

FOR MOST OF OUR HISTORY, whatever was learned about the human body came from looking under the skin and poking around between the various organs, vessels, and bones. Since most of the specimens available for such investigation were invariably and understandably dead, assumptions about even the most fundamental workings relied heavily on myth and imagination. And so it remained until some four hundred years ago, when new discoveries sparked a revolution in understanding how the body works. One of these breakthroughs literally changed people's view of the world.

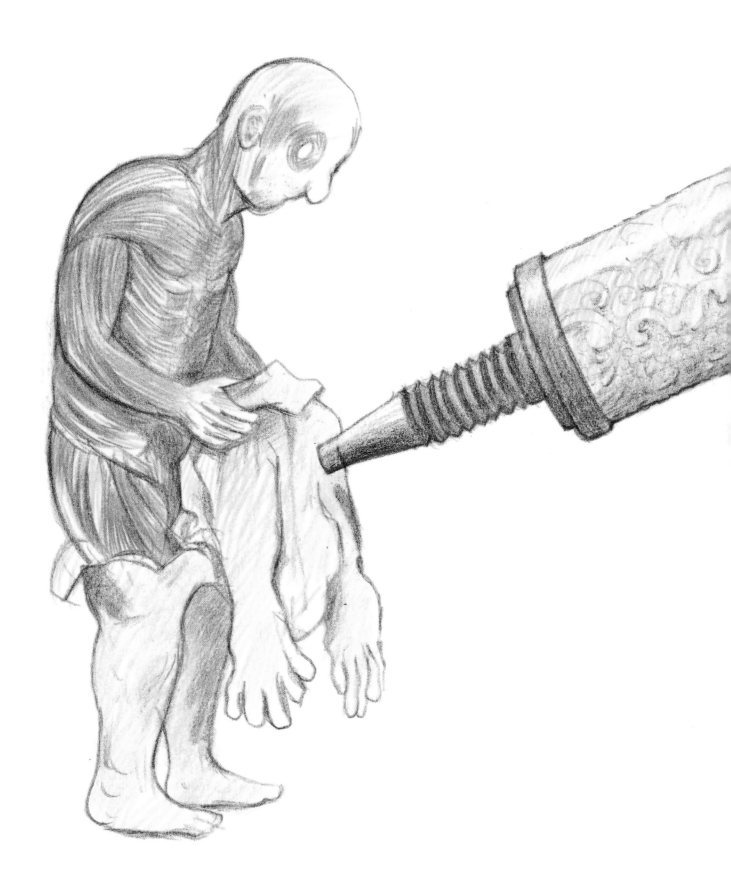

The invention of the microscope made it possible to see objects that were invisible to the naked eye. Among those "objects" were tiny, self-contained living units called cells. From apple trees to zebras, all living things are made of cells. Each of us is built of vast numbers of them, with estimates ranging up to a hundred trillion. Put a wafer-thin slice of any body organ under the microscope and you will see just a few of them.

Early cell observers noted that each of these structures had an outer boundary, the cell membrane, surrounding clear cytoplasm that contained a nucleus. Cytoplasm was thought to be just a featureless jelly until the first half of the twentieth century, when a new breed of microscope came on the scene.

13

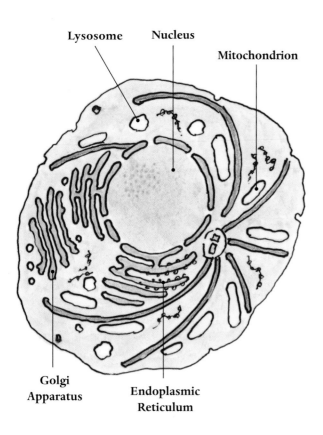

Lysosome   Nucleus

Mitochondrion

Golgi
Apparatus

Endoplasmic
Reticulum

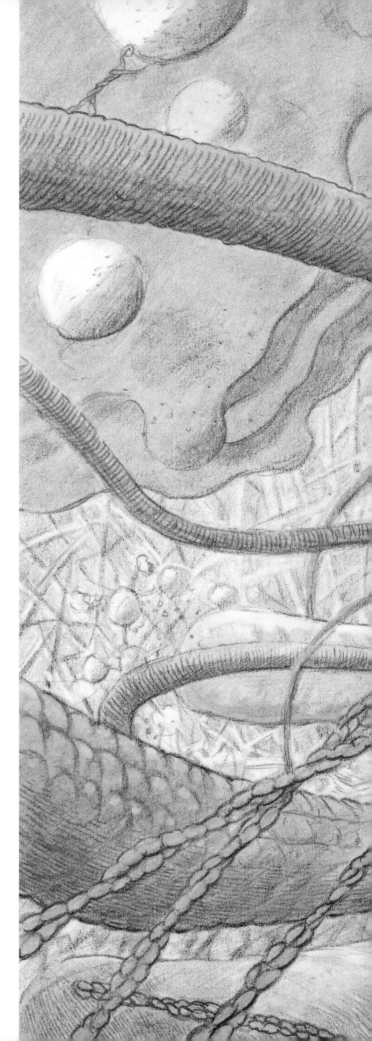

The electron microscope, with powers of magnification far beyond those of light microscopes, revealed that unlike the simple monastic rooms after which they were named, cells are actually bustling little worlds, each filled with distinct structures that have their own particular function. The largest such structure is the nucleus, which serves as the main library and oversees all operations. Manufacturing and transport are the responsibility of the endoplasmic reticulum and the Golgi apparatus. The energy to run a cell is provided by a collection of power plants called mitochondria. And lysosomes, the cell's junkyards, handle recycling.

There are a few things, however, that even the electron microscope cannot see, and these include atoms, the raw materials from which cells are made.

How Big Is Small?

Everything, including yesterday's lunch, this book, Mount Everest, Smudge the terrier, even distant galaxies, is made of atoms. You alone require some five trillion trillion of them. Obviously, they are quite small, but to get some sense of just how small requires a brief detour. Smudge is chasing a tennis ball across the lawn at Battery Park on the tip of Manhattan. If that ball were a single atom, a typical body cell at the same scale would extend all the way to Central Park Zoo, a distance of five miles (eight kilometers).

Battery
Park

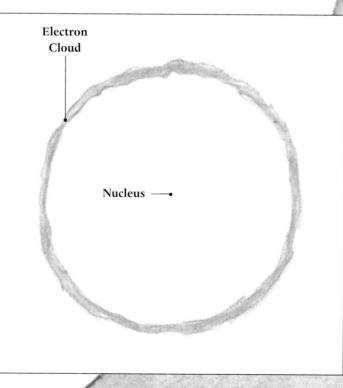

Empire State Building

Central Park Zoo

MANHATTAN

Electron Cloud

Nucleus ⟶

Despite its size, however, every atom is an entity unto itself. Imagine that same tennis ball without its rubber shell, just the fuzz. At its center, and barely visible, would be a small, dense nucleus of minute particles called protons and neutrons. Whizzing around the nucleus—like planets orbiting the sun—are even tinier particles called electrons. Impossible to locate precisely because of their constant movement, they are described as an electron cloud or, for our purposes, the "fuzz." It is the different number of particles in different atoms that distinguish one kind from another.

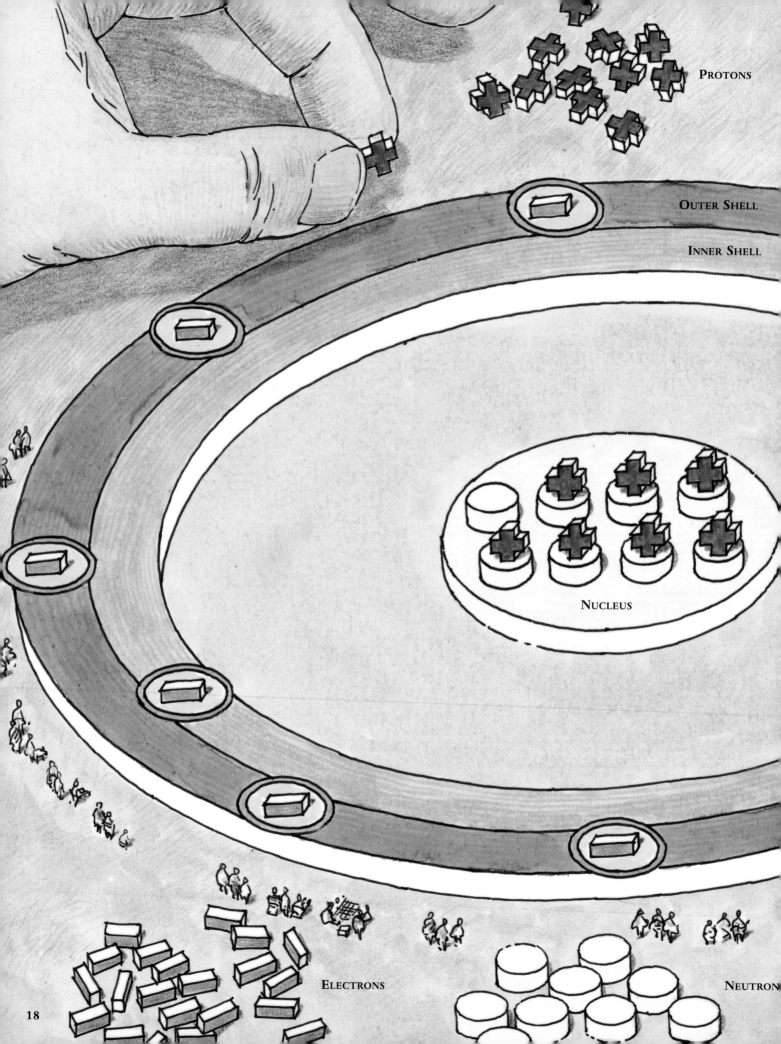

PROTONS

OUTER SHELL

INNER SHELL

NUCLEUS

ELECTRONS

NEUTRON

18

BUILDING ATOMS

Left to their own devices, most kinds of atoms will contain the same number of electrons and protons and, occasionally, neutrons. Protons have a positive (+) electrical charge. Electrons have an equally strong negative (–) charge. It is the attraction between positive and negative charges that holds an atom together.

Electrons travel around the nucleus in specific orbits called shells. Each shell can hold only a certain number of electrons, and as each one reaches capacity, a new one is formed. The oxygen atom under construction on the facing page has eight electrons. Two fill up the innermost shell, and six more occupy all but two of the eight slots in the second shell. Atoms with more than ten electrons require a third shell, and so on.

When the outermost shell of an atom is full and there are no more electrons to place, that particular atom is said to be stable. This is not usually the case, however. Most atoms, such as oxygen with its two empty spaces, spend their lives continually seeking fulfillment.

Of the approximately twenty-four different kinds of atoms required, 95 percent of the human body is made of just these four:

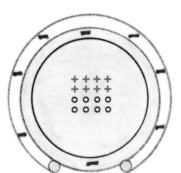

OXYGEN

CARBON

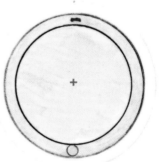

HYDROGEN

NITROGEN

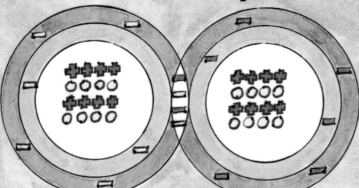

OXYGEN MOLECULE (O₂)

MAKING MOLECULES

In their quest for a full outer shell, atoms willingly sacrifice their individual identities. Through countless chemical reactions they bond with each other to build communities of various shapes and sizes called molecules.

HYDROGEN

HYDROGEN

One kind of bond is achieved by sharing electrons. When two oxygen atoms, for instance, share two of their electrons with each other, they fill their respective outer shells and in the process form an oxygen (O_2) molecule, the active ingredient in the air we breathe.

Most interactions, however, happen between atoms of different types. Hydrogen, with its solitary electron, needs just one more to fill its single shell. If hydrogen and oxygen each share an electron, hydrogen becomes stable. If a second hydrogen atom joins the group, all three atoms enjoy stability. The happy result of this union is a single molecule of water (H_2O).

The sharing of electrons between atoms isn't always equal, and that's certainly the case with water molecules. The oxygen atom's big nucleus exerts much more pull on the shared electrons than the smaller nucleus of each hydrogen atom. Because electrons have a negative charge, this inequality makes the oxygen atom slightly negative and each hydrogen atom slightly positive.

Since opposites attract, the oxygen atom in one water molecule is drawn to a hydrogen atom in another water molecule. Though the bonds that form are weak and readily broken—more like casual friends than permanent partners—they hold water molecules together and ensure that within a particular temperature range, water is liquid, rather than gas. This is more than merely convenient. Liquid water is the medium in which a cell's chemical reactions take place. No water, no life!

WATER
MOLECULE
(H_2O)

Weak Bond

OXYGEN

IONS AND SOLUTIONS

Most atoms are "happiest" bound together as molecules. Though many achieve this bonded state by sharing electrons, some have other ideas. Sodium (Na) atoms, for instance, have just one electron in their outermost shell, while chlorine (Cl) atoms have seven. If sodium gives that solitary electron to chlorine, both achieve stability. Since the sodium atom now contains more protons than electrons, it has a positive (+) electrical charge. The chlorine atom, having gained an electron, is now negatively (–) charged. Electrically charged atoms are called ions, and oppositely charged ions stick together. In this case the result of bonding between Na^+ and Cl^- ions is sodium chloride, or common table salt.

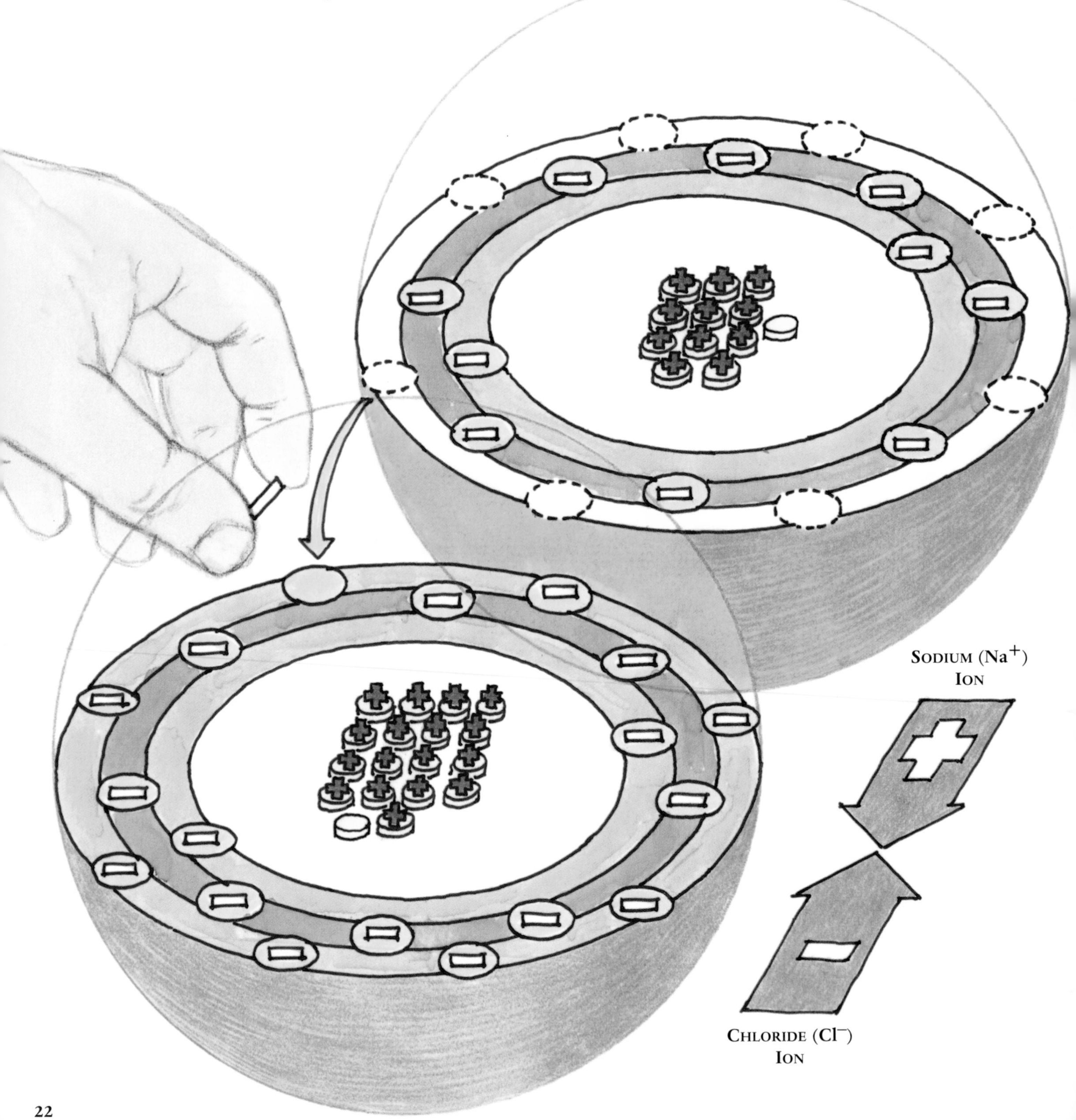

SODIUM (Na^+)
ION

CHLORIDE (Cl^-)
ION

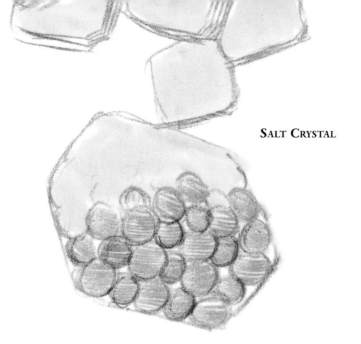

SALT CRYSTAL

All molecules possess a kind of energy that makes them move. When dropped into water, vibrating sodium chloride molecules become surrounded by faster-moving water molecules. Because water molecules are slightly charged, their negative ends surround and isolate Na^+ ions while their positive ends do the same to Cl^- ions. This interaction dissolves the salt crystals and produces a salt solution.

The ability of water to dissolve ionic molecules is vitally important to the way we work. Sodium ions, for example, play a key role in moving and controlling the body. Molecules formed by the sharing of electrons can dissolve too, but only if one part has a slightly positive charge and another a slightly negative one. These are called polar molecules. Glucose, the body's main energy supplier and a polar molecule, works because of its ability to interact with water molecules to make a glucose solution.

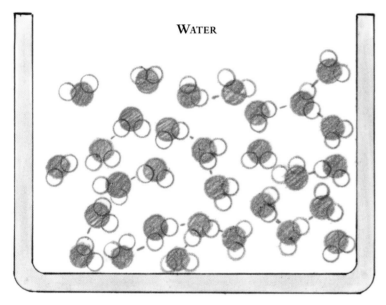

WATER

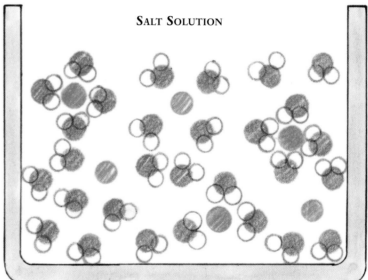

SALT SOLUTION

Ions and molecules dissolved in water bounce off each other at random, spreading naturally from an area of high concentration to one of low concentration until an even distribution is achieved. This process is called diffusion. It happens in gases too, although there the molecules move even faster. That's why if someone "breaks wind" at one end of a room, it's not long before everyone else shares the experience.

DIFFUSION

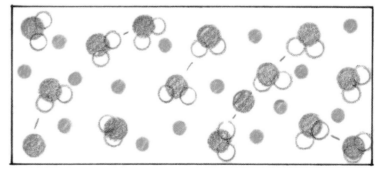

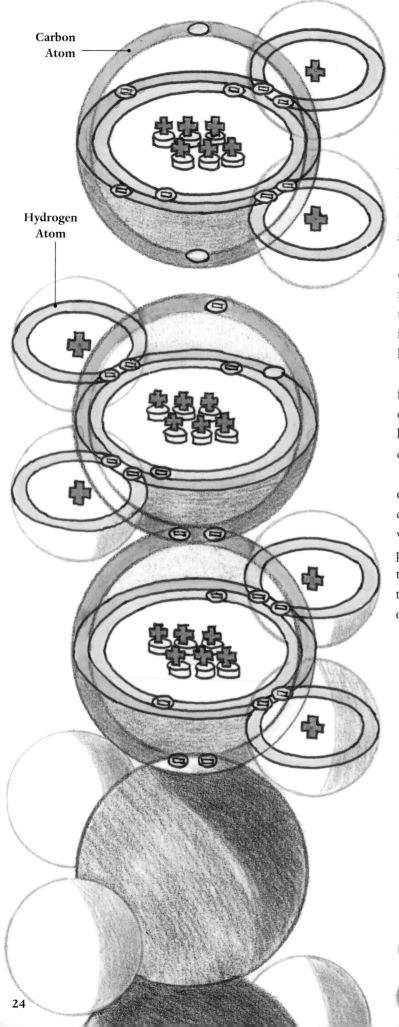

Carbon Atom

Hydrogen Atom

CARBON BACKBONE

We humans, along with every other living thing on earth, are put together using a set of molecules built around atoms of carbon. With only four electrons in their outer shell, carbon atoms are built to bond. They readily form chains and rings that serve as molecular "backbones" to which are attached other electron-sharing atoms, such as hydrogen, oxygen, nitrogen, and phosphorus.

The resulting molecules are stable and at the same time capable of taking part in the myriad chemical reactions that make our cells tick. Each of these carbon-based molecules is uniquely suited to its role inside the body. Among the most important are carbohydrates, proteins, nucleic acids, and lipids.

Many lipids, including fats and oils, have molecules built from fatty acids—long chains composed almost entirely of carbon atoms sharing electrons with each other and with hydrogen add-ons. Fatty acids don't have any electrical charges, so they are nonpolar and don't dissolve in water.

One group of lipids, called phospholipids, are major players in the construction of cell membranes. Two fatty acid chains are connected to a third molecule called glycerol, which in turn is bonded to a fourth molecule containing phosphorus. This last molecule is polar—part of it is negatively charged, and part of it positively charged. Having electrical charges at the phosphorus end but not at the fatty acid end makes phospholipids ideally suited to their job.

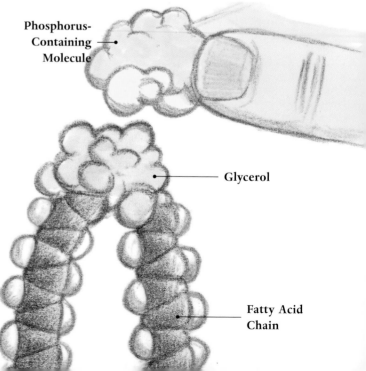

Phosphorus-Containing Molecule

Glycerol

Fatty Acid Chain

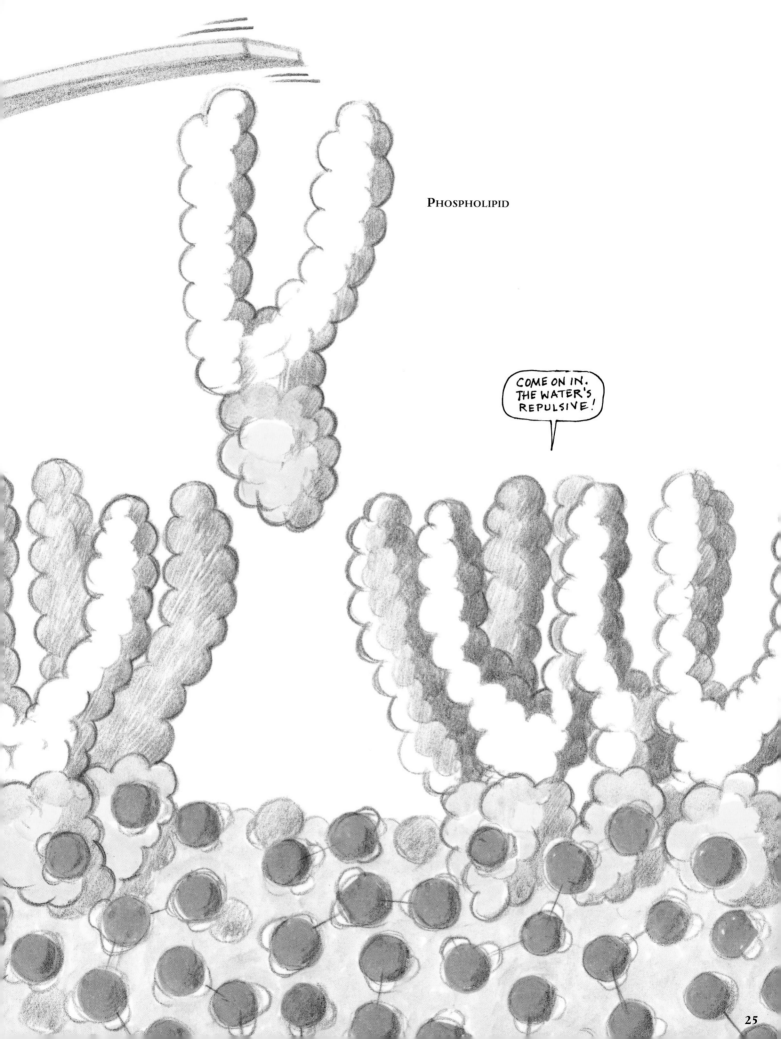

PHOSPHOLIPID

COME ON IN. THE WATER'S REPULSIVE!

25

Tail to Tail

Membrane-making phospholipids lead a double life. Their polar end, or "head," is attracted to water. Their non-polar end, or "tail," is repelled by it. When they are all in the pool together, they arrange themselves so that their heads face and mix with water molecules while their tails point in the opposite direction. For complete isolation, the tails spontaneously line up tip to tip, creating a flexible—yet water-free—double layer. This remarkable construction is the basis of the membrane that surrounds not only cells but many of their internal components. Around one-fifth of membrane lipid is made up of cholesterol, which helps stabilize the otherwise mushy membrane.

Between the expanses of lipids are numerous proteins. Some provide channels through the membrane to control the movement of substances in and out of the cell. Others serve as message receptors to allow communication between one cell and another. Still others act as markers that enable patrolling defense cells to identify them as part of the body and not a foreign intruder.

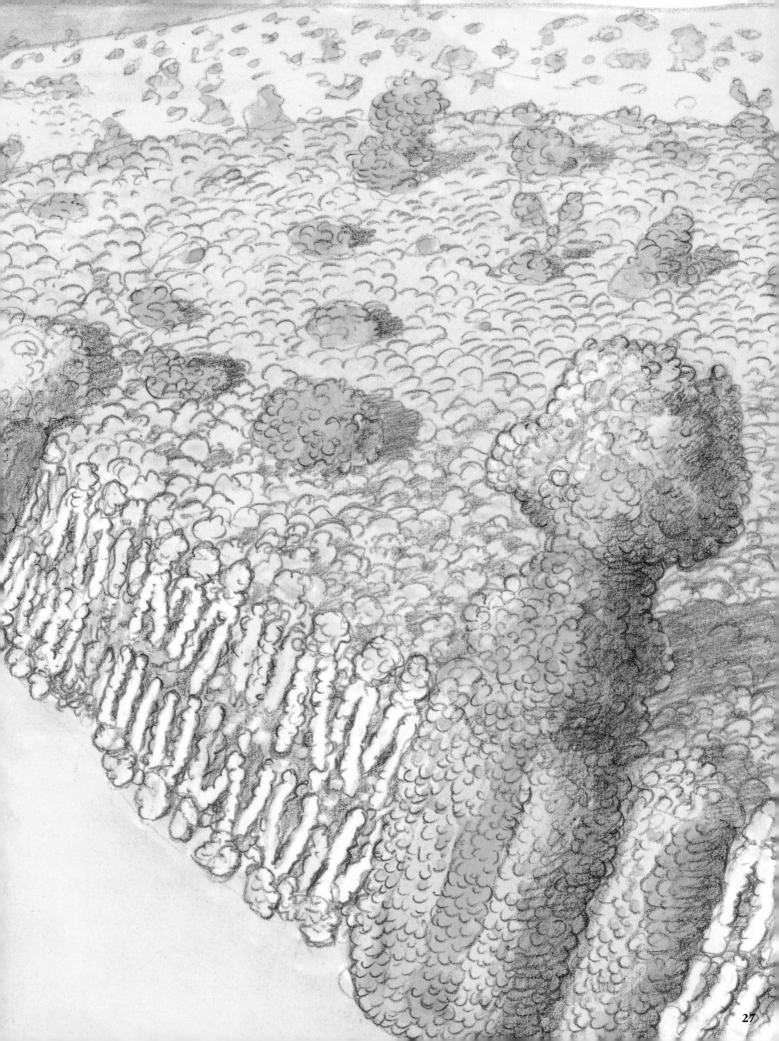

STRETCH AND SQUEEZE

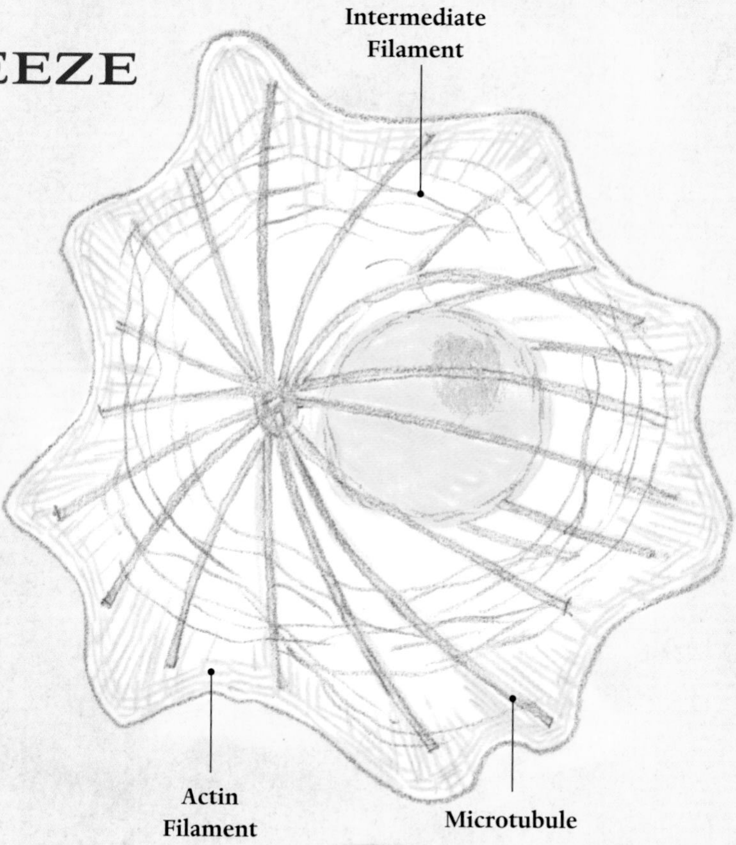

Without its poles and ropes a tent would collapse into a shapeless heap. The same goes for cells. Without a well-organized and adaptable internal support structure, a cell would have all the dynamism of a deflated balloon. Although it varies from cell to cell, this framework, or cytoskeleton, is assembled primarily from three components.

Microtubules are the largest in diameter. Stiff but bendable, they extend from a structure near the nucleus and push outward on the cell membrane, giving it shape.

A network of actin filaments—the smallest in diameter—concentrated mainly just below the membrane braces and strengthens it, rather like the struts of a geodesic dome. Actin filaments also crisscross the interior of the cell, pulling the membrane toward the center, opposing the outward push of the microtubules.

Intermediate filaments, the third component of the cytoskeleton, weave throughout the cell and hold everything in place. They connect the actin filaments to the microtubules and the cell membrane to the nucleus.

Intermediate Filament

Actin Filament

Microtubule

TWISTING STRANDS

It is the cytoskeleton's job not only to provide support for a cell but also to rearrange that support in response to changing forces. To make this possible, each of its various components is built from slightly different protein subunits that can easily be assembled or disassembled.

It takes two strands of protein subunits twisted around each other like a double string of pearls to build each actin filament.

To produce the microtubules, protein subunits stick together in rows. Arranged side by side but slightly staggered, these rows create the effect of a spiraling wall.

Intermediate filaments are made from short lengths of twisted protein attached end to end to form longer strands that spiral around each other.

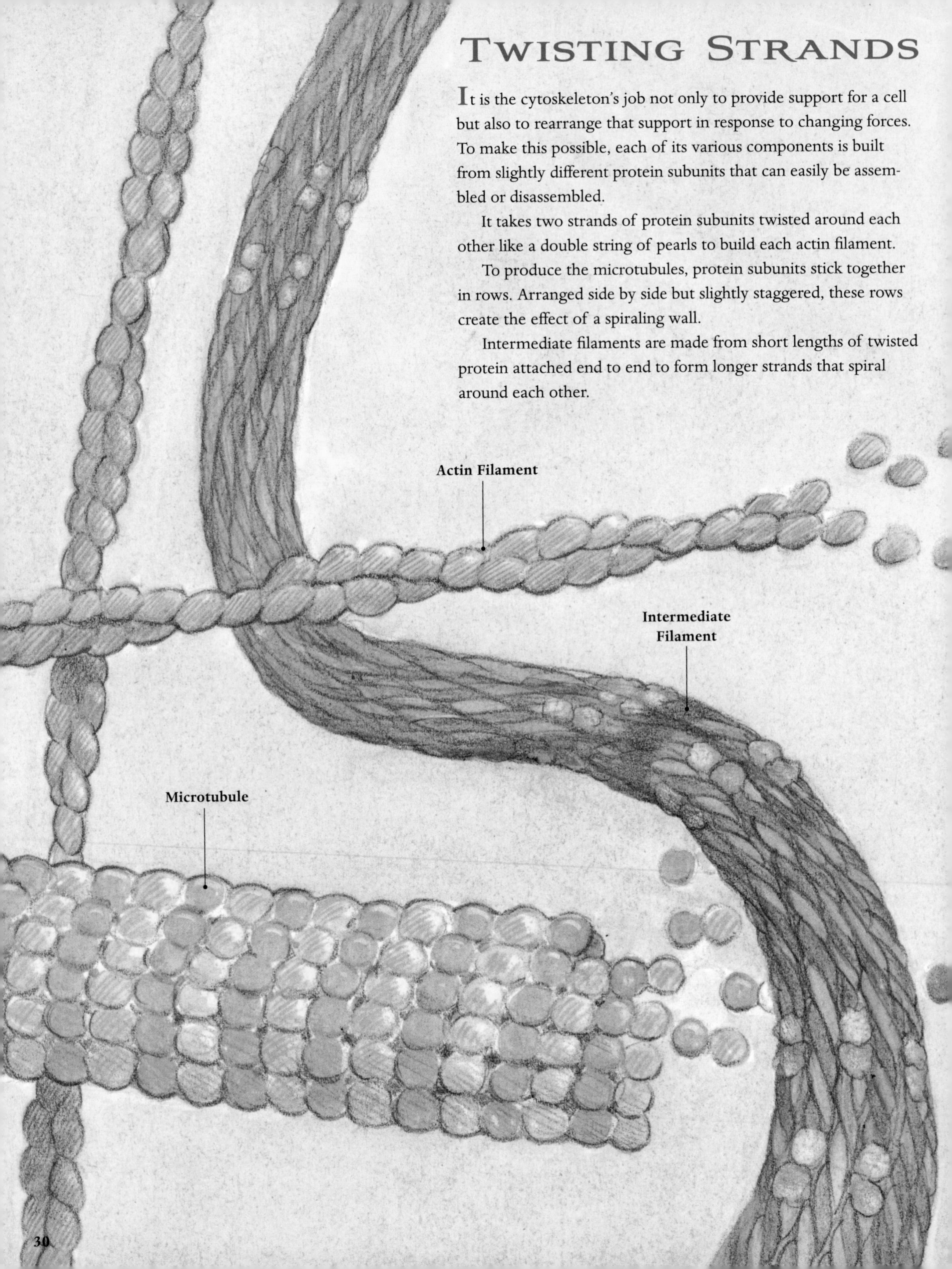

Actin Filament

Intermediate Filament

Microtubule

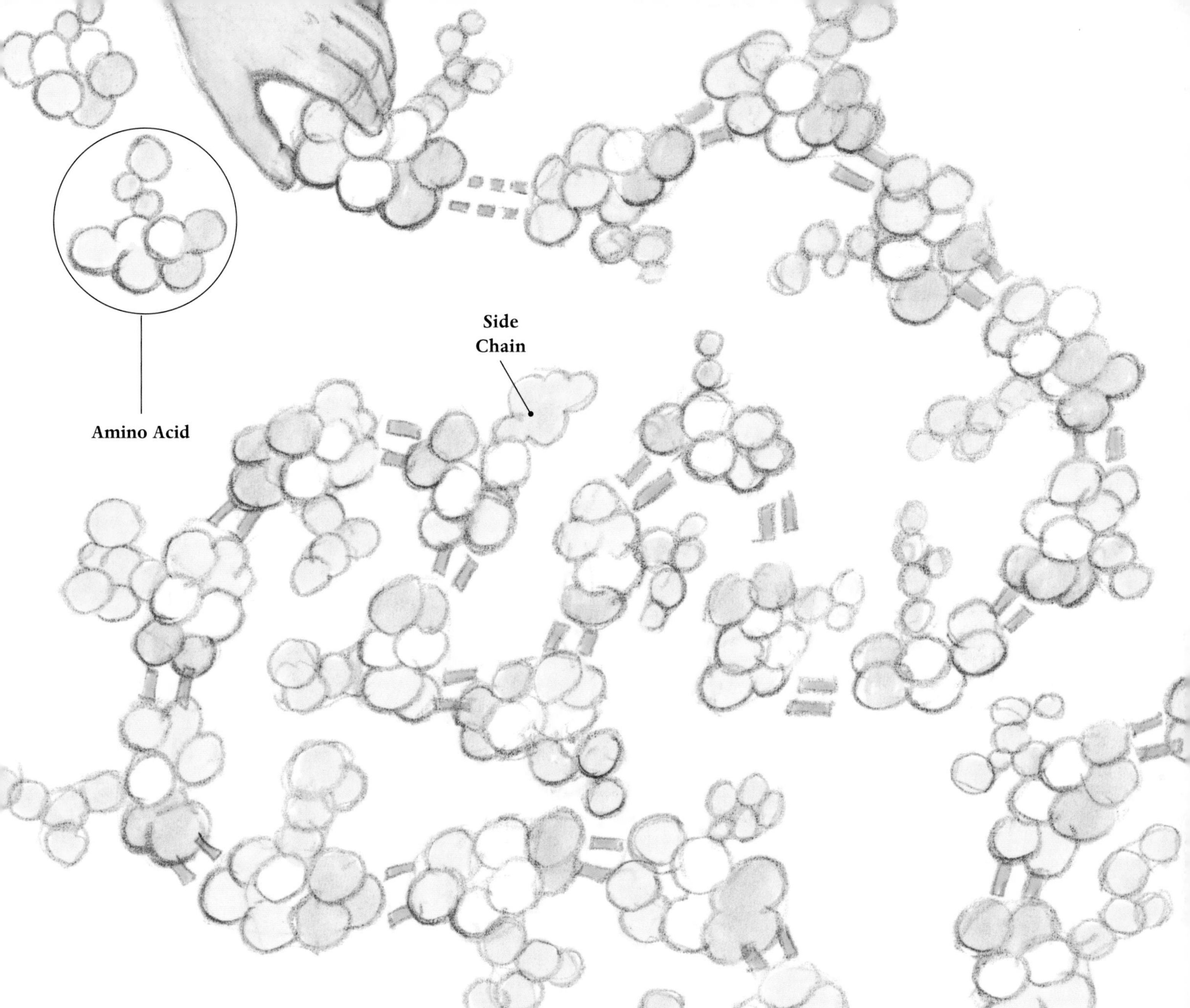

Amino Acid

Side Chain

BUILDING BLOCKS

Whether providing structural support (as we have seen), accelerating chemical reactions (enzymes), immobilizing germs (antibodies), or carrying messages (hormones), proteins are the most versatile of all molecules and are essential for making living systems work.

Regardless of what they do, all proteins are constructed from just twenty different kinds of building blocks called amino acids. These small molecules are built with the same common "core," but each has a unique projecting side chain. Bonds between the amino acids link them together like charms on a bracelet. Other bonds then cause the resulting chain to twist and fold into a specific protein. The final shape depends on the precise number and order of the amino acids. Any deviation means that the protein cannot do its job.

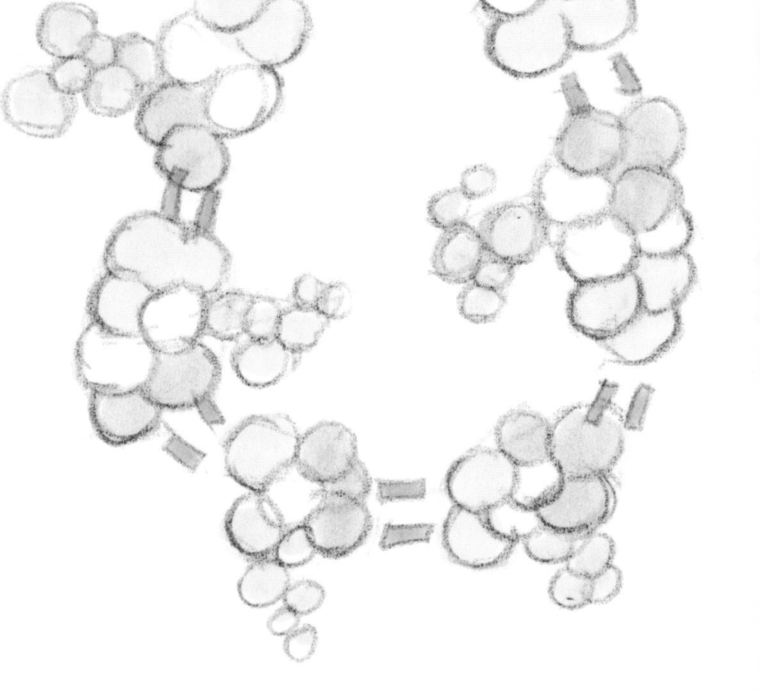

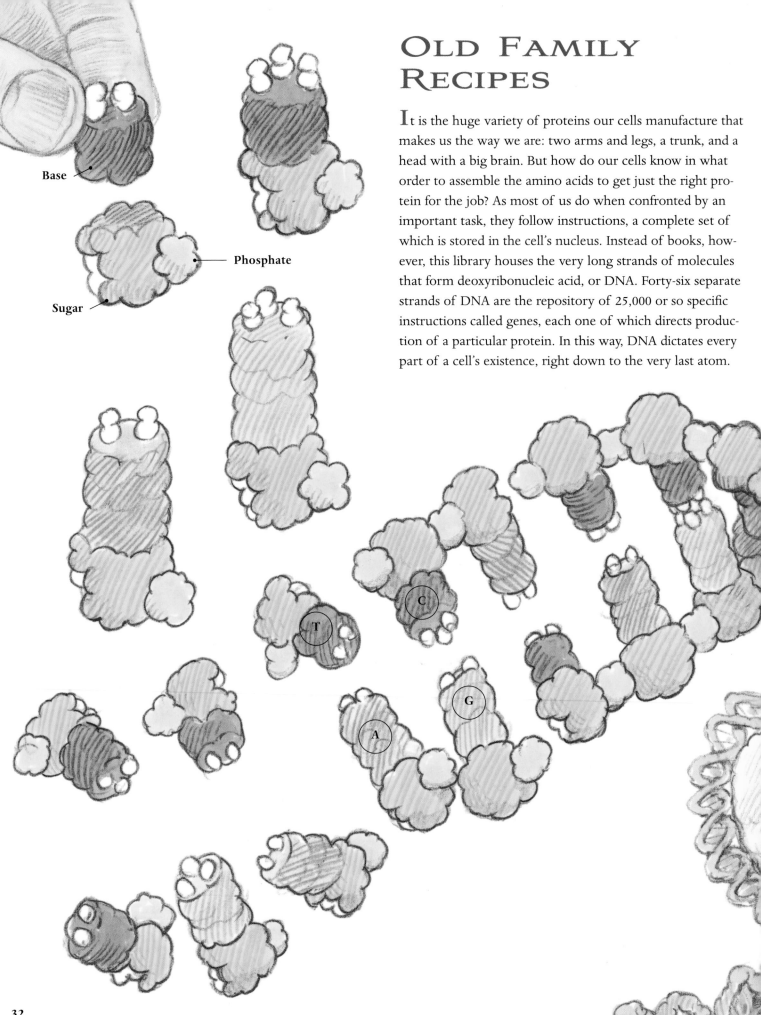

Base

Phosphate

Sugar

OLD FAMILY RECIPES

It is the huge variety of proteins our cells manufacture that makes us the way we are: two arms and legs, a trunk, and a head with a big brain. But how do our cells know in what order to assemble the amino acids to get just the right protein for the job? As most of us do when confronted by an important task, they follow instructions, a complete set of which is stored in the cell's nucleus. Instead of books, however, this library houses the very long strands of molecules that form deoxyribonucleic acid, or DNA. Forty-six separate strands of DNA are the repository of 25,000 or so specific instructions called genes, each one of which directs production of a particular protein. In this way, DNA dictates every part of a cell's existence, right down to the very last atom.

Nucleotides are the building blocks of DNA, and each has three component molecules: a sugar, a phosphate, and a base. The sugar and phosphate molecules of adjacent nucleotides link up to form the "backbone" from which the bases project. There are four kinds of bases—adenine (A), guanine (G), cytosine (C), and thymine (T). The order in which they are assembled provides the instructions for building proteins.

Left to its own devices, a single strand of DNA would, like proteins, quickly fold into a tangled wad and become very difficult to "read." To keep the instructions legible, a second parallel strand is attached to the first by weak bonds that form between opposing bases. This bonding is very specific: A bonds only with T, and C only with G. Other forces between the molecules cause this ladder-like arrangement to twist itself into the familiar spiral formation called a double helix.

DNA DOUBLE HELIX

Globular Protein

Every nucleus holds just over 6 feet (1.8 meters) of DNA. And each of the forty-six strands is neatly wrapped around small groups of globular proteins. This shorter, better-organized arrangement is the state in which DNA is found during normal cell operations. In addition to packing DNA more efficiently, these proteins also play a part in regulating which genes are "switched on" in which cells.

COPYING INSTRUCTIONS

Since damage to its DNA could easily compromise the normal functioning of a cell, this precious set of instructions can never be checked out of the nuclear library. And even if it could, the openings or pores in the envelope surrounding the nucleus are not big enough to allow such huge molecules to migrate out into the cytoplasm.

Making the instructions available is the job of a gifted copycat called ribonucleic acid, or RNA. Copying begins when the section of DNA containing the relevant gene is uncoiled and the strands separated to expose its bases. With one of the strands acting as a template, free-floating RNA nucleotides position their bases opposite their complements. At the same time, these RNA nucleotides form their own backbone by bonding with each other through their sugar and phosphate groups. The resulting copy is a short, single strand of RNA that is small enough to pass through pores.

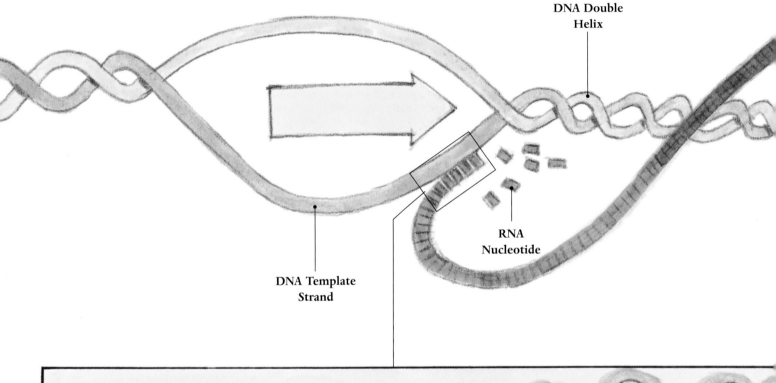

DNA Double Helix

DNA Template Strand

RNA Nucleotide

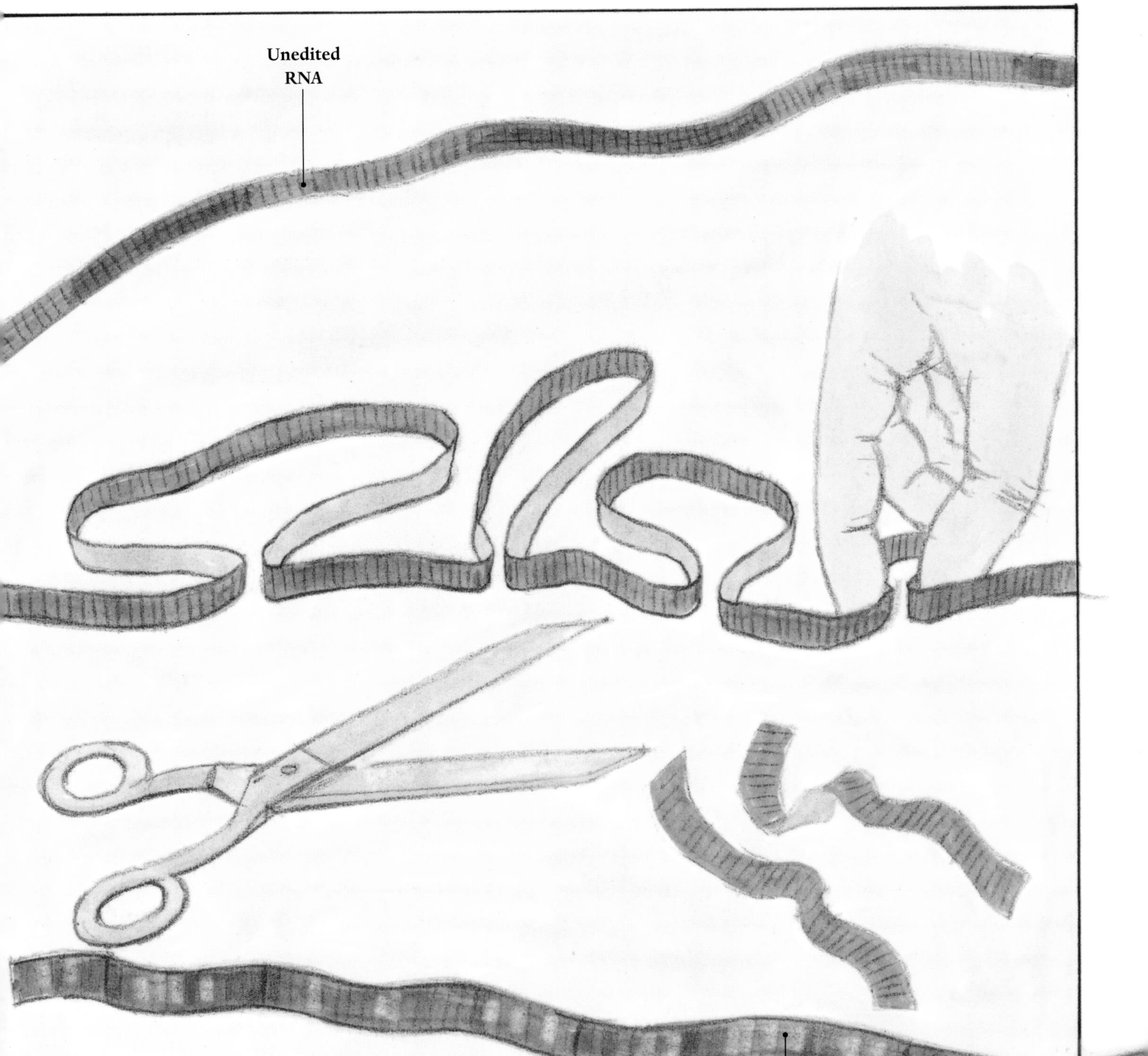

**Unedited
RNA**

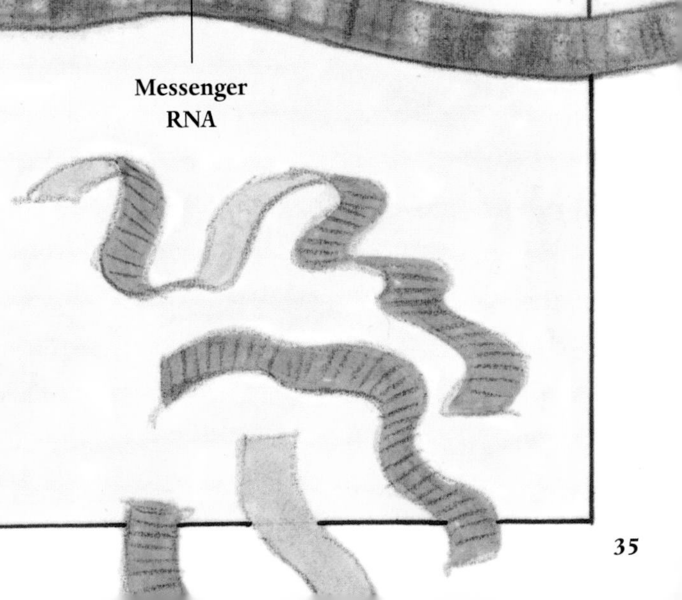

CUT AND SPLICE

Imagine reading a novel in which the heart-stopping plot
was repeatedly interrupted by a bunch of pages written in a
language you couldn't read. A gene is much like that. Its
sequence of meaningful bases is littered with vast expanses
of unintelligible "text." And, since it copies the gene directly,
so is the RNA. Before heading out into the cytoplasm, the
RNA must first be edited. Enzymes snip out the offending
passages, then splice together the "working" portions of the
gene. The RNA version of DNA, now called messenger
RNA (mRNA), is ready to be translated into a protein.

**Messenger
RNA**

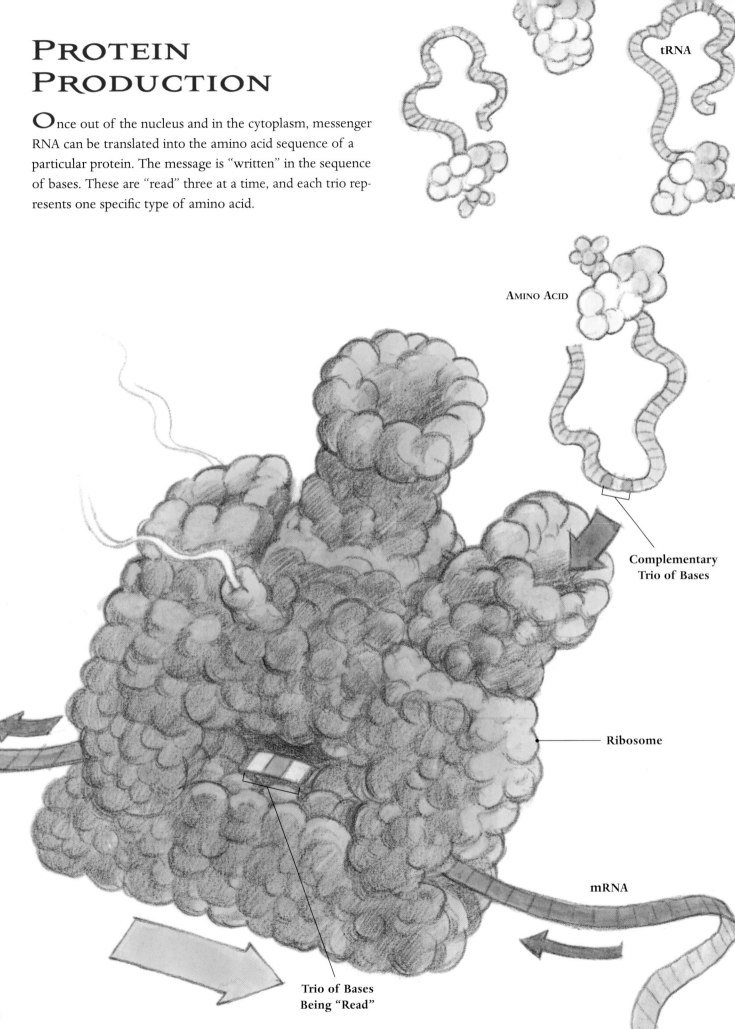

PROTEIN PRODUCTION

Once out of the nucleus and in the cytoplasm, messenger RNA can be translated into the amino acid sequence of a particular protein. The message is "written" in the sequence of bases. These are "read" three at a time, and each trio represents one specific type of amino acid.

tRNA

AMINO ACID

Complementary
Trio of Bases

Ribosome

mRNA

Trio of Bases
Being "Read"

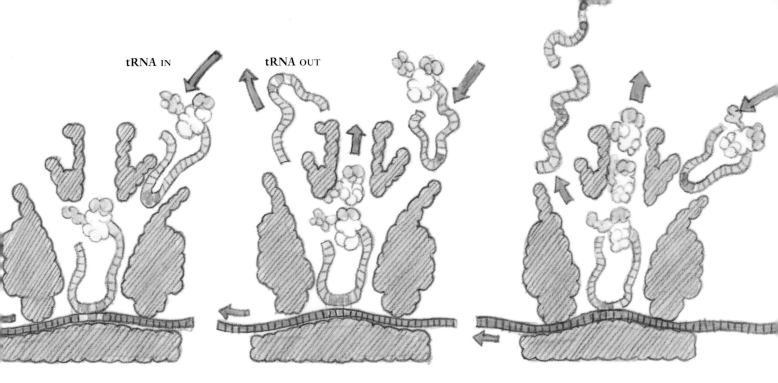

The translation process begins when mRNA enters a ribosome, the cell's protein-making machine. As soon as the first three bases are in position, a specific amino acid is delivered to the ribosome by another type of RNA called tRNA that bears a trio of bases complementary to those on mRNA. The ribosome then "feeds" the mRNA through to "expose" the next three bases. A new amino acid enters—its complementary tRNA label matching the new trio on mRNA—and forms a bond with the first amino acid. This process is repeated over and over, gradually pushing the newly formed protein chain—with its precise sequence of amino acids—out into the cytoplasm, where it folds into its unique shape. Usually a single mRNA molecule is threaded simultaneously through a whole row of ribosomes to make protein production more efficient.

PROTEIN MOLECULE
FOLDING INTO ITS
UNIQUE SHAPE

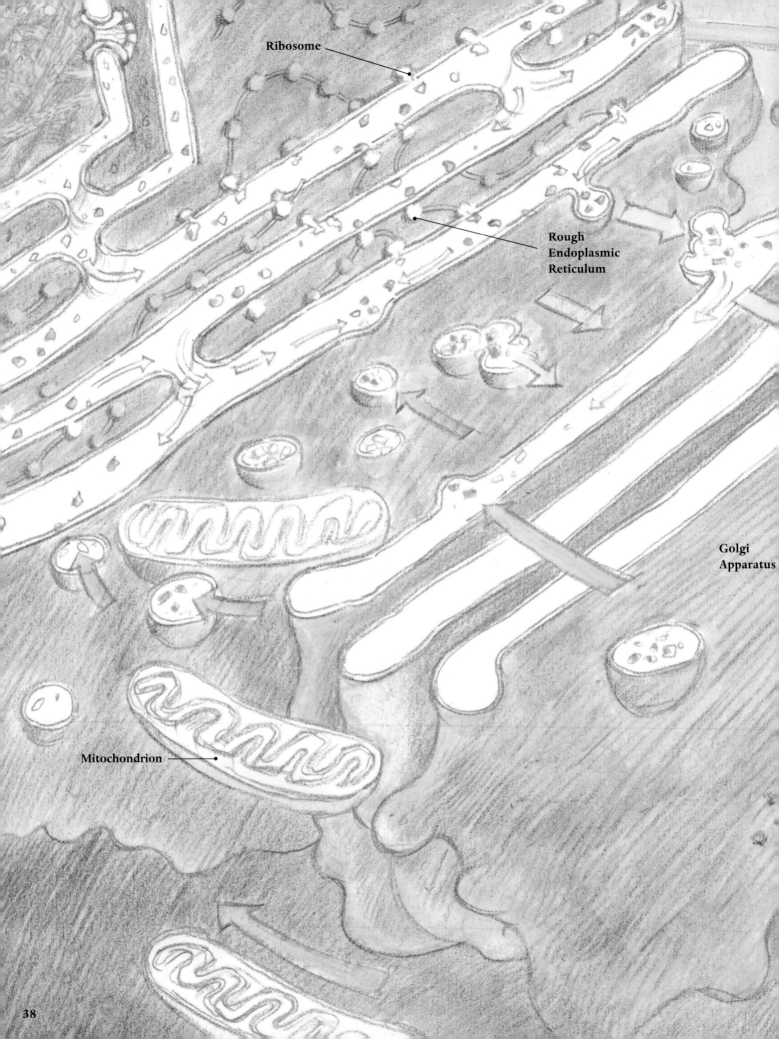

Ribosome

Rough
Endoplasmic
Reticulum

Golgi
Apparatus

Mitochondrion

Microtubule

EXPORTS

Cell Membrane

Membrane
Sac

Lysosome

IMPORTS

PACK AND SHIP

Making proteins is one thing. Getting them where they are needed is another. A large percentage of proteins are assembled in ribosomes attached to factory complexes called rough endoplasmic reticulum (RER). Once folded into their working shapes—and whether destined for places either inside or outside the cell—these proteins are packed aboard membrane sacs that when fully laden are pinched off from the membrane of the RER and transported to the cell's shipping department, the Golgi apparatus.

Inside the chambers of the Golgi apparatus these proteins are trimmed, tagged, and sorted. Those due for export are repacked in membrane sacs, which are then pulled along tubes of the cytoskeleton to the cell membrane, where they fuse to discharge their contents. Some of the sacs leaving the Golgi are filled with powerful digestive enzymes. Called lysosomes, they fuse with other sacs carrying the remains of various parts of the cell, such as worn-out mitochondria. As the remains are digested, breakdown products escape into the cytoplasm so they can be reused. These include amino acids that are built into proteins.

Whether making or breaking molecules, the millions of controlled chemical reactions that take place in each cell every second are known collectively as metabolism, and like any other kind of work, metabolism requires energy.

The favored energy supplier for most cells is glucose—a member of the carbohydrate family—although fatty acids are also an important fuel source for muscles and some other tissues.

RICOCHET

The energy to be harnessed from glucose is trapped in the bonds that hold its atoms together. To be useful, it must first be released and then stored in specialized energy-dispensing molecules called ATP.

If glucose is the energy equivalent of money in your bank account, ATP is the cash in your pocket—readily available and universally accepted. It is everywhere in the cell, and when it is called upon to fuel a reaction, it easily sheds one of its phosphates to release the needed energy.

Breaking down either glucose or fatty acids to their bare bones—carbon dioxide and water—to unleash trapped energy is a potentially hazardous business. If either of these molecules were to be dismantled in a single step, all that stored energy would escape in the form of heat and we would burst into flames. To avoid such an unpleasant consequence, cells break fuel down in a series of controlled reactions that liberate energy gradually, in safe amounts. The relatively small amount of heat released serves to keep our insides warm.

The first phase of energy release from glucose happens in the cytoplasm. In the course of ten* steps and with pin-ball wizardry, glucose ricochets from one enzyme to the next, changing and fragmenting as it goes. And yet even after all this, only two molecules of ATP have been produced, along with two molecules of a substance called pyruvate.

*Step 4 results in two different molecules. One follows the upper pathway shown here (6, 7, 8, 9, 10) to pyruvate. The other must be converted by a fifth step before it can follow that same path.

ATP

ADP

GLUCOSE

Enzyme

8

7

6

3

2

1

MITOCHONDRION

Pyruvate

10

9

10

10

9

4

7

8

6

5

41

Pyruvate

OXYGEN

HYDROGEN
CARRIER

OXYGEN IN

MITOCHONDRION

PUMPING IONS

Only 10 percent of the energy locked inside glucose molecules is released in the cytoplasm. For the remaining 90 percent, our cells turn the job over to their personal power plants, the mitochondria. These specialized structures enjoy a degree of independence from the all-controlling nucleus by being equipped with their own DNA. This allows them to divide when a cell's demands suddenly increase, quickly doubling the amount of available energy.

Each mitochondrion has two membranes—a smooth outer sac and a folded inner sac. Enzymes belonging to the inner sac work in a sequence of small steps to break pyruvate down into the waste carbon dioxide we breathe out and, more important, into energy-carrying hydrogen.

A mechanism embedded in the folded membrane then breaks down the hydrogen atoms into protons (H^+) and energy-rich electrons. The electrons gradually give up this energy so it can be used to pump the protons into the space between the membranes. As these protons then stream back into the inner space to restore the equilibrium on both sides of the folded membrane, their movement generates enough ATP to satisfy the cell's energy requirements.

As a finale to this process, the molecules of oxygen we continually breathe in finally reveal their function. They mop up energy-depleted electrons and hydrogen ions to form that most benign of waste products, water.

42

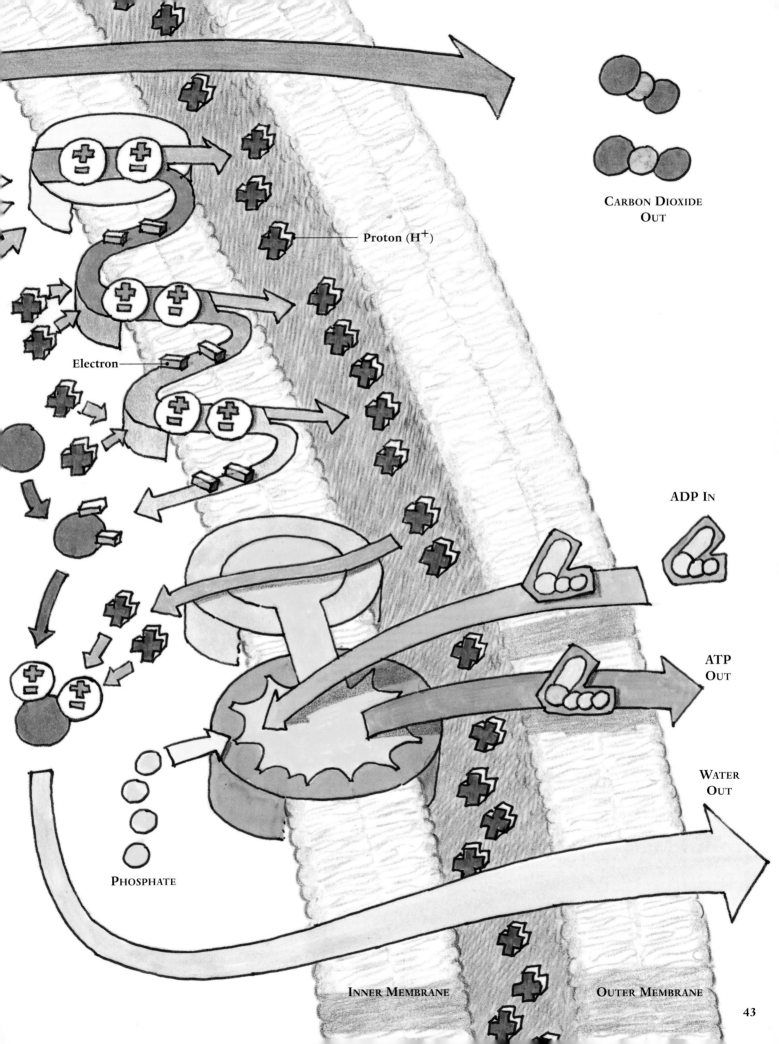

CARBON DIOXIDE
OUT

Proton (H+)

Electron

ADP IN

ATP
OUT

WATER
OUT

PHOSPHATE

INNER MEMBRANE

OUTER MEMBRANE

THE GREAT DIVIDE

Each of us starts out as a single cell. And we would all stay that way were it not for cell division, the process by which a "parent" cell makes the ultimate sacrifice and splits itself into two identical offspring. One or both of the offspring soon become "parents" themselves and they too divide. Repeat this a few million times and you eventually have enough cells to be you.

Cell division not only provides more cells simply so we can grow, but also generates new cells to fill vacancies left by their worn-out or short-lived predecessors and to repair any damage.

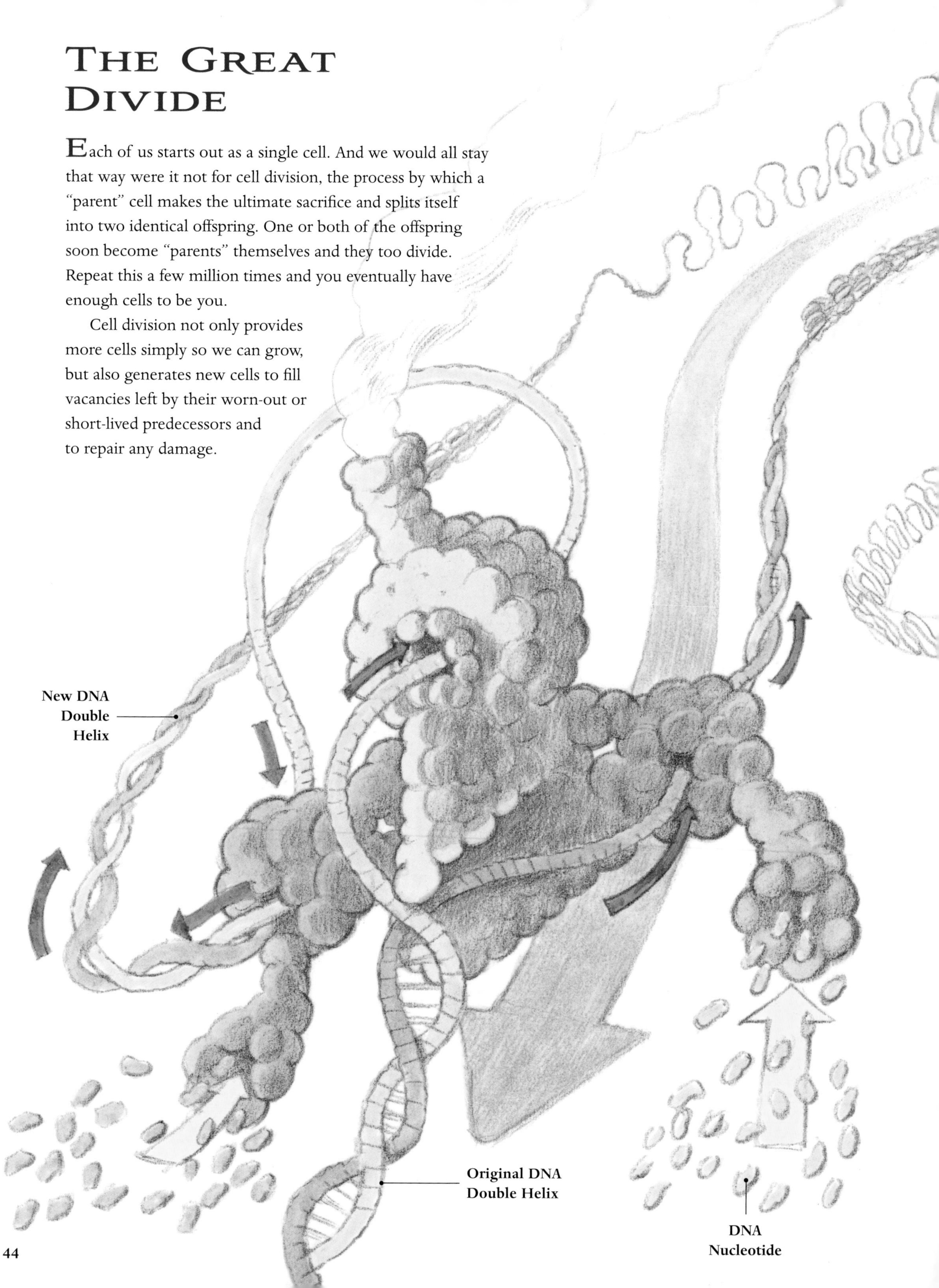

New DNA Double Helix

Original DNA Double Helix

DNA Nucleotide

REPLICATING DNA

Since cells can build a body only if each of them is working with the right instructions, every parent cell must make an exact copy of its DNA, one for each offspring, before it begins to divide.

Replication begins when a molecular contraption built primarily of enzymes assembles itself around one end of a DNA molecule. It carefully uncoils a short section to expose the bases along both strands. Free-floating DNA nucleotides then attach themselves to these strands in an order that precisely complements the order of the bases. As the machine rumbles along, each strand, along with its "new" and perfectly matched partner, twists into a double helix to produce a pair of identical DNA molecules.

After being packaged with various proteins, each strand continues to twist and loop into a more compressed form. The two identical, highly compressed strands, called chromatids, then become linked to form a chromosome.

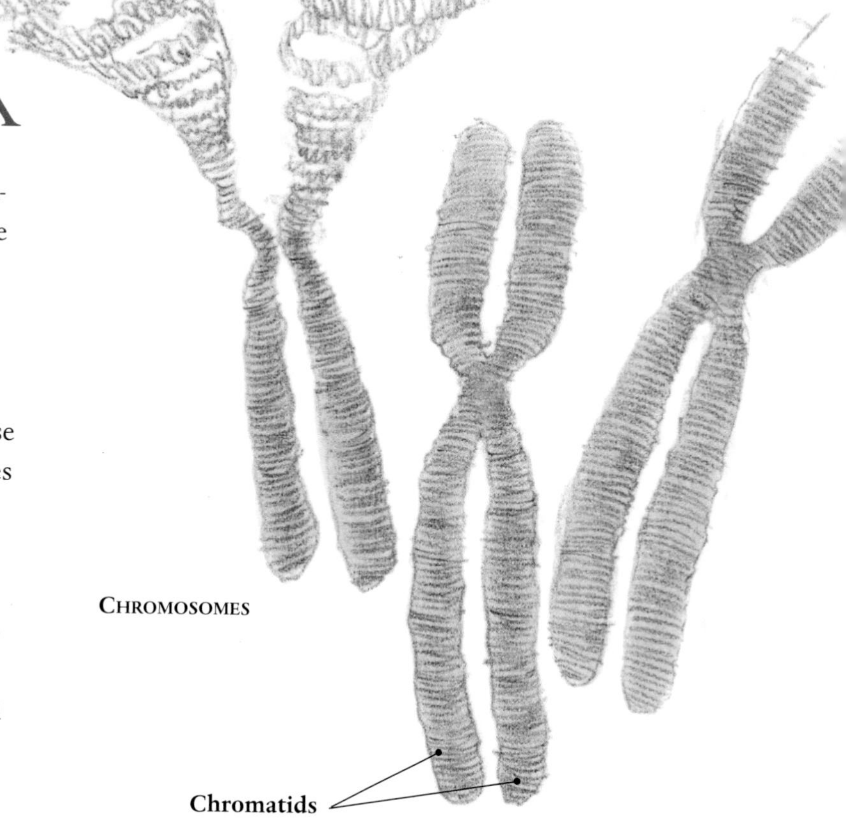

CHROMOSOMES

Chromatids

45

ANOTHER OPENING, ANOTHER SHOW

The DNA molecules that make up every cell's instruction kit are fragile and easily broken. Only a carefully choreographed sequence of events can divide a cell into two while still providing each of the offspring with identical, undamaged copies of those DNA instructions.

But before a cell can divide, new proteins must be built, mitochondria and other components duplicated, DNA replicated, and ATP stockpiled. These preparations happen during a period called interphase. Following interphase, cell division begins in earnest with mitosis. It has five stages, each of which flows seamlessly into the next. Early on in mitosis, DNA is condensed into less breakable chromosomes that can be separated and relocated.

After mitosis, the cell, with its chromosomes now accurately duplicated and dispersed, finally splits in two. Given the drama of cell division, you might well think the show is over, but before you can say "three cheers for mitosis," interphase has already started preparing for the next performance.

1

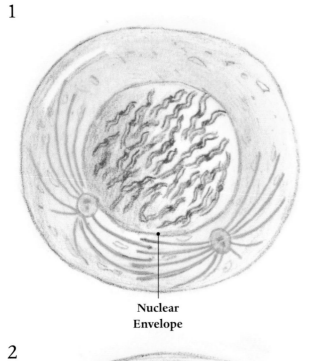

Nuclear Envelope

2

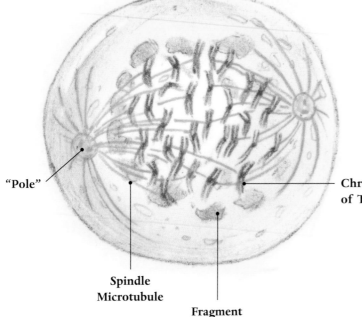

"Pole"

Spindle Microtubule

Fragment

Chromosome Consisting of Two Chromatids

1. PROPHASE

As mitosis begins, each pair of replicated DNA threads shorten to form linked chromatids that together make a chromosome. The cell's "normal" cytoskeleton is dismantled and replaced by an arrangement of microtubules called a spindle that will oversee the choreography.

2. PROMETAPHASE

As the nuclear envelope disintegrates, the two structures from which the microtubules of the spindle originated move around to form the "poles" at each end of the cell. One set of tubes from each pole then meets at the center of the cell and overlaps with its counterpart. A second set links each chromatid to opposite poles.

3. METAPHASE

Tugged and shoved by the spindle, all forty-six chromosomes gather for a farewell line dance at the spindle's equator, the midway point between the poles.

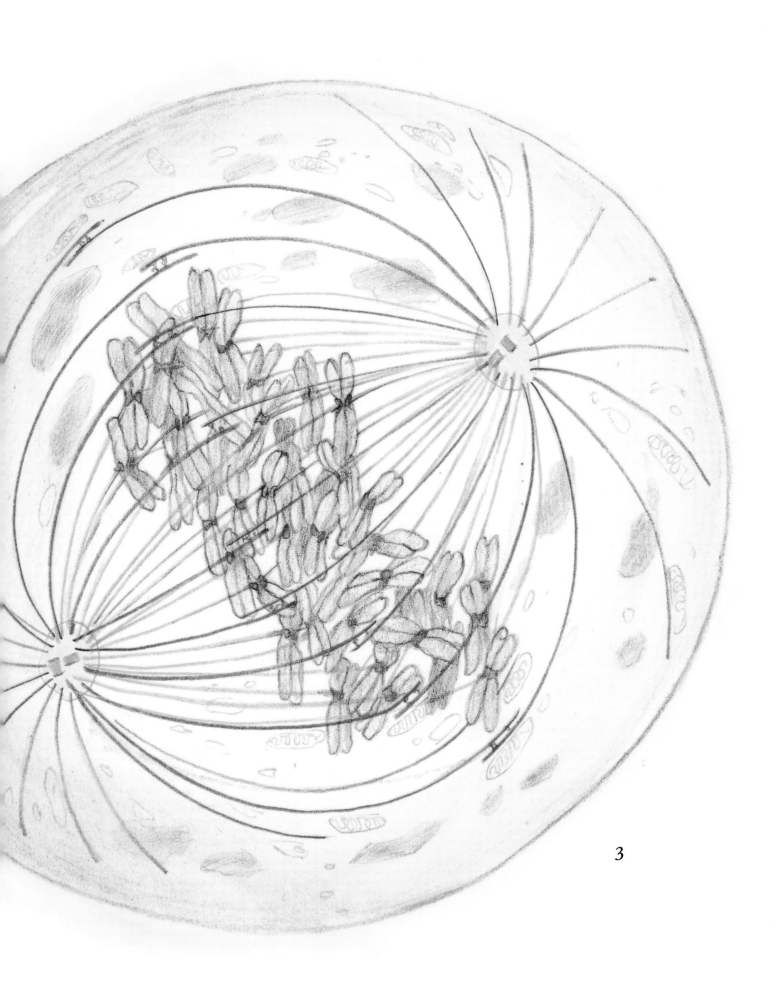

3

4. ANAPHASE

Suddenly the identical chromatids of each chromosome part company. Now called chromosomes in their own right, each is pulled to the opposite pole while overlapping microtubules push those poles apart.

4

5. TELOPHASE

When chromosomes reach their destination at either end of the still elongating cell, they detach from the spindle. With a nuclear envelope reassembling around them, they safely uncoil. The spindle is dismantled and disappears, leaving only a ring of actin filaments and myosin "motor" proteins at the equator. Actin and myosin also cause the contraction of muscle cells that make us move.

6

6. CYTOKINESIS

With mitosis complete, the cell now contains two chromosome-filled nuclei. But not for long. The ring of actin filaments and myosin encircling the cell's midsection begins to contract and eventually pinches the cell in half, creating two identical orphans.

WHERE'S MOM?

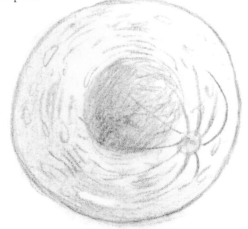

CELL SPOTTER'S GUIDE

Running an organization as complex as the human body is all about teamwork. And as with any successful team, division of labor among the body's cells is vital. For example, branching neurons carry messages, spherical fat cells store energy, long muscle fibers move the body, and dough-nut-shaped red blood cells carry oxygen. These and all the other cell types inside a body are the offspring of the same single fertilized egg and therefore must have identical DNA. So how is it that these cells can look and act so different?

Just as we don't read all the recipes in a cookbook to make an omelet, so each type of cell needs only a portion of its gene instructions to do its job. In each type of cell, genes that "shape" that cell for its specialized role are "switched on" while genes that aren't needed are "switched off." That's what makes a neuron a neuron and not a red blood cell.

The body cells shown here—a sample from the two hundred or so different types found in the body—are drawn at the same scale to indicate the wide range of shapes and relative sizes. To give an idea of "real" size, the period at the end of this sentence is just a little bigger than the actual size of the egg shown below.

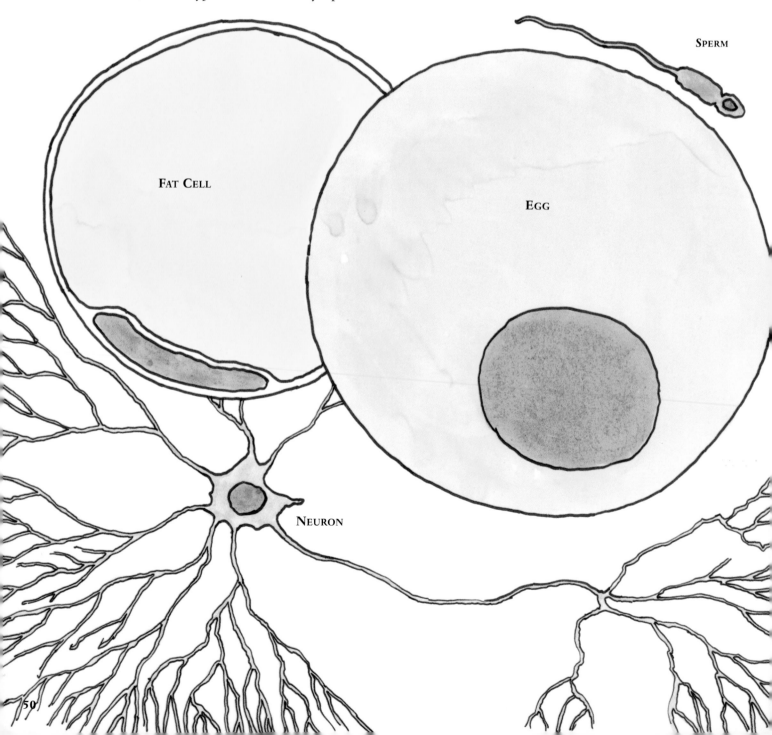

FAT CELL

SPERM

EGG

NEURON

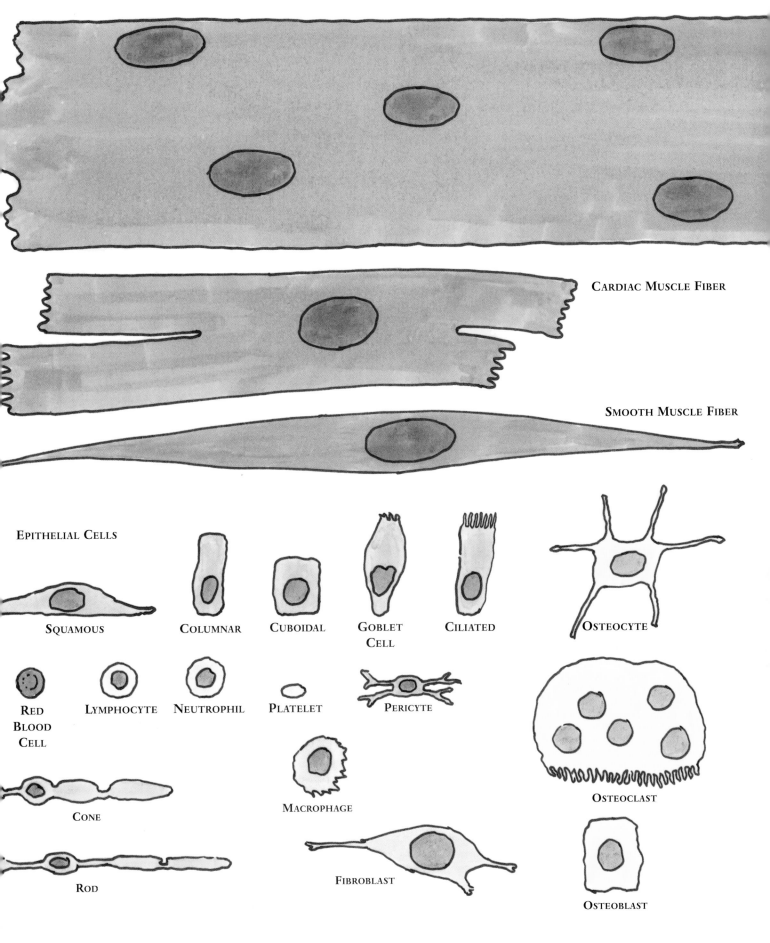

SKELETAL MUSCLE FIBER

CARDIAC MUSCLE FIBER

SMOOTH MUSCLE FIBER

EPITHELIAL CELLS

SQUAMOUS

COLUMNAR

CUBOIDAL

GOBLET CELL

CILIATED

OSTEOCYTE

RED BLOOD CELL

LYMPHOCYTE

NEUTROPHIL

PLATELET

PERICYTE

OSTEOCLAST

CONE

MACROPHAGE

ROD

FIBROBLAST

OSTEOBLAST

TIES THAT BIND

Your body is constructed from a collection of tissues. Each tissue is a close-knit community of like-minded cells working together. Four tissue types predominate: epithelial tissues line cavities and form exterior surfaces; muscle tissues create movement; nervous tissues maintain control; and connective tissues support all the others. Within tissues, cells of the same type are held together by materials they secrete themselves, but for additional strength and stability, many tissues also rely on special junctions between their cells.

Anchor proteins just inside the membranes of adjacent cells are locked together by link proteins. These anchor proteins are attached either to a band of rods running around the inside of the cell membrane or to cables that cross the cell. To further strengthen tissue, the bases of its cells are connected to an underpinning membrane of interwoven fibers.

In some tissues, protein molecules in adjacent cell membranes form a quilt-like pattern that tightly binds the cells together. This arrangement prevents anything from leaking between cells, forcing it instead to travel through the cells, where its movement can be controlled.

Cells must be able to communicate with each other. Those in close proximity communicate directly through channels made of clusters of proteins. These allow small molecules such as sugars and amino acids to pass from one cell to another.

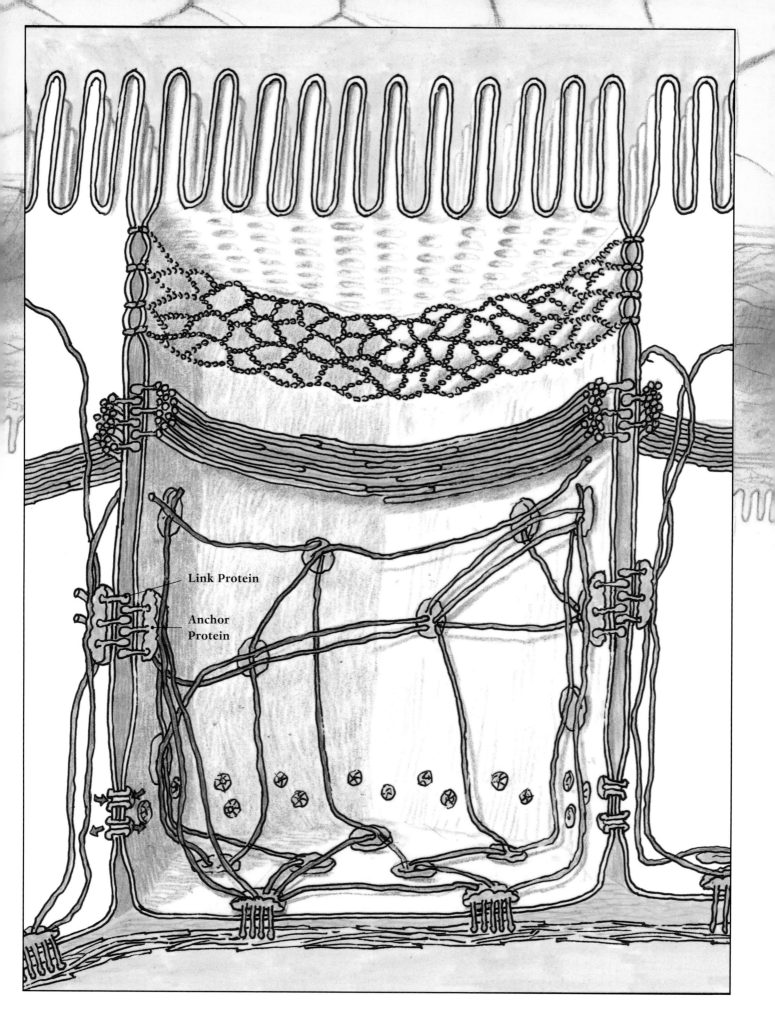

Link Protein

Anchor
Protein

53

TISSUES THAT CONNECT

The most abundant and widespread tissue in the body is connective tissue. In its many forms, which include bone, cartilage, and fat, these tissues tie other tissues together, as well as supporting and protecting them.

It is the flexibility and toughness of the substances produced by connective tissue cells that hold the body together. In bone this substance can bear great weight. In tendons and ligaments it can withstand tension.

The most widely distributed connective tissue is the loose tissue that underpins epithelial and other tissues. It contains cells called fibroblasts that secrete a gel-like matrix crisscrossed by collagen fibers for strength and elastin fibers for elasticity. Both collagen and elastin are members of the protein family. Water trapped inside the matrix forms the tissue fluid through which cells obtain their nutrients from the bloodstream and into which they eliminate their waste.

Connective tissues join forces with other tissue types to make specialized organs such as the heart, stomach, and brain. Selected organs pool their expertise to create systems. And twelve or so systems work as one to make a human being.

MATRIX

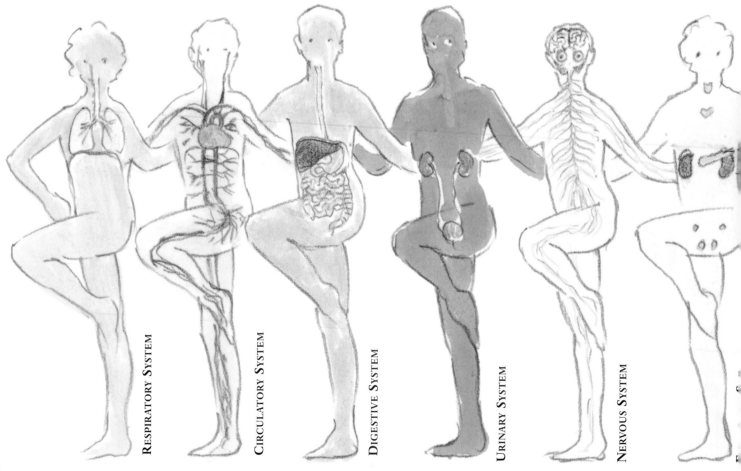

RESPIRATORY SYSTEM

CIRCULATORY SYSTEM

DIGESTIVE SYSTEM

URINARY SYSTEM

NERVOUS SYSTEM

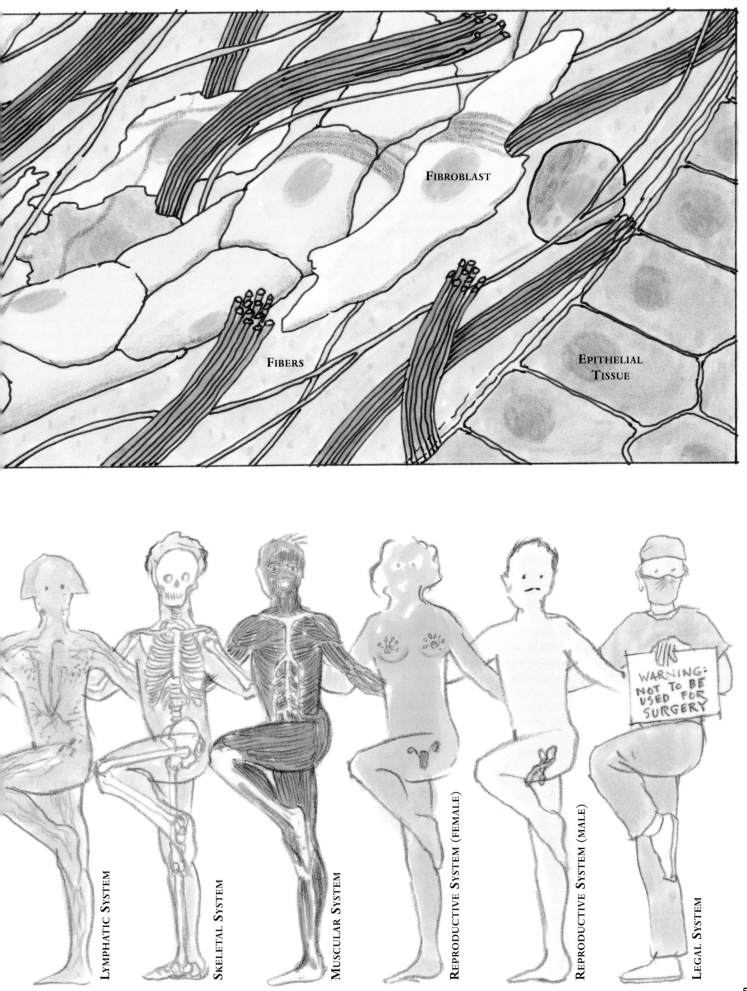

FIBROBLAST

FIBERS

EPITHELIAL
TISSUE

WARNING:
NOT TO BE
USED FOR
SURGERY

LYMPHATIC SYSTEM

SKELETAL SYSTEM

MUSCULAR SYSTEM

REPRODUCTIVE SYSTEM (FEMALE)

REPRODUCTIVE SYSTEM (MALE)

LEGAL SYSTEM

55

CHAPTER 2

AIR TRAFFIC CONTROL

BREATHING IS A NATURAL PROCESS THAT, unlike eating or drinking, we have to do continuously. All of our cells need oxygen in order to release the energy that keeps them and us alive. The efficient and carefully controlled act of sucking air into our lungs and blowing it out several times each minute is the first step in ensuring they get it.

The second step, the speedy and constant delivery of oxygen to the cells themselves, is the responsibility of the heart and bloodstream, the latter of which also gathers waste carbon dioxide to be released out into the atmosphere.

If one or the other system breaks down, life becomes much more difficult. But until that happens, we rarely think about or appreciate either process.

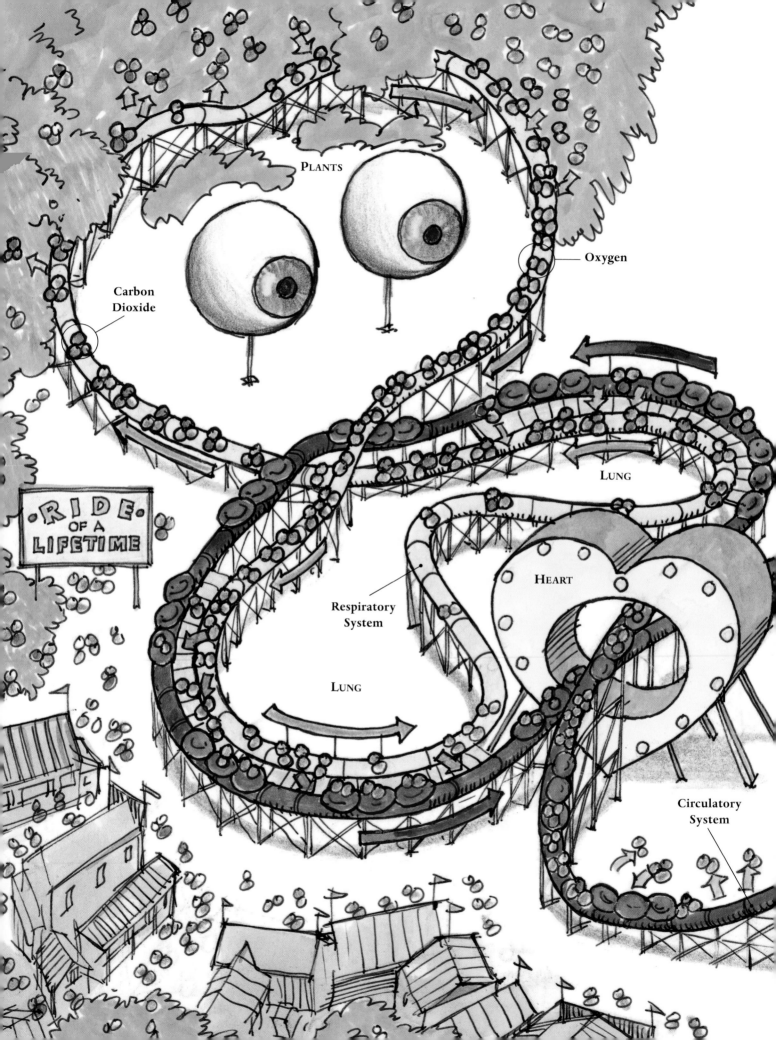

SUPPLY CHAIN

Consuming oxygen and generating carbon dioxide happen day and night for the lifetime of most organisms on the planet, including us. As oxygen is being used up, it is replaced by a process called photosynthesis that happens in trees, ferns, and countless other plants. During the day, this vegetation soaks up carbon dioxide and, using the energy of sunlight, combines it with water to make the food it needs. Photosynthesis, like any metabolic process, produces waste.

Fortunately for us, that waste is oxygen.

To take in an adequate supply of oxygen molecules and get them where they are needed, our cells have constructed a pair of distinct but mutually dependent systems. The first, the respiratory system, draws oxygen into the lungs and sends waste carbon dioxide out. The second, the circulatory system, delivers that fresh oxygen from the lungs to each and every cell and carries the waste back.

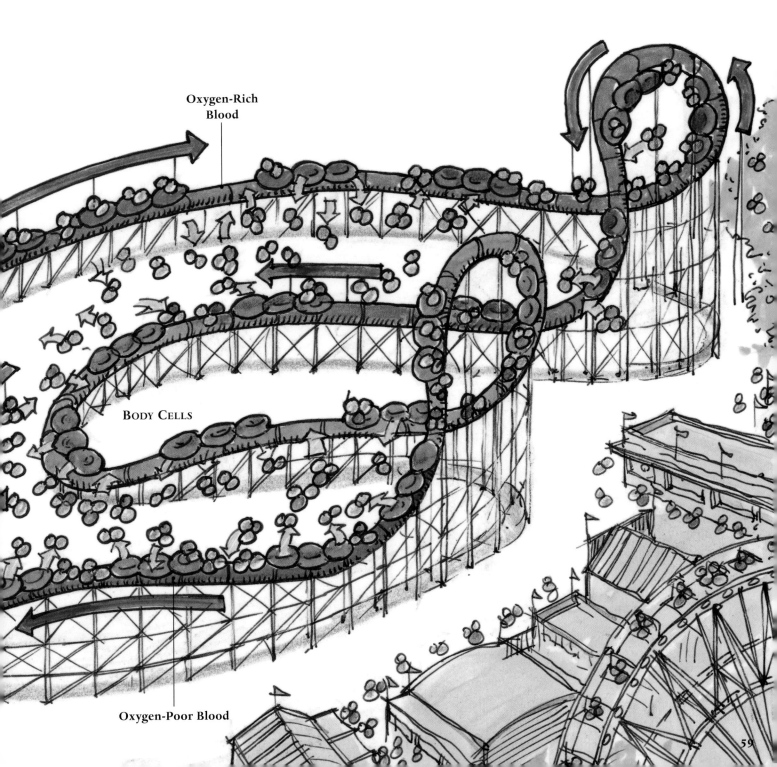

Oxygen-Rich Blood

BODY CELLS

Oxygen-Poor Blood

GOOD THING WE BROUGHT THE MACHETE.

NOSE JOB

The air we breathe is full of dust, skin flakes, insect body parts, clothing fibers, and pollen grains, not to mention bacteria and other germs. Our easily damaged lungs need air that is not only clean but also moist and warm.

Behind our nostrils are the two halves of the nasal cavity, both lined by a membrane that is sticky with mucus. As air is drawn in, large particles are filtered out by a tangle of coarse hairs. Upon entering the nasal cavities, the airflow is then disrupted by a number of curved projections, and any remaining particles are flung into the mucus. Tiny hairlike projections called cilia sway from side to side, sweeping "dirty" mucus backwards through the nasal cavity to the throat, from which it will pass to the stomach for digestion.

As it is being cleaned, air is warmed by heat escaping from blood vessels and moistened by water vapor that evaporates from the wet nasal lining.

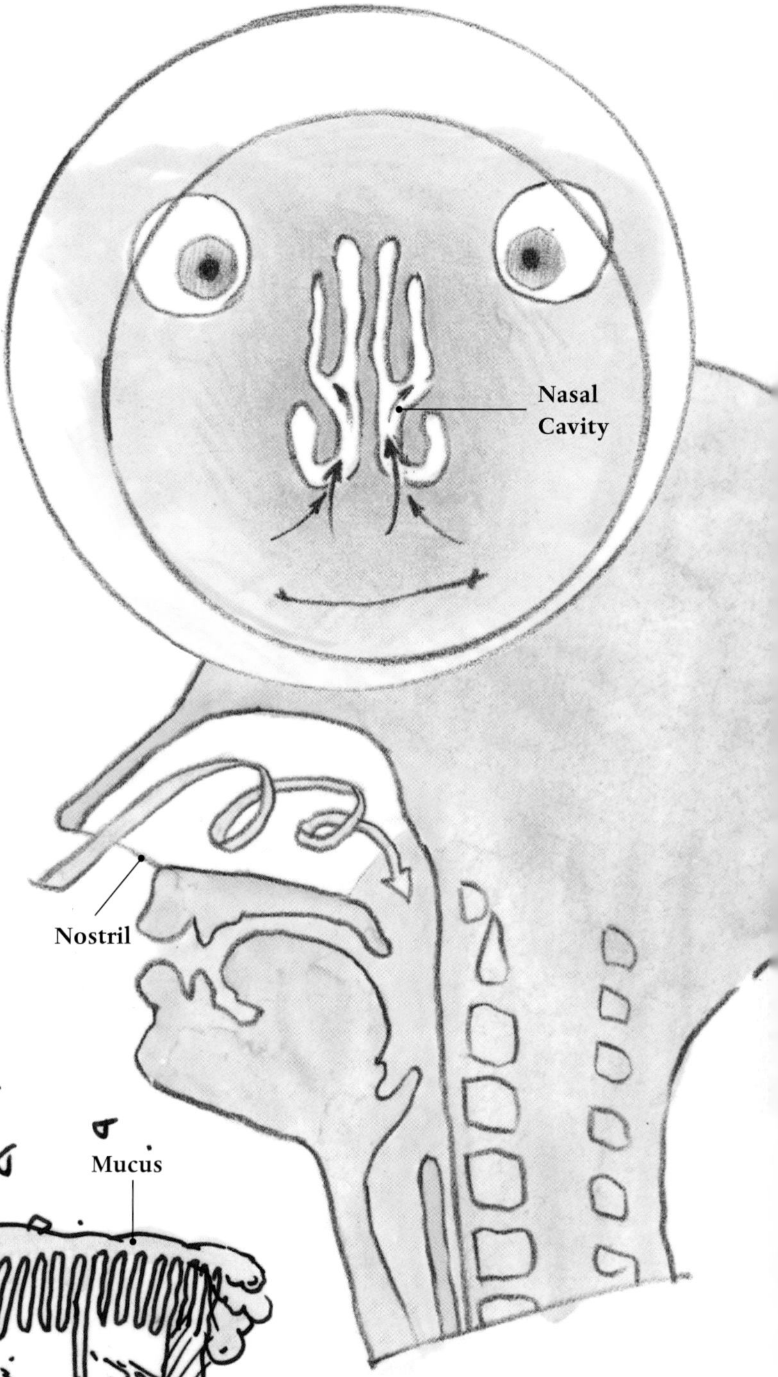

Nasal Cavity

Nostril

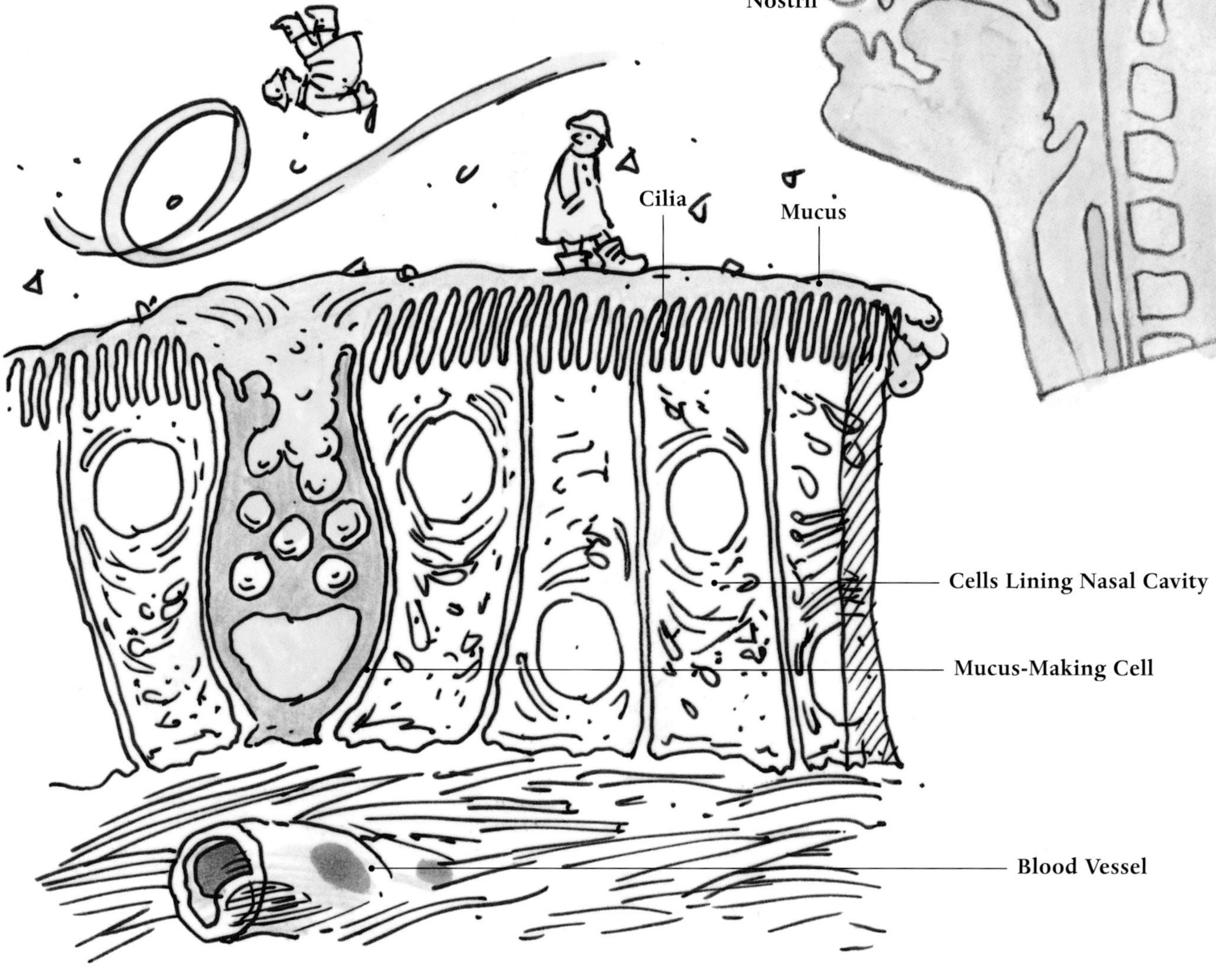

Cilia

Mucus

Cells Lining Nasal Cavity

Mucus-Making Cell

Blood Vessel

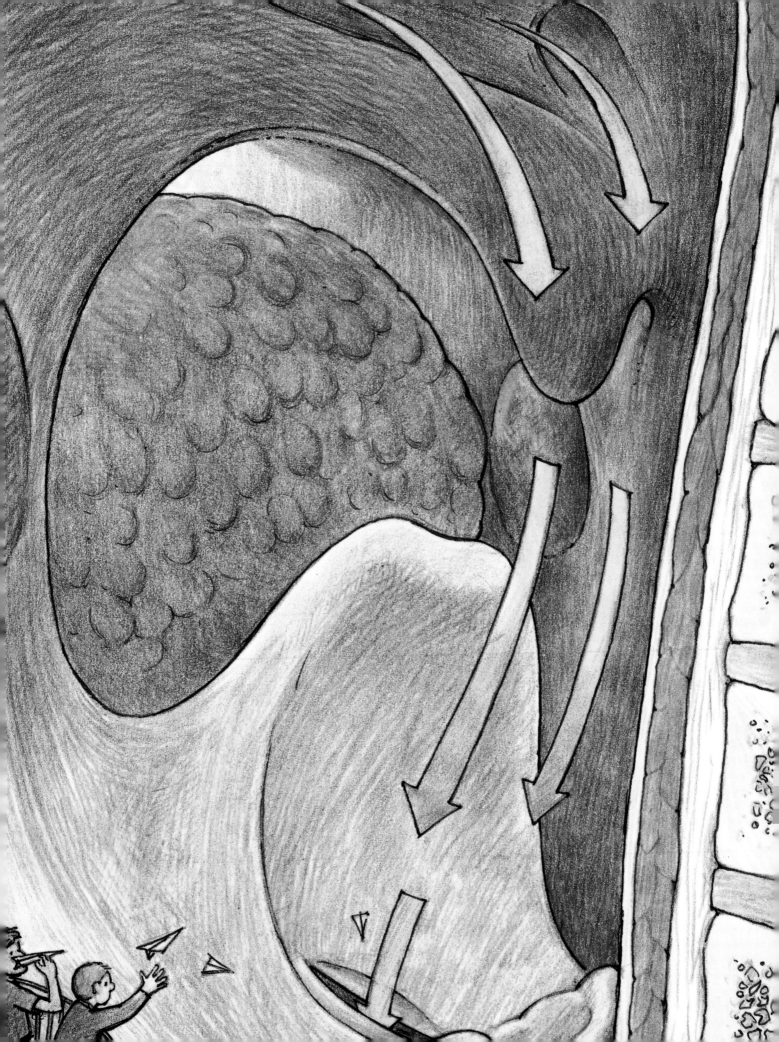

OPEN AIRWAY

For part of their journey, air and food have a common pathway—the throat. Newly cleaned air from the nasal cavity passes through the throat, larynx, and trachea to reach the lungs; food from the mouth exits the throat through the esophagus on its way to the stomach. When we swallow food or drinks, breathing is briefly interrupted as a flap of cartilage called the epiglottis temporarily covers the opening to the larynx. This protects the airway from potential catastrophe by making sure food "goes down the right way."

C-shaped bands of cartilage reinforce the trachea and keep it from collapsing inward as we inhale. The cartilage stops at the back of the trachea, allowing the esophagus to expand into the airway momentarily as food passes through.

The air-filtering process that started in the nose continues inside the trachea as mucus and cilia trap and redirect all unwanted visitors. In this case, however, dirt- and germ-laden mucus is swept upward to the throat, ready for a quick trip to the stomach and destruction.

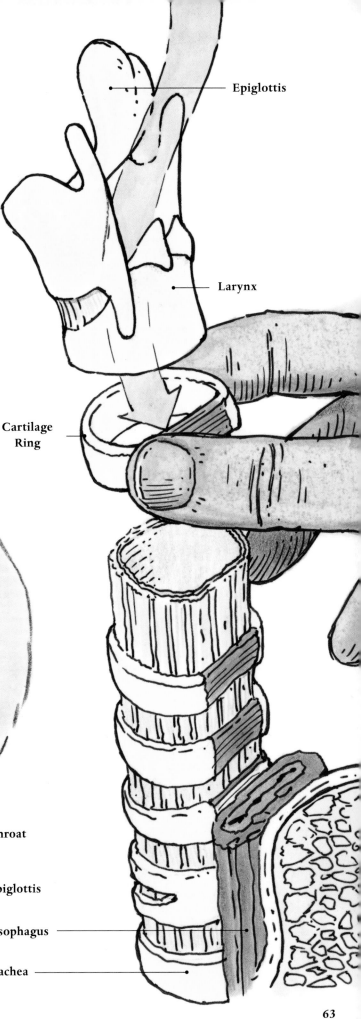

Epiglottis

Larynx

Cartilage Ring

Esophagus

Trachea

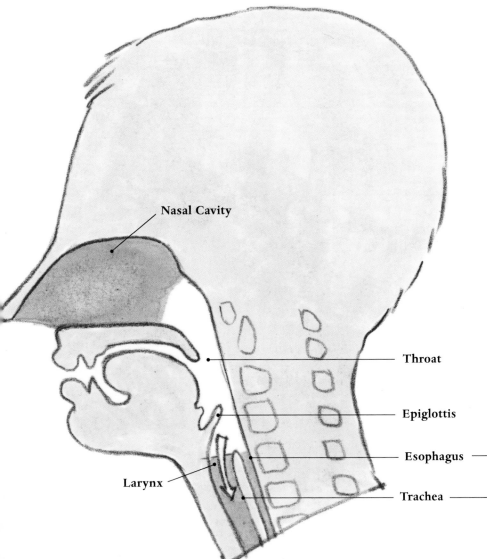

Nasal Cavity

Throat

Epiglottis

Larynx

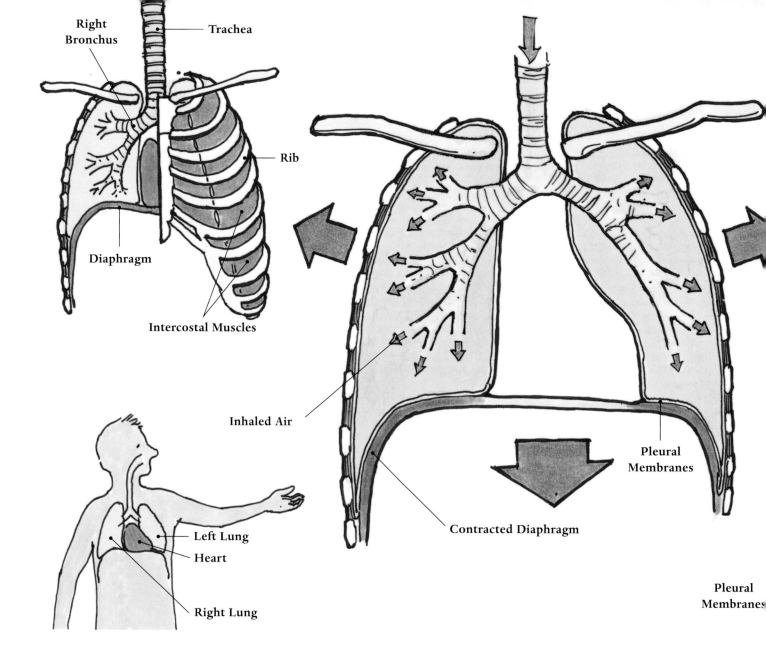

Right Bronchus

Trachea

Rib

Diaphragm

Intercostal Muscles

Inhaled Air

Contracted Diaphragm

Pleural Membranes

Pleural Membranes

Left Lung

Heart

Right Lung

TAKE A DEEP BREATH

Deep in the chest and just above the heart, the trachea divides to form the left and right bronchi that carry air into and out of the lungs. The lungs and heart "sit" on the diaphragm, a domed sheet of muscle that seals off the chest cavity from the abdomen below. All three organs are protected by a "cage" of ribs attached in front to the sternum, in the rear to the backbone, and to each other by intercostal muscles. Each lung is further enclosed by two layers of tissue called pleural membranes. The inner layer is attached to the lungs' surface, the outer layer to the chest cavity and diaphragm. Lubricating fluid trapped in the narrow space between the layers allows them to slide against each other but not to pull apart.

In order to expand and draw in air, lungs depend entirely on the diaphragm and intercostal muscles. When the diaphragm contracts it flattens and pulls the lungs downward while contraction of the intercostal muscles causes the rib cage and the lungs to move upward and outward. As the space inside the lungs increases, air pressure inside them decreases to below that outside the body. This pressure difference causes air from the outside to flow through the nose and down to the lungs, bringing with it fresh supplies of oxygen.

Diaphragm

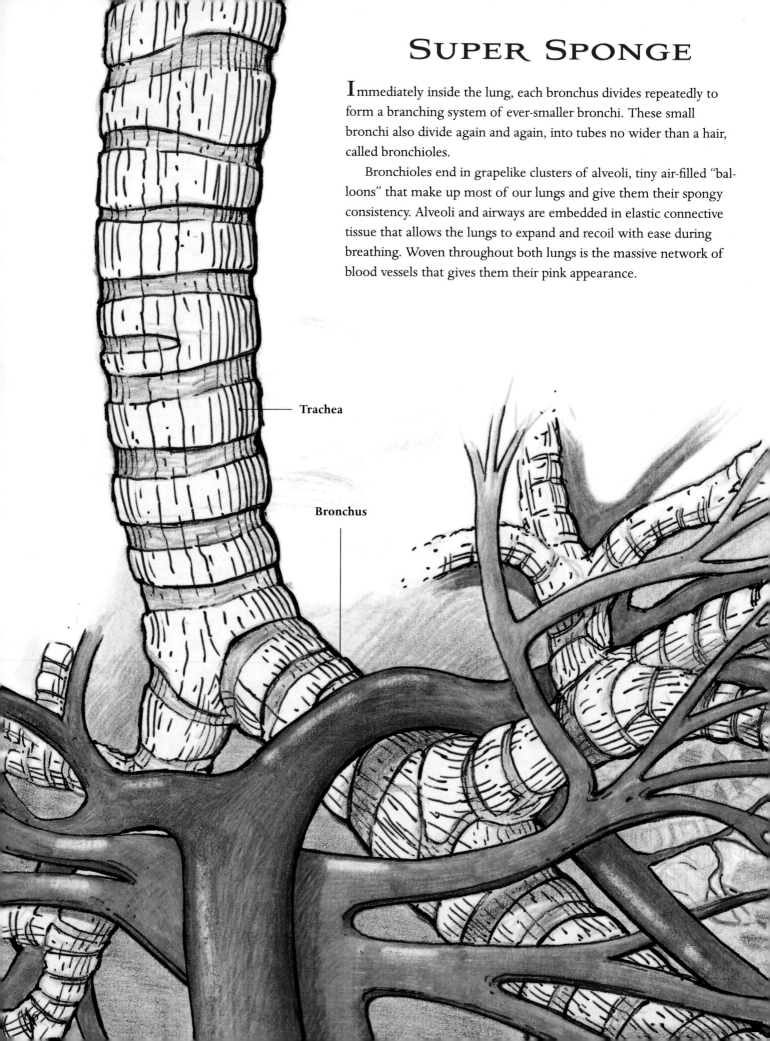

SUPER SPONGE

Immediately inside the lung, each bronchus divides repeatedly to form a branching system of ever-smaller bronchi. These small bronchi also divide again and again, into tubes no wider than a hair, called bronchioles.

Bronchioles end in grapelike clusters of alveoli, tiny air-filled "balloons" that make up most of our lungs and give them their spongy consistency. Alveoli and airways are embedded in elastic connective tissue that allows the lungs to expand and recoil with ease during breathing. Woven throughout both lungs is the massive network of blood vessels that gives them their pink appearance.

Trachea

Bronchus

There are 150 million microscopic alveoli in each lung, covered by a web of tiny capillaries through which an endless flow of blood dumps carbon dioxide and picks up oxygen. Despite their small size, these thin-walled, interconnected air bags take up most of the space inside the lungs. If it were possible to flatten out all the alveoli from both lungs, we'd be looking at a rectangle of moist epithelium approximately 30 feet (9 meters) high and 25 feet (7.7 meters) wide with a sheet of blood flowing down one side and open air on the other.

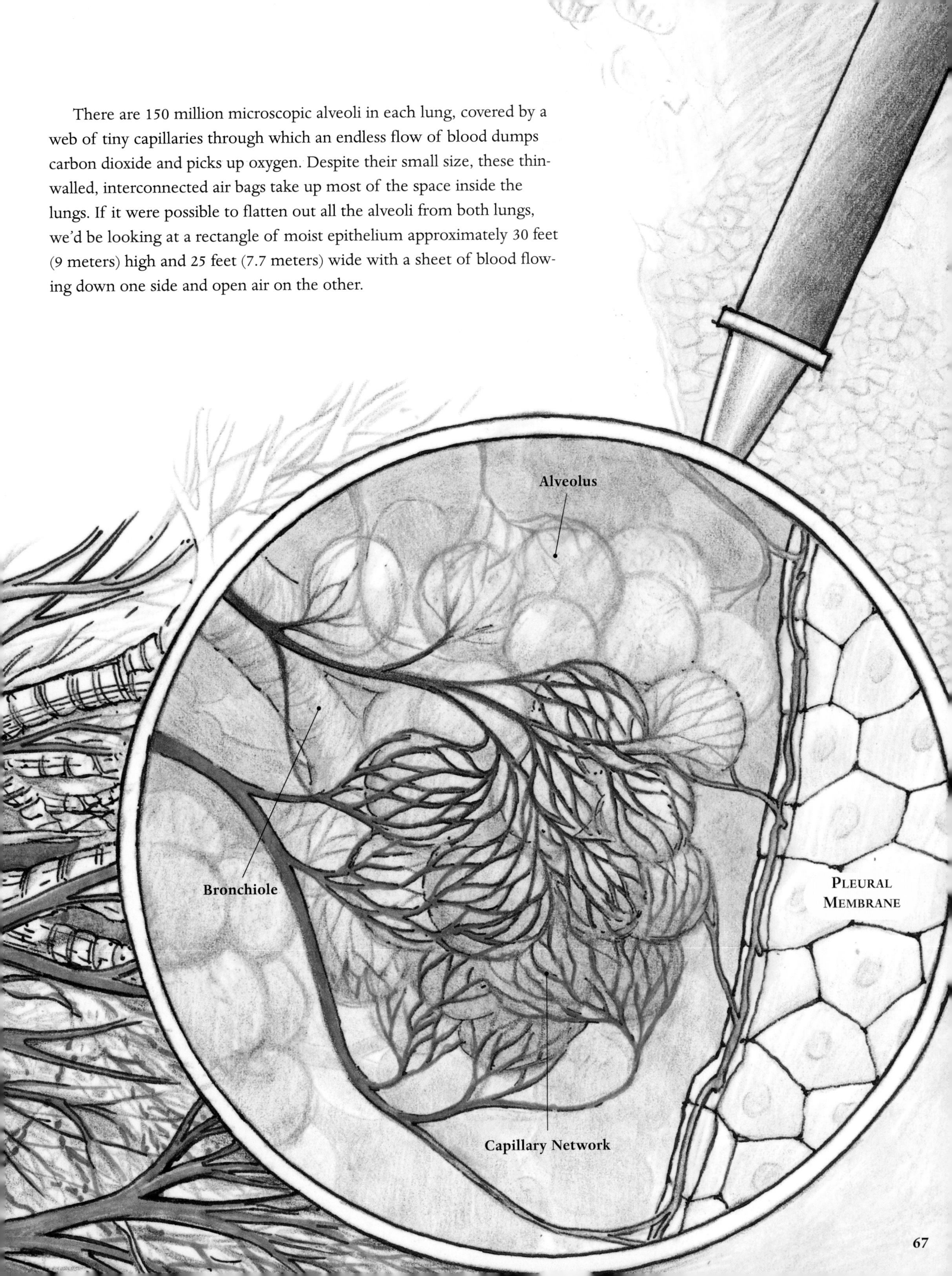

Alveolus

Bronchiole

PLEURAL MEMBRANE

Capillary Network

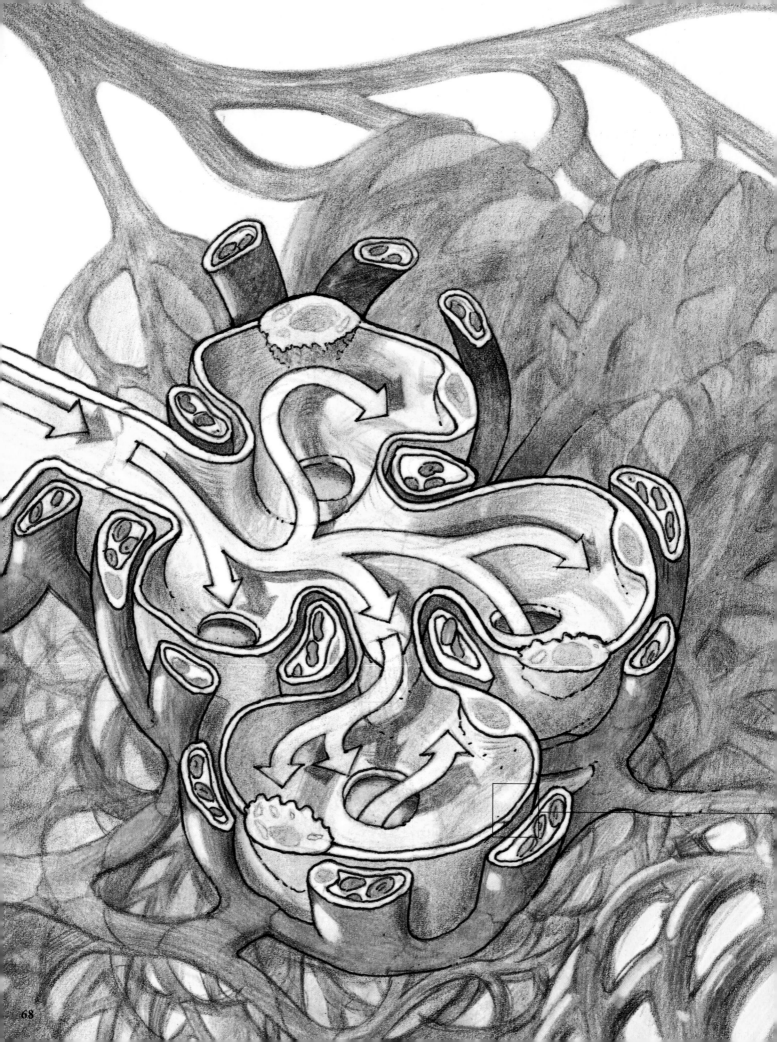

Drop-off and Pickup #1

The exchange of oxygen and carbon dioxide is fast. Each air-filled alveolus is separated from an adjacent blood-filled capillary by a membrane just four ten-thousandths of an inch (0.001 millimeter) thick. That membrane consists of the wall of the alveolus, the wall of the capillary, and the flimsy basal lamina between them.

Gas exchange is also economical. Because it relies on diffusion—the natural movement of molecules from areas of high concentration to areas of low concentration—no energy is consumed. Oxygen diffuses across the membrane into the capillary and is picked up by red blood cells and spirited away. Breathing in keeps levels of oxygen high inside the alveolus, while the constant removal of oxygen by the bloodstream keeps oxygen levels low in the capillary.

Special cells in the alveolar walls add something called surfactant to the watery lining of the alveolus. Surfactant prevents the water molecules from sticking together, which could cause the alveolus to collapse between breaths, with fatal consequences.

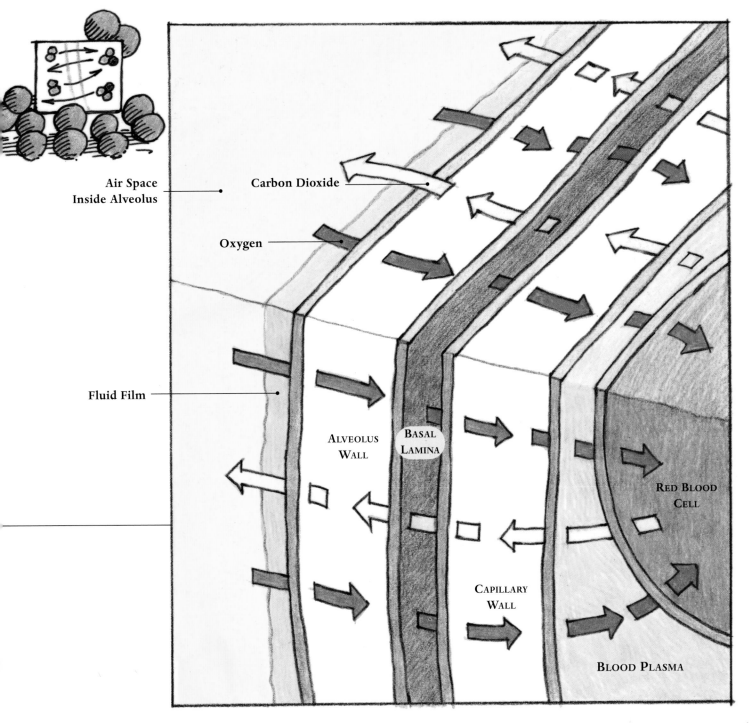

Air Space
Inside Alveolus

Carbon Dioxide

Oxygen

Fluid Film

ALVEOLUS
WALL

BASAL
LAMINA

RED BLOOD
CELL

CAPILLARY
WALL

BLOOD PLASMA

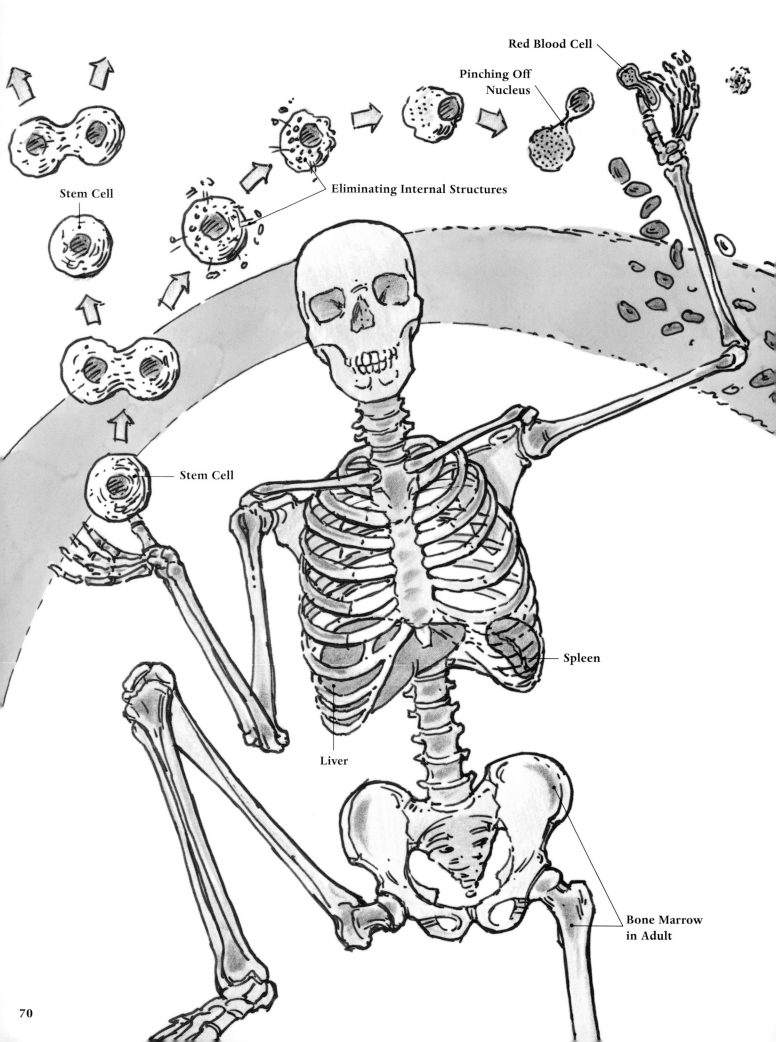

Stem Cell

Eliminating Internal Structures

Pinching Off Nucleus

Red Blood Cell

Stem Cell

Spleen

Liver

Bone Marrow in Adult

RED CELLS IN THE LIMELIGHT

Red blood cells lead a very full but relatively short life. They are derived—at a rate of around two million per second—from constantly dividing, unspecialized stem cells in the marrow found inside certain bones. Within bone marrow the developing red blood cell produces as much hemoglobin as it can hold, even pinching off and expelling its nucleus to create more room. By the time it enters the circulatory system, each cell has also become perfectly contoured for picking up and unloading oxygen as rapidly as possible.

For approximately 120 days, each red blood cell travels throughout the body, using its relative smallness and flexibility to reach even the most distant cells. This process is not without wear and tear, however, and eventually red blood cells become too fragile to continue their work. They will have passed through an organ called the spleen many times on their travels, but at the end of their run, they are trapped there once and for all. It is primarily in this organ, next to the stomach, that each hemoglobin molecule is broken down. Its iron and amino acids are salvaged for reuse and the rest is converted to bile pigments, which are shipped via the bloodstream to the liver for elimination.

A DAY AT THE SPLEEN

Worn-Out Red Blood Cell

Amino Acids

Iron

Bile Pigments

TO THE LIVER

PARKING FOR SPLEEN ONLY

THE DYNAMIC DUO TIMES FOUR

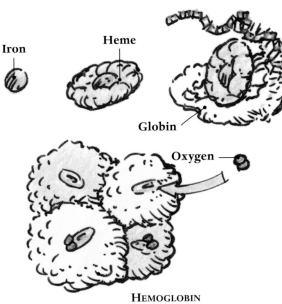

Iron

Heme

Globin

Oxygen

HEMOGLOBIN

Hemoglobin is a complex oxygen-carrying molecule constructed from four subunits. Each consists of a heme group and a protein called globin. The heme group forms a ring around an atom of iron, the part of the molecule that binds oxygen. Heme absorbs certain wavelengths of light and reflects others, giving hemoglobin its red color. The folded globin molecule completely envelops the heme group and then links up with the three similar subunits to form one of the 250 million hemoglobin molecules inside each red blood cell. With four heme groups, each hemoglobin molecule can carry four oxygen molecules. That's a staggering total of one billion oxygen molecules carried by each of the trillions of red blood cells in our bodies.

EVERYBODY INTO THE POOL

Like cartilage and bone, blood is a connective tissue, but it's the only one made of cells floating in a liquid. Blood is a distributor, delivering essentials to cells and removing their wastes. It's a regulator, spreading heat around the body to keep our insides at a steady 98.6°F (37°C). And it's also a protector, with leak-fixing capabilities and an army of germ killers.

Blood may appear red, but the liquid part is actually a watery, straw-colored fluid. Called plasma, this fluid transports dissolved items such as food (glucose, amino acids,

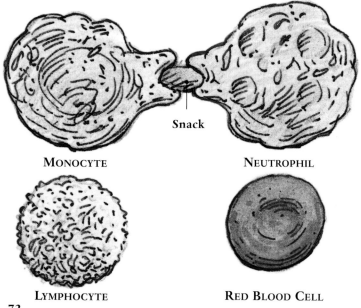

MONOCYTE

NEUTROPHIL

Snack

LYMPHOCYTE

RED BLOOD CELL

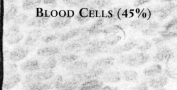

PLASMA (55%)

BLOOD CELLS (45%)

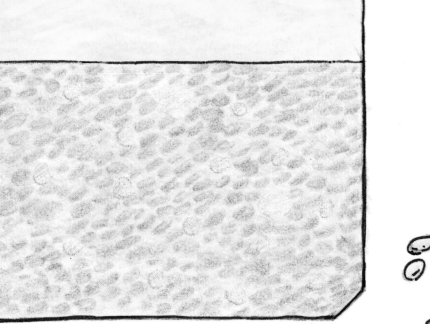

and fats), hormones, wastes (carbon dioxide and urea), and various ions. Plasma also carries several types of proteins involved in blood clotting, defense, and maintaining water balance.

Suspended in plasma are several types of cells, all from the red bone marrow production site. While red blood cells make up 99 percent of this population, white blood cells are far more diverse. They include germ-eating neutrophils and monocytes and antibody-releasing lymphocytes, linchpins of the immune system. Finally there are platelets, the pluggers of leaks and initiators of blood clotting. These bud from huge bone marrow cells called megakaryocytes.

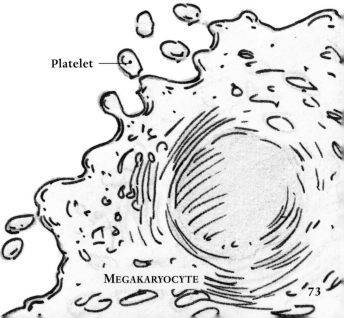

Platelet

MEGAKARYOCYTE

FRIEND OR FOE?

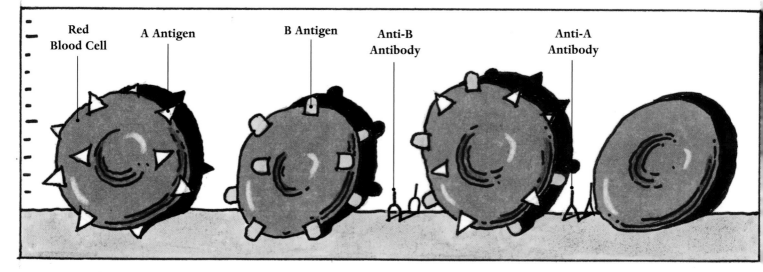

Red Blood Cell   A Antigen   B Antigen   Anti-B Antibody   Anti-A Antibody

Just as we have our own identities, so too do our red blood cells. Attached to their surface are specific antigens—molecular markers made from carbohydrates and proteins. The presence or absence of these antigens determines which blood group a person belongs to. A antigens identify group A blood, B antigens denote group B blood, A and B antigens together produce group AB blood, and blood with neither antigen is classified as group O.

A and B antigens are particularly important when it comes to blood transfusions. A problem can arise because of antibodies, chemicals in blood plasma—the liquid in which red blood cells float—that bind to any "foreign" cells or proteins and mark them for destruction. Group A blood contains antibodies that will target B antigens, while group B blood contains antibodies that will target A antigens. If, for example, group B blood is inadvertently given to a group A person, the anti-A antibodies in donated blood are rapidly diluted—because the quantity of blood given in a transfusion is a fraction of that already circulating in the recipient—and have little effect. But anti-B antibodies in the recipient's plasma make the donated group B red cells clump together. This can block blood vessels and result in painful and sometimes fatal consequences.

Group AB blood has neither anti-A nor anti-B antibodies so potentially it can receive blood of any group. Group O blood contains both anti-A and anti-B antibodies, and so can only receive group O blood. In fact, because its red cells lack A and B antigens, group O blood can also be given to people with A, B, or AB blood type.

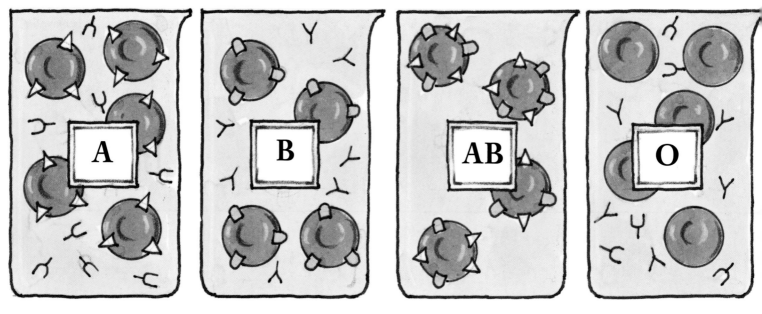

A   B   AB   O

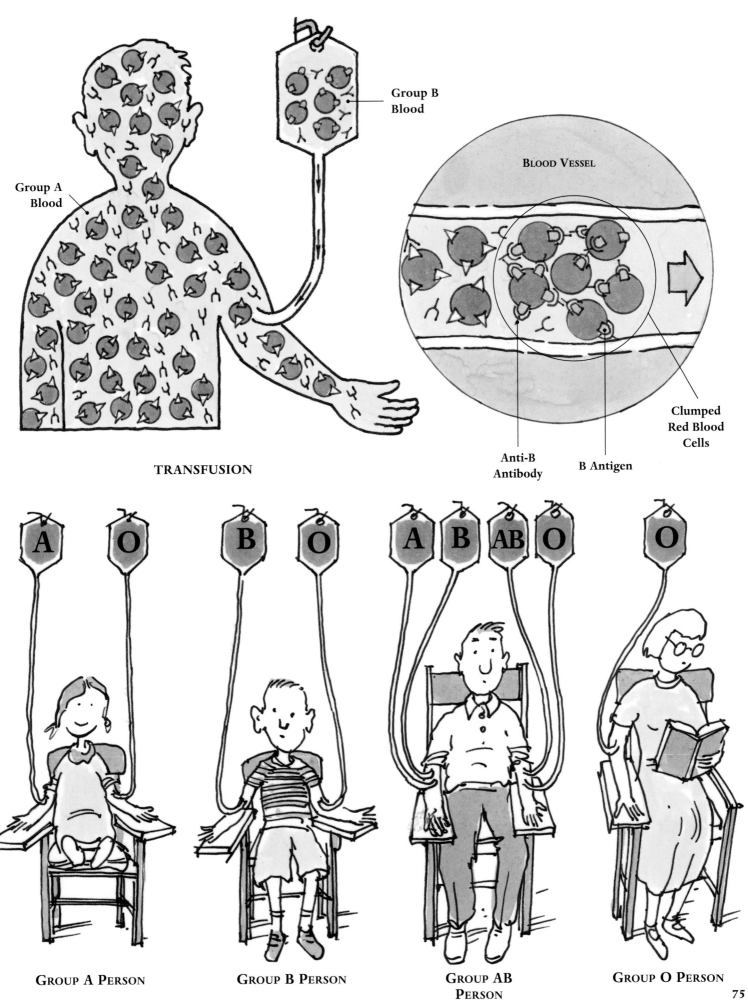

Group A
Blood

Group B
Blood

TRANSFUSION

BLOOD VESSEL

Anti-B
Antibody

B Antigen

Clumped
Red Blood
Cells

GROUP A PERSON

GROUP B PERSON

**GROUP AB
PERSON**

GROUP O PERSON

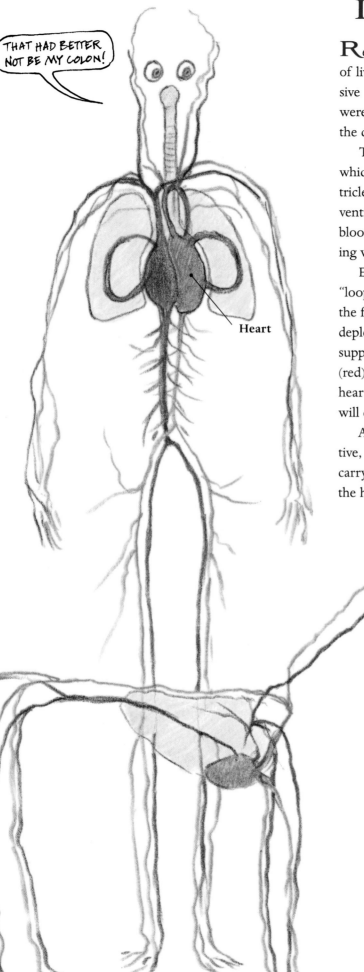

IN CIRCULATION

Reaching everywhere from toes to teeth, a vast network of living tubes carries blood to where it's needed. As extensive as this delivery system is, however, it would be useless were it not for the heart, the mighty pump at the core of the circulatory system.

The heart has two halves—left and right—both of which are divided into two chambers, an atrium and a ventricle. The atrium receives blood and passes it on to the ventricle, which in turn sends it on its way. It takes a red blood cell sixty seconds to make a complete roundtrip, during which it enters and leaves the heart not once but twice.

Each half of the heart pumps blood through a separate "loop" of the blood-vessel network. At the beginning of the first loop, the right half of the heart pumps oxygen-depleted blood (blue) to the lungs, where it picks up fresh supplies. This loop is then completed by oxygen-rich blood (red) leaving the lungs and returning to the left side of the heart. From here it enters the second, much larger loop that will carry it around the body.

Arteries carry blood from the heart to muscle, connective, and all other types of tissues. Microscopic capillaries carry blood through the tissues, and veins bring it back to the heart.

RIGHT LUNG

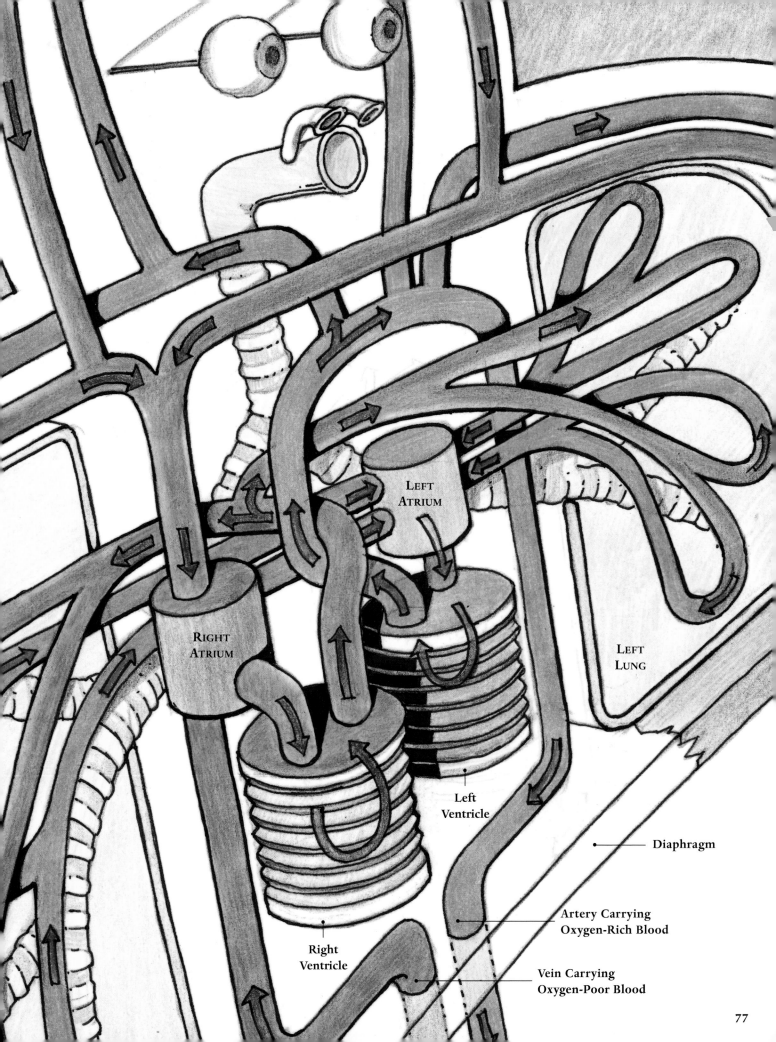

LEFT
ATRIUM

RIGHT
ATRIUM

LEFT
LUNG

Left
Ventricle

Diaphragm

Right
Ventricle

Artery Carrying
Oxygen-Rich Blood

Vein Carrying
Oxygen-Poor Blood

Never Tiring

Most of the wall enclosing all four chambers of the heart is made up of cardiac muscle, a type of muscle unique to the heart. It consists of branching muscle cells firmly anchored to each other, bundled, and reinforced by connective tissue fibers that prevent tearing when the cells contract.

Try clenching your fist repeatedly without stopping. The arm and hand muscles that power this movement will soon tire. The same isn't true for cardiac muscle. Its cells can work nonstop for a lifetime because they generate much more energy than regular cells, including other kinds of muscle cells. Large numbers of bigger-than-normal mitochondria occupy around one-quarter of the space inside each cell.

The copious amounts of oxygen and fuel required by mitochondria to release energy are provided by the heart's own dedicated blood supply. So important is this supply that the first arteries to branch off the aorta—the main artery leaving the heart's left side—are the two coronary arteries. If this supply becomes blocked or fails for some reason, the heart and therefore the entire body are soon in trouble.

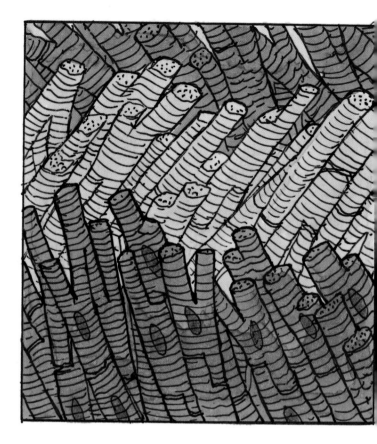

CARDIAC MUSCLE

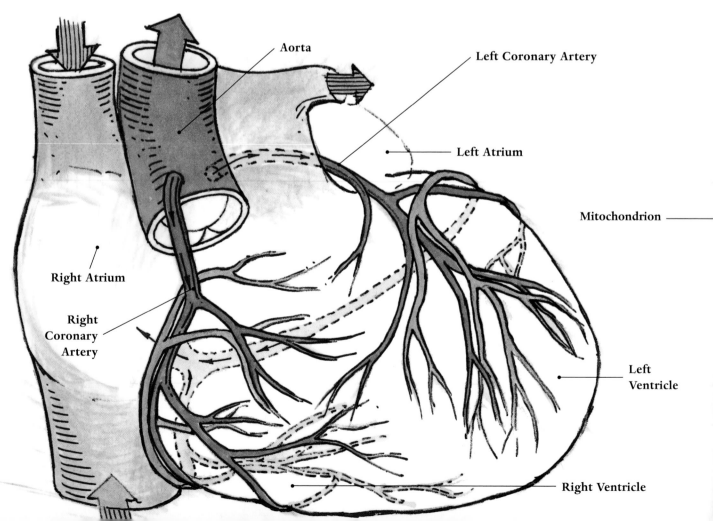

Aorta

Left Coronary Artery

Left Atrium

Mitochondrion

Right Atrium

Right Coronary Artery

Left Ventricle

Right Ventricle

CARDIAC MUSCLE CELL

ANCHORING JUNCTION

BE NOT STILL

Successful operation of the heart depends on two sets of special valves that enforce a one-way flow of blood. Although these valves are very thin, they are resilient enough to withstand a lifetime's pummeling.

The exits from both ventricles—only the left one is shown here—are guarded by valves made up of three pockets. When the ventricles contract, the force of blood flowing into the artery flattens each pocket against the wall. When the heart relaxes, blood flows backwards toward the ventricles and fills the pockets, causing them to swell and seal off the opening.

The valve between each atrium and ventricle consists of downward-pointing flaps. When the ventricle contracts, blood is pushed against the flaps, forcing them into their closed, self-sealing position. Cords made of collagen anchor the flaps in this position and prevent them from being blown inside out like an umbrella in a gale. It is this delicate-looking but surprisingly tough arrangement that prevents blood from flowing back into the atrium.

During each heartbeat, the atria and ventricles of both sides of the heart relax and contract in exactly the same sequence.

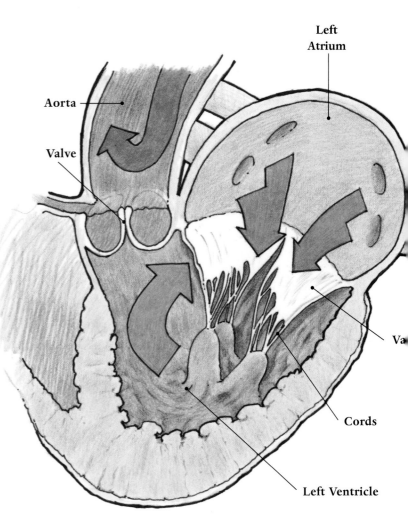

Left Atrium

Aorta

Valve

Va

Cords

Left Ventricle

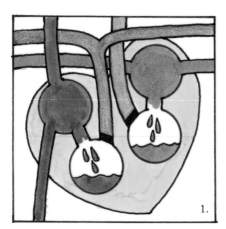

1.

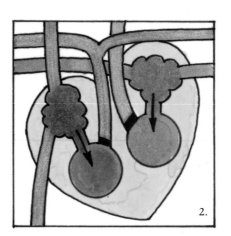

2.

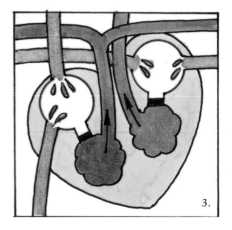

3.

1. All four chambers of the heart are relaxed. Oxygen-poor blood from the body flows into the right atrium and on to the right ventricle. Oxygen-rich blood from the lungs enters the left atrium and ventricle. Backward pressure from blood that left during the last heartbeat keeps the valves guarding the exits from the ventricles firmly shut to prevent backflow of blood.

2. Now the two atria contract together and squeeze their remaining blood into the ventricles.

3. Both ventricles contract together, forcing open the valves as oxygen-poor blood is pumped out of the right side of the heart to the lungs and oxygen-rich blood exits the left side of the heart toward the rest of the body. At the same time the valves between atria and ventricles slam shut to stop blood from returning to the atria.

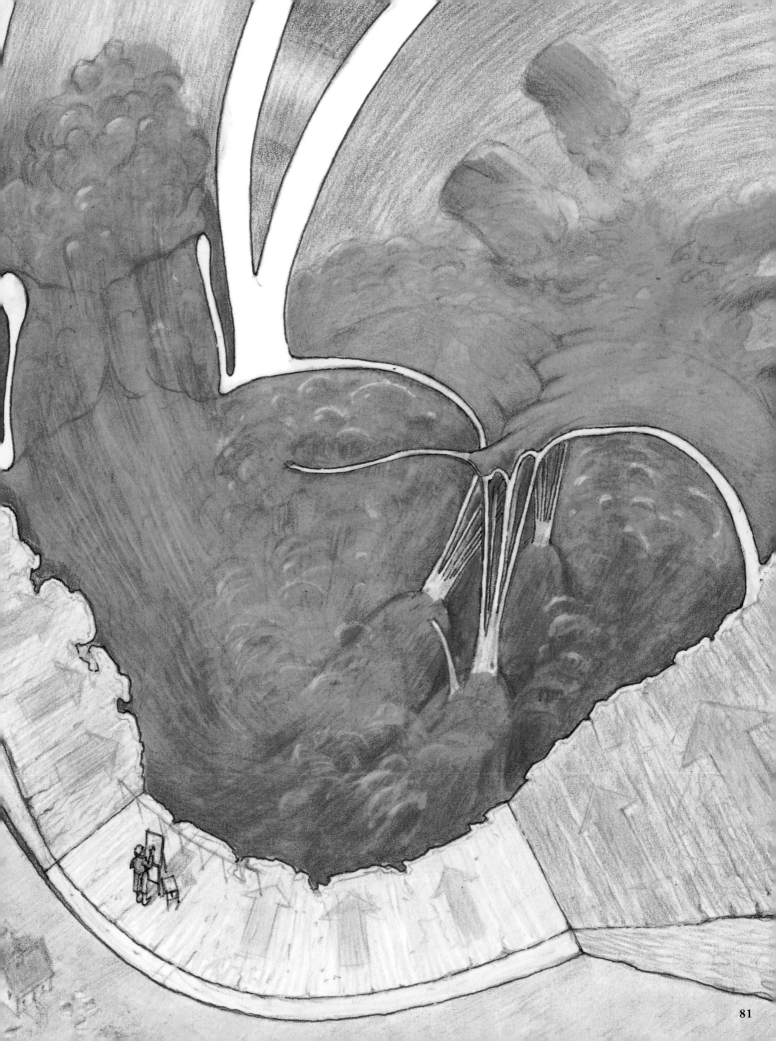

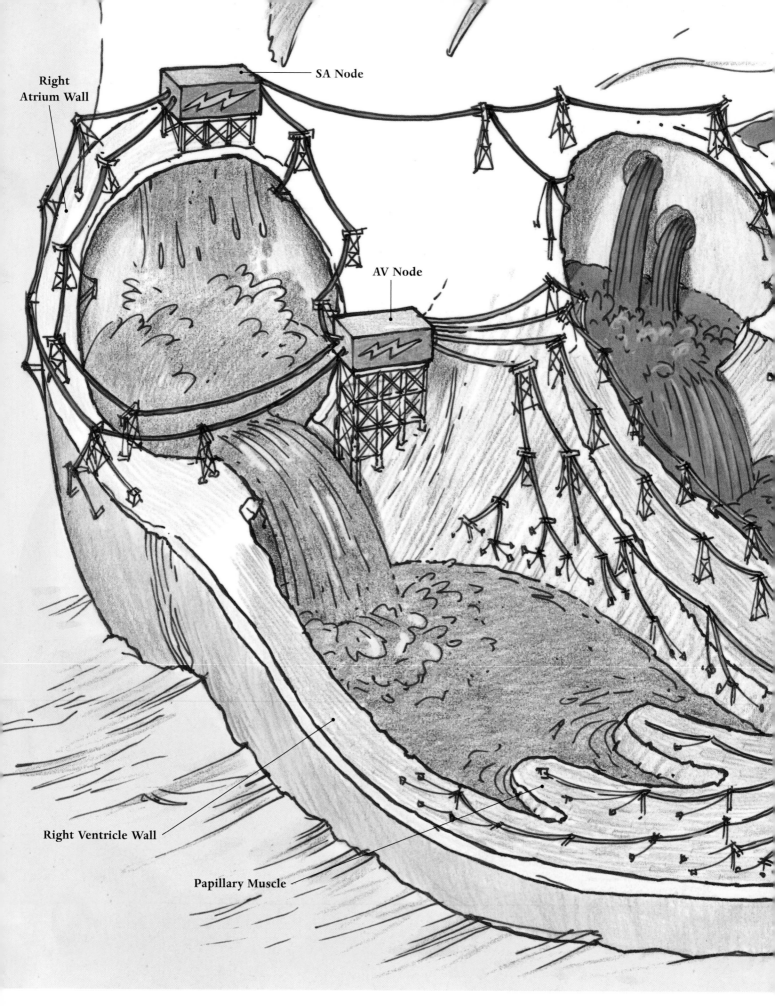

SA Node

Right
Atrium Wall

AV Node

Right Ventricle Wall

Papillary Muscle

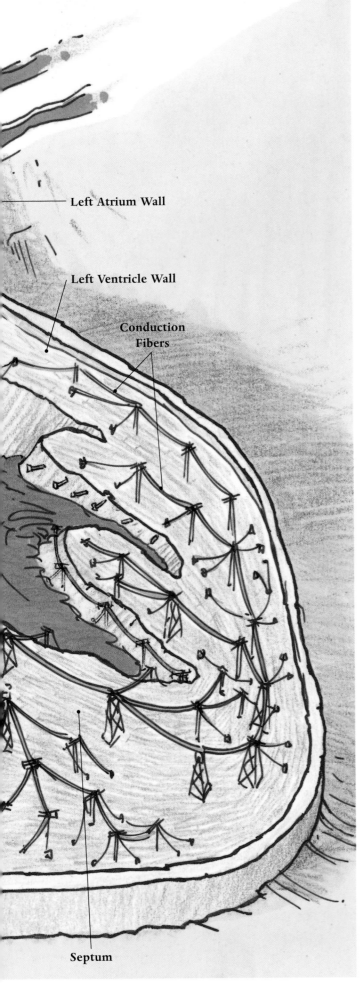

Left Atrium Wall

Left Ventricle Wall

Conduction Fibers

Septum

SETTING THE PACE

A control system with split-second timing ensures that the heart's atria contract just before the ventricles. Without it, contraction would be chaotic and the heart's pumping action feeble. The key to this control is a bundle of special cells called the SA node, the heart's natural pacemaker. With the ability to "fire" spontaneously, these cells stimulate the contraction of heart muscle cells and maintain the pace of the beating heart.

Impulses from the SA node spread through the walls of the right and left atria, ensuring that both chambers contract together. At the same time, these impulses travel directly through conduction fibers made of modified heart muscle cells to a second bundle of cells called the AV node. Since this is the only electrical connection between the atria and the ventricles, there is a slight delay to give the atria time to finish contracting before impulses proceed to the ventricles.

From the AV node, impulses then speed along bundles of conduction fibers through the septum, the wall that separates the right and left ventricles. Left and right branches of these bundles further divide into a network of fibers that supply the ventricle walls. The papillary muscles contract first—tugging on the cords to stop their valves from turning inside out—followed by the ventricles themselves.

After a slight pause to let the two ventricles relax, the next wave of impulses is sent out by the SA node, an event repeated seventy or more times a minute.

MUSCLE CELLS LEFT TO THEIR OWN DEVICES

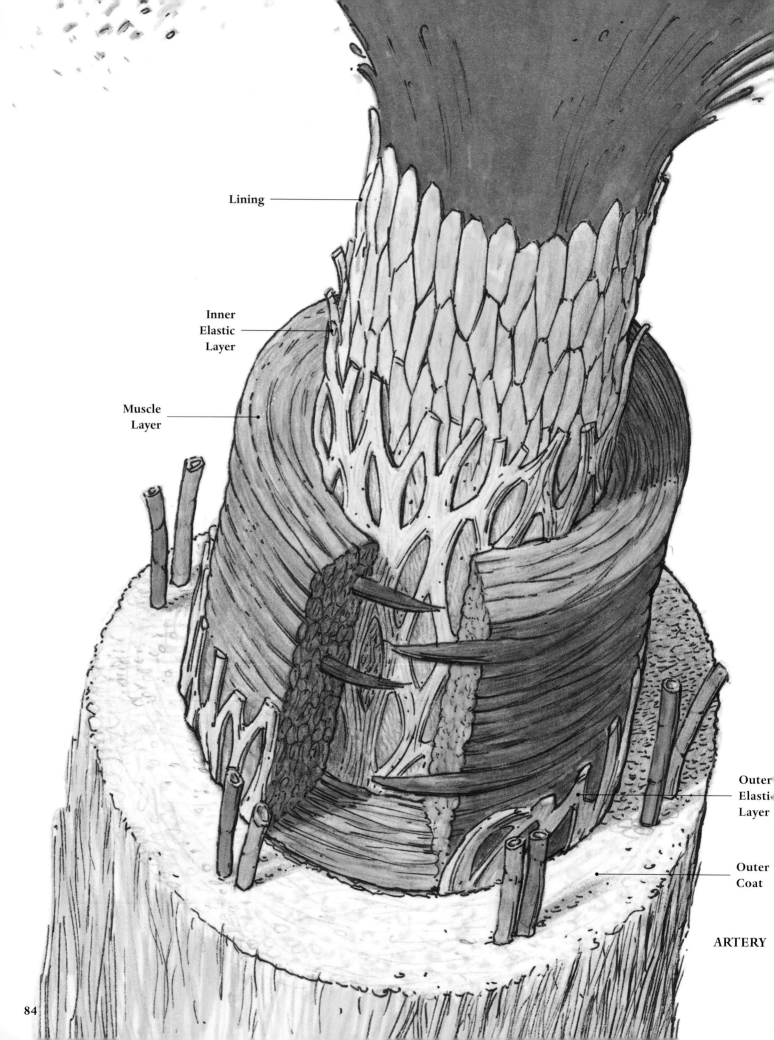

Lining

Inner
Elastic
Layer

Muscle
Layer

Outer
Elastic
Layer

Outer
Coat

ARTERY

84

FEEL THE PULSE

There's a fast and easy way to discover how quickly your heart is beating. Press two fingers against the thumb side of your wrist and you should feel the surge of blood that is being pumped along the radial artery by a single heartbeat. This is your pulse. Count the number of pulses in a minute, and that's your heart rate.

The radial artery is a branch of an artery that itself is an offshoot of the inch-wide aorta that carries oxygen-rich blood from the heart's left ventricle. All arteries have a thick wall with layers of elastic and muscular tissues to resist the high blood pressure generated by the heart's contraction.

Elasticity allows an artery to expand as the heart forces blood along it and then recoil to push blood onward as the heart relaxes. This ensures that blood flow is smooth and continuous, not punctuated by stops and starts. It's this expansion and recoil that is felt as a pulse in the radial artery at the point where it passes over the hardness of the forearm's radius bone.

As arteries branch farther and get smaller, their elasticity decreases and muscle content increases. Under instructions from the brain, the muscle layer can contract or relax to control blood flow to a particular tissue.

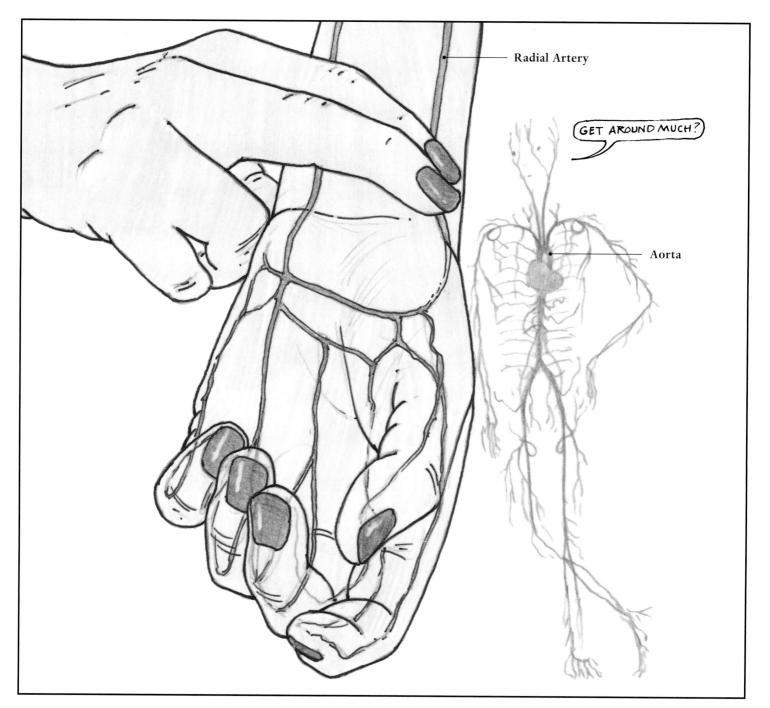

Radial Artery

GET AROUND MUCH?

Aorta

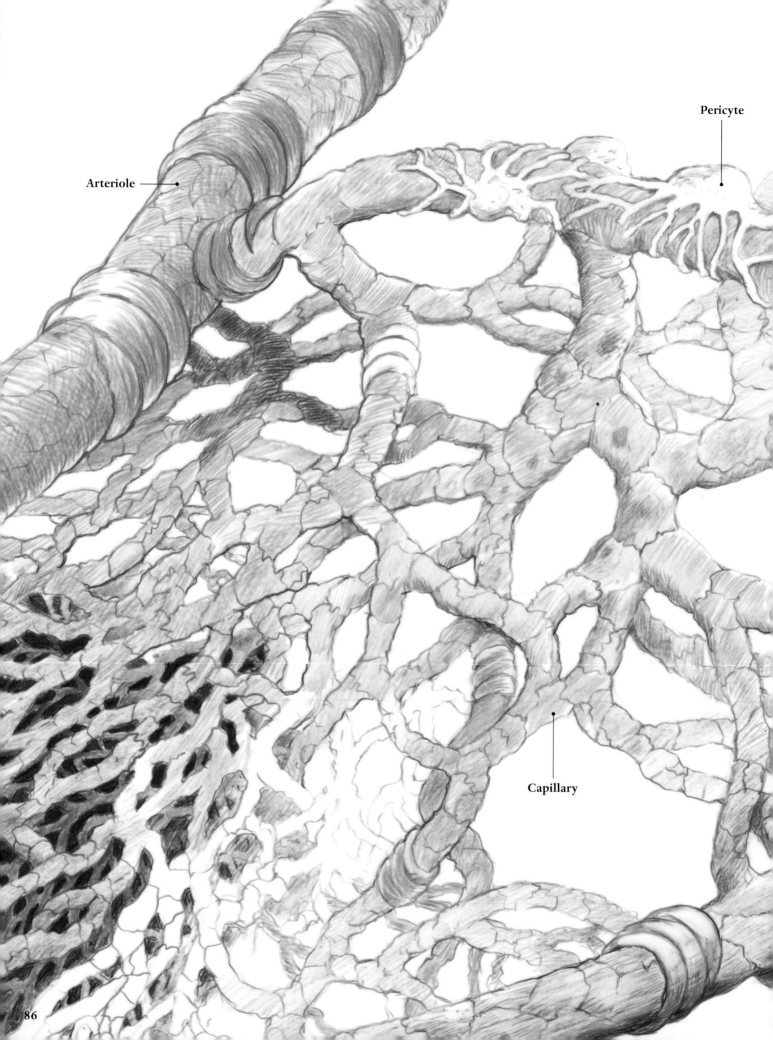

Arteriole

Pericyte

Capillary

DELIVERY SERVICE

If arteries and veins are the highways of the circulatory system, capillaries are the side streets through which deliveries are made to the body's trillions of cellular customers.

As they penetrate organs and tissues, the narrowest arteries divide into even finer arterioles, the smallest of which are wrapped in spiraling smooth muscle fibers. Arterioles divide further to make capillaries, the narrowest of all blood vessels, with an internal diameter just wide enough to allow red blood cells free passage. The wall of a capillary is very thin, consisting of a single layer of cells sometimes reinforced by spider-shaped cells called pericytes. The branching capillaries form a network called a capillary bed that weaves its way through the tissue, ensuring that no cell is far from its supplier. These capillaries then merge to form slightly larger vessels called venules that unite to form the veins that will return blood to the heart.

Venule

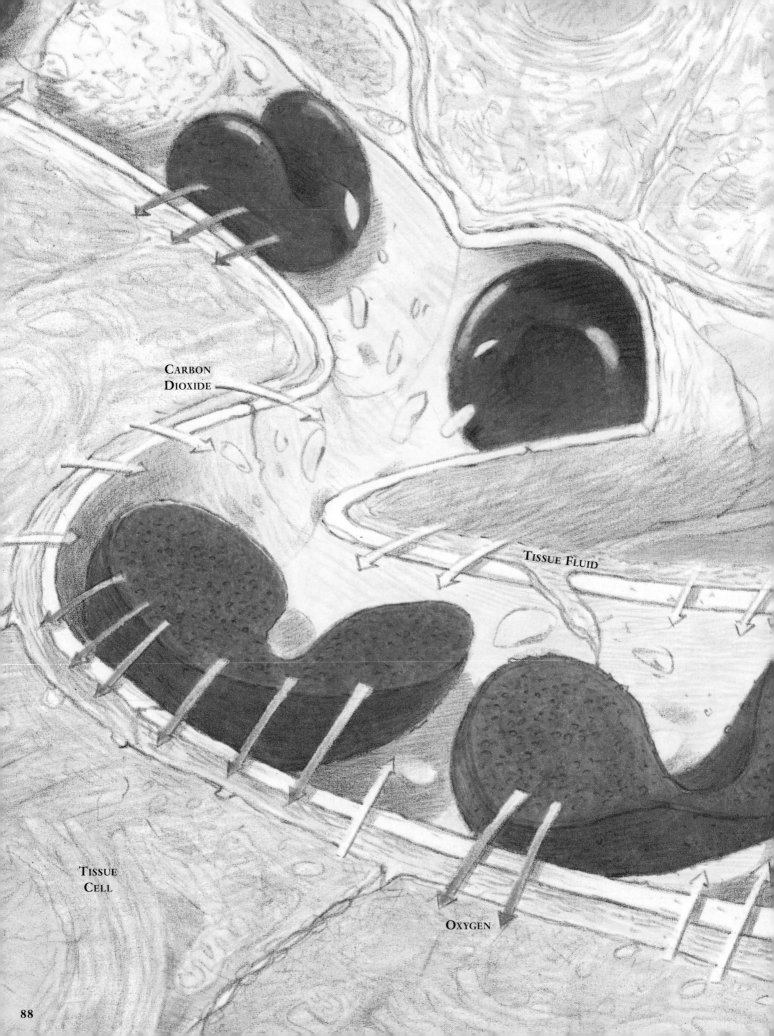

CARBON
DIOXIDE

TISSUE FLUID

TISSUE
CELL

OXYGEN

88

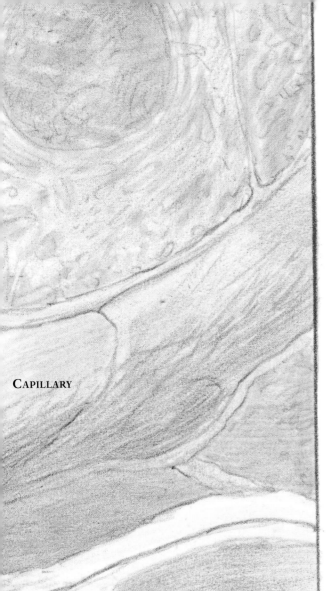

CAPILLARY

DROP-OFF AND PICKUP #2

Imagine floating, totally contented, in a warm lake that supplies all your needs and removes your wastes. For you that's pure fantasy, but for your body's cells it's everyday life. Cells are "bathed" in a fluid that provides a stable, nurturing environment with a constant temperature and chemical composition. And it's through this tissue fluid that substances are exchanged between capillaries and tissue cells.

Between the cells that form capillaries there are a number of tiny openings that make these vessels quite leaky. This is not sloppy construction but rather the means by which fluid containing simple molecules, such as glucose and amino acids, can flow into the surrounding tissues. Once there, these molecules diffuse toward and into cells where their concentration is much lower than it was in capillary blood.

Just as it picked up oxygen in the oxygen-rich lungs, hemoglobin inside red blood cells unloads it here in the oxygen-poor tissues. Hampered by the narrowness of the capillaries, red blood cells move slowly and in line, giving them more time to unload their cargo. Oxygen diffuses from blood, where it is plentiful, into the surrounding tissue, where it is constantly consumed. Waste carbon dioxide similarly diffuses along the reverse route, to be picked up by the blood—particularly in the plasma—and returned to the lungs.

BACK FOR MORE

Whether blood is returning to the heart from the lungs or from the rest of the body, it does so through veins. After leaving the tissues, veins merge and increase in diameter, eventually joining up with two large vessels, both of which empty into the right atrium. The superior vena cava carries blood from the head, arms, and upper body. The inferior vena cava delivers it from the rest of the body.

Veins have a layered wall that matches that of arteries, except that it's much thinner. Blood pressure inside veins is far lower than in arteries, so there is no need for the thick wall that prevents arteries from bursting when the ventricles contract. The downside to lower pressure is that blood tends to flow backwards, away from the heart, under its own weight. To overcome this, larger veins are equipped with valves similar to those that control the exits from the ventricles. As blood flows backwards, it fills both halves of each valve, thereby shutting off further backflow.

Most blood is still being pushed through the veins by pressure from the heart. But where veins pass through skeletal muscles, their contents get an extra boost. As these muscles contract, they squeeze the veins, forcing most blood "upward" through the valves. Valves downstream are closed by blood sent in the opposite direction.

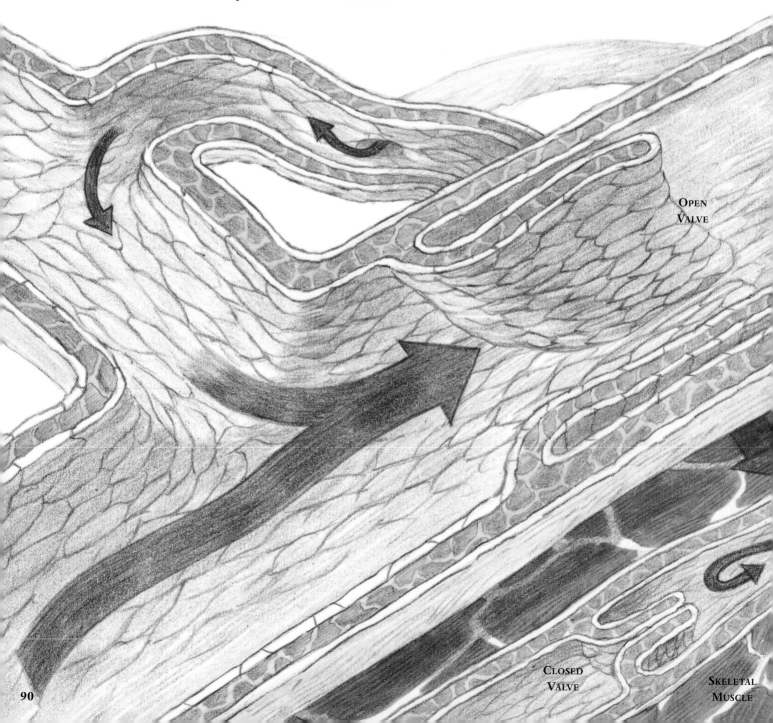

OPEN
VALVE

CLOSED
VALVE

SKELETAL
MUSCLE

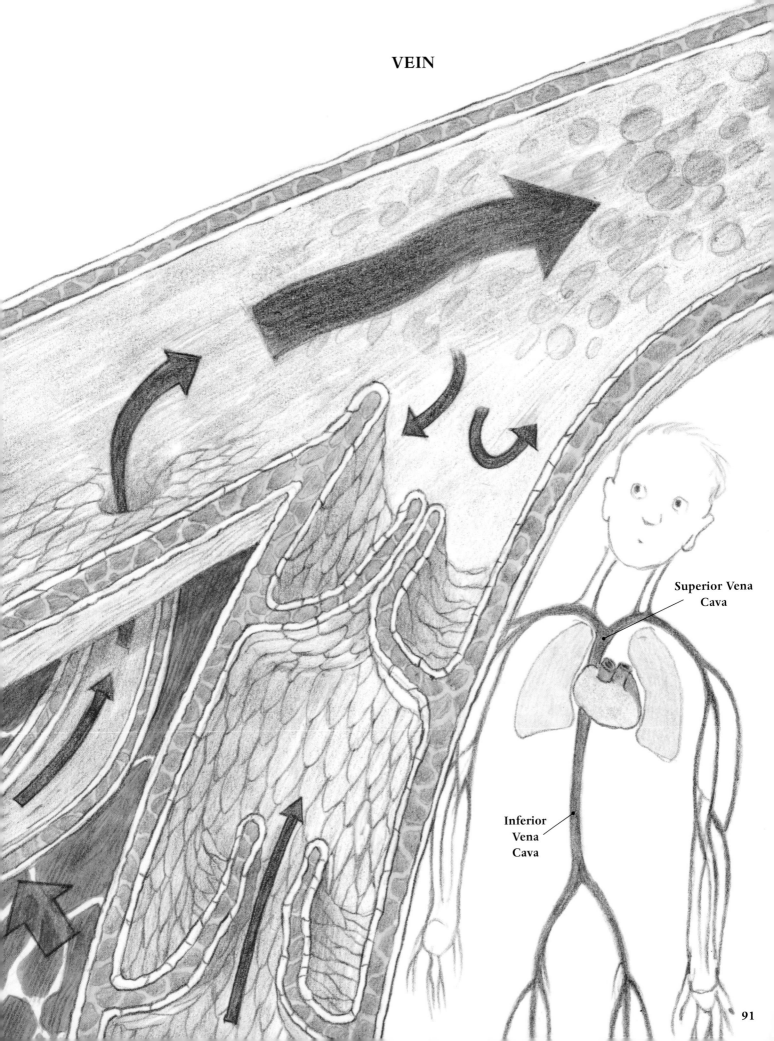

Superior Vena
Cava

Inferior
Vena
Cava

BREATHE OUT

As a result of the exchange of gases between alveoli and the bloodstream, the air in the lungs now contains more carbon dioxide and less oxygen than the air that was breathed in.

Exhaling this "stale" air is a more passive process than inhaling fresh air. The diaphragm relaxes and is returned to its original dome shape by the upward pressure of the stomach and other organs in the abdomen as they return to their original locations. The layer of intercostal muscles that raised the ribs also relaxes, letting gravity pull the rib cage down and inward. Together these actions decrease the space inside the chest, squeezing the lungs so that air pressure inside them is now greater than that outside. Air is forced up the bronchioles, bronchi, and trachea and out through the nose and mouth.

This "quiet" exhalation is what happens when we are not that active. When we exercise, however, our body needs to exhale faster to get rid of the extra carbon dioxide produced by hard-working muscles. Muscles lining the abdomen contract, forcing the abdominal organs up against the diaphragm, causing it to rise beyond its normal dome shape. Another layer of intercostal muscles pulls the rib cage down and inward. As a result, space inside the chest is reduced even further and the air is expelled that much faster.

HEART

REMOVED FOR RESTORATION

Diaphragm

MAKING SOUNDS

Whether you are singing, shouting, or soliloquizing, the sounds that emerge from your mouth have their origins in your larynx. Feel the lower section of the front of your neck as you speak and you feel the larynx moving as it does its job.

The larynx is built of cartilage. A complete ring called the cricoid cartilage is fastened to the top of the trachea. A larger curved plate called the thyroid cartilage is hinged to the sides of the cricoid, and two smaller pieces called the arytenoid cartilages sit on top of the cricoid cartilage. Stretched between the thyroid cartilage and the arytenoid cartilages is a pair of ligaments. We can't see them because each is buried within a folded membrane. These membranes are our vocal cords.

During normal breathing the cords are widely separated. But when we feel the need for vocal communication a complex assortment of muscles surrounding the larynx moves the various cartilages to close and tighten the vocal cords. The steady rhythm of inhalation and exhalation is briefly interrupted by a controlled blast of air from the lungs. The closed, stretched vocal cords vibrate with a buzzing sound that is amplified and given timbre by the "organ pipe" throat and nasal cavity before being crafted into recognizable words by tongue, lips, and cheeks. The tighter and closer together the vocal cords are, the higher the pitch of the sounds; the faster the air moves between them, the louder the sounds.

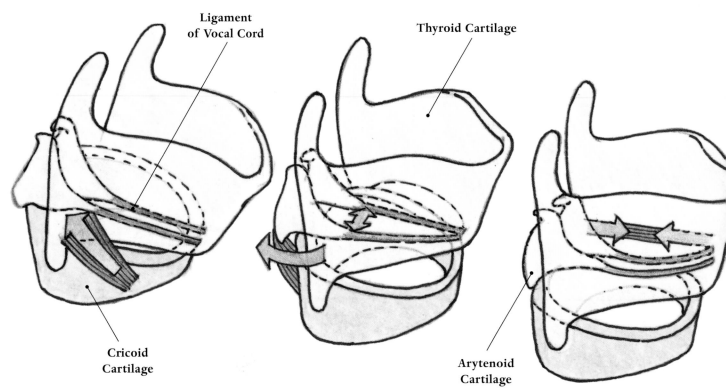

Ligament of Vocal Cord

Thyroid Cartilage

Cricoid Cartilage

Arytenoid Cartilage

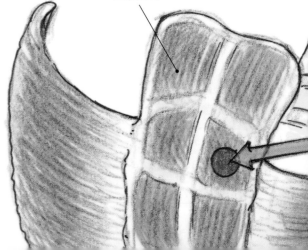

Stretch Receptor

Intercostal Muscles

Diaphragm

Abdominal Muscles

CHANGING DEMANDS

When we're active our muscles work harder and consume more energy than when we're taking a nap. To generate this extra energy, muscles need more oxygen and glucose. That, in turn, requires faster breathing, to get more oxygen into the body, and a quicker heart rate, to pump supplies to muscles as fast as possible.

Breathing is controlled by a "center" in the brain stem at the base of the brain. This center receives a constant stream of information about what is happening in various parts of the body. Stretch receptors in muscles and joints tell the center how hard muscles are working, while those in the lungs indicate how inflated they are. Receptors in the walls of large blood vessels warn of rising levels of waste carbon dioxide as muscles contract faster. In response to all this information the center instructs the diaphragm, intercostal, and abdominal muscles to increase the rate and depth of breathing.

Although basic heart rate is controlled by the heart itself, it can be increased or decreased by another center in the brain stem, the cardiac center. This area also receives information from carbon dioxide receptors. So, when the body becomes more active, the cardiac center tells the heart's SA and AV nodes to pick up the pace.

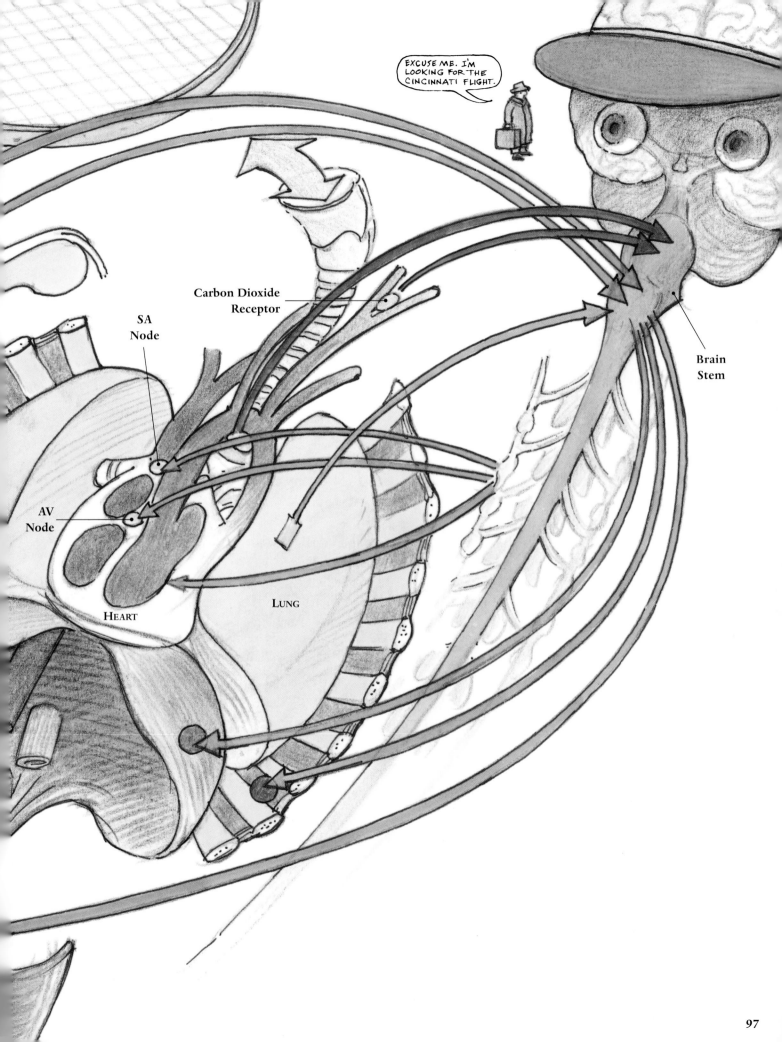

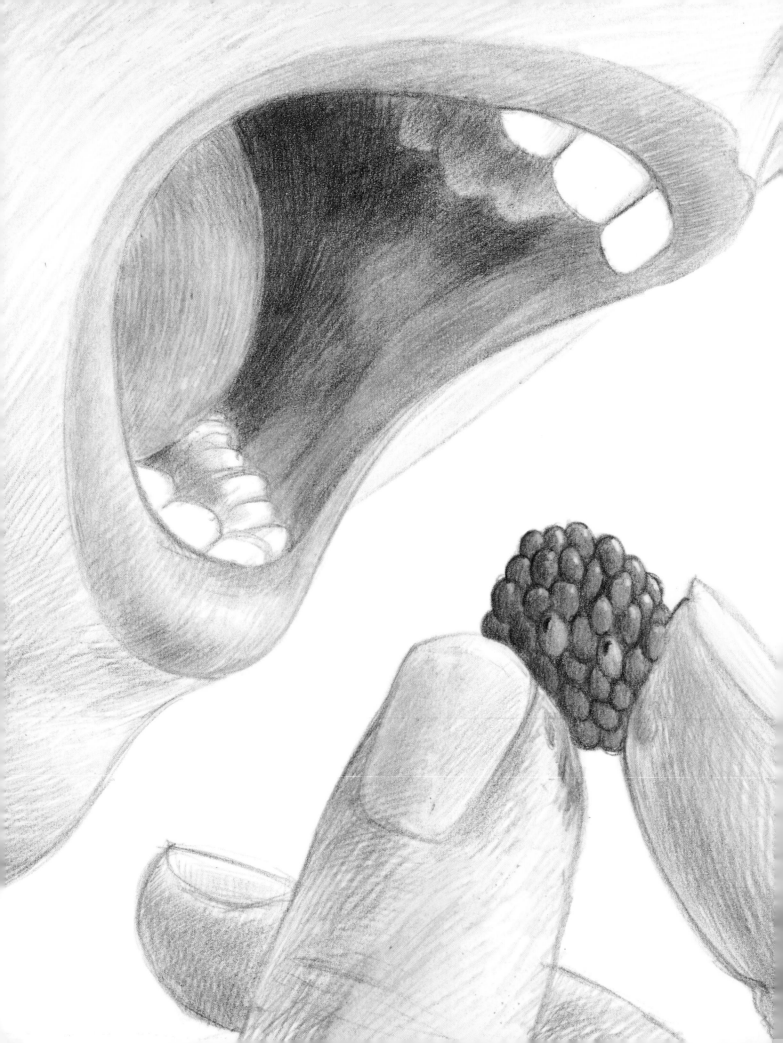

CHAPTER 3
LET'S EAT

FOOD SUPPLIES THE RAW MATERIALS for growth and repair, as well as the energy to make cells work. Without it, they would shut down and we would die. Yet most of the mouthwatering and nourishing foods passing our lips are at that instant quite useless as far as the body is concerned. The simple substances it needs remain locked inside sandwiches, steaks, strawberries, and sushi until the digestive system goes to work and its "disassembly line" breaks down complex foods to release usable nutrients.

For most of us, what happens to food inside the body once a meal has been consumed is something of a mystery. But, as with so many aspects of the human body, this is a journey well worth taking. Why should food have all the fun?

WHAT'S FOR DINNER?

On the menu today it's baked snapper with butter, pasta, steamed broccoli, and sliced tomato. But it could just as easily have been stir-fried tofu with noodles, a pepperoni pizza, chicken curry with rice, or a cheese omelet with french fries and green salad. The choices and combinations are endless, and that's important. It's the colors, shapes, aromas, tastes, and memories of different foods that tempt us to the table, ensuring that our bodies get the nutrients that are essential for life.

Nutrients are the substances in food that maintain the body and make it work. Most of what we eat is made up of carbohydrates, proteins, and fats. Nutrients needed in smaller amounts, but still vital, are vitamins and minerals. Also on the list are fiber and water. By supplying some protein, carbohydrate, fat, and certain vitamins and minerals, the snapper meal provides many of our nutrient needs. But not all. Our diet should comprise a mix of foods that supply all necessary nutrients in the right amounts.

CARBOHYDRATES

Complex carbohydrates, particularly starch, are found in foods such as pasta, bread, rice, potatoes, and cereals. During digestion starch is broken down to the simple sugar glucose, the body's main source of energy.

FIBER

This collection of stringy, indigestible substances is found in plant foods such as broccoli, beans, and bananas. It stretches intestinal muscles, making them more efficient so they push unwanted waste out of the body even more quickly.

VITAMINS AND MINERALS

Only needed in tiny amounts, vitamins and minerals are nonetheless essential for growth and good health. Most vitamins come from fresh fruit and vegetables, with some also found in fish, meat, dairy, and eggs. Minerals, such as calcium and iron, also help the body perform optimally. The best sources are vegetables, dairy, meat, and some fish.

FATS

Dairy food, meat, seeds, and nuts all supply fats, as do vegetable oils. Fat is digested into fatty acids, which are used as an energy source and to make cell membranes. Or they are rebuilt into fat that, under the skin, insulates the body and helps to keep us warm.

PROTEINS

Rich sources of proteins are fish, lean meat, poultry, and beans. Once digested, proteins supply the body with amino acids. These building blocks are reassembled by cells into different proteins used for construction, as enzymes, and a myriad of other roles.

WATER

More than 50 percent of our body is water. It provides the liquid medium in which substances dissolve and react inside cells, not to mention the basis of our internal transport systems—blood and lymph. Water comes not just from drinks but also from all but the driest foods.

SMELL EPITHELIUM

Nerve Signa

Smell Receptor

Cilia

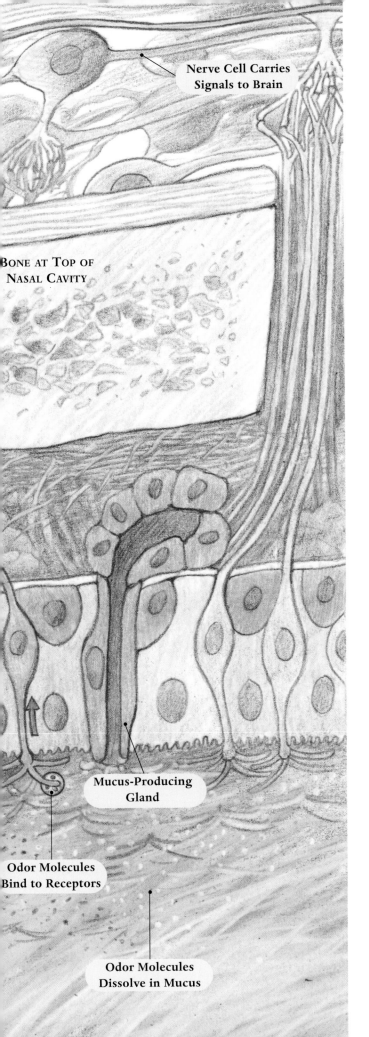

Nerve Cell Carries
Signals to Brain

BONE AT TOP OF
NASAL CAVITY

Mucus-Producing
Gland

Odor Molecules
Bind to Receptors

Odor Molecules
Dissolve in Mucus

SMELL SENSATIONS

It may be no match for a bloodhound's, but our sense of smell can still distinguish between some 10,000 different odors. Smelling begins in the nasal cavity, the space behind the nose that is split into two halves. In the upper reaches of each half, a thumbnail-size patch of specialized epithelium is home to millions of smell receptor cells. Each is tipped with a bunch of hairlike cilia that house odor receptors. Once inhaled, odor molecules dissolve in watery mucus and bind to the receptors on the cilia. The smell receptor sends a signal to the smell center of the brain, where the odor is "identified."

The cilia of each receptor cell carry just one type of receptor, but that receptor can respond to several different odor molecules. What's more, different parts of each odor molecule bind to different receptors. Having received information from a range of receptors, the brain pieces it all together to identify a particular smell. This may, for example, warn us that something is burning or reassure us that it's just cooking. Messages also go to the brain's emotional and memory center, the limbic system. That's why certain smells evoke certain feelings or recall special memories.

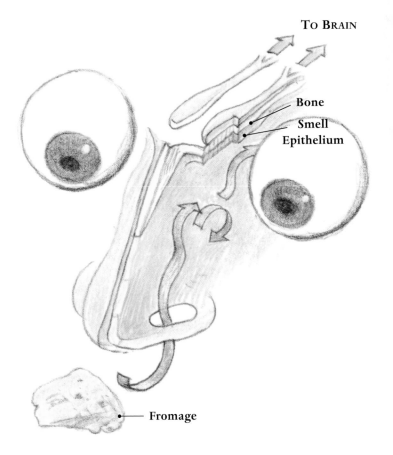

TO BRAIN

Bone

Smell
Epithelium

Fromage

MUSHROOM-
SHAPED PAPILLA

SPIKY PAPILLA

GOOD TASTE

Tasting is an essential part of eating. Tastes we identify as
pleasant boost our appetite. Any that are bitter or sour warn
us that what we are about to swallow may be poisonous.
Both of these aspects of taste depend on around 10,000 tiny
taste detectors called taste buds on the tongue's surface.

Look at your tongue in a mirror and you'll see that its
surface is covered with tiny bumps, or papillae. Of the three
types of papillae—mushroom-shaped, big with a ridge, and
spiky—only the first two house taste buds. As food is
maneuvered by the tongue, its smaller molecules, such as
sugars or salts, dissolve in watery saliva and flow into taste
buds. Here they are detected by receptor cells, which send
signals to taste centers in the brain that allow us to distinguish five basic tastes—sweet, salty, sour, bitter, and savory
umami.

Spiky papillae lack taste buds, but their tough tips allow
the tongue to grip food, including slippery ice cream. They
also sense heat, cold, touch, pressure, and even the pain
caused by eating hot peppers. It's these sensations, combined with tastes and smells, that give us an appreciation of
flavor. And, as anyone with a bad cold will testify, smell is
the senior partner. Without a sense of smell, flavors are just
plain bland.

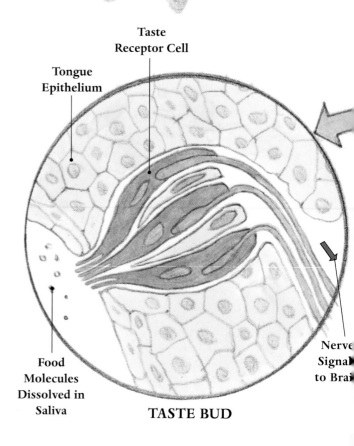

Tongue
Epithelium

Taste
Receptor Cell

Food
Molecules
Dissolved in
Saliva

Nerve
Signal
to Brain

TASTE BUD

104

BIG PAPILLA
SURROUNDED BY A RIDGE

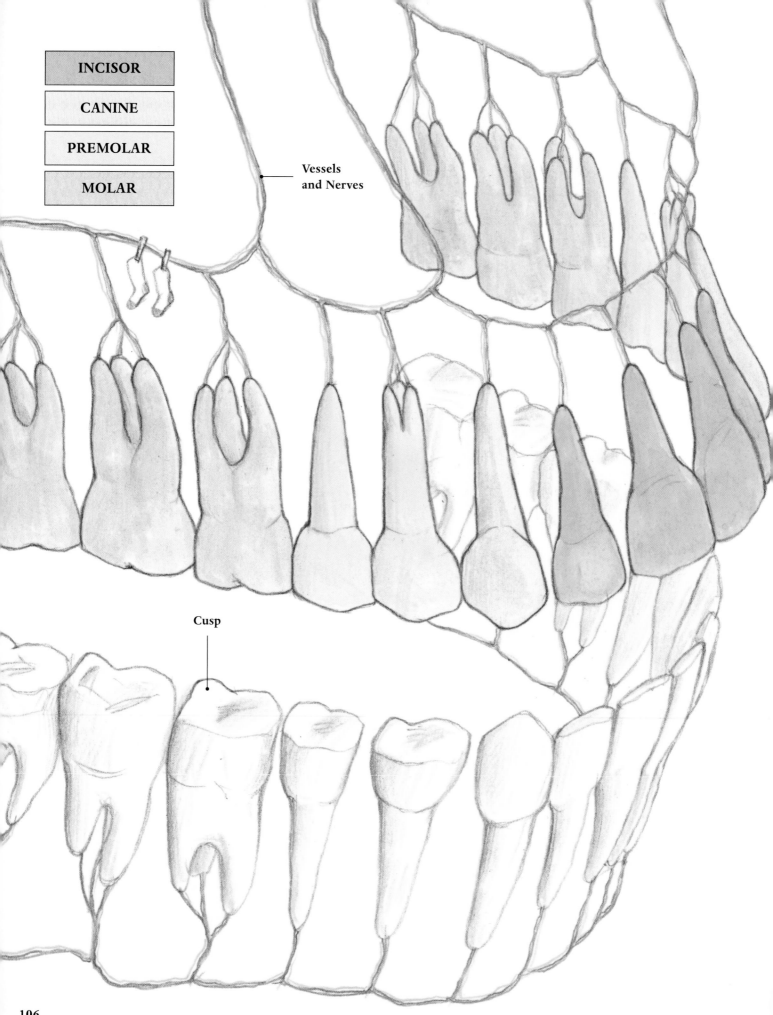

INCISOR

CANINE

PREMOLAR

MOLAR

Vessels
and Nerves

Cusp

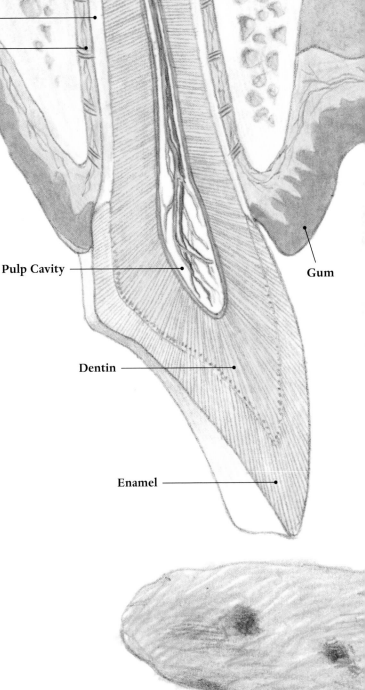

Jawbone

"Cement" Layer

Anchoring Ligament

Pulp Cavity

Gum

Dentin

Enamel

SLICE AND CRUSH

Unlike pythons or pelicans, we humans cannot swallow our meals in one big gulp. Food must be broken down into small pieces before it can be swallowed. Performing this opening act of digestion is a chewing machine armed with teeth, powered by muscles, and lubricated by saliva.

A thirty-two-piece dental tool kit—an upgrade from the twenty-piece childhood version—deals effortlessly with our eclectic diet. Chisel-shaped incisors slide past each other to chop and slice food. Pointed canines grip, pierce, and tear. Premolars with broad crowns and twin cusps, or peaks, crush and chew. And massive, multicusped molars lock together to grind food into small pieces.

To withstand years of chewing, a tooth must be hard-wearing and firmly anchored. The white, exposed part of the tooth—the crown—is covered by enamel, the body's hardest material. Incredibly strong yet lifeless, enamel is underpinned by living, bonelike dentin. This also forms the tooth's root, which slots into a socket in a jawbone where it is "cemented" firmly in place. Within dentin, the pulp cavity contains blood vessels that supply food and oxygen to the cells in living tooth tissues, and nerves, which provide sensation. Connecting crown to root, the neck of the tooth is gripped by the gum, a tight collar that prevents disease-causing bacteria from gaining access to the root.

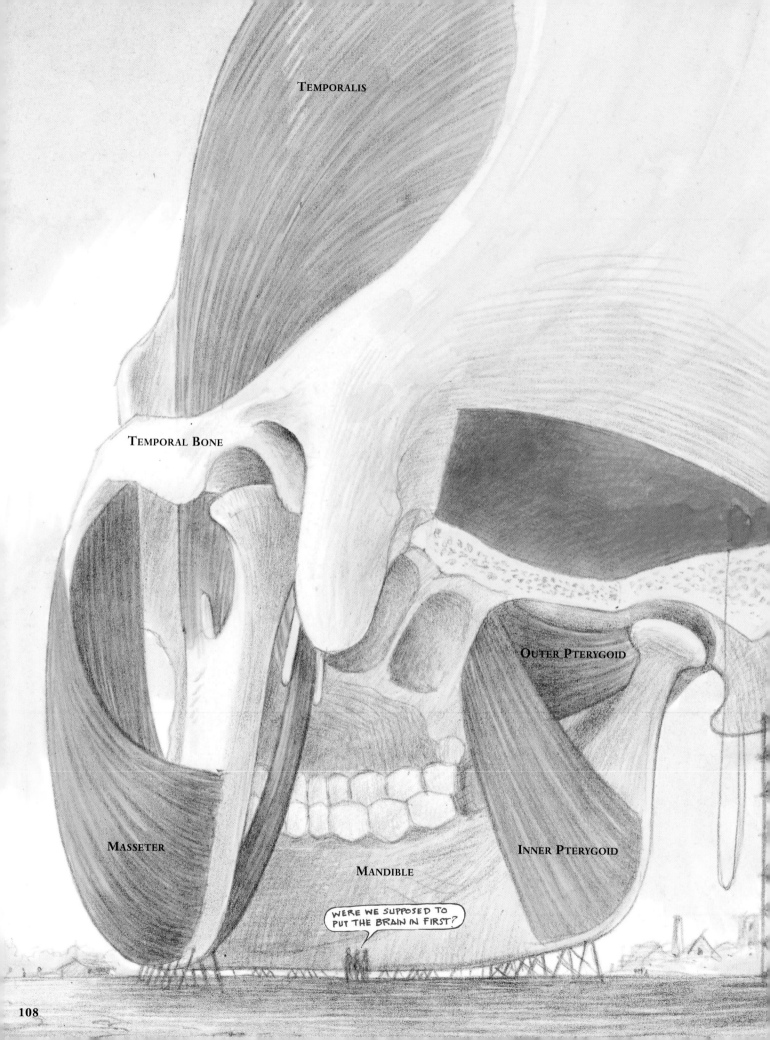

TEMPORALIS

TEMPORAL BONE

OUTER PTERYGOID

MASSETER

INNER PTERYGOID

MANDIBLE

WERE WE SUPPOSED TO PUT THE BRAIN IN FIRST?

POWER BEHIND THE CROWNS

Four pairs of jaw muscles—the masseter, temporalis, inner pterygoid, and outer pterygoid—power biting and chewing. Their job is to move the mandible, or lower jaw, so that the teeth not only come into contact but do so with the necessary force. The mandible connects with the temporal bones on each side of the skull through two highly specialized joints. So flexible are these joints that they permit different movements according to which muscles are in charge. The most powerful, the masseter and temporalis, lift the mandible, generating food-crushing pressure between the back teeth equivalent to a car running over your foot. The inner pterygoid pulls the jaw from side to side to promote a grinding action. The outer pterygoid makes the chin jut out, while the temporalis pulls it back. Together, these actions allow the upper and lower sets of teeth to grip and tear food to get it into the mouth, and then crush and grind it.

Other muscles help too. The circular muscle around the mouth presses the lips together to draw food in and stop it from falling out, unless you insist on talking while eating. Cheek muscles make sure that food stays between the teeth during chewing.

SEA OF SALIVA

The aroma, sight, and now the taste of food have already triggered the release of saliva into the mouth along ducts that lead from three pairs of salivary glands. Every day some two to three pints (1–1.5 liters) of saliva—mostly water with a dash of mucus, germ-killing lysozyme, and the starch-digesting enzyme amylase—trickle into the mouth cavity to keep it moist and disinfected. But at mealtimes the slow trickle turns into a flood that, in the turmoil of chewing, is mixed with food fragments by the curling, twisting tongue. Slippery mucus in saliva glues food particles together, lubricating them for a smoother passage down the throat. At the same time, amylase begins the chemical transformation of the starchy elements of the meal into sugar, a job made more efficient by shredding and grinding of food into smaller pieces.

Once food has been thoroughly chewed, the tongue sculpts it into an easy-to-swallow lump or bolus and pushes it to the back of the throat for the next stage of the journey.

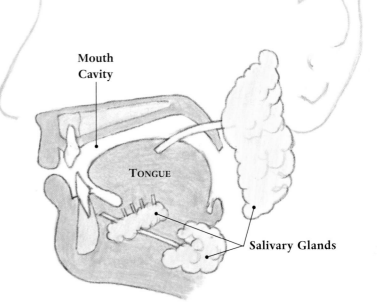

Mouth
Cavity

TONGUE

Salivary Glands

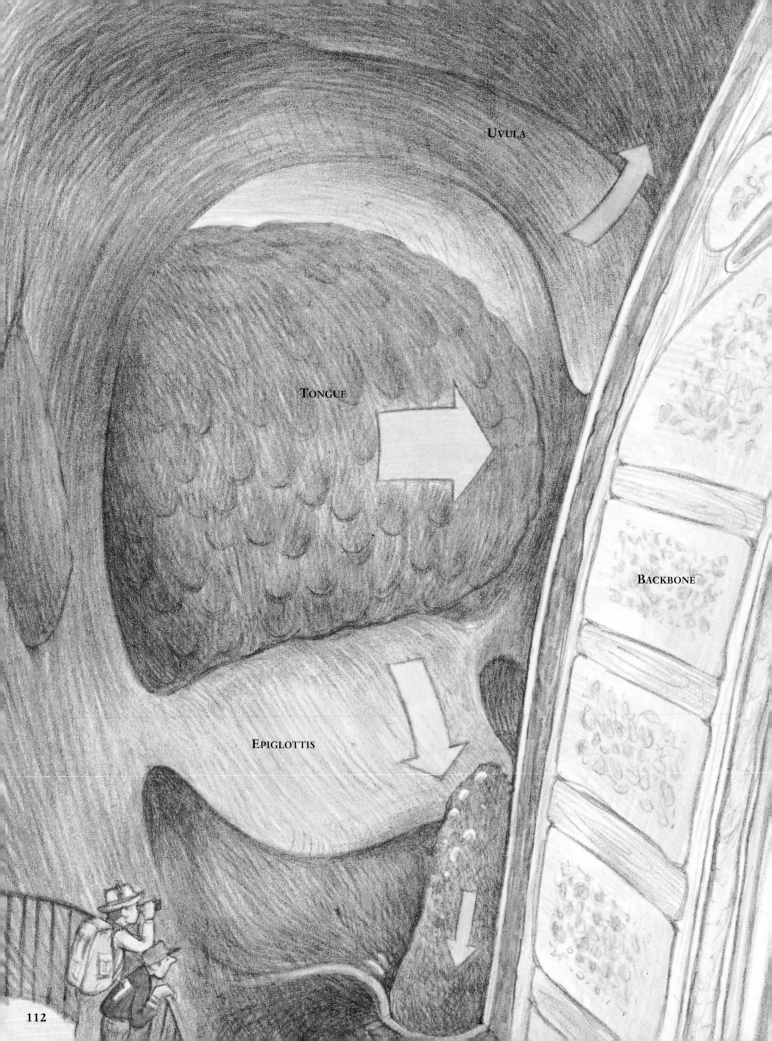

UVULA

TONGUE

BACKBONE

EPIGLOTTIS

Down the Hatch

Swallowing starts when the tongue forces the slippery food bolus into the throat and triggers an unstoppable sequence of events. As throat muscles contract to propel the bolus into the esophagus, the tube that leads to the stomach, three other possible exit routes are blocked. The uvula, the fleshy projection that dangles over the throat's entrance, lifts upward to stop food intruding into the nasal cavity. The tongue, still pushing backwards, prevents an unwanted return of food to the mouth cavity. And as breathing temporarily ceases, the larynx rises and its hinged cover, the epiglottis, flaps downward to block the airway to the lungs and prevent choking.

It isn't gravity that gets food from throat to stomach. The esophagus actively pushes the bolus. It can do this because it has the same basic structure as the rest of the alimentary canal—the "tube" that runs from mouth to anus. Its lining secretes mucus to reduce friction. Wraparound circular muscles contract behind the bolus and relax in front of it to force it downward. Lengthwise longitudinal muscles relax behind the bolus but contract in front to open up the normally closed passage. The resulting wave of contraction and relaxation, called peristalsis, gets food from throat to stomach in just six seconds. So powerful and gravity defying is peristalsis that food will reach the stomach even if you choose to eat upside down.

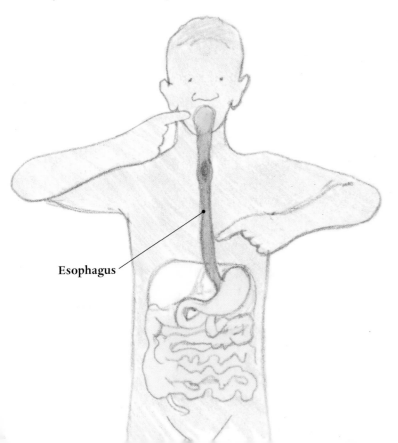

Esophagus

LONGITUDINAL MUSCLES

CIRCULAR MUSCLES

LINING OF ESOPHAGUS

BOLUS

CHURN AND STORE

The stomach is basically a bag between the esophagus and the small intestine. Its lining secretes an acidic digestive fluid called gastric juice, and its wall contains not two but three layers of muscle—longitudinal, circular, and oblique—each oriented in a different direction. Powerful contractions of these muscles churn food, mix it with gastric juice, and push it toward the stomach's exit. As this happens the entrance to the stomach closes to prevent food and acid from traveling back up the esophagus, and its exit, a ring of muscle called the pyloric sphincter, contracts to prevent the flow of food into the duodenum—the first section of the small intestine—until processing is completed.

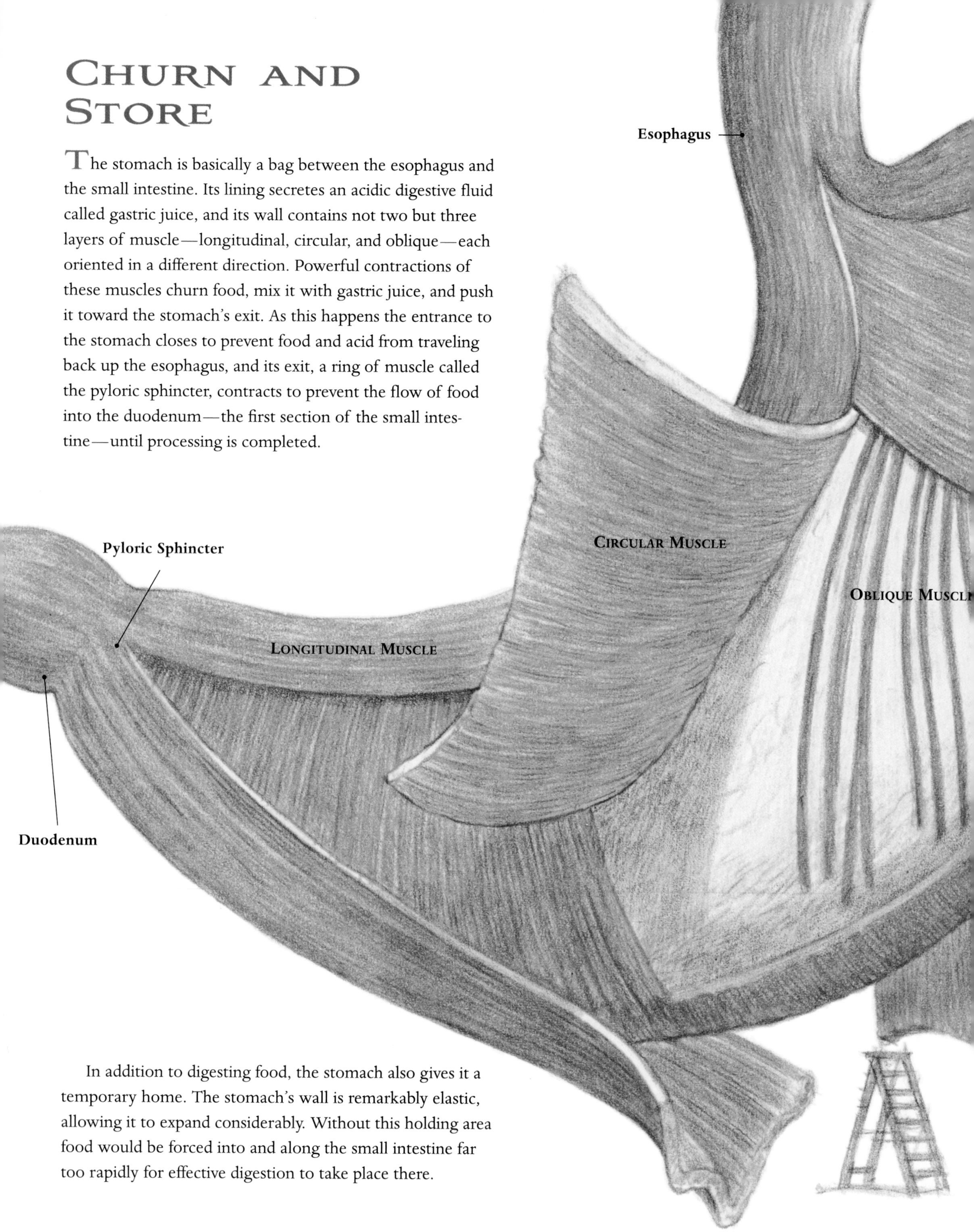

Esophagus →

Circular Muscle

Oblique Muscle

Pyloric Sphincter

Longitudinal Muscle

Duodenum

In addition to digesting food, the stomach also gives it a temporary home. The stomach's wall is remarkably elastic, allowing it to expand considerably. Without this holding area food would be forced into and along the small intestine far too rapidly for effective digestion to take place there.

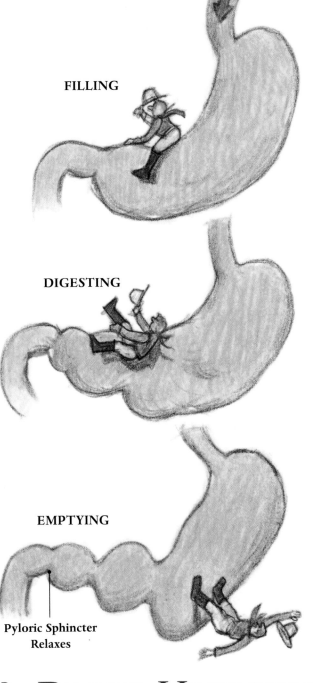

FILLING

DIGESTING

EMPTYING

Pyloric Sphincter Relaxes

A BRIEF HISTORY OF CHYME

As food arrives from the esophagus, peristalsis moves it toward the opposite end of the stomach, where the most vigorous churning, kneading, and mixing of food with gastric juice takes place. After several hours of processing, the pyloric sphincter relaxes slightly and contraction of stomach muscles pumps small squirts of a soupy mix of partially digested food called chyme into the duodenum. The pyloric sphincter also acts as a filter. It closes automatically if any large food particles attempt to pass through, ensuring that only liquid chyme reaches the duodenum. Those large particles are dispatched backwards for further digestion.

Stomach

ACID BATH

Every day gastric glands deep in the stomach's lining make four pints (two liters) of corrosive juice and release it through millions of holes called gastric pits. Cells halfway down the glands produce the ingredients for hydrochloric acid, although they aren't combined until they've been secreted into the gland itself. Deeper down, other cells

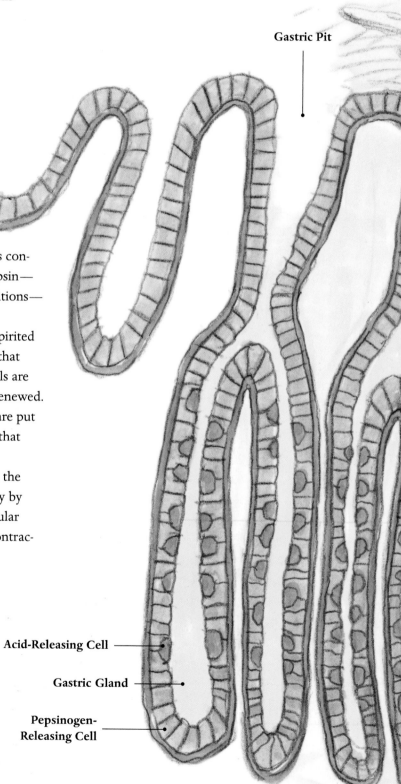

Gastric Pit

release an inactive enzyme called pepsinogen. This is converted by hydrochloric acid to the active enzyme pepsin—the only digestive enzyme to work best in acid conditions—that accelerates the breakdown of proteins in food.

To avoid digesting itself, the stomach mounts a spirited defense. Lining cells produce a thick mucus coating that prevents contact with gastric juice. Any damaged cells are rapidly replaced, and each week the entire lining is renewed. However, the destructive properties of gastric juice are put to good use by killing most disease-causing bacteria that enter the body in food and drink.

The thought, sight, smell, or taste of food causes the brain to signal the stomach to get ready for a delivery by releasing extra gastric juice and contracting its muscular walls. As the stomach empties, both secretion and contraction decrease.

Acid-Releasing Cell

Gastric Gland

Pepsinogen-Releasing Cell

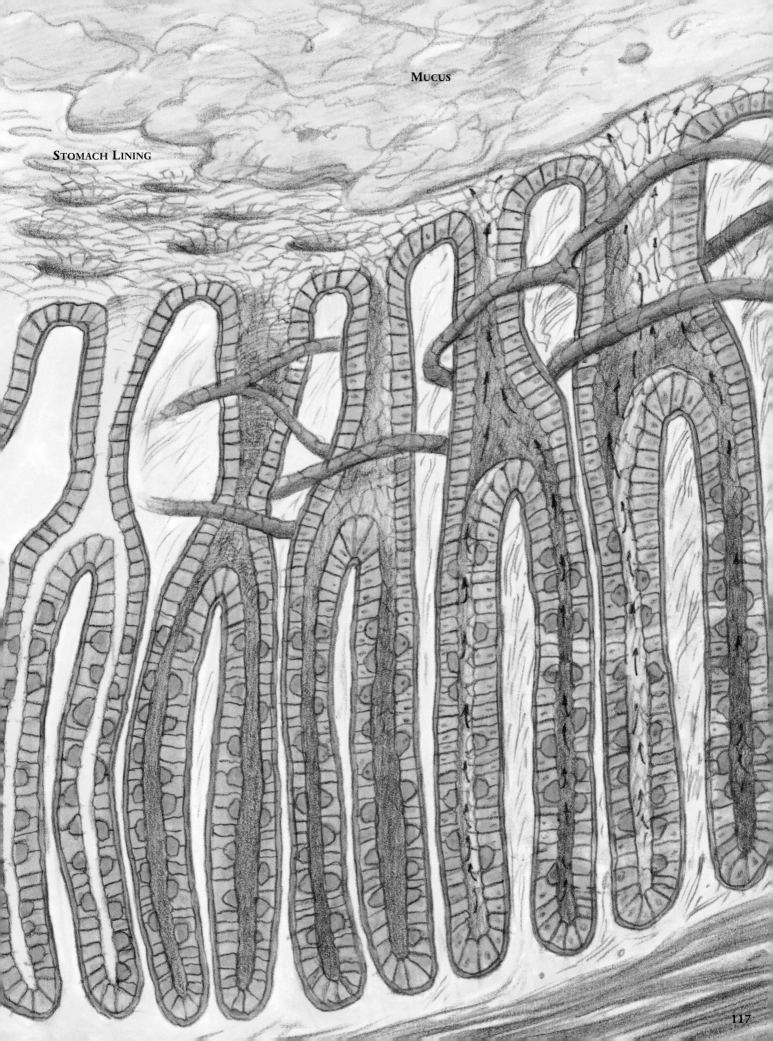

MUCUS

STOMACH LINING

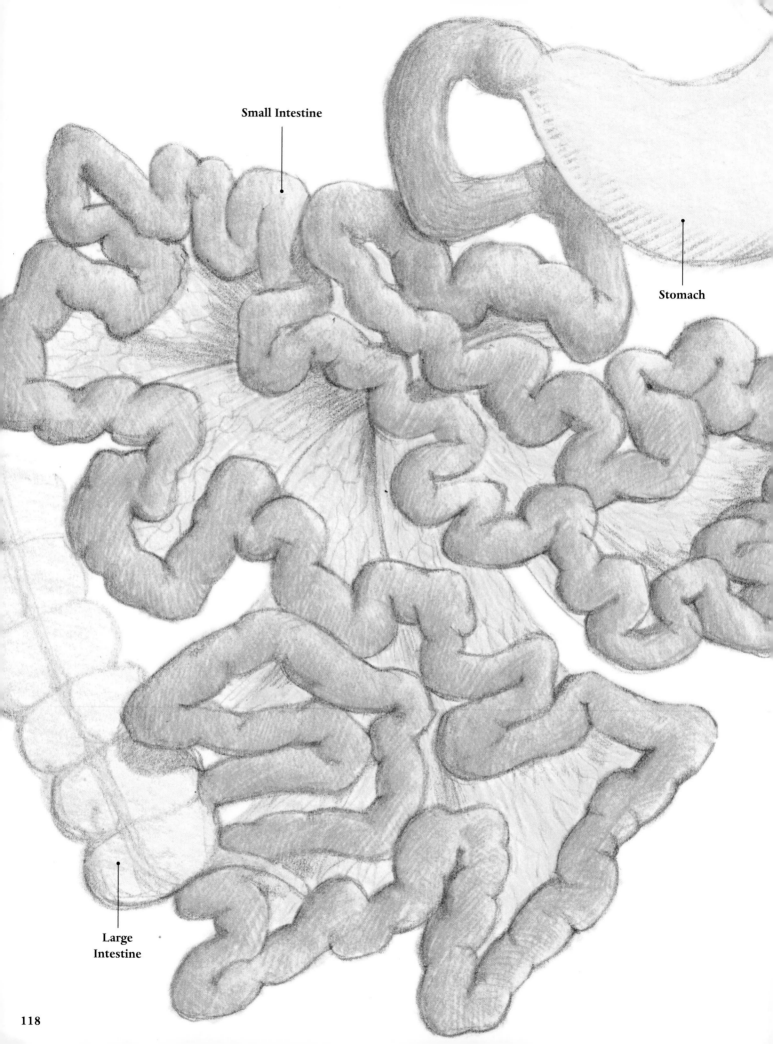

Small Intestine

Stomach

Large
Intestine

118

DIGEST AND ABSORB

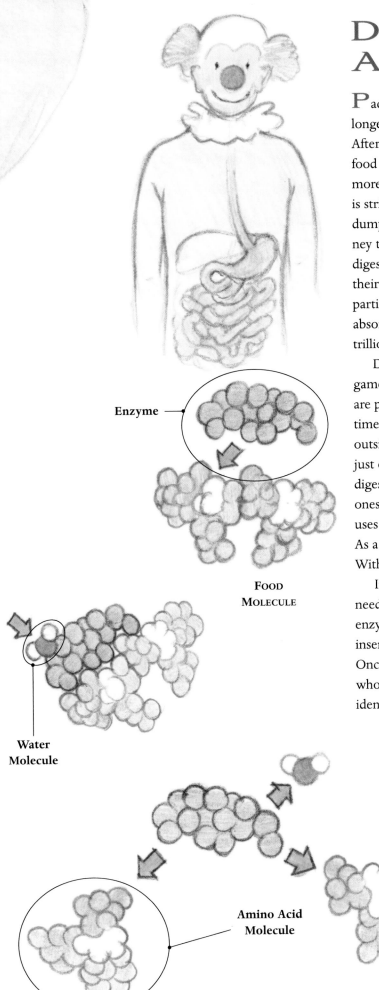

Enzyme

FOOD MOLECULE

Water Molecule

Amino Acid Molecule

Packed inside the abdomen, the small intestine is the longest and most important part of the digestive system. After leaving the stomach, well-mashed but barely digested food is moved along 20 feet (6 meters) of small intestine no more than one inch (2.5 centimeters) wide. Along the way it is stripped of its nutrients, leaving just watery waste to be dumped into the large intestine. In the course of that journey two things happen. First, food molecules are completely digested by an array of enzymes that break them down to their basic building blocks. Second, these building blocks—particularly glucose, amino acids, and fatty acids—are absorbed into the bloodstream and dispatched for use by trillions of body cells.

Digestion without enzymes would be like a football game without players—no action and no result. Enzymes are proteins that speed up by thousands or even millions of times the rate at which chemical reactions—both inside and outside cells—take place. Each kind of enzyme is suited to just one type of chemical reaction. In the alimentary canal, digestive enzymes break down big food molecules into small ones. They do this by accelerating a chemical reaction that uses water molecules as scissors to "cut up" big molecules. As a result, a meal is soon reduced to simple components. Without enzymes this would be impossible.

In this illustration a molecule made of two amino acids needs to be split. First the molecule attaches to just the right enzyme, fitting like a key in a lock. A water molecule is then inserted to break the bond between the two amino acids. Once they are liberated, the enzyme, unchanged by the whole process, is free to repeat the process with another identical molecule.

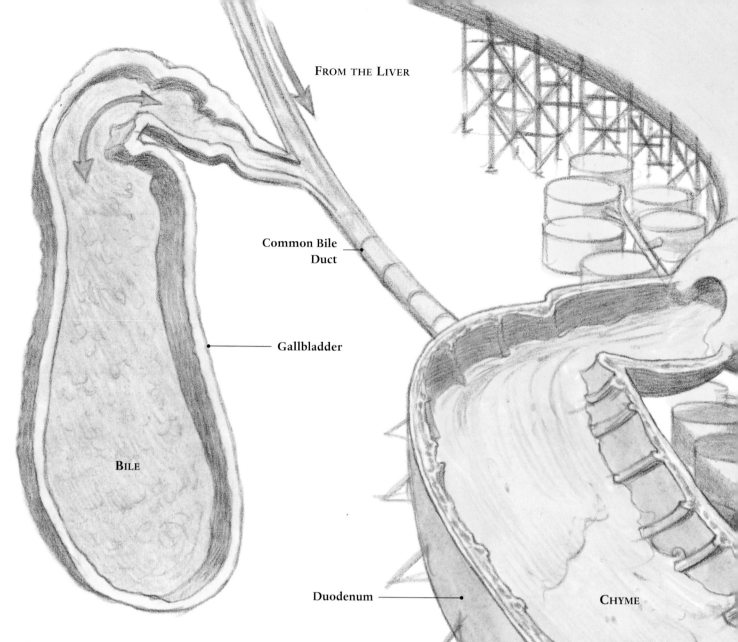

Common Bile
Duct

Gallbladder

BILE

Duodenum

CHYME

OPENING SHOTS

Short but busy are words that aptly describe the duodenum, the first loop of the small intestine. It's here that chyme from the stomach is prepared for the final phase of digestion. The opening shots in this campaign are provided by the liver and pancreas, the exports of which—bile and pancreatic juice, respectively—empty into the duodenum. Both liquids are alkaline, and when they mix with newly arrived chyme they transform it from highly acidic to just alkaline. This change is essential because the battery of digestive enzymes that operate in the small intestine will work only in a slightly alkaline environment. Furthermore, without the ingredients contained in bile and pancreatic juice, digestion in the small intestine would grind to a halt.

Liver

STOMACH

PANCREAS

Pancreatic
Duct

PANCREATIC JUICE

BILE

Roughly the size of a kiwi fruit, the gallbladder (opposite) is a muscular bag that stores, concentrates, and releases bile, a greenish liquid made by the liver, to which it is connected. When chyme arrives in the duodenum, the gallbladder contracts and squeezes its contents along the common bile duct. As well as excretory products, bile also contains bile salts. In the small intestine these convert large fat globules into tiny droplets that are much more easily broken down by fat-digesting enzymes.

Clusters of cells inside the pancreas make pancreatic juice, which is released into the duodenum through the opening shared with the common bile duct. Pancreatic juice contains enzymes that break down carbohydrates, proteins, fats, and nucleic acids. Much like pepsin in the stomach, the enzymes that break down proteins are activated only in the duodenum to prevent them from destroying the cells that made them.

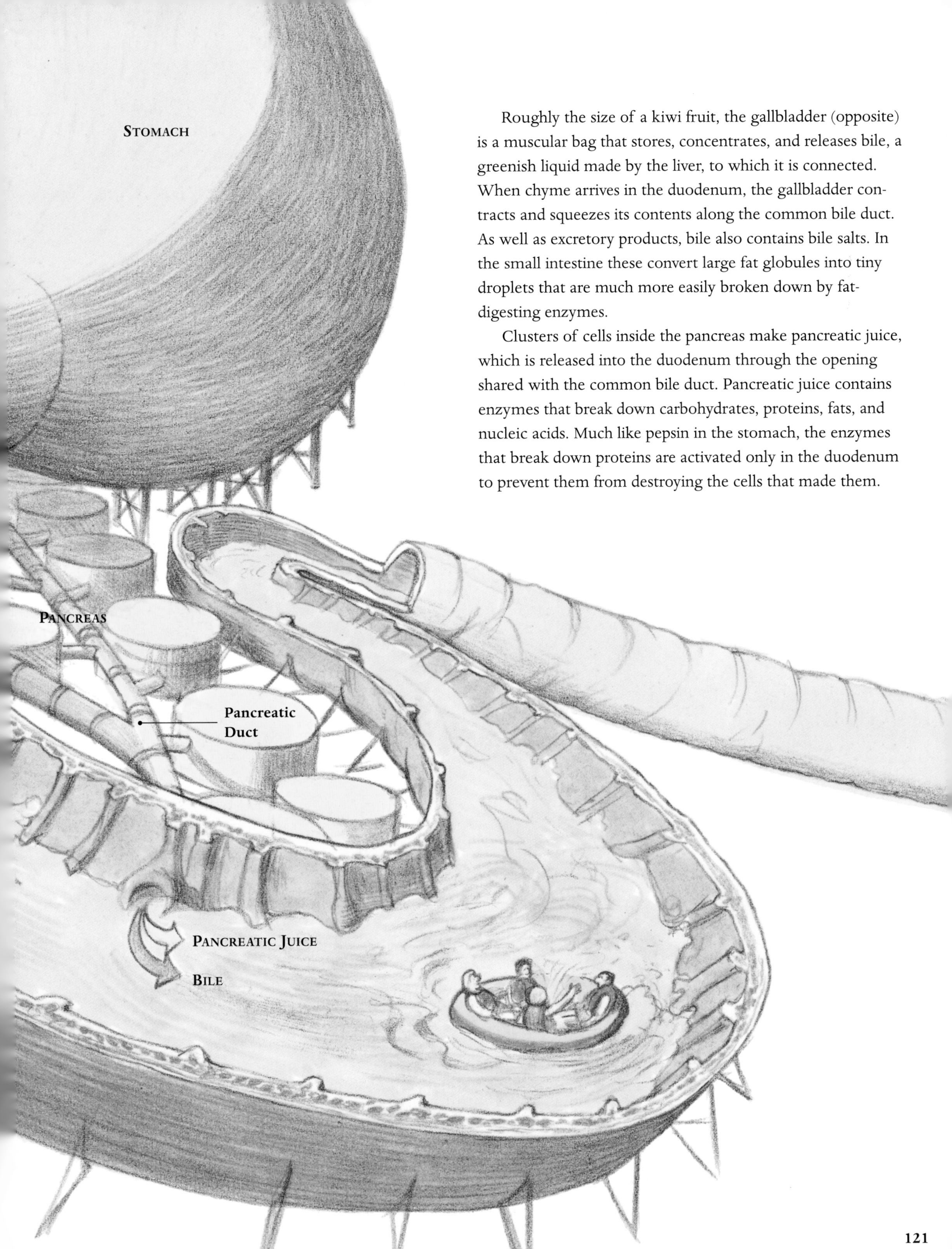

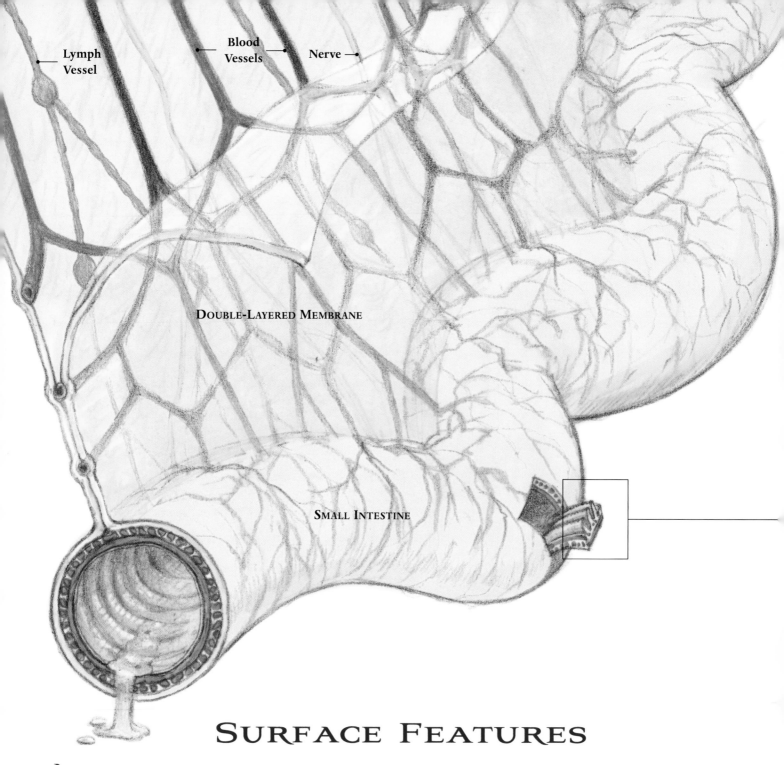

Lymph Vessel

Blood Vessels

Nerve →

Double-Layered Membrane

Small Intestine

SURFACE FEATURES

As the small intestine continues beyond the duodenum, it is supported from the rear wall of the abdomen by a double-layered membrane. Sandwiched between its two layers are blood and lymph vessels, which carry newly digested food away from the small intestine, and nerves, which instruct the intestine's muscular walls to move still digesting food.

Thanks to its considerable length, the small intestine has plenty of time to both break food down and to absorb its products. Its surprisingly large internal surface—produced by folds and villi—also plays an important role in the process. Running around the inside of the small intestine,

circular folds slow the flow of chyme, creating more opportunity for digestion and absorption. Slimy with watery intestinal juice, these folds are covered by millions of tiny projections called villi that provide the location for both the final stage of digestion and the absorption of its products.

As in the esophagus, but not with such power, peristalsis moves food along the small intestine. In addition, contraction of circular muscles in sections of the small intestine produces an effect called segmentation that sloshes chyme back and forth, mixing it with pancreatic enzymes and bringing it into contact with villi.

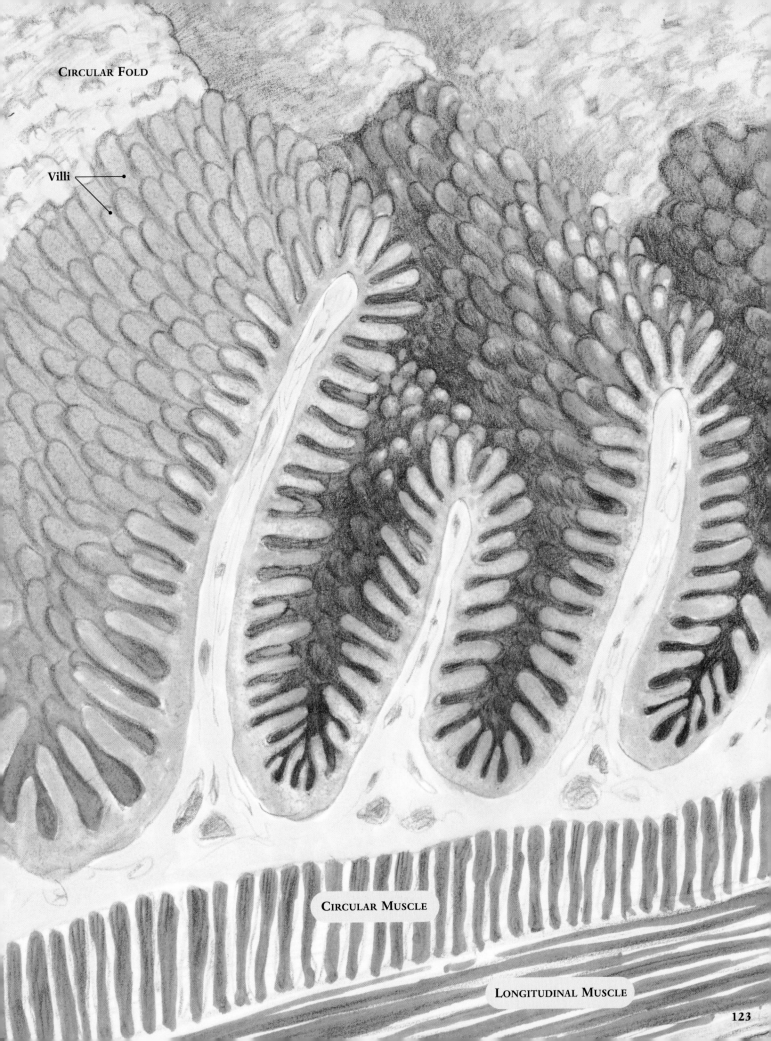

CIRCULAR FOLD

Villi

CIRCULAR MUSCLE

LONGITUDINAL MUSCLE

123

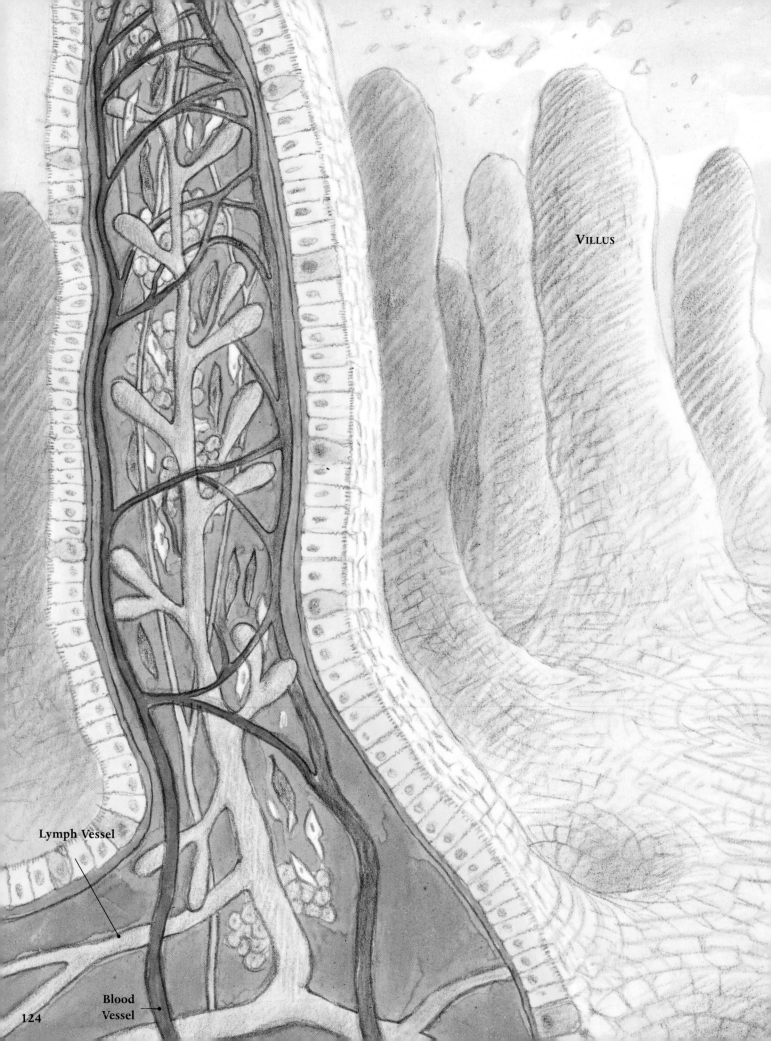

VILLUS

Lymph Vessel

Blood
Vessel

124

Microvilli

CROSSING THE BORDER

The tiny villi that project from the lining of the small intestine each have tiny projections of their own. A microscopic view of the surface of the epithelial cells covering a villus reveals a mass of microvilli. Attached to these microvilli are the enzymes that complete the digestion of carbohydrates to glucose and of proteins to amino acids; the digestion of fats to fatty acids has already been achieved by pancreatic juice enzymes. By providing a massive surface where digestion and the absorption of end products can happen side by side, microvilli greatly increase the efficiency of both processes.

Inside each villus is a network of blood capillaries and a branch of the lymphatic system. Glucose and amino acids are absorbed into capillaries and carried off to the liver for processing. Fatty acids are reassembled into fats and pass into lymphatic vessels before being deposited into the bloodstream. Villi also absorb most of the water contained in food, saliva, gastric juice, and other secretions, as well as the bile salts that aided fat digestion, which, as an act of good housekeeping, are sent back to the liver for recycling.

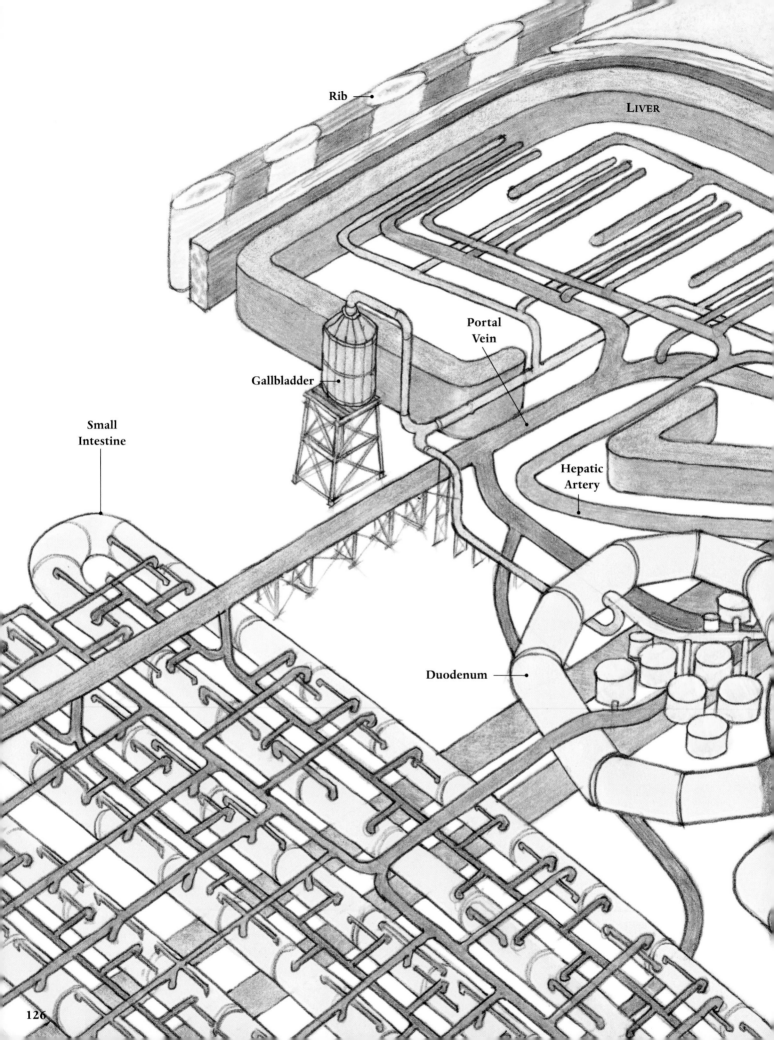

Rib

LIVER

Portal
Vein

Gallbladder

Small
Intestine

Hepatic
Artery

Duodenum

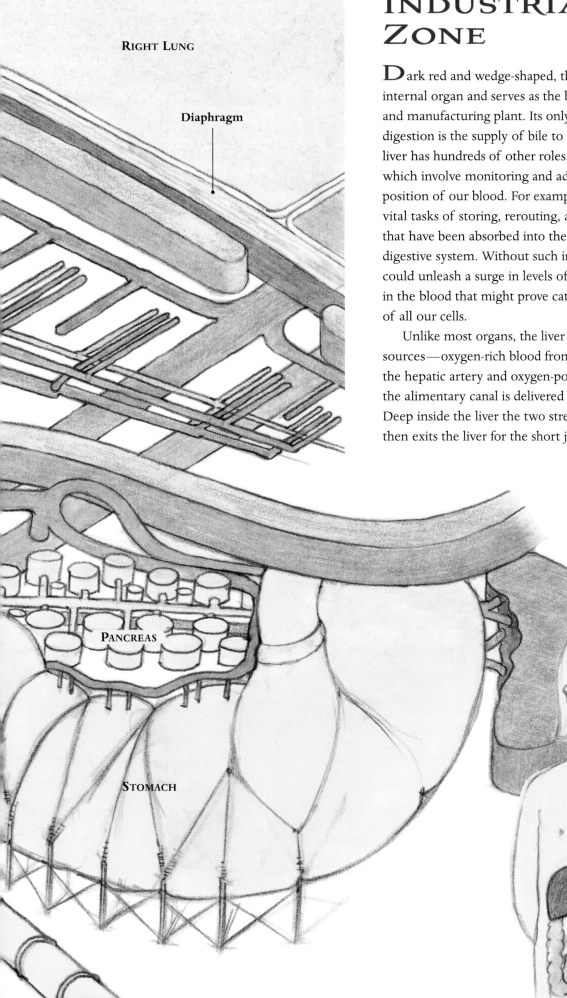

RIGHT LUNG

Diaphragm

PANCREAS

STOMACH

INDUSTRIAL ZONE

Dark red and wedge-shaped, the liver is our largest internal organ and serves as the body's primary processing and manufacturing plant. Its only direct contribution to digestion is the supply of bile to the duodenum, but the liver has hundreds of other roles, the most important of which involve monitoring and adjusting the chemical composition of our blood. For example, liver cells perform the vital tasks of storing, rerouting, and transforming nutrients that have been absorbed into the bloodstream from the digestive system. Without such intervention, every meal could unleash a surge in levels of sugars and other nutrients in the blood that might prove catastrophic to the well-being of all our cells.

Unlike most organs, the liver takes in blood from two sources—oxygen-rich blood from the heart arrives through the hepatic artery and oxygen-poor but food-rich blood from the alimentary canal is delivered through the portal vein. Deep inside the liver the two streams mix. Processed blood then exits the liver for the short journey back to the heart.

TOWARD THE
HEART

Central Vein

Venule

Arteriole

Branch of
Bile Duct

LOBULE

PROCESSING PLANT

Looked at from the outside, the liver gives few clues about its inner workings—apart from the deep red color hinting at a rich blood supply. At the microscopic level, however, all is revealed. Here are the liver's workhorses, the ultimate multitaskers of the cellular world. Called hepatocytes, these cells are organized into thousands of six-sided units called lobules, each the size of a sesame seed. Inside a lobule, sheets of hepatocytes line the maze of broad, leaky capillaries that converge inward toward a central vein. At the corners of the lobule are three vessels, two carrying blood into the liver and one carrying bile out. An arteriole brings blood from the heart, while a venule brings blood from the alimentary canal. As blood passes through the maze on its way to the central vein, hepatocytes have enough time to clean it and adjust its composition. Traveling in the opposite direction along narrow tubes is bile secreted by hepatocytes and destined for the duodenum.

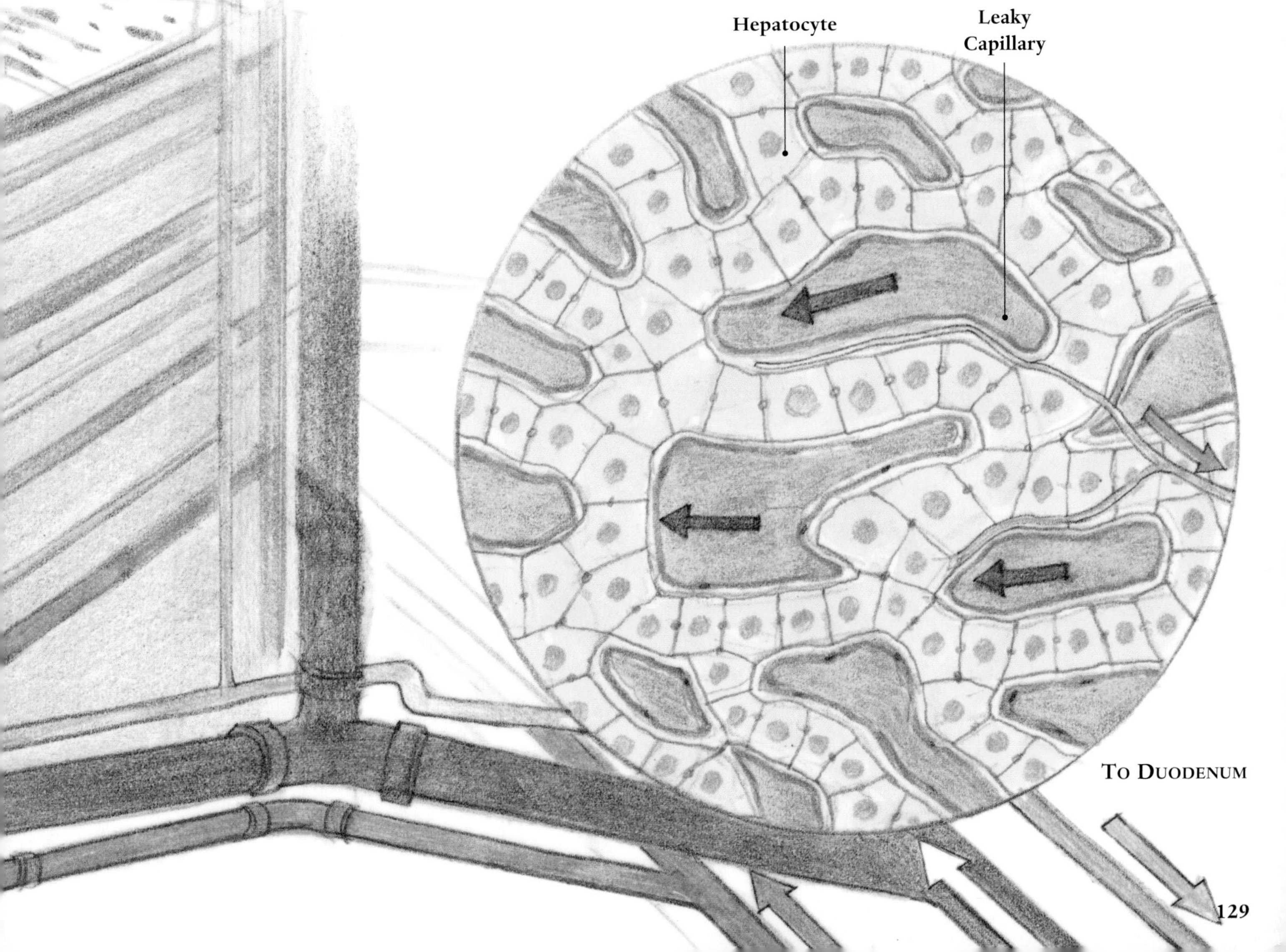

Hepatocyte

Leaky Capillary

TO DUODENUM

BLOOD PLASMA

HEPATOCYTE

Bile-Carrying
Canal

LIVER CAPILLARY

MACROPHAGE

LIVER CELLS

The cells that form the liver's capillaries have holes in them. As blood courses along, plasma and small molecules leak through these openings to reach the billions of hepatocytes that scrutinize and regulate blood's composition. Among their most important roles, they store glucose when there's too much in the blood and release it when there's too little, thereby ensuring that body cells experience neither feast nor famine when it comes to fuel supplies. They also store fats and certain minerals, including iron recycled from old red blood cells, and vitamins A, B_{12}, D, E, and K.

The hepatocytes package fatty acids for shipment around the body, manufacture cholesterol, an important component of cell membranes, and make blood proteins, such as those involved in clotting. They cannot store excess amino acids, but these can be converted into other useful substances. Also in the liver is the combining of bile pigments—produced by breaking down hemoglobin from worn-out red blood cells—and bile salts to form bile, which plays a vital role in fat digestion.

Other roles for the liver include removing and breaking down a wide range of drugs from the blood, deactivating hormones so that they act only for a limited time, and housing macrophages that filter blood by extracting and destroying bacteria and other debris.

RED BLOOD CELL

PANCREATIC ISLET

PANCREAS

Vein
(To the Liver via
the Portal Vein)

SEE! IT'S RIGHT
BEHIND MY
STOMACH.

PANCREAS REVISITED

As well as making digestive enzymes and releasing them into the duodenum, the pancreas has another role to play. Scattered among its clusters of enzyme-secreting cells are a million or so tiny glands known as pancreatic islets that release two all-important hormones called glucagon and insulin that ensure our cells are never short of fuel.

A cell without glucose is like a car without gas—it simply stops working. Glucose is the cell's main energy source, one that must be on tap twenty-four hours a day. Without the intervention of glucagon and insulin, levels of blood glucose would surge after meals and plummet between them. Very high levels of glucose actually inhibit its uptake by cells, while very low glucose levels are insufficient to meet a cell's needs. What the pancreatic hormones do, through their opposing actions, is to maintain a near constant level of glucose in the blood in order to guarantee that our cells have a steady supply regardless of whether we are stuffed or starving, active or asleep.

PANCREATIC HORMONES

Inside pancreatic islets there are two types of hormone-making cells. Alpha cells produce glucagon, a hormone that triggers an increase in blood glucose, and beta cells release insulin, which decreases the amount of glucose in circulation. Both hormones are secreted into capillaries that eventually drain into the portal vein, the highway to the liver. The cell membranes of both alpha and beta cells are dotted with special receptors that "sense" how much glucose is flowing past them in the blood so that they "know" how much hormone to release.

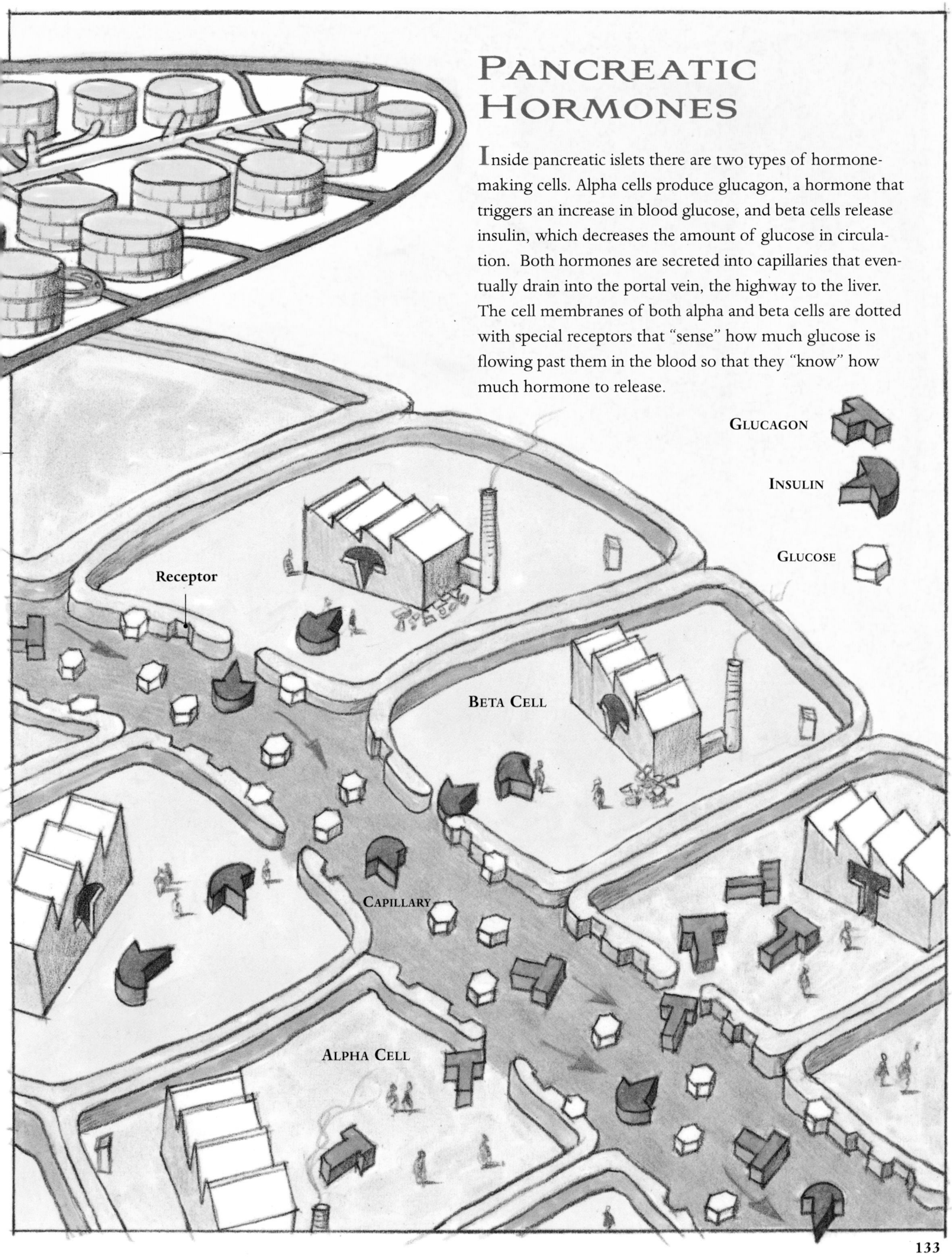

GLUCAGON

INSULIN

GLUCOSE

Receptor

BETA CELL

CAPILLARY

ALPHA CELL

CONTROLLING GLUCOSE

As blood flows past them, both alpha and beta cells in the pancreas act as tiny fuel sensors. When glucose molecules fill or don't fill receptors in their membranes, they respond in opposite ways. In times of a glucose glut, beta cells increase the supply of insulin, which in turn tells liver and other cells to take steps to reduce blood glucose levels. In times of glucose scarcity, alpha cells release more glucagon, which instructs liver cells to increase blood glucose levels. Working together around the clock, both types of hormones perform an elegant and essential glucose balancing act.

TOO MUCH GLUCOSE (AFTER MEALS)

1. Beta cells react to high glucose levels by releasing more insulin; glucagon production by alpha cells decreases.
2. Insulin binds to liver cells, which triggers the joining together of glucose molecules from the blood to make glycogen, a big molecule that stores energy inside liver cells.
3. Insulin binds to tissue cells, encouraging them to take up glucose from blood and use it to release energy.
   Blood glucose levels go down.

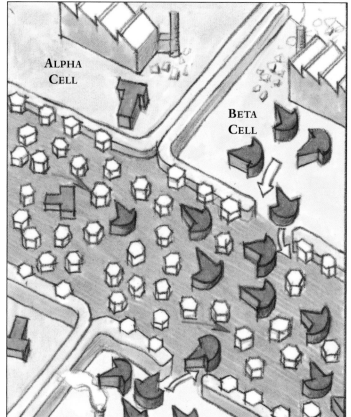

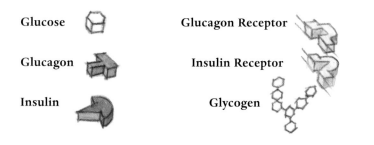

Glucose		**Glucagon Receptor**	
Glucagon		**Insulin Receptor**	
Insulin		**Glycogen**	

TOO LITTLE GLUCOSE (BETWEEN MEALS)

1. Alpha cells react to low glucose levels by releasing extra glucagon; insulin production by beta cells falls.
2. Glucagon binds to liver cells, triggering both the breakdown of glycogen to glucose and the release of glucose into the blood.
3. Glucagon does not target tissue cells, but low insulin levels mean that these cells do not deplete blood glucose.
   Blood glucose levels go up.

Neither insulin nor glucagon lasts long in the bloodstream. Within minutes they are mopped up and destroyed by the liver to stop them from accumulating and interfering with the sensitive glucose control process.

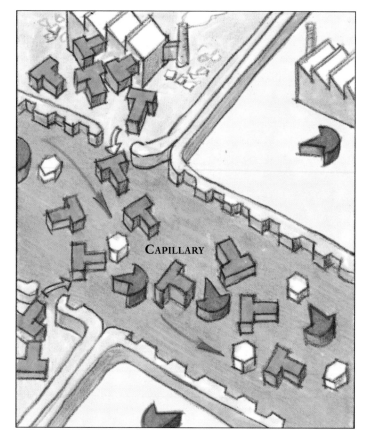

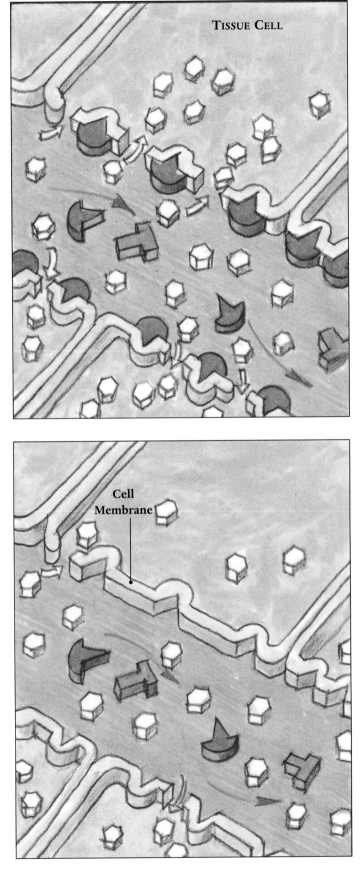

TISSUE CELL

Cell
Membrane

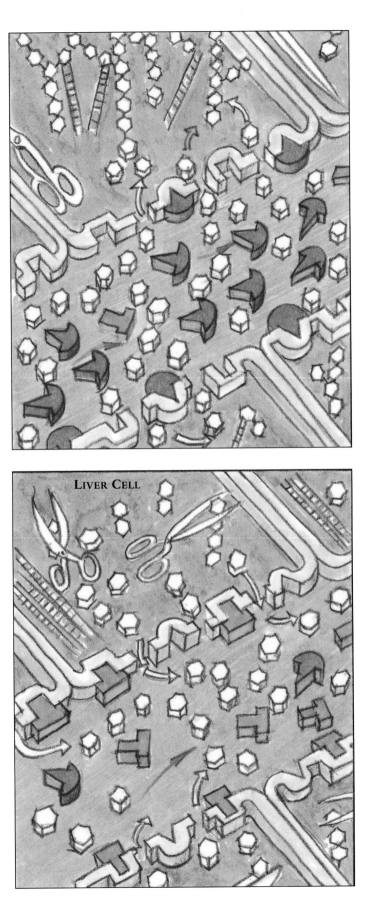

LIVER CELL

INSIDE KIDNEYS

Digested food provides the raw materials for metabolism. One major waste product of metabolism is urea, made in the liver from excess amino acids. Since metabolic wastes can poison the body, it is essential that they be efficiently and expeditiously eliminated. Our kidneys perform a crucial part of this task by continuously filtering the blood. In addition to removing waste, they extract excess water and salts from the blood to ensure that its volume and concentration remain constant. The mix of waste and water forms urine, which the kidneys then pass on for disposal.

Each kidney is divided into three zones—the cortex, medulla, and pelvis. The cortex and medulla are home to a million nephrons, the tiny blood-filtering units that produce urine. The hollow pelvis funnels urine into the ureter for its onward journey.

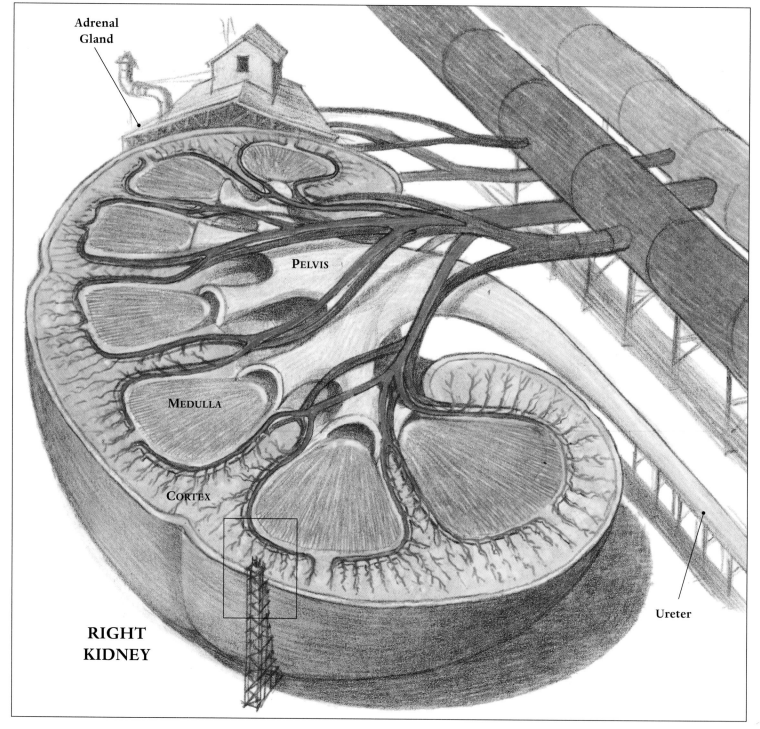

Adrenal Gland

PELVIS

MEDULLA

CORTEX

RIGHT KIDNEY

Ureter

MEDULLA

CORTEX

NEPHRON

COLLECTING DUCT

RESTROOMS

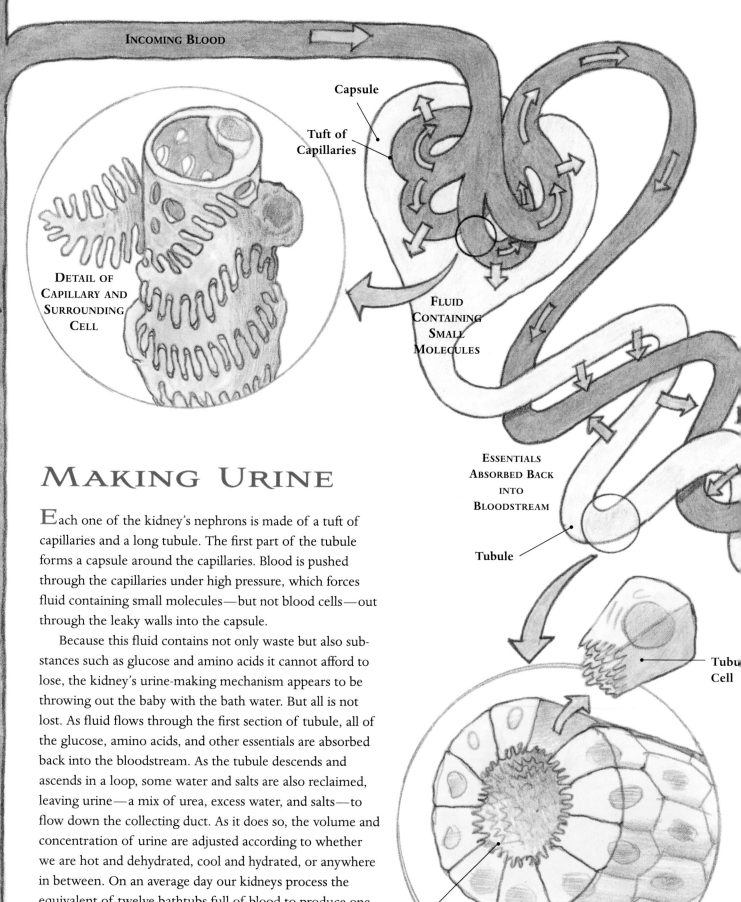

Capsule

Tuft of
Capillaries

DETAIL OF
CAPILLARY AND
SURROUNDING
CELL

FLUID
CONTAINING
SMALL
MOLECULES

ESSENTIALS
ABSORBED BACK
INTO
BLOODSTREAM

Tubule

Tubule
Cell

Microvilli
Provide
Large
Surface for
Absorption

MAKING URINE

Each one of the kidney's nephrons is made of a tuft of capillaries and a long tubule. The first part of the tubule forms a capsule around the capillaries. Blood is pushed through the capillaries under high pressure, which forces fluid containing small molecules—but not blood cells—out through the leaky walls into the capsule.

Because this fluid contains not only waste but also substances such as glucose and amino acids it cannot afford to lose, the kidney's urine-making mechanism appears to be throwing out the baby with the bath water. But all is not lost. As fluid flows through the first section of tubule, all of the glucose, amino acids, and other essentials are absorbed back into the bloodstream. As the tubule descends and ascends in a loop, some water and salts are also reclaimed, leaving urine—a mix of urea, excess water, and salts—to flow down the collecting duct. As it does so, the volume and concentration of urine are adjusted according to whether we are hot and dehydrated, cool and hydrated, or anywhere in between. On an average day our kidneys process the equivalent of twelve bathtubs full of blood to produce one big soda bottle full of urine.

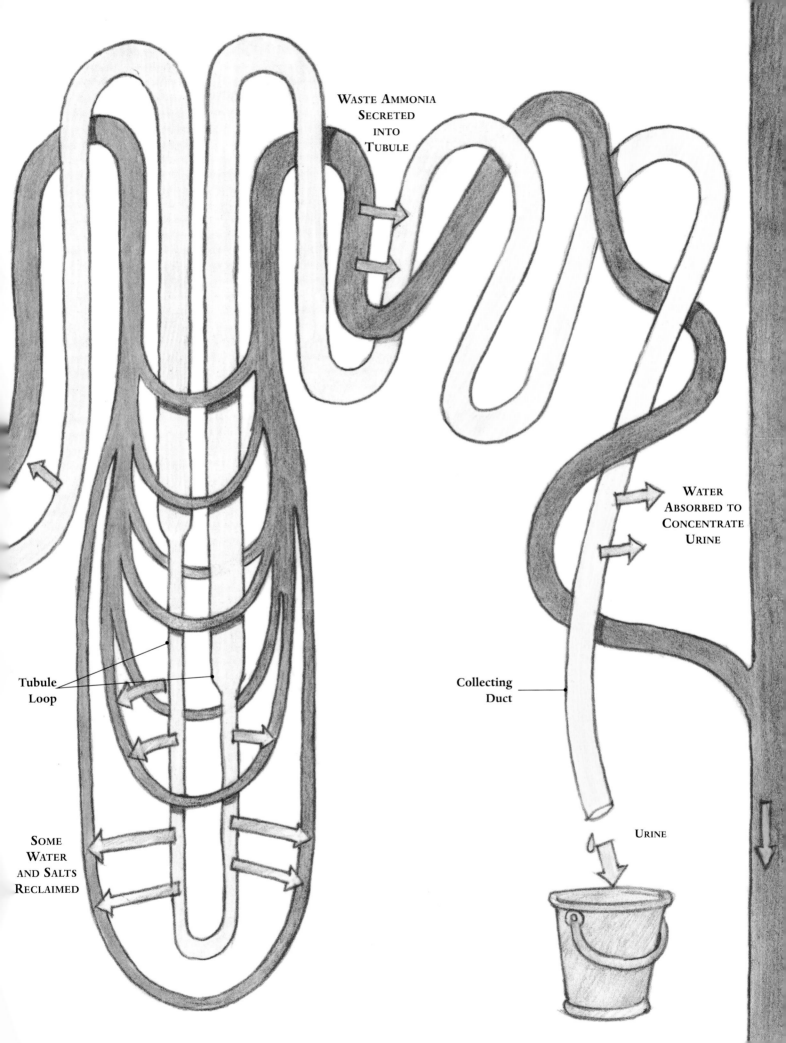

WASTE AMMONIA
SECRETED
INTO
TUBULE

WATER
ABSORBED TO
CONCENTRATE
URINE

Collecting
Duct

Tubule
Loop

SOME
WATER
AND SALTS
RECLAIMED

URINE

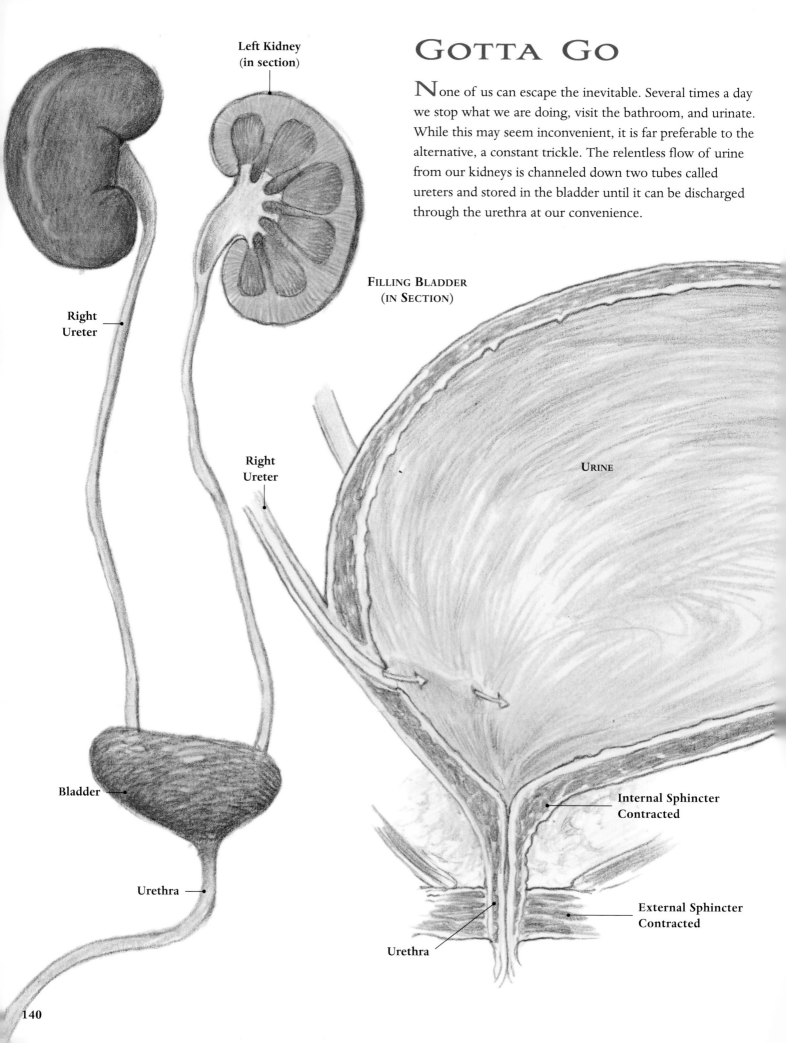

**Left Kidney
(in section)**

GOTTA GO

None of us can escape the inevitable. Several times a day we stop what we are doing, visit the bathroom, and urinate. While this may seem inconvenient, it is far preferable to the alternative, a constant trickle. The relentless flow of urine from our kidneys is channeled down two tubes called ureters and stored in the bladder until it can be discharged through the urethra at our convenience.

**FILLING BLADDER
(IN SECTION)**

**Right
Ureter**

**Right
Ureter**

URINE

Bladder

**Internal Sphincter
Contracted**

Urethra

**External Sphincter
Contracted**

Urethra

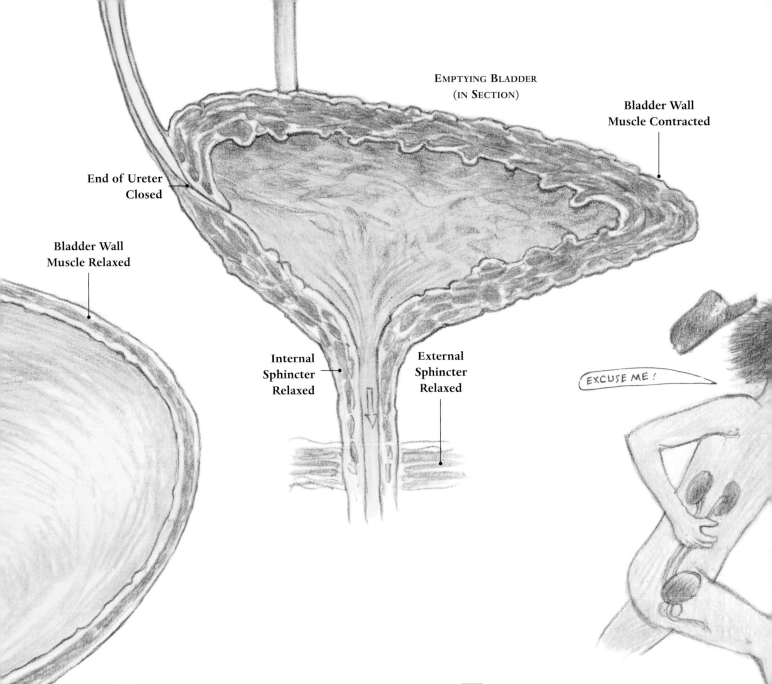

EMPTYING BLADDER
(IN SECTION)

Bladder Wall
Muscle Contracted

End of Ureter
Closed

Bladder Wall
Muscle Relaxed

Internal
Sphincter
Relaxed

External
Sphincter
Relaxed

EXCUSE ME !

FILLING

Each ureter gently massages urine from one of the kidneys by peristalsis to an opening at the rear of the bladder, a muscular and remarkably stretchy storage bag. Urine pressure inside the bladder closes this opening enough to prevent backflow but still allows urine to enter. The urethra is the tube that will carry urine to the outside. Currently it is closed by an internal sphincter, which encircles the bladder-urethra junction, and, lower down, by an external sphincter that is under our control. Its muscular wall relaxed, the bladder becomes rounder as it fills with urine. Stretch receptors in the bladder's muscular wall tell the nervous system how full it is.

EMPTYING

Initially the bladder is "told" to keep its wall muscle relaxed and sphincters tightly closed. But once a reasonable volume of urine has accumulated, messages reach the brain and we feel the urge to urinate. Involuntary signals from the brain stem contract the bladder wall muscle and relax the sphincters. We can, if we want, override this reflex action and keep the voluntary external sphincter shut. But as more urine accumulates, the need to empty the bladder becomes more urgent. Eventually, we have to relax the external sphincter and allow the bladder wall muscle to contract, rhythmically squeezing urine out through the urethra. The bladder soon returns to its original size, internal folds reappear, and refilling begins.

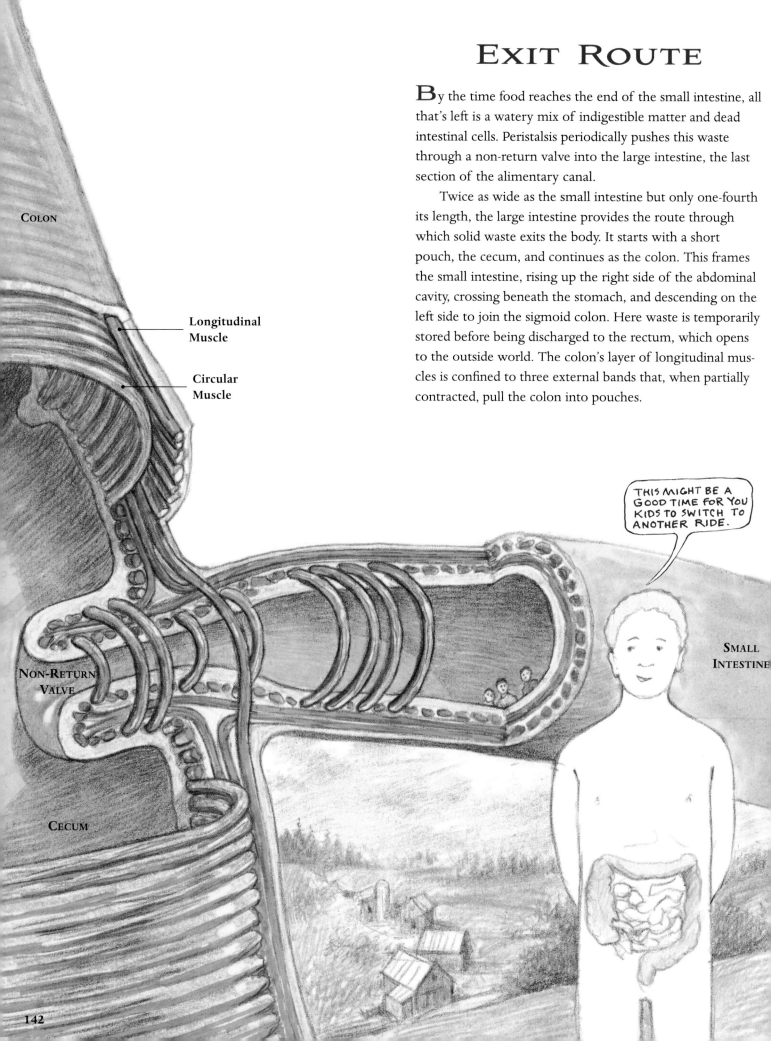

EXIT ROUTE

By the time food reaches the end of the small intestine, all that's left is a watery mix of indigestible matter and dead intestinal cells. Peristalsis periodically pushes this waste through a non-return valve into the large intestine, the last section of the alimentary canal.

Twice as wide as the small intestine but only one-fourth its length, the large intestine provides the route through which solid waste exits the body. It starts with a short pouch, the cecum, and continues as the colon. This frames the small intestine, rising up the right side of the abdominal cavity, crossing beneath the stomach, and descending on the left side to join the sigmoid colon. Here waste is temporarily stored before being discharged to the rectum, which opens to the outside world. The colon's layer of longitudinal muscles is confined to three external bands that, when partially contracted, pull the colon into pouches.

COLON

Longitudinal Muscle

Circular Muscle

NON-RETURN VALVE

CECUM

THIS MIGHT BE A GOOD TIME FOR YOU KIDS TO SWITCH TO ANOTHER RIDE.

SMALL INTESTINE

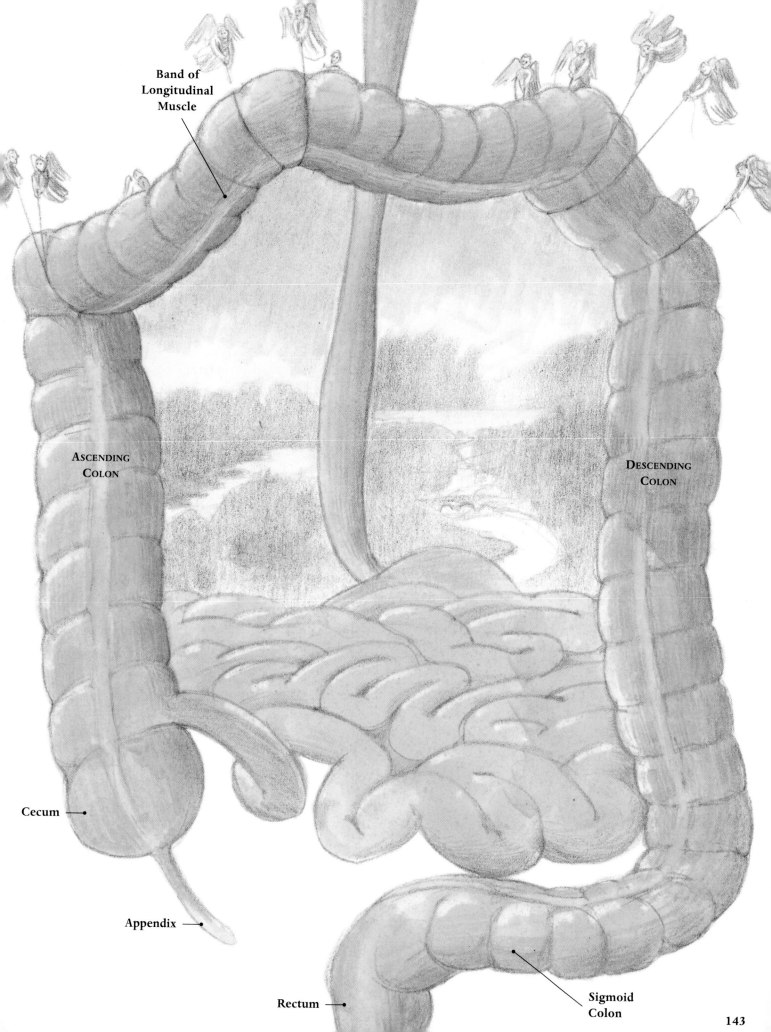

Band of
Longitudinal
Muscle

ASCENDING
COLON

DESCENDING
COLON

Cecum

Appendix

Rectum

Sigmoid
Colon

143

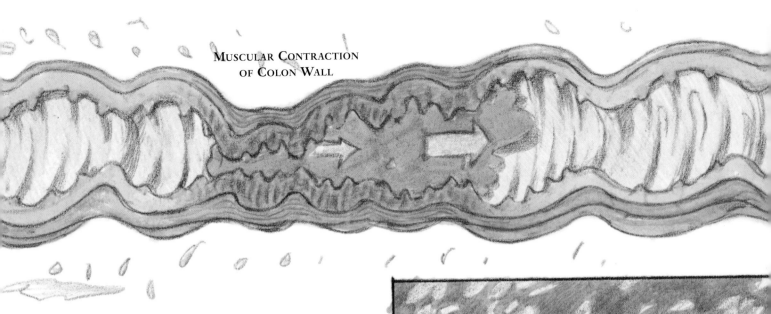

MAKING FECES

There's an obvious change in terrain as we move from small to large intestine. Gone are the circular folds and villi, reflecting the fact that the colon—the longest section of the large intestine—has no digestive role. Instead, its job is to propel waste material toward the anus so it can be pushed out of the body. During that journey, water is absorbed through the intestinal lining into the bloodstream, an action that helps the body avoid dehydration and makes the once watery waste—now called feces—semisolid and more manageable.

Warm and wet, the colon is an ideal home for trillions of bacteria that usually live in peace with their host. Bacteria manufacture the substances that give feces and wind their characteristic odors and use converted bile pigments to color feces brown. They also work on waste to release sugars and vitamins that we can use.

Usually the muscular contractions of the walls produce a slow, sluggish movement of feces that allows time for water to be absorbed. But three or four times a day—triggered by the arrival of food in the stomach—a powerful wave of peristalsis called a mass movement forces feces into the sigmoid colon, where they are stored until liberated by defecation. During the twelve to thirty-six hours it takes to get from cecum to anus, each pound (450 grams) of watery waste is converted to five ounces (150 grams) of feces. Up to half of that weight is made up of living and dead bacteria.

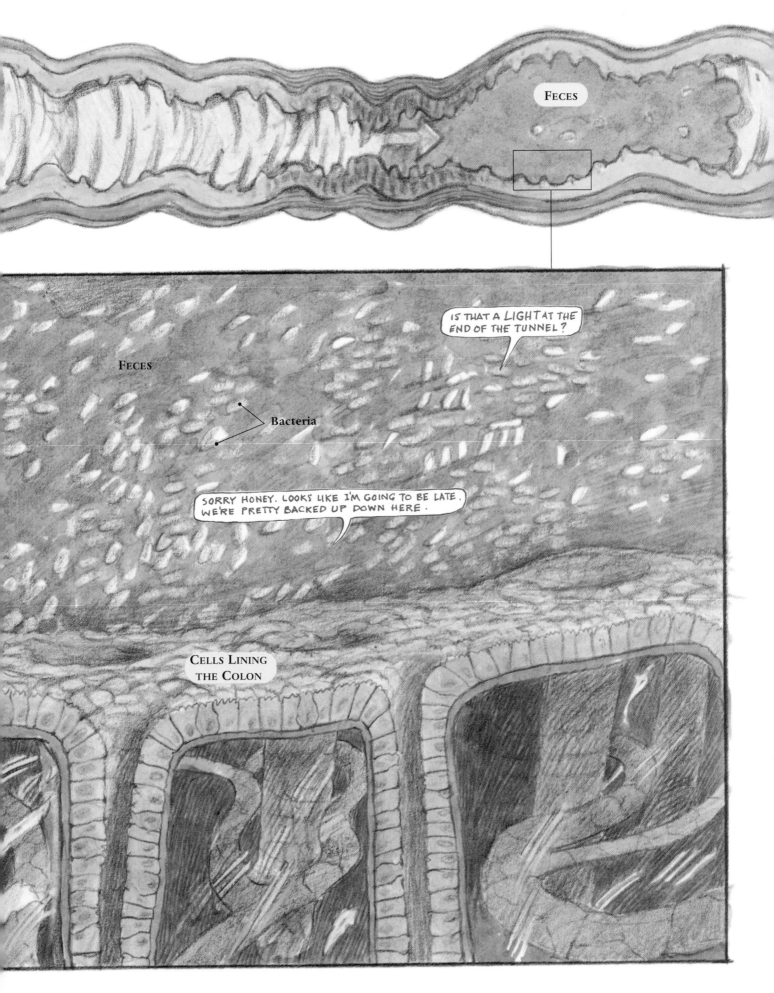

Journey's End

The final act of the digestive process is familiar to all of us. It is defecation, the elimination of feces along the rectum and the short anal canal and out through the anus. Surrounding the anus are two sphincters that act as drawstrings. The internal anal sphincter is controlled automatically. The external one does what you tell it to. Unless, that is, its owner is a baby or toddler; they need diapers because they haven't yet learned to control their external sphincter.

Once "seated" in the bathroom, we make a conscious decision to relax the external sphincter and let contraction of the rectum push the feces out through the open anus. Extra help comes from two sources. Contraction of abdominal muscles and the diaphragm provide additional downward pressure on the rectum, especially during "straining." And contraction of the levator ani muscle lifts the anal canal to pull the anus over the exiting feces. Once finished, we wash our hands, because feces are teeming with bacterial passengers that might cause us harm.

DEFECATION REFLEX

When the rectum is empty, both sphincters are contracted and the anus stays closed. But when feces are pushed into the rectum, they stretch the rectal wall and trigger a sequence of responses called the defecation reflex.

1. Stretch receptors in the rectal wall send sensory messages to the spinal cord.
2. Signals from the spinal cord instruct muscles in the wall of the sigmoid colon and rectal wall to contract, thereby squeezing the feces.
3. These signals also tell the internal sphincter to relax.
4. When pressure in the rectum builds to a certain level, the external sphincter also starts to relax.
5. As sensory messages reach the brain, we feel an urge to defecate.
6. Fortunately, motor signals speeding in the opposite direction order the external sphincter to stay firmly contracted until we decide to defecate.

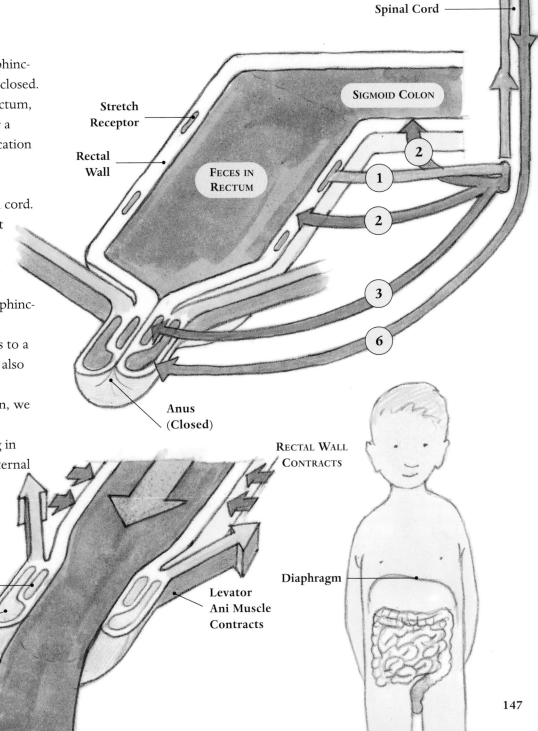

Spinal Cord

SIGMOID COLON

Stretch Receptor

Rectal Wall

FECES IN RECTUM

Anus (Closed)

Internal Sphincter Relaxed

External Sphincter Relaxed

Levator Ani Muscle Contracts

RECTAL WALL CONTRACTS

Diaphragm

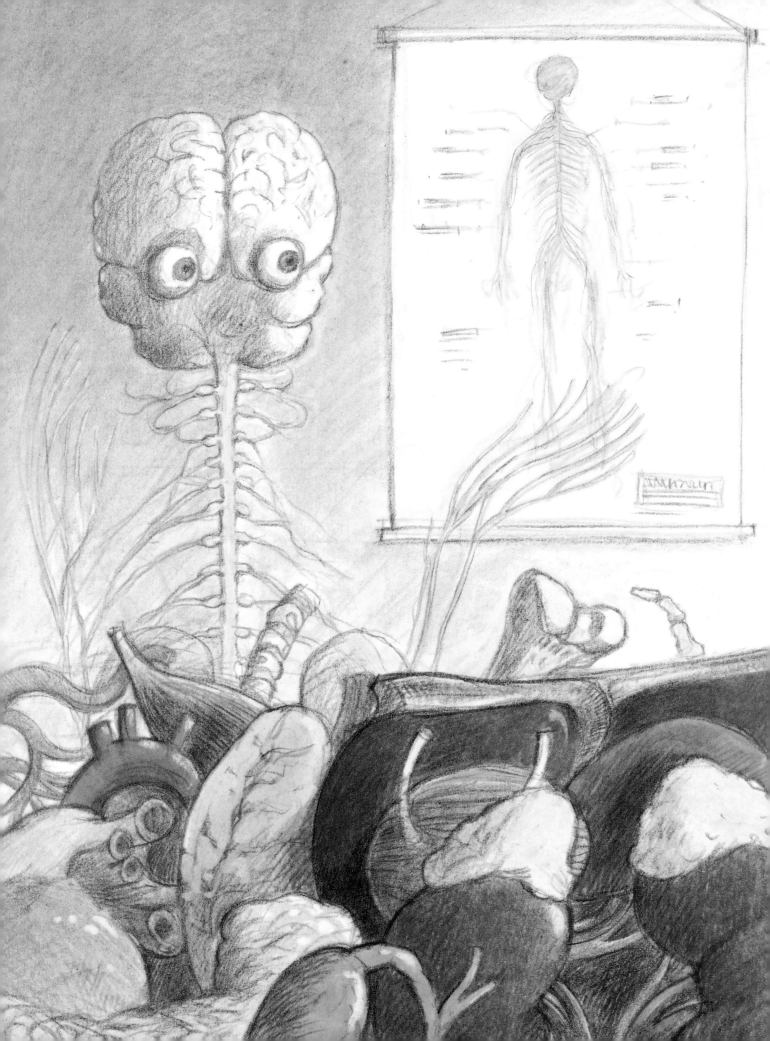

CHAPTER 4

WHO'S IN CHARGE HERE?

OVER THE PAST TWO HUNDRED YEARS, clever researchers have focused the amazing power of the brain on itself, building an unprecedented understanding of its architecture and workings as well as those of the entire nervous system. We now know how this lightning-fast communication network enables us to taste lemons, feel pain, remember birthdays, read and write books, tell bad jokes, and contemplate the universe—and how its internal "autopilot" ensures the smooth running of our bodies even as we sleep.

There are, of course, still many mysteries about how the brain works. But if we are, as we like to believe, the smartest creatures on Earth, then surely it's just a matter of time until we solve them.

DENDRITE

CELL BODY

NEURON

COMMUNICATORS

The human body could not possibly function without its nervous system. With cool efficiency and split-second timing, this complex communication network analyzes and collates an endless stream of incoming signals and then fires off instructions to coordinate every aspect of the way we work.

Axon Branches of
Another Neuron

Made up of the brain and spinal cord, as well as the nerves that link them with every part of the body, the nervous system consists largely of interconnected cells called neurons. Like all cells, neurons are microscopic, but some, such as the ones that pass down your leg and "talk" to your toes, are extremely long. A neuron receives signals from other neurons through spiky projections called dendrites. These signals then pass through its cell body to a single longer projection called an axon, which transmits them either to the tissue it controls or to the next neuron.

The ability of a neuron to receive, carry, and pass on high-speed electrical signals depends on the distribution of ions along both sides of its cell membrane. There are both positive and negative ions, but the positive ions—sodium and potassium—are what concern us here. When the neuron is resting and not transmitting, sodium ions predominate just outside the membrane and potassium ions predominate just inside. Members of both groups pass through the membrane to the opposite side in an attempt to even out their numbers. Potassium ions, however, are better escape artists. They can leak out far more easily than sodium ions can leak in. This leaves the cell with more positive ions outside, which in turn creates an excess of negative charge inside.

Although pumps in the membrane continually eject sodium ions and bring back potassium ions, they can't eliminate the imbalance, only stabilize it. So when a neuron is resting, its inside is negatively charged with respect to its outside.

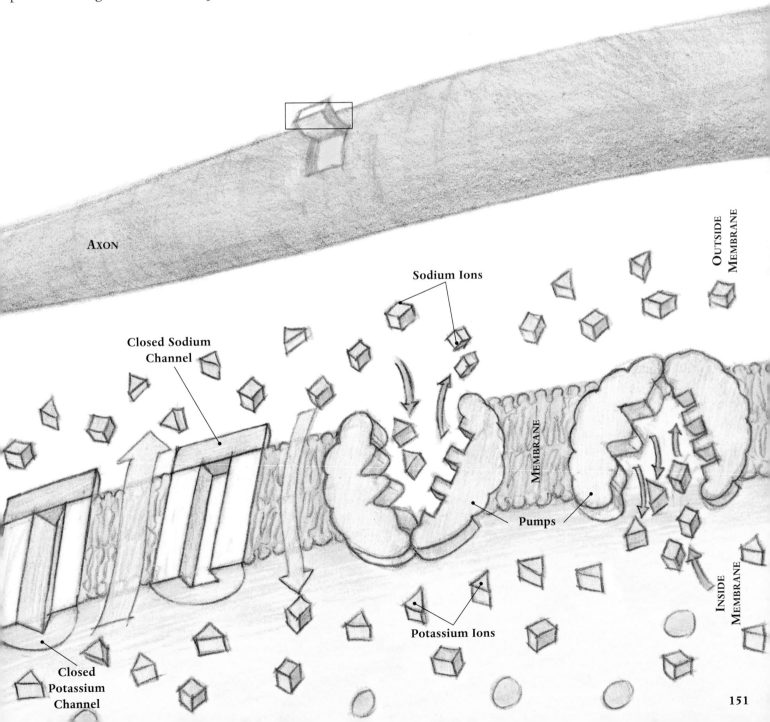

AXON

OUTSIDE MEMBRANE

Sodium Ions

Closed Sodium Channel

MEMBRANE

Pumps

Closed Potassium Channel

Potassium Ions

INSIDE MEMBRANE

SENDING SIGNALS

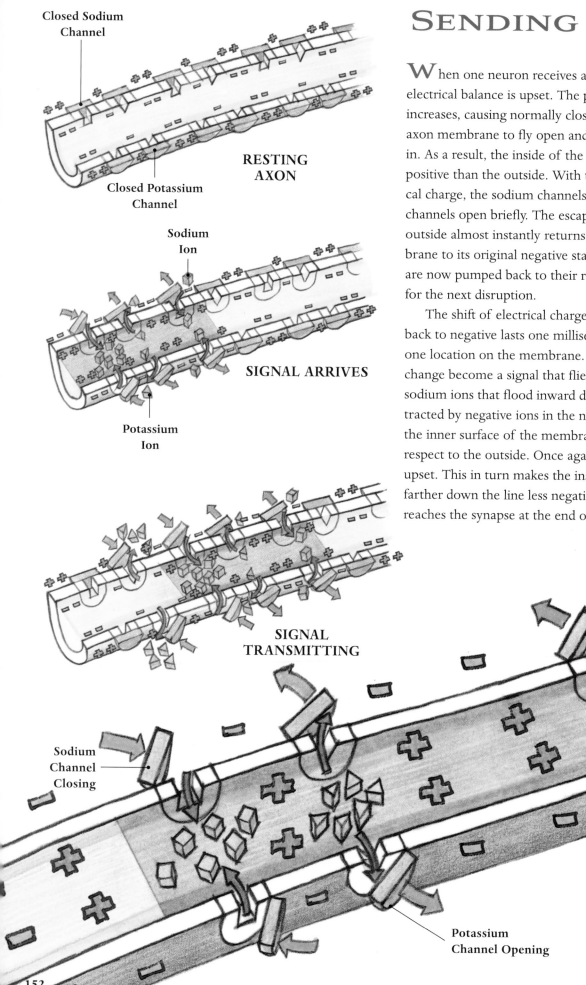

Closed Sodium Channel

RESTING AXON

Closed Potassium Channel

Sodium Ion

SIGNAL ARRIVES

Potassium Ion

SIGNAL TRANSMITTING

Sodium Channel Closing

Potassium Channel Opening

Sodium Channel Opening

When one neuron receives a signal from another, its electrical balance is upset. The positive charge inside its axon increases, causing normally closed sodium channels in the axon membrane to fly open and allow sodium ions to rush in. As a result, the inside of the axon becomes much more positive than the outside. With this sudden reversal of electrical charge, the sodium channels slam shut and the potassium channels open briefly. The escape of potassium ions to the outside almost instantly returns the inner surface of the membrane to its original negative state. Just as speedily, all escapees are now pumped back to their rightful resting positions, ready for the next disruption.

The shift of electrical charge from negative to positive and back to negative lasts one millisecond and happens at only one location on the membrane. So how does this electrical change become a signal that flies along the axon? The positive sodium ions that flood inward during the upheaval are attracted by negative ions in the next part of the axon, making the inner surface of the membrane there less negative with respect to the outside. Once again the balance is suddenly upset. This in turn makes the inside of the membrane even farther down the line less negative and so on until the signal reaches the synapse at the end of the line.

At a synapse, one neuron communicates with another but they do not actually touch. Though the gap separating them is extremely small, it is wide enough to stop the signal in its tracks. The bulbous tip at the end of neuron number one's axon contains membrane-enclosed sacs filled with neurotransmitter molecules. Arrival of a signal causes the sacs to fuse with the neuron membrane, open, and release neurotransmitter molecules into the gap. These molecules rapidly reach a dendrite of neuron number two and bind to its receptors. Channels in the dendrite membrane open, allowing ions to enter and upset the normal electrical charge. This in turn stimulates the axon of neuron number two to send its own signal speeding along to the next synapse.

After the event, which lasts just one millisecond, neurotransmitter molecules in the gap are either destroyed or reclaimed and recycled. Open sacs reform and are refilled with neurotransmitter molecules.

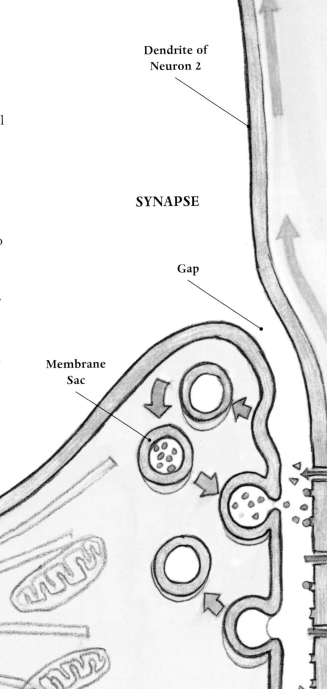

Dendrite of Neuron 2

SYNAPSE

Gap

Membrane Sac

Axon of Neuron 1

Neurotransmitter Molecule

Receptor

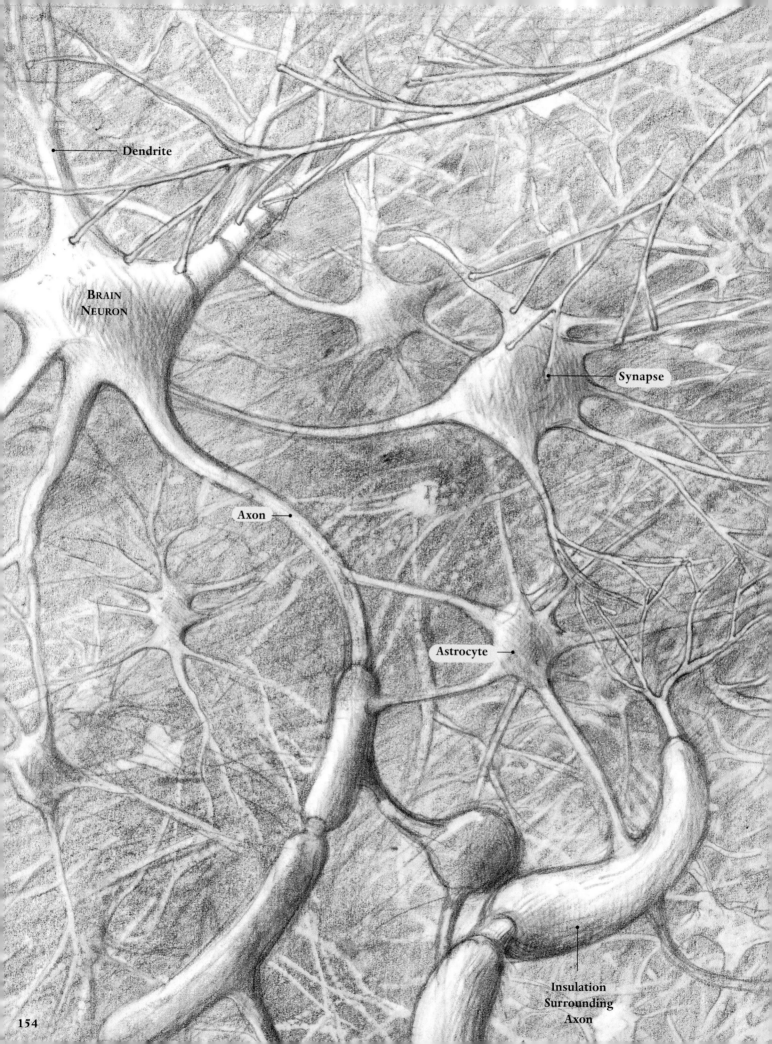

Dendrite

BRAIN
NEURON

Synapse

Axon

Astrocyte

Insulation
Surrounding
Axon

Neuron Network

Around 100 billion neurons are found in the brain, where they form a communications network of unrivaled processing power. Through its dendrites and axon branches, each neuron can make contact with hundreds or thousands of others. It is this unimaginably large number of connections that generates the brain's awesome power. Most of this work happens in the six layers of nerve cells—the gray matter—that form the cerebral cortex, the thin outer layer of the brain. Emerging from beneath the cortex, long axons carry signals to and from other parts of the brain and the body. They are wrapped with insulation to increase the speed at which their signals travel. Together these axons form the white matter.

As numerous as they may be, brain neurons are dependent on ten times as many support cells, including star-shaped astrocytes that support and feed neurons and ensure that they operate with maximum efficiency.

GRAY MATTER OF THE
CEREBRAL CORTEX

WHITE MATTER

FROM LAYERS TO LOBES

Together, the cerebral cortex and its underlying white matter form the cerebrum, the largest and uppermost part of the brain. To squeeze as much of itself as possible into the limited space of the skull, the hard-working cortex folds into many ridges and grooves. The longest and deepest groove splits the cerebrum into left and right halves, or hemispheres. Other major grooves help delineate the frontal, parietal, occipital, and temporal lobes of each hemisphere, named for the skull bones that overlie them.

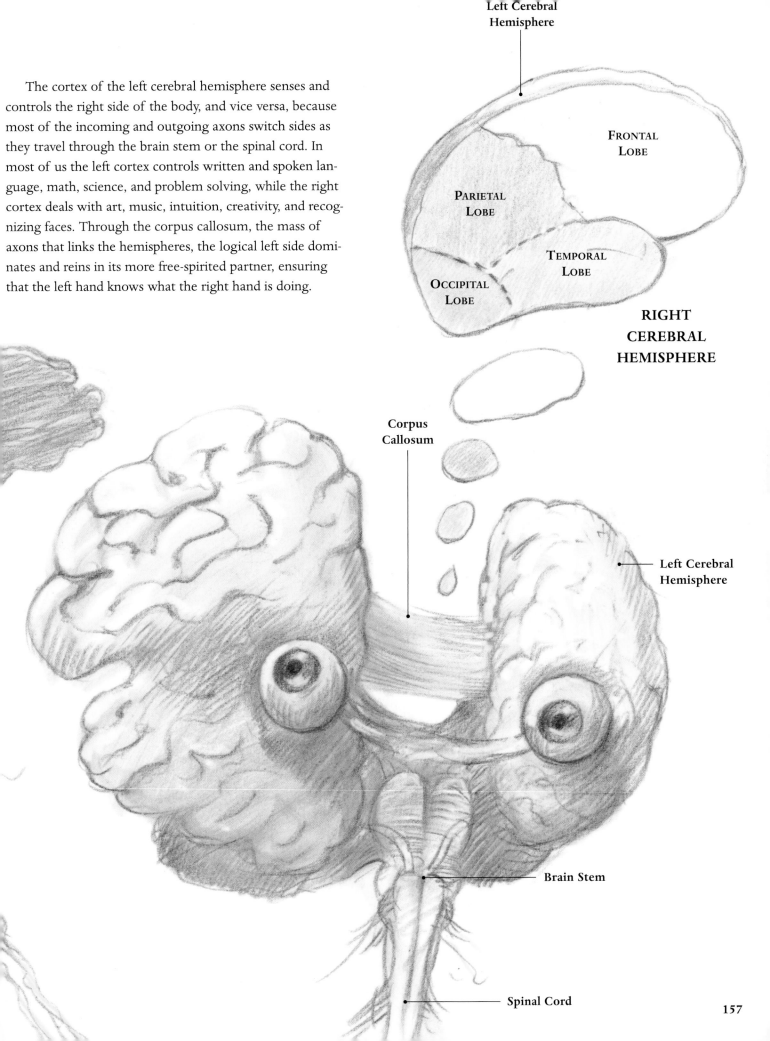

The cortex of the left cerebral hemisphere senses and controls the right side of the body, and vice versa, because most of the incoming and outgoing axons switch sides as they travel through the brain stem or the spinal cord. In most of us the left cortex controls written and spoken language, math, science, and problem solving, while the right cortex deals with art, music, intuition, creativity, and recognizing faces. Through the corpus callosum, the mass of axons that links the hemispheres, the logical left side dominates and reins in its more free-spirited partner, ensuring that the left hand knows what the right hand is doing.

Left Cerebral Hemisphere

FRONTAL LOBE

PARIETAL LOBE

TEMPORAL LOBE

OCCIPITAL LOBE

RIGHT CEREBRAL HEMISPHERE

Corpus Callosum

Left Cerebral Hemisphere

Brain Stem

Spinal Cord

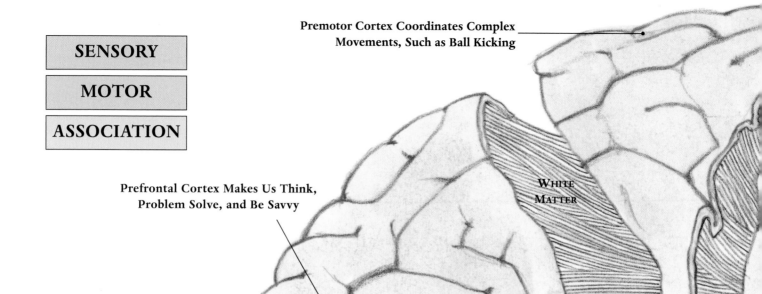

SENSORY

MOTOR

ASSOCIATION

Premotor Cortex Coordinates Complex Movements, Such as Ball Kicking

Prefrontal Cortex Makes Us Think, Problem Solve, and Be Savvy

WHITE MATTER

Broca's Area Produces Speech

MAPPING THE CORTEX

Reading these words, thinking about lunch, remembering a birthday, and kicking a ball all have something in common. To happen, each requires a mass firing of selected groups of neurons in the cerebral cortex. Here messages are received, decisions made, memories stored, and instructions sent out. Different areas of the cerebral cortex perform different tasks. With the exception of Wernicke's and Broca's areas, which appear only on the left hemisphere (shown here), both sides are similarly divided.

All areas of the cortex fall into one of three categories. Sensory areas analyze input from sensors and sense organs. Motor areas instruct skeletal muscles to contract and move the body. Association areas, which make up more than three-quarters of the cortex, interpret sensory input and control functions such as thought, creativity, and memory.

Auditory Association Cortex Identifies Sounds

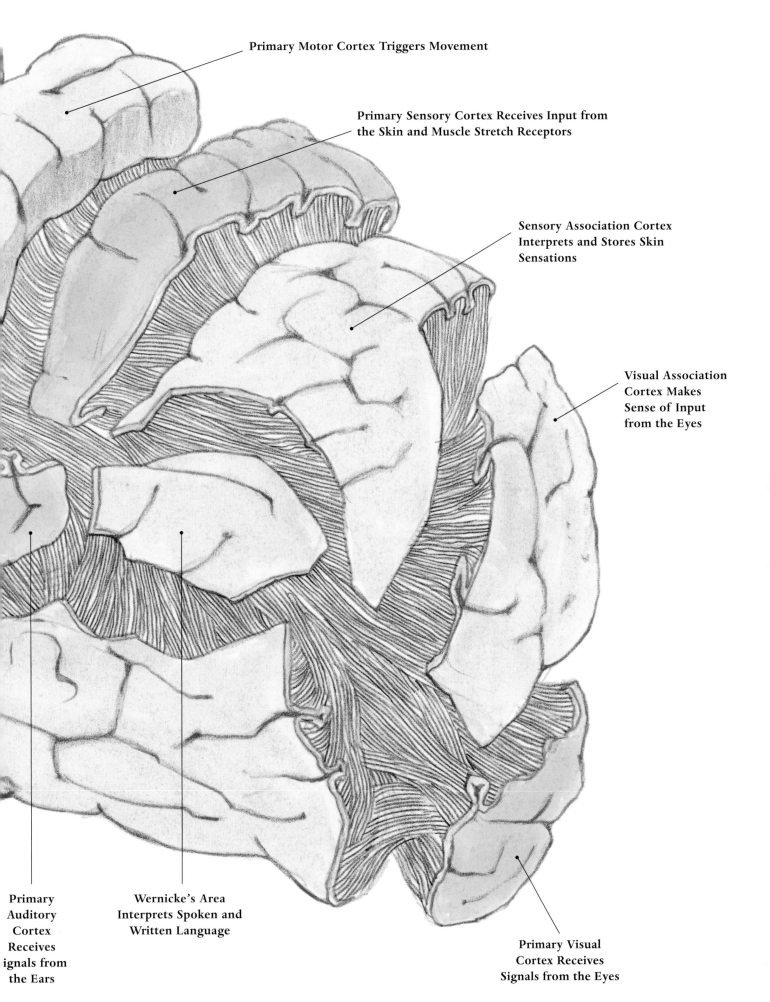

Primary Motor Cortex Triggers Movement

Primary Sensory Cortex Receives Input from
the Skin and Muscle Stretch Receptors

Sensory Association Cortex
Interprets and Stores Skin
Sensations

Visual Association
Cortex Makes
Sense of Input
from the Eyes

Primary
Auditory
Cortex
Receives
Signals from
the Ears

Wernicke's Area
Interprets Spoken and
Written Language

Primary Visual
Cortex Receives
Signals from the Eyes

159

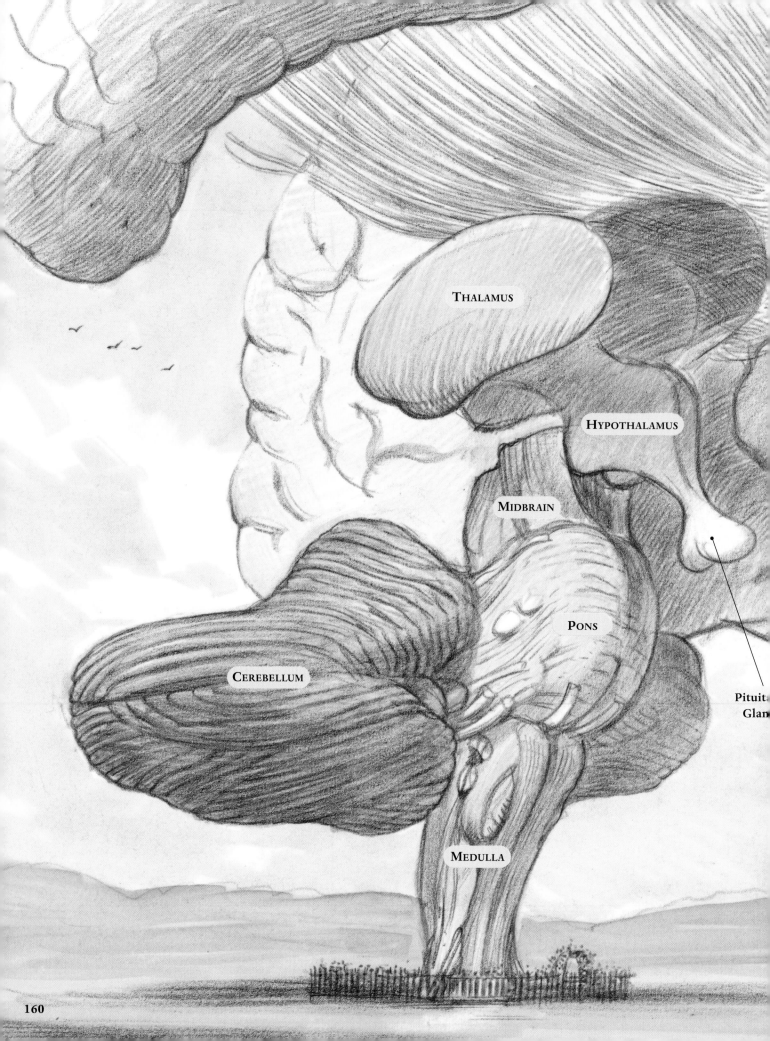

THALAMUS

HYPOTHALAMUS

MIDBRAIN

PONS

CEREBELLUM

Pituita
Glan

MEDULLA

LEFT CEREBRAL HEMISPHERE

INNER STRUCTURES

Not all of the working parts of the brain are displayed on the hills and valleys of its cerebrum. The thalamus and hypothalamus, the brain stem, and the cerebellum are "inner structures" that also have key roles to play.

The thalamus and hypothalamus are nestled between the cerebral hemispheres, above the brain stem. Every second, the brain is bombarded with a mass of sensory information telling it what is happening inside and outside the body. The egg-shaped thalamus relays these sensory messages to the cerebral cortex. At the same time, it edits and filters input to prevent the cerebrum from going into information overload and "crashing." Just below the thalamus, the hypothalamus is vested with an importance totally out of proportion to its small size. For example, it is the control center of the autonomic nervous system, a branch of the nervous system that automatically regulates heart rate, blood pressure, breathing rate, and many other processes in response to changing conditions inside and outside the body. Among many other roles, the hypothalamus also oversees whether we feel hungry or thirsty, keeps our internal temperature at a steady level, and wakes us up after a good night's sleep.

The brain stem (midbrain, pons, and medulla oblongata, or medulla) provides the pathways for axons carrying messages between the spinal cord and the "higher" parts of the brain. Under the supervision of the hypothalamus, it also regulates many automatic functions upon which our survival depends, including sleep. The midbrain is a reflex center that controls movement of the eyes and head as things change around us. The pons relays signals between the motor cortex of the cerebrum and the cerebellum. The medulla regulates heart rate, breathing rate, and blood pressure.

The cerebellum, with its left and right lobes, lies behind the pons and medulla. This "little brain" enables the body to maintain its posture and move in a smooth and coordinated way.

SUPPORT AND NURTURE

If our brain weren't floating in some kind of liquid, it could suffer the same fate as a beached whale and be crushed by its own weight. Instead of salt water, however, our brains live in and are protected by a clear liquid called cerebrospinal fluid.

Cerebrospinal fluid is made from blood carefully filtered through clusters of special capillaries. These capillaries are surrounded by a layer of tightly connected cells that deny entry to anything in the blood that might threaten the brain. Around one pint (500 milliliters) of cerebrospinal fluid is produced daily in four centrally located cavities called ventricles. These are linked to each other, to the space that surrounds the brain and spinal cord, and to the spinal cord's central canal.

Cerebrospinal fluid flows from the ventricles and into the space below the skull, where it acts as a cushion, giving the brain buoyancy and protecting it from knocks and blows. Although the brain's hungry neurons already demand a prodigious blood supply—one-fifth of the heart's output for an organ that accounts for only one-fiftieth of the body's weight—cerebrospinal fluid also helps to nurture and feed the brain as it bathes its surfaces. Having done its job, it then passes into broad canals called sinuses, where it mixes with blood that is on its way back to the heart.

Ventric

CEREBELLUM

Vein Carrying Blood
Toward the Heart

Central Canal of
Spinal Cord

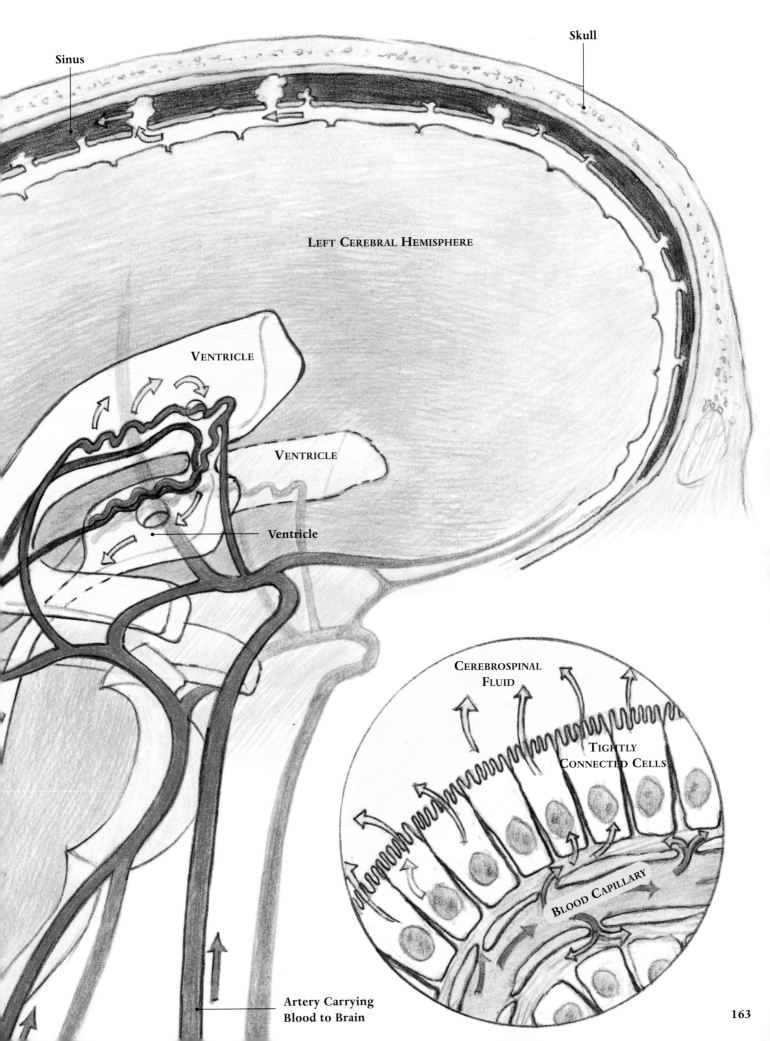

Sinus

Skull

LEFT CEREBRAL HEMISPHERE

VENTRICLE

VENTRICLE

Ventricle

CEREBROSPINAL
FLUID

TIGHTLY
CONNECTED CELLS

BLOOD CAPILLARY

Artery Carrying
Blood to Brain

163

Brain Protection

The comparison may be unappetizing, but if you could prod your brain it would have the feel of warm Jell-O. Such delicacy means that the slightest pressure could cause serious damage by destroying irreplaceable neurons. To protect their crowning achievement, our cells have fashioned a strong, multilayered, shock-absorbing case.

A gentle tap on the side of the head meets with solid resistance from the outer layer of that case—the skull. The dome that surrounds the brain is constructed of thin, curved bones with sawtooth edges that are locked together in immovable joints called sutures. This self-bracing arrangement gives the skull enormous strength.

Beneath the bone is a series of membranes. The first of these is the thick and tough dura mater. It has two layers, the innermost of which folds inward in places to form partitions that check the movement of the brain, much as a seat belt restrains a car passenger. Beneath the dura mater is the arachnoid, and below that is the brain-hugging pia mater.

The space between the arachnoid and pia mater is crossed by a web of strands, invaded by major blood vessels and filled with cerebrospinal fluid. This acts as a liquid cushion to support the brain and to stop it from bouncing off the skull when the head rapidly accelerates or decelerates.

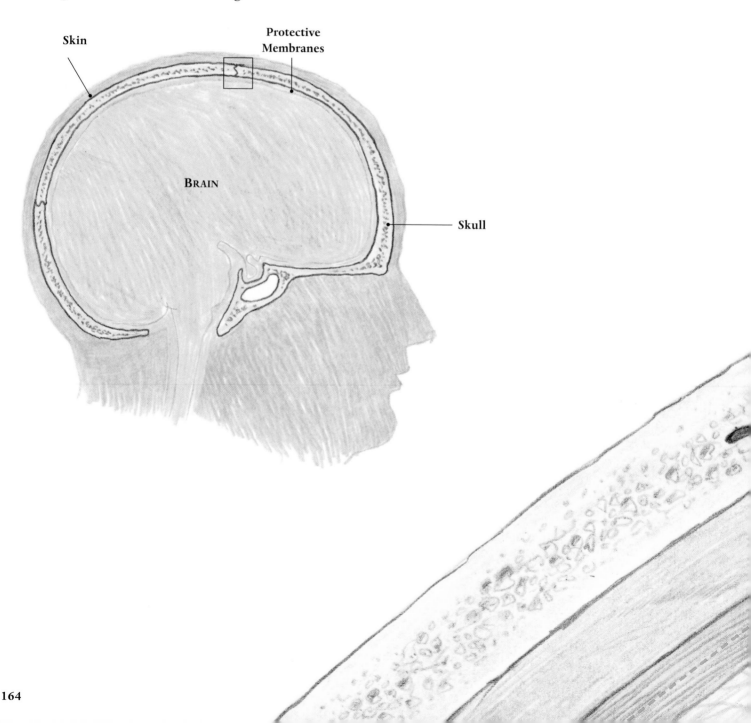

Skin

Protective Membranes

BRAIN

Skull

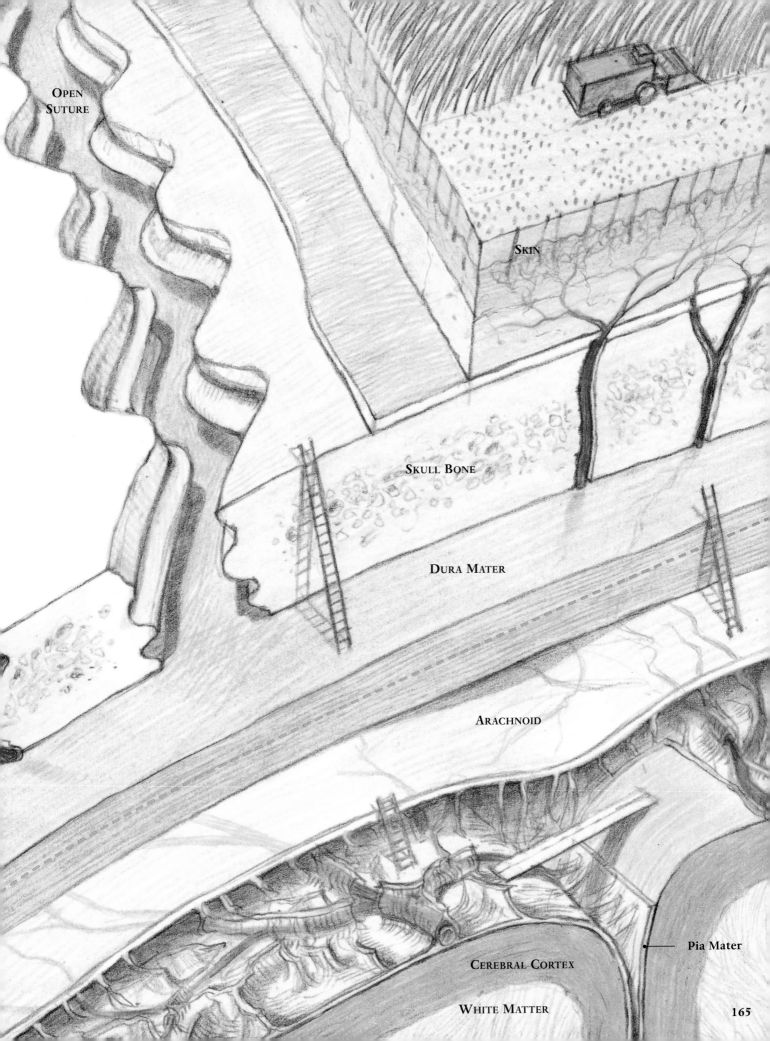

OPEN SUTURE

SKIN

SKULL BONE

DURA MATER

ARACHNOID

CEREBRAL CORTEX

Pia Mater

WHITE MATTER

165

MAKING SENSE

A baby's cry. The blue ocean on a sunny day. Rotten eggs. A juicy peach. Soft velvet. We can experience these and millions of other stimuli because of our senses—hearing, vision, smell, taste, and touch.

Our connection with the world depends on input from sensory receptors, and different sensory receptors respond to different stimuli. Mechanoreceptors in the ear, skin, and internal organs fire when distorted by touch, stretching, pressure, or vibration. Photoreceptors in the eye are switched on by light. Chemoreceptors in the tongue and nose respond to substances dissolved in water.

Thermoreceptors in the skin detect changes in temperature. Nociceptors in the skin and internal organs react to painful stimuli.

Touch receptors in the skin are just modified dendrites at the end of sensory neurons. But those for hearing, vision, smell, and taste are distinct, specialized cells. Smell receptors project into the nasal cavity, while taste receptors are clumped in taste buds on the tongue. Those for hearing and sight are housed in dedicated sense organs—the ears and eyes.

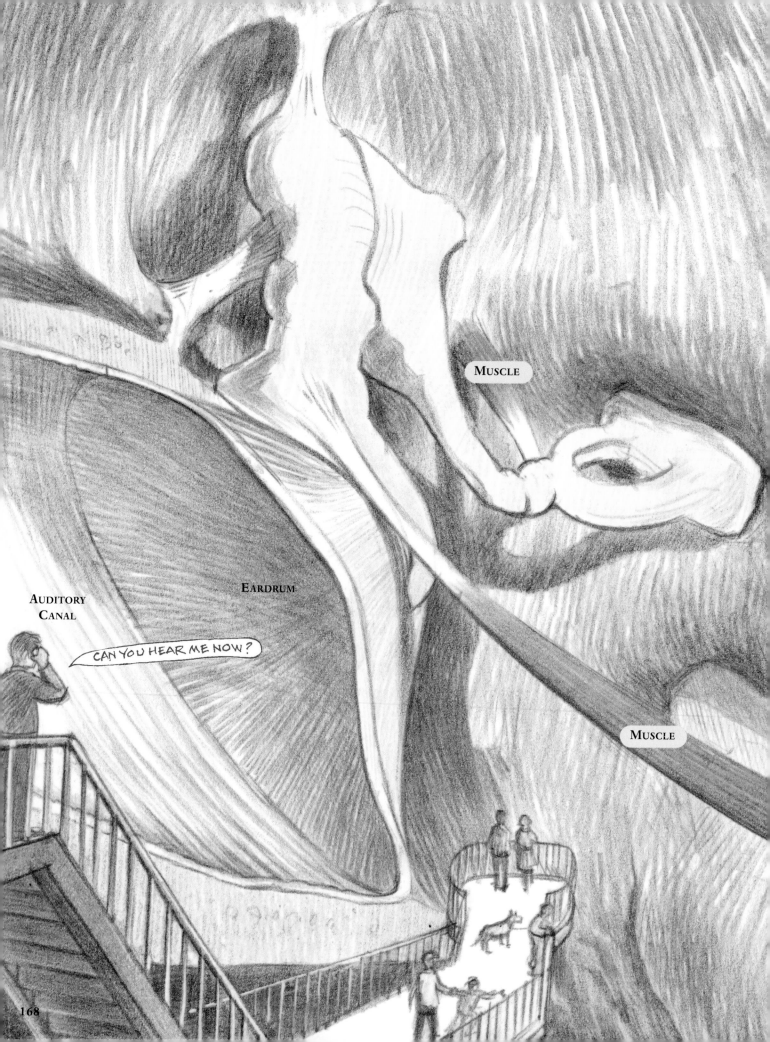

WAVES TO VIBRATIONS

Drop a pebble into water, and visible waves ripple outward from the splash point. Pluck a guitar string, and invisible waves travel outward through the air, are captured by the ears, and ultimately interpreted as sounds by the brain.

Whatever their source, sound waves are funneled by the outer ear into the auditory canal, the inner end of which is blocked by the eardrum, a thin, taut membrane that vibrates when the sound waves strike.

Behind the eardrum is the middle ear, an air-filled space spanned by a chain of three tiny bones that connect the eardrum to the membrane-covered oval window at the entrance to the inner ear. When the eardrum reverberates, the chain moves in and out like a piston, amplifying the vibrations and transmitting them to the oval window. To prevent damage to delicate inner parts of the ear, two tiny muscles keep the bones' movements in check when very loud noises are heard.

The inner ear is a labyrinth of channels surrounded by bone, lined by membranes, and filled with fluid. One branch leads to the semicircular canals that comprise our organs of balance, while another, the spiral-shaped cochlea, is the site of sound detection.

The cochlea is divided lengthwise into three parallel ducts. The first begins at the oval window and extends to the tip of the spiral. There it connects with a second duct, which makes the return trip, ending at another membrane-covered window. Between the two is the self-contained duct that houses the receptors that convert sound vibrations into electrical signals.

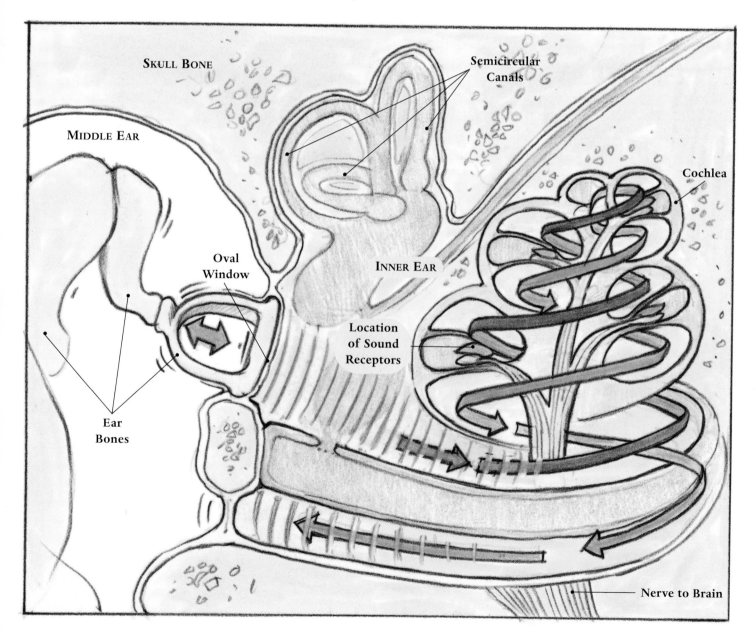

Hearing Things

Every time sound waves arrive in the ear, the oval window moves in and out, generating pressure waves in the cochlea. These are detected by rows of hair cells that are housed within the cochlea's central duct and rest on its lower membrane. Projecting from the top of each cell are stiffened "hairs"—not the same as the hairs on your head—of varying lengths. The tips of the tallest ones are enmeshed in an overarching gel-like membrane and linked to their shorter neighbors by tiny fibers. At its base each hair cell forms a synapse with a sensory neuron.

The arrival of pressure waves causes the lower membrane to vibrate and the hair cells to move, making their longest enmeshed "hairs" bend from side to side. These movements stretch the fibers between the "hairs," thereby opening channels in the membrane that covers them. This action triggers the release of neurotransmitter molecules across the synapse to the sensory neuron, which generates signals and sends them to the brain.

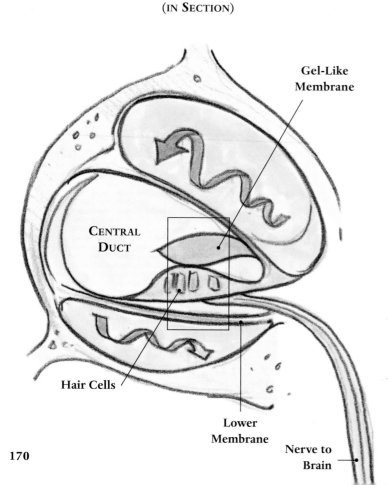

**COCHLEA
(IN SECTION)**

Gel-Like
Membrane

CENTRAL
DUCT

Hair Cells

Lower
Membrane

Nerve to
Brain

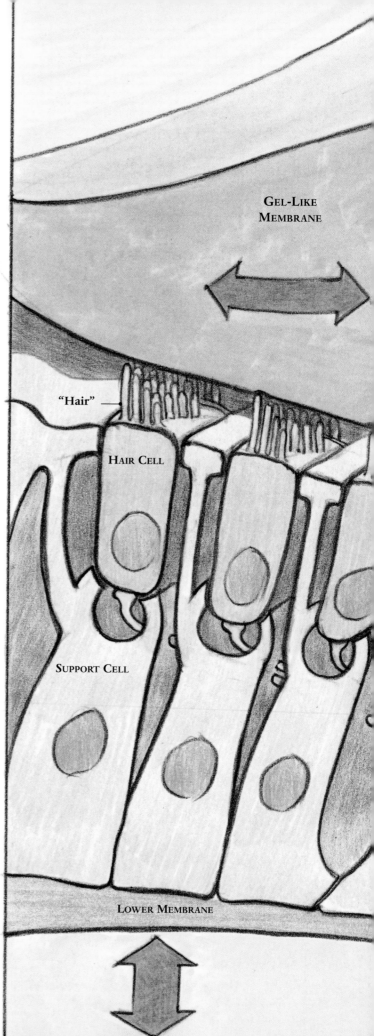

GEL-LIKE
MEMBRANE

"Hair"

HAIR CELL

SUPPORT CELL

LOWER MEMBRANE

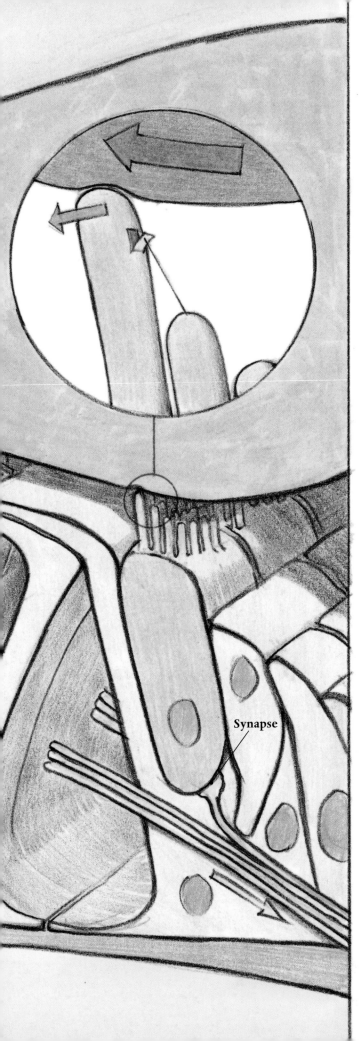

Traveling by way of the medulla, midbrain, and thalamus, signals from each ear—left and right—go to the primary auditory cortex on both sides of the brain. Here we are made conscious of the pitch, volume, and direction of sounds. Different pitches are identified by cells at particular points along the cochlea's central canal—high-pitched sounds trigger hair cells near the oval window, low-pitched sounds affect hair cells near the tip of the cochlea. Louder sounds make the membranes vibrate more vigorously, giving the hair cells a rough ride so they fire more rapidly. Sound direction is determined by which ear detects the sound first, even by a split second.

Adjacent to the primary auditory cortex is the larger auditory association cortex. This is the area of the brain that allows us to distinguish between speech, screeching tires, and a dropped pin.

Synapse

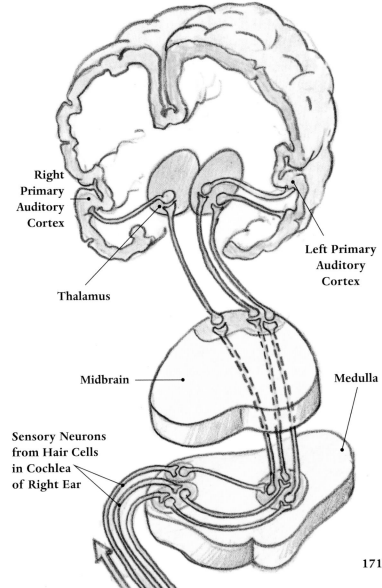

Right Primary Auditory Cortex

Left Primary Auditory Cortex

Thalamus

Midbrain

Medulla

Sensory Neurons from Hair Cells in Cochlea of Right Ear

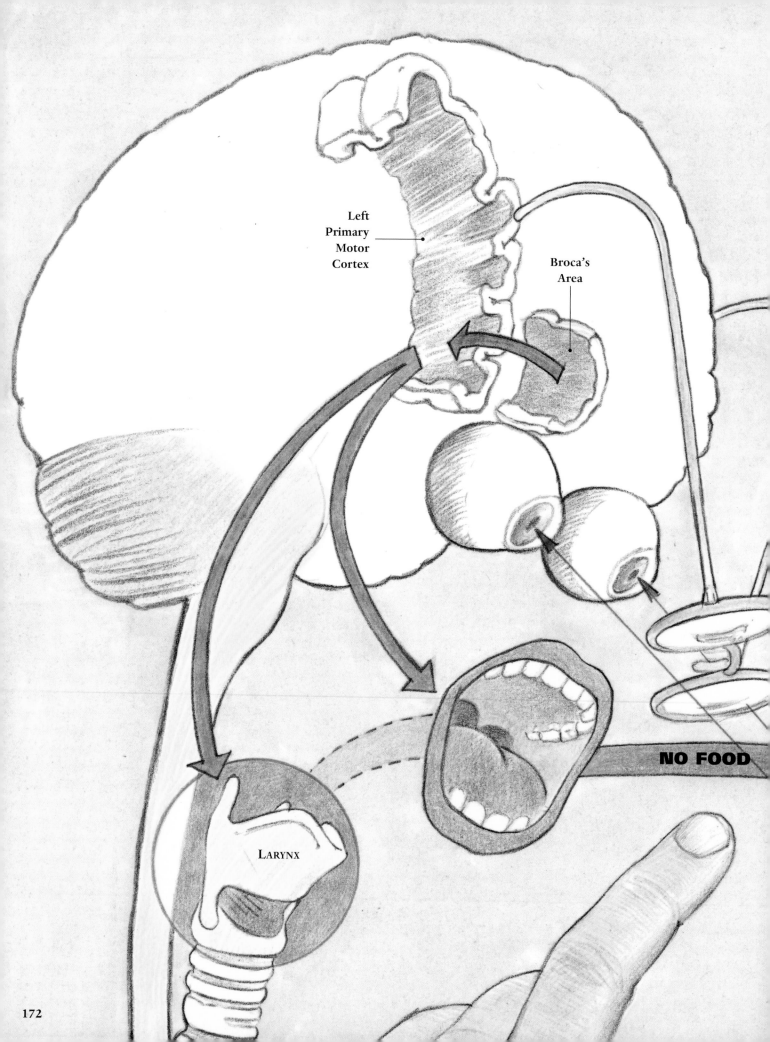

Left
Primary
Motor
Cortex

Broca's
Area

LARYNX

NO FOOD

THE SPOKEN WORD

Only humans can enjoy the luxury of communicating with each other using a structured language with its own library of words. As with so many aspects of brain operation, there is still much to be explained about how we make and understand words, phrases, or entire sentences. But here is what seems to be happening when someone speaks to us and we reply.

The "language cortex" consists of Broca's and Wernicke's areas, each named for the nineteenth-century physician who discovered it and both located in the left cerebral hemisphere on either side of the primary auditory cortex. Sound signals from the ears travel via the thalamus to the auditory cortex. If those signals represent "speech" and

not just meaningless sounds, they are relayed to Wernicke's area, which attaches meaning to words and gives sentences structure. This information then travels to Broca's area, where an appropriate response to the heard message is put together. From here signals are sent to those areas of the motor cortex that control the muscles of the sound-producing larynx, as well as those of the jaws, lips, and tongue that shape raw sounds into recognizable speech.

Wernicke's area also analyzes input from the visual cortex. So if you see something written that relates to what you are hearing, the message is enhanced and your understanding is clearer.

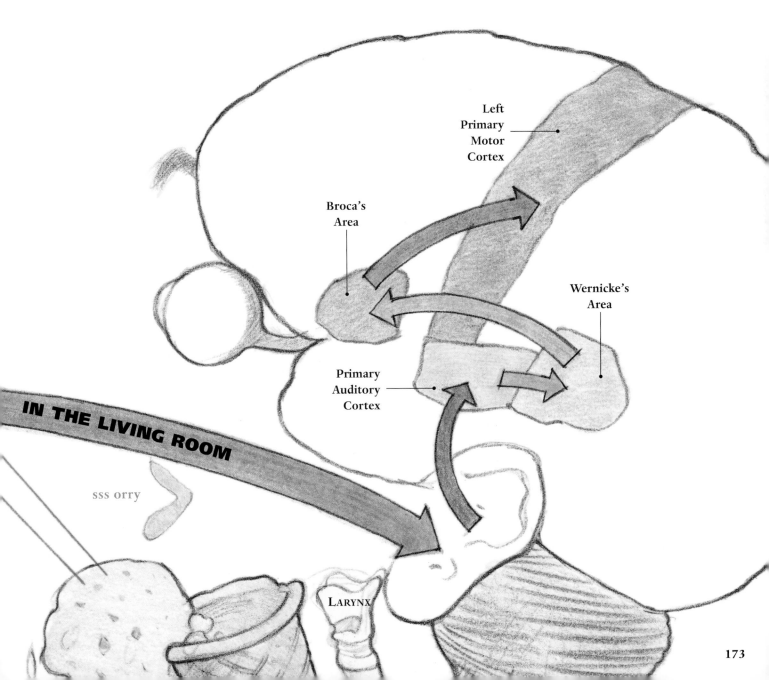

Left Primary Motor Cortex

Broca's Area

Wernicke's Area

Primary Auditory Cortex

IN THE LIVING ROOM

sss orry

LARYNX

173

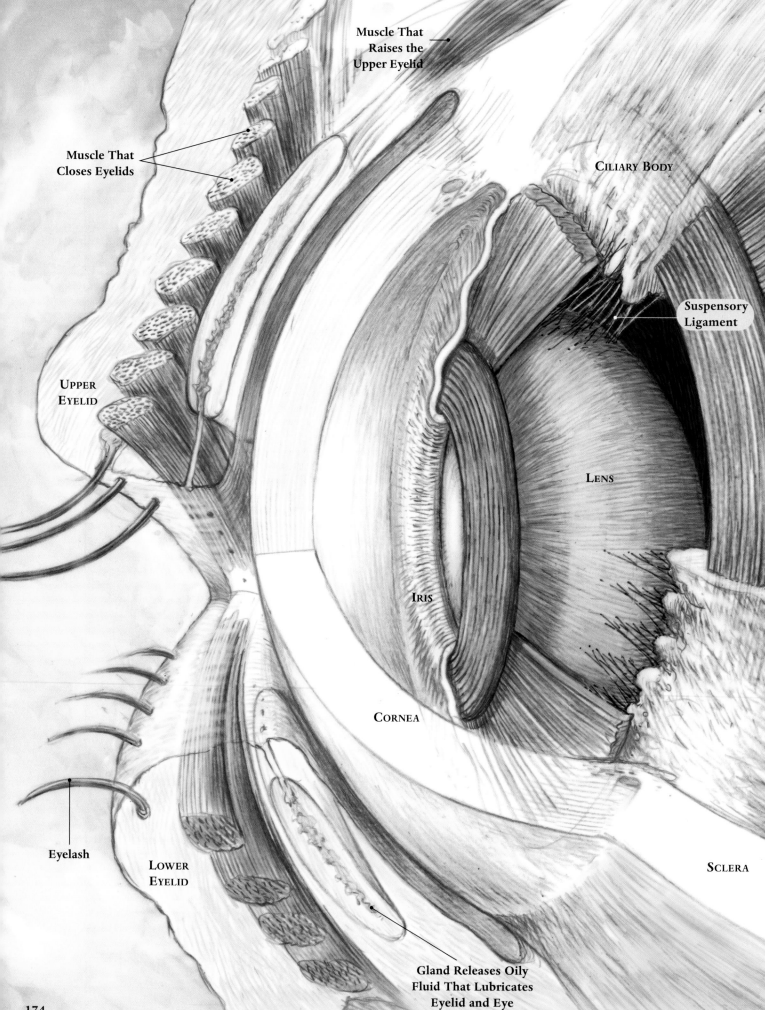

Muscle That
Raises the
Upper Eyelid

Muscle That
Closes Eyelids

CILIARY BODY

Suspensory
Ligament

UPPER
EYELID

LENS

IRIS

CORNEA

Eyelash

LOWER
EYELID

SCLERA

Gland Releases Oily
Fluid That Lubricates
Eyelid and Eye

Eyes Front

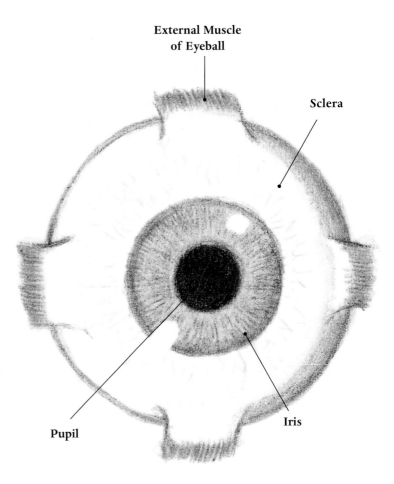

External Muscle of Eyeball

Sclera

Iris

Pupil

Whenever we humans chat, unless we are shy or have something to hide, we look at the eyes of the individual we are addressing. Or, more precisely, at the one-sixth of the eyeball that is not tucked away within a fat-padded bony socket in the skull and that is exposed after every blink of the protective eyelid.

Just behind each eyelid is the sclera, the tough white protective coat that completely encases the eyeball except at the front, where the clear cornea provides a circular window through which light rays can enter.

Behind the cornea, the colored iris regulates the amount of light passing through its central opening—the pupil—and onto the light-sensitive retina beyond it.

Our eyes must be able to work in all kinds of light, and the iris makes sure we are neither blinded by bright light nor rendered helpless in dim conditions.

Adjustment of pupil size is automatic. It's a perfect example of the balancing act performed by opposing divisions of the body's automatic controller, the autonomic nervous system. Under their control are two sets of smooth muscle fibers in the iris—radial fibers that resemble the spokes of a bicycle wheel and circular fibers that run concentrically around the pupil.

BRIGHT LIGHT

When bright light hits the retina, the autonomic nervous system sends signals to the circular muscle fibers. The fibers contract, shrinking the pupil and protecting delicate light receptors within the eye.

DIM LIGHT

When there isn't much light, the autonomic nervous system triggers contraction of the radial muscles of the iris. These pull the pupil wide open to admit as much light as possible.

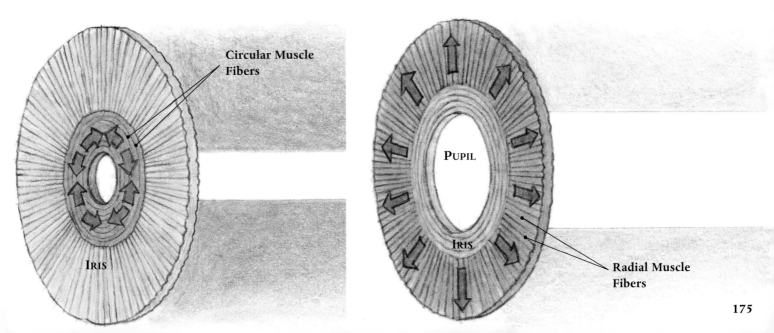

Circular Muscle Fibers

IRIS

PUPIL

IRIS

Radial Muscle Fibers

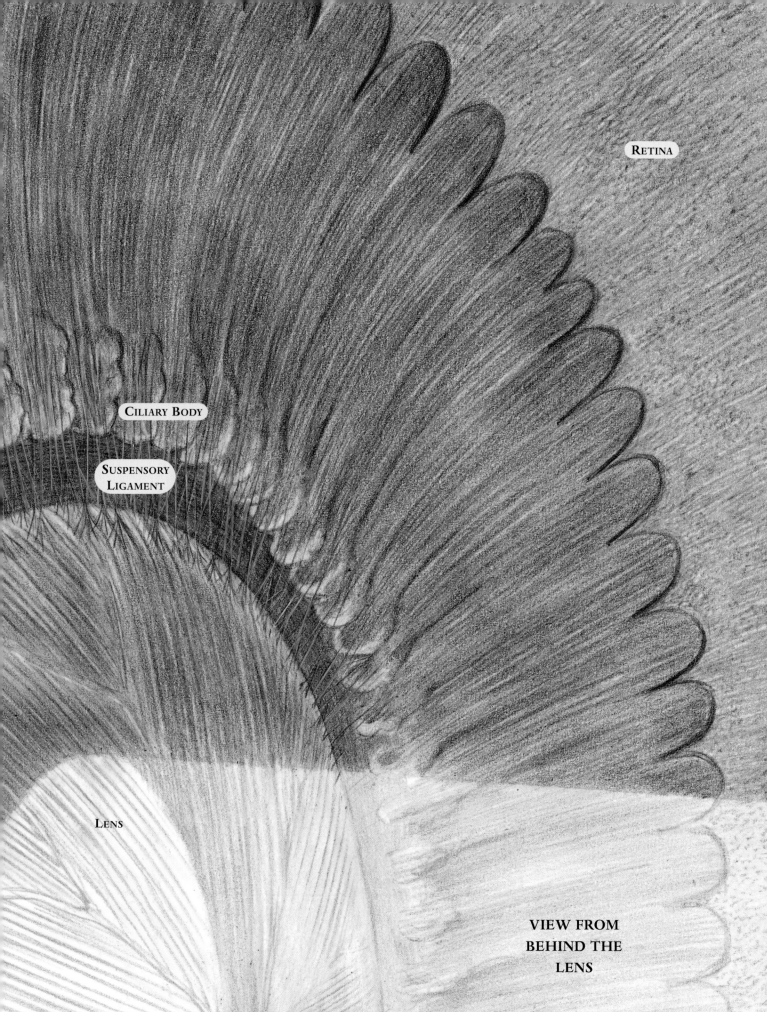

RETINA

CILIARY BODY

SUSPENSORY
LIGAMENT

LENS

VIEW FROM
BEHIND THE
LENS

176

IN FOCUS

The eyeball has two interior spaces. A clear gel called vitreous humor fills the much larger rear space, while watery aqueous humor fills the front one. Being under slight pressure, both humors push outward, giving the eyeball its shape. Between humors the lens is held upright by the fine fibers of the suspensory ligament, itself surrounded by a ring of smooth muscle called the ciliary body. The lens completes the bending of light rays started by the cornea, thereby projecting a sharp, upside-down, and reversed image onto the light-sensitive retina lining most of the rear section of the eyeball. Between the retina and sclera is the dark choroid layer, the blood vessels of which supply them with nutrients and oxygen.

Although the cornea does most of the focusing, it cannot cope both with parallel light rays from distant objects and diverging light rays from nearby objects. The lens, under orders from the autonomic nervous system, is far more versatile.

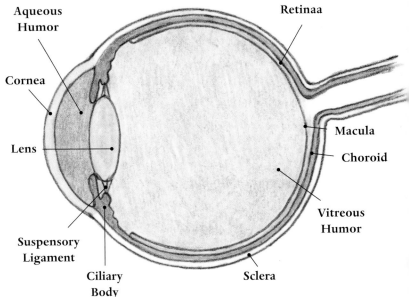

HORIZONTAL SECTION OF THE EYEBALL

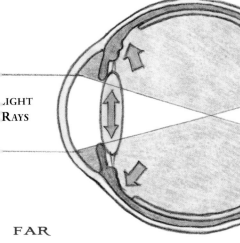

FAR

When we look into the distance, the ciliary body relaxes. This allows outward pressure from the humors to expand the muscle ring, thereby pulling on the suspensory fibers. The lens is made thinner, minimizing any bending effect it may have on the light passing through it.

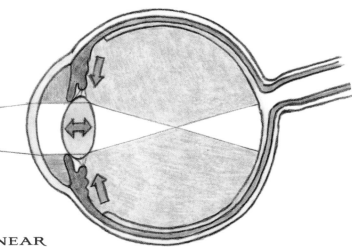

NEAR

If we look at objects close by, the ciliary body is instructed to contract. As the suspensory fibers slacken, the naturally elastic lens becomes fatter, so that it bends light and has greater focusing power than when it was thinner.

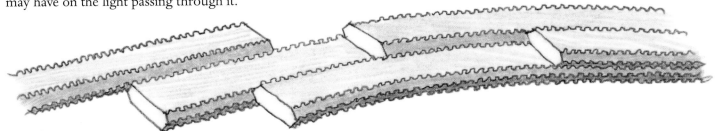

TRANSPARENT AND ELASTIC

The lens is constructed from highly specialized interlocking cells that are long, narrow, and very thin. Having lost most of their internal structures, these cells are filled with crystallins—special proteins that make the lens both transparent and flexible. Like the cornea, the lens has no blood supply to compromise its transparency. Instead, nourishment is absorbed from the aqueous and vitreous humors.

CONES AND RODS

Vision is our foremost sense. Nearly three-quarters of the body's sensory receptors are assigned to the eyes, specifically to the retina, the thin layer that marks the beginning of the path from light to information. Key to the operation of the retina are photoreceptor cells called rods and cones. The 120 million rods in each eye work best in dim light, specializing in fuzzy monochrome images and peripheral vision. The eye's 6 million cones operate best in bright light, detecting colors and providing most detail. Most cones are confined to the macula, that part of the retina upon which light falls when we look directly at something. There are three types of cones, one for red light, one for blue, and one for green. By combining their input, the brain can "see" in full color.

The outermost tips of both rods and cones jut into a layer of dark, pigmented cells. At their other ends they synapse with neurons that, in turn, synapse with ganglion cells, the axons of which merge to form the optic nerve. To reach rods and cones, light must first pass through this veritable obstacle course.

Both rods and cones have an outer and inner segment. The outer segment contains a stack of membrane-enclosed discs. Embedded in the membrane are visual pigments, each consisting of a protein combined with light-absorbing retinal. When light hits the discs, the kinked retinal molecule straightens and detaches from its protein. This alters the electrical charge across the membrane, a charge passed on to a ganglion cell, which then fires, sending nerve signals to the brain. Visual pigments rapidly reform, ready for reuse. Worn-out discs are removed from the tips of rods and cones daily, and their components are recycled by pigment layer cells.

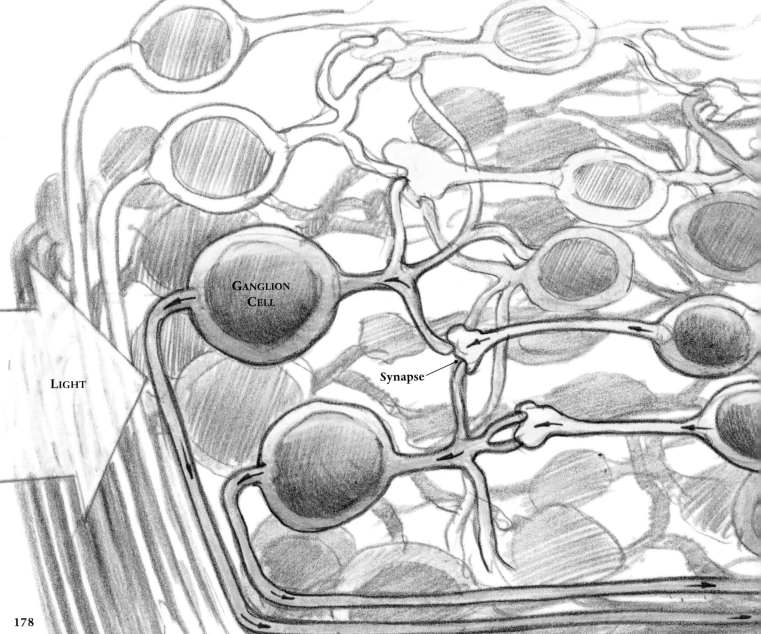

GANGLION
CELL

Synapse

LIGHT

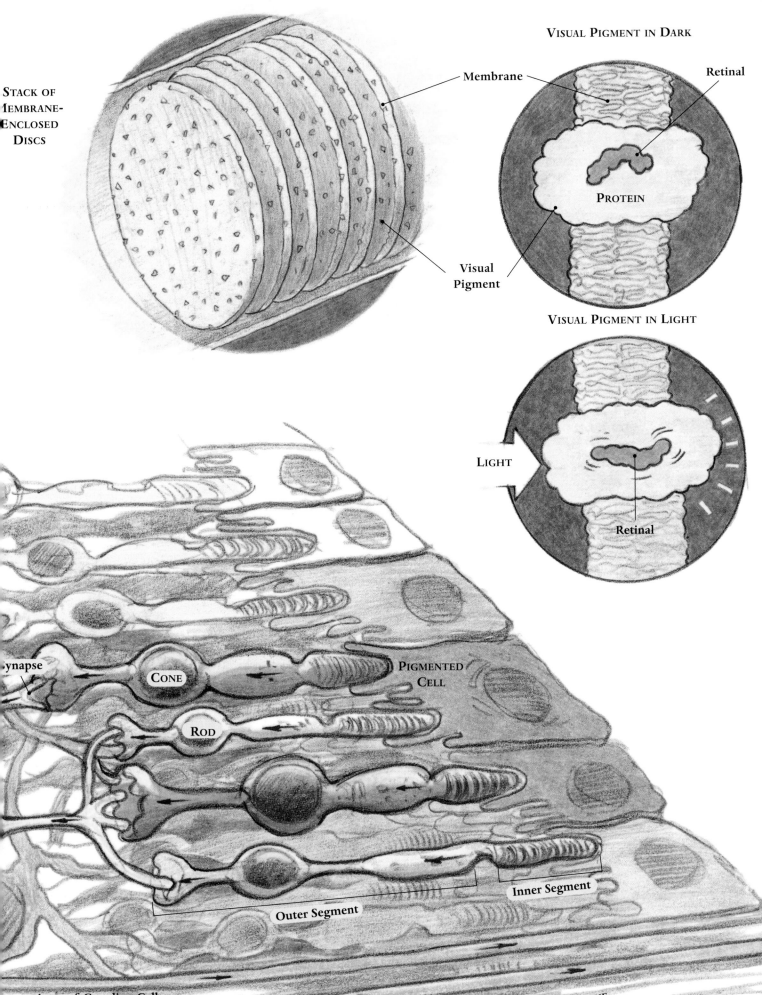

STACK OF
MEMBRANE-
ENCLOSED
DISCS

VISUAL PIGMENT IN DARK

Membrane

Retinal

PROTEIN

Visual
Pigment

VISUAL PIGMENT IN LIGHT

LIGHT

Retinal

Synapse

CONE

ROD

PIGMENTED
CELL

Inner Segment

Outer Segment

Axon of Ganglion Cell

TO OPTIC NERVE

179

EYES TO BRAIN

Our eyes transform light from the outside world into signals that our brain then converts into pictures. To avoid overloading the brain with an unadulterated stream of information, processing starts in the retina. In each eye, crude signals from all 126 million rods and cones must first pass through just one million ganglion cells, a process that eliminates weak signals. The stronger ones continue on to the brain through a million axons that are bundled together to form one of the two optic nerves.

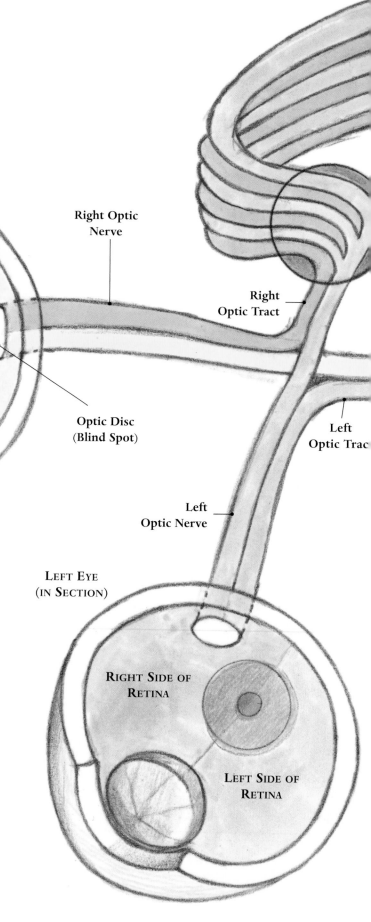

Right Optic Nerve

Right Optic Tract

Left Optic Tract

Optic Disc (Blind Spot)

Left Optic Nerve

RIGHT EYE (IN SECTION)

LEFT EYE (IN SECTION)

RIGHT SIDE OF RETINA

LEFT SIDE OF RETINA

Shortly after leaving the eyes, axons from the inner half of each retina cross over before continuing their journey along either left or right optic tract. This means that the left optic tract carries signals from the left side of each eye's retina while the right optic tract handles signals from the right side of each retina. But because the lens reversed the image projected on each retina, the left optic tract is actually carrying information from the right part of the visual field—what the eye "sees"—and the right tract is carrying information from the left. Each tract then enters a part of the thalamus, where specific layers of neurons process signals arriving from ganglion cells in the retina that specialize in detecting either movement or color and shape. Once refined, these signals are sent on to the primary visual cortex.

A few axons from both optic tracts never make it to the thalamus. They go directly to the midbrain, where their signals help in the control of eye movements and pupil size.

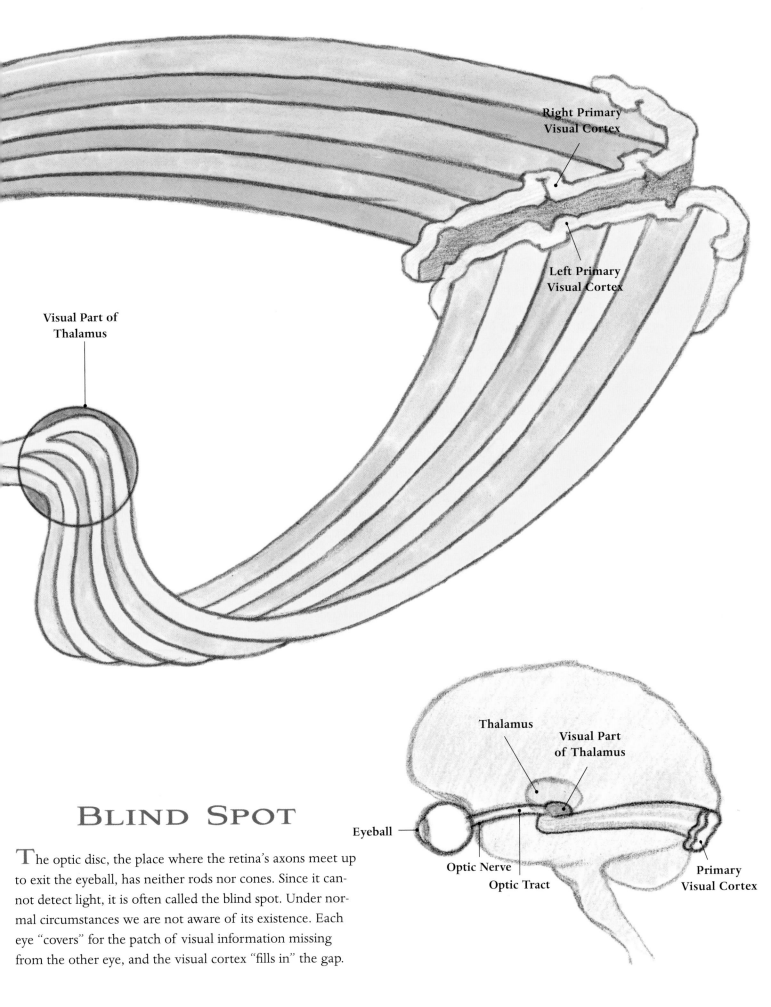

Right Primary Visual Cortex

Left Primary Visual Cortex

Visual Part of Thalamus

Thalamus

Visual Part of Thalamus

Eyeball

Optic Nerve

Optic Tract

Primary Visual Cortex

BLIND SPOT

The optic disc, the place where the retina's axons meet up to exit the eyeball, has neither rods nor cones. Since it cannot detect light, it is often called the blind spot. Under normal circumstances we are not aware of its existence. Each eye "covers" for the patch of visual information missing from the other eye, and the visual cortex "fills in" the gap.

Seeing Things

Turning electrical signals from the eyes into a full-color, action-packed 3D movie presents quite a challenge for the visual cortex, but not an impossible one. It breaks down this massive task into smaller, more manageable operations. Information about color, shape, and movement is processed separately by progressively more sophisticated parts of the cortex. Only at the end of this process is the "big picture" put together.

The starting point for image making is the primary visual cortex, where each neuron receives input from several neurons in the visual part of the thalamus. This means the quality of information is higher—instead of just responding to spots of light, some neurons respond to bars of light at specific angles, others to movement of bars of light, and still others to their color.

Streams of separate information are then forwarded to the secondary visual cortex. Each of its neurons receives signals from many primary visual cortex neurons, which, again, increases the information level so that neurons can now, for example, respond to corners and edges. As the information passes through each subsequent level of the visual cortex, the message becomes more complex.

After initial processing, signals from the visual cortex travel along two linked pathways in each cerebral hemisphere. Shapes and colors are analyzed along the lower "WHAT?" pathway so that objects can be recognized in the temporal lobe. Signals related to movement take the upper "WHERE?" pathway to the parietal lobe, where motion and navigation are determined. Parts of the WHAT? and WHERE? pathways also compare inputs from right and left eyes to give the "picture" depth and distance.

**Visual Part
Thalamus**

**Where?
Pathway**

**What?
Pathway**

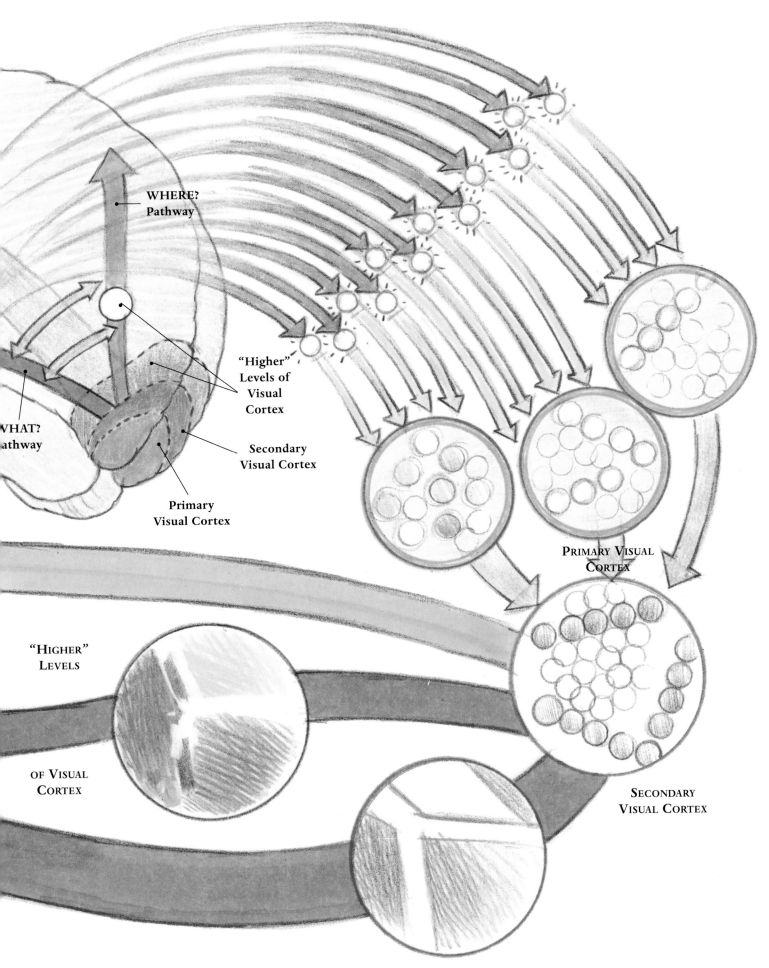

WHERE?
Pathway

WHAT?
Pathway

"Higher"
Levels of
Visual
Cortex

Secondary
Visual Cortex

Primary
Visual Cortex

PRIMARY VISUAL
CORTEX

SECONDARY
VISUAL CORTEX

"HIGHER"
LEVELS

OF VISUAL
CORTEX

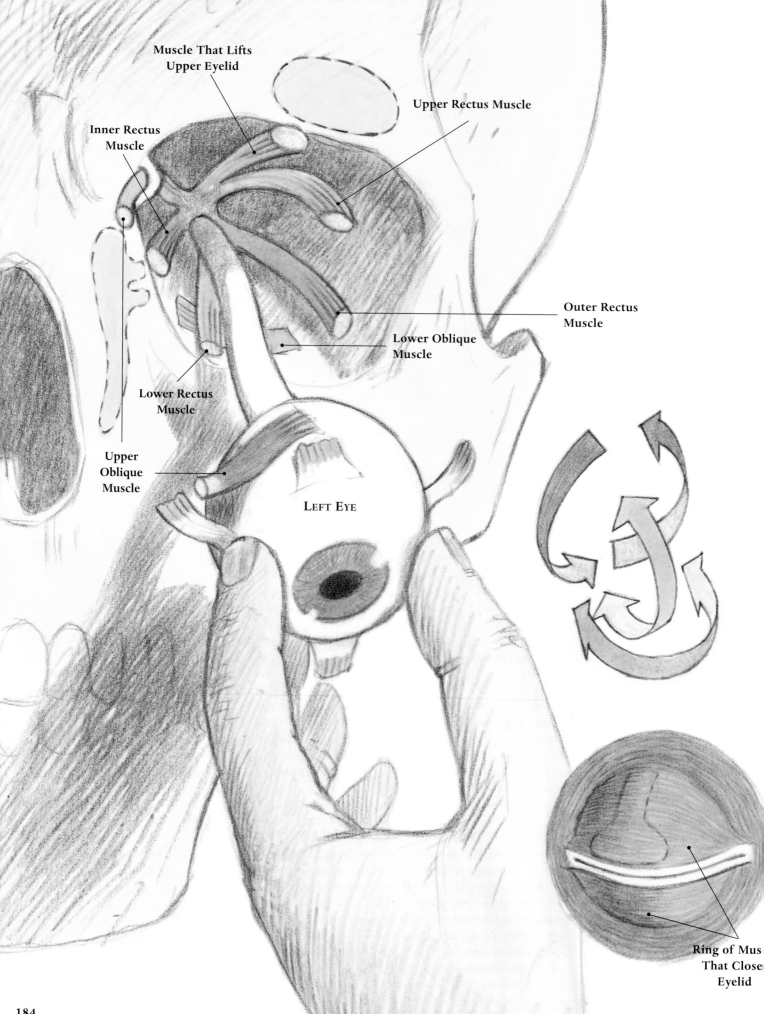

Muscle That Lifts
Upper Eyelid

Inner Rectus
Muscle

Upper Rectus Muscle

Outer Rectus
Muscle

Lower Oblique
Muscle

Lower Rectus
Muscle

Upper
Oblique
Muscle

LEFT EYE

Ring of Mus
That Close
Eyelid

SWIVEL AND BLINK

Eyes are not fixed in place, rigidly staring straight ahead. They swivel in their sockets, moved by six straplike muscles that are anchored to bone at one end and to the sclera at the other. The four rectus muscles move the eye up and down and from side to side. The two oblique muscles move the eye either down and inward or up and outward.

Eye muscles generate two basic types of movement. Slow movements point the eyes at objects of interest or track objects as they move in front of us. Tiny and rapid, jerky movements scan motionless objects so that light from all parts of them land at the center of the macula. Under the brain's control, both eyes move together in the same direction.

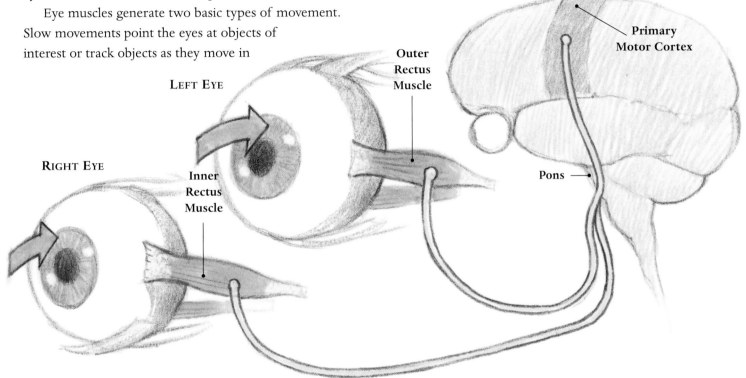

LEFT EYE

RIGHT EYE

Outer Rectus Muscle

Inner Rectus Muscle

Primary Motor Cortex

Pons

Without giving it a thought, we blink automatically up to fifteen times a minute. Like a vertical windshield wiper, the upper eyelid spreads tears across the surface of the eye to wash away dust and irritants and keep the cornea moist and lubricated, and with such speed that vision remains uninterrupted. Tears are released continuously along ducts by tear glands above the eye, then drain through two tiny openings in the eye's inner corner into a duct that empties into the nasal cavity. That's why crying—excess tears—and a runny nose go together.

The eyelids are closed by a ring of muscle that surrounds the eye socket. Lifting the larger upper eyelid to open the eyes is another muscle that runs back along the top of the eye socket. The lower eyelid has no comparable muscle and basically just sits there.

Blinking can also be provoked by outside stimuli. Sudden intense light or a rapidly approaching object both trigger reflex blinking that protects the eye from damage. And, of course, there is voluntary unilateral blinking—better known as winking!

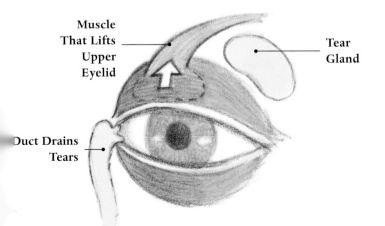

Muscle That Lifts Upper Eyelid

Tear Gland

Duct Drains Tears

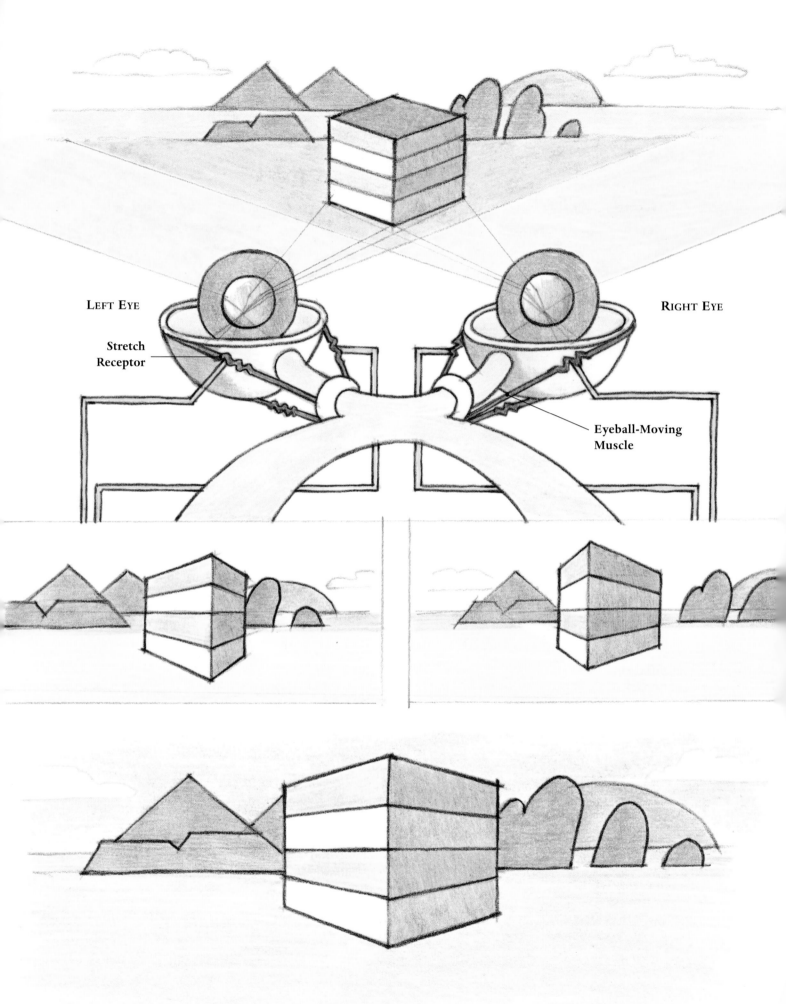

LEFT EYE

RIGHT EYE

Stretch
Receptor

Eyeball-Moving
Muscle

DEPTH AND DISTANCE

Reaching out for something with both eyes open is easier than doing it with one eye closed. That's because, by comparing information from both eyes, our brain allows us to gauge depth and distance. Our left eye sees a view of the outside world that differs from but overlaps with the view seen by our right eye. The visual cortex uses these slightly different inputs to construct a stereoscopic, or three-dimensional, picture of our surroundings.

Other cues help our brain locate things in space. When we look at distant objects our forward-facing eyes point straight ahead, but to view closer objects they must both rotate inward. Signals from stretch receptors in eyeball-moving muscles "tell" the brain whether its owner is looking at a distant or nearby object. Further cues include the fading of colors and the converging of straight lines, such as railroad tracks, with distance. For stereoscopic vision to work, however, what we are looking at has to be in focus.

OUT OF FOCUS

Our eyes should automatically focus light from any object whether near or distant, but for many people they don't. Farsightedness and nearsightedness are both common problems.

FARSIGHTEDNESS

If the eyeball is too short, light rays from near objects focus behind the retina. The eye attempts unsuccessfully to deal with this by making the lens fatter in order to project a sharp image on the retina, but nearby objects are still seen as a blur. Glasses or contact lenses are needed to make light rays converge before they enter the eye.

NEARSIGHTEDNESS

Where the eyeball is too long, light rays from distant objects are focused in front of the retina and appear as a blur. Nearby objects pose no problem because the thickness of the lens is increased to produce a sharp image on the retina. This time glasses or contact lenses are worn to make light rays diverge before entering the eye.

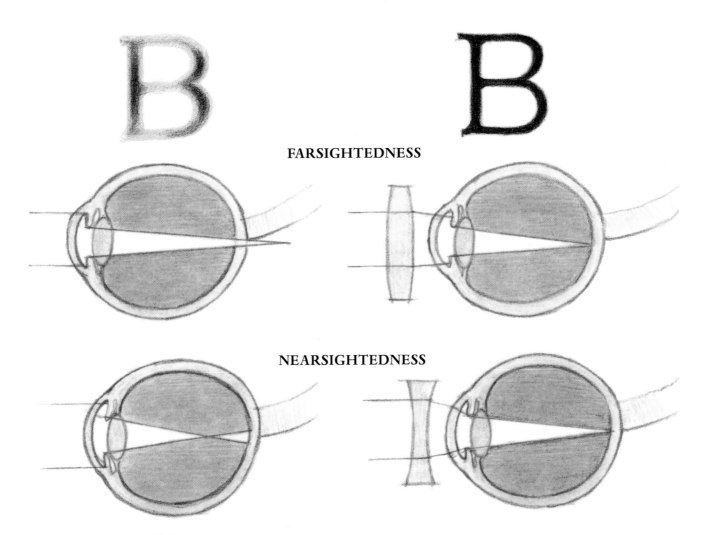

FARSIGHTEDNESS

NEARSIGHTEDNESS

Brain

Spinal Cord

Nerve

BUNDLE OF NERVES

It may be a smart operator, but the brain cannot work in isolation. Without the ability to receive updates and send out instructions, it would be powerless. That's where the spinal cord and nerves come in.

The spinal cord runs down the back and acts as a conduit for information to and from all parts of the body. Together the brain and spinal cord form the central nervous system, the management division of the nervous organization. Linking the central nervous system to the rest of the body is the peripheral nervous system—a network of nerves with branches reaching even the farthest extremity. Paired cranial nerves arising from the brain supply mainly the head and neck, while short spinal nerves fanning out from both sides of the spinal cord give rise to nerves that deal with the rest of the body.

Each nerve contains thousands, sometimes millions, of parallel axons, collected into several bundles that are enclosed, along with some fat padding, by a tough outer covering. This arrangement protects delicate axons but also allows the nerve to bend during movement. Most nerves carry the axons of both sensory and motor neurons. Sensory neurons convey signals toward the central nervous system while motor neurons carry them in the opposite direction. Wrapped around the axons of both types of neurons are support cells that form layers of insulation called a myelin sheath. There are small gaps or nodes between one support cell and the next where the axon is exposed. Signals "jump" from node to node, making their speed of transmission much faster than in noninsulated neurons. This is particularly important when messages are traveling over long distances.

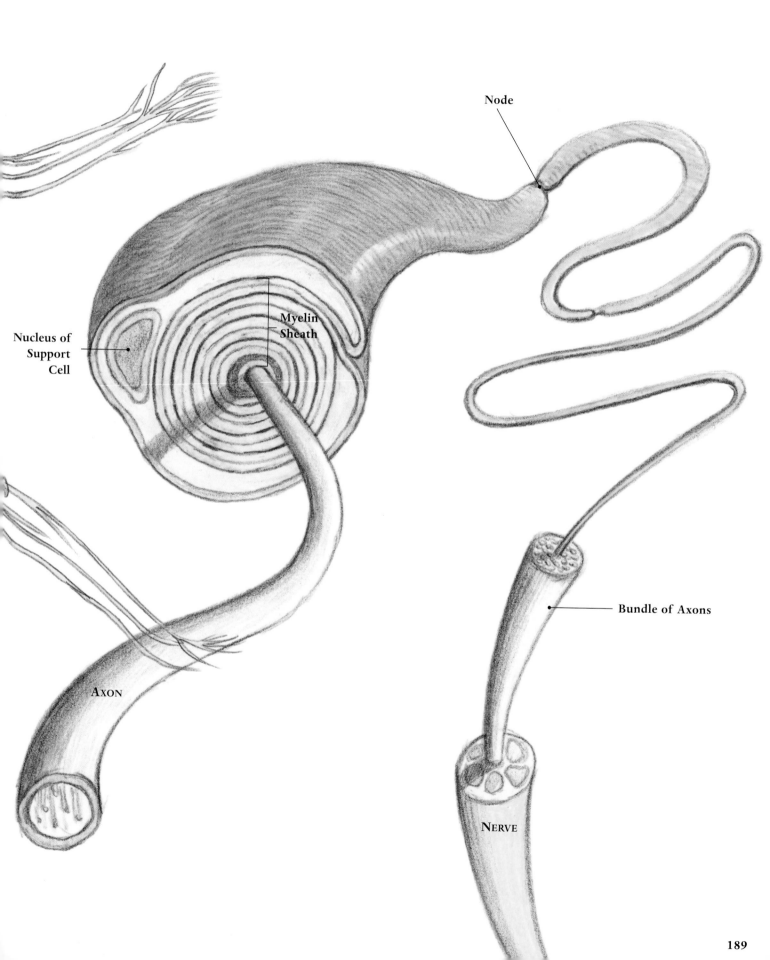

Node

Myelin
Sheath

Nucleus of
Support
Cell

Bundle of Axons

AXON

NERVE

UP, DOWN, AND SIDEWAYS

The spinal cord is constantly buzzing with activity. It receives signals from and dispatches signals to the body. It relays signals to and from the brain, and it also processes some incoming information. With so much going on at the same time, the pathways that carry signals to, from, and within the spinal cord need to be highly organized.

All the nerves in the body—except those in the head and parts of the neck—connect with the spinal cord through short spinal nerves, each of which has two roots. The back root carries sensory information from touch, heat, or pain receptors into the cord. The front root carries motor information, such as instructions to move or scratch, to the appropriate part of the body.

Unlike the brain, the spinal cord's white matter is on the outside, surrounding an H-shaped core of gray matter.

Incoming signals to the spinal cord arrive through the axons of sensory neurons that upon entering the cord either immediately synapse with linking neurons in the gray matter or travel through the white matter to communicate with other neurons or with the brain itself.

Outgoing signals are dispatched through the axons of motor neurons. Their cell bodies in the spinal cord's gray matter receive instructions either from the brain or, by way of linking neurons, from incoming sensory neurons. Many motor neurons carry signals to skeletal muscles that cause them to contract and move the body. Motor neurons serving the autonomic nervous system communicate with cardiac muscle, smooth muscle, and various glands to regulate processes we are generally unaware of, such as heart rate or pupil size.

Spinal Cord

Cell Body of Sensory Neuron

One of the Vertebrae That Enclose and Protect Spinal Cord

Motor Neuron Carrying Signals to Skeletal Muscles

Motor Neuron of Autonomic Nervous System

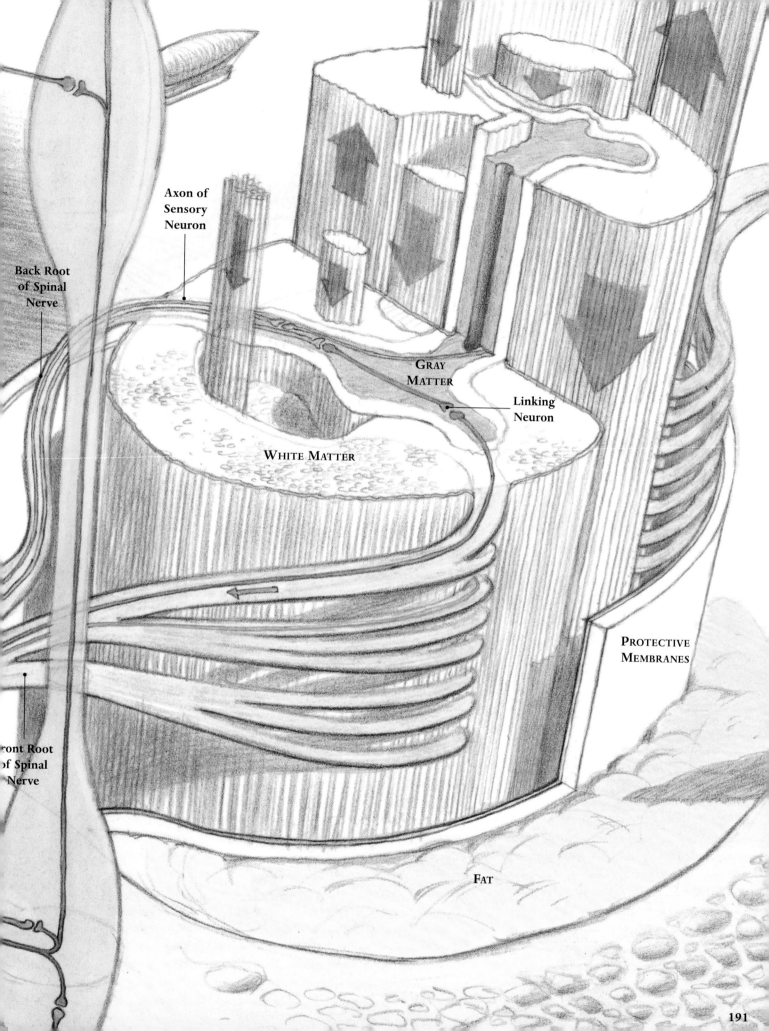

Axon of
Sensory
Neuron

Back Root
of Spinal
Nerve

Gray
Matter

Linking
Neuron

White Matter

Front Root
of Spinal
Nerve

Protective
Membranes

Fat

SOFT TOUCH

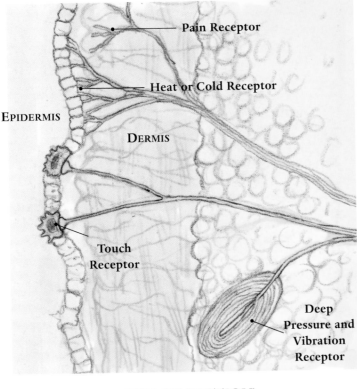

Pain Receptor

Heat or Cold Receptor

EPIDERMIS

DERMIS

Touch Receptor

Deep Pressure and Vibration Receptor

SKIN (IN SECTION)

Stroke a cat and you will feel the softness of her fur and the warmth of her body. If she licks your hand you will feel the roughness of her tongue. When she falls asleep in your lap you'll feel her weight pressing down on you. And when she starts purring, you'll pick up the vibrations. You can feel these sensations because your skin houses a battery of receptors that when stimulated send signals to your brain's sensory cortex, where they are decoded and "felt." Some receptors detect light touch; others respond only when squashed by heavy pressure or when vibrated. Still others are triggered by heat or cold. By interpreting input from different receptors, the brain gives us a lot of information about the objects we are touching. And when the cat sinks her teeth into your hand, there are receptors for that too.

NERVE

Each section of the sensory cortex receives impulses from receptors located in a particular region of the body. The extent of areas dedicated to some body parts are way out of proportion to the size of those parts. The tongue, lips, hands, and fingers have far more representation than, say, the elbow or knee. That's because they carry many more sensory receptors. These differences in representation are shown clearly by a sensory homunculus (opposite). This distorted figure has body parts of such size as to reflect the relative area each occupies in the sensory cortex. He also has a mean forehand.

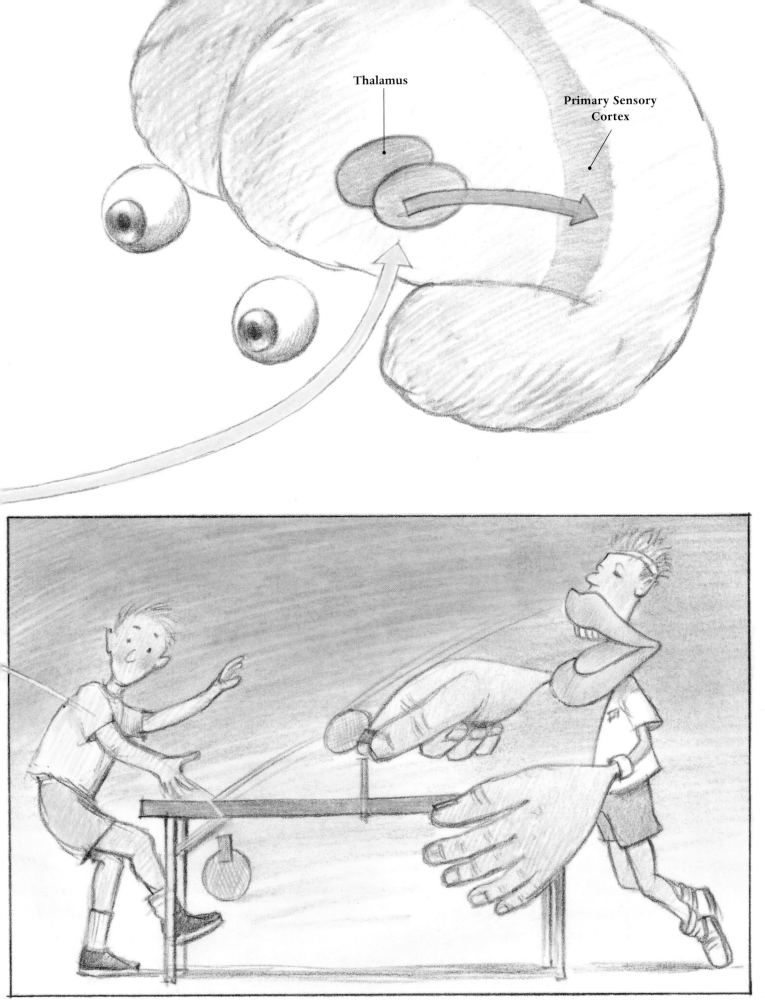

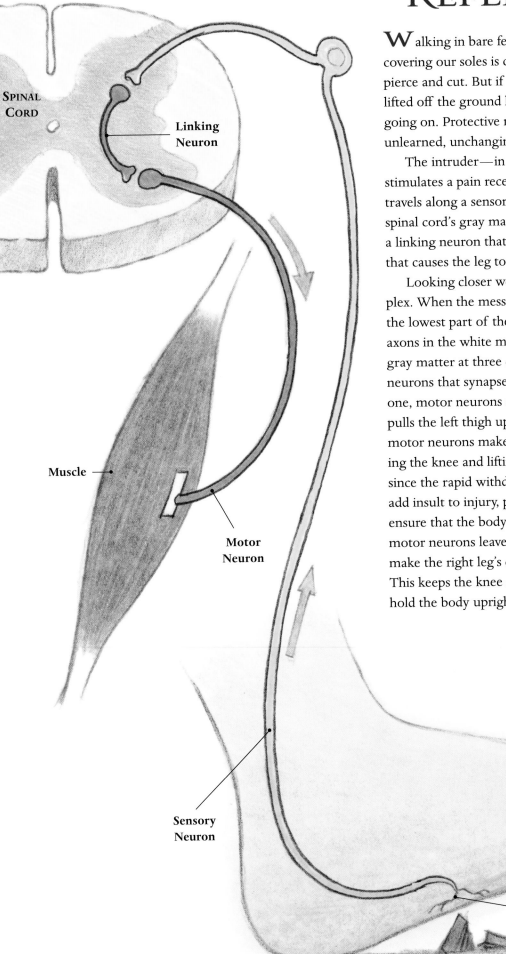

REFLEX ACTION

Walking in bare feet is always risky. Even though the skin covering our soles is comparatively thick, sharp objects can pierce and cut. But if this does happen, the foot is rapidly lifted off the ground long before the brain realizes what is going on. Protective reflexes such as this are hard-wired, unlearned, unchanging, and unconscious.

The intruder—in this case a piece of broken glass—stimulates a pain receptor to fire, generating a signal that travels along a sensory neuron to the spinal cord. In the spinal cord's gray matter the sensory neuron synapses with a linking neuron that relays its message to a motor neuron that causes the leg to be pulled upward.

Looking closer we see that things are a little more complex. When the message from the injured left foot arrives at the lowest part of the spinal cord, it is relayed upward along axons in the white matter. Branches from these axons enter gray matter at three different levels to synapse with linking neurons that synapse with motor neurons. At level number one, motor neurons stimulate the iliopsoas muscle, which pulls the left thigh upward, while at level number three motor neurons make the hamstring muscles contract, bending the knee and lifting the foot away from the ground. But since the rapid withdrawal of one of our feet could easily add insult to injury, parallel nerve messages are needed to ensure that the body stays upright. At level number two, motor neurons leave the opposite side of the spinal cord to make the right leg's quadriceps femoris muscle contract. This keeps the knee straight, thereby stiffening the leg to hold the body upright.

Spinal Cord

Linking Neuron

Muscle

Motor Neuron

Sensory Neuron

Pain Receptor

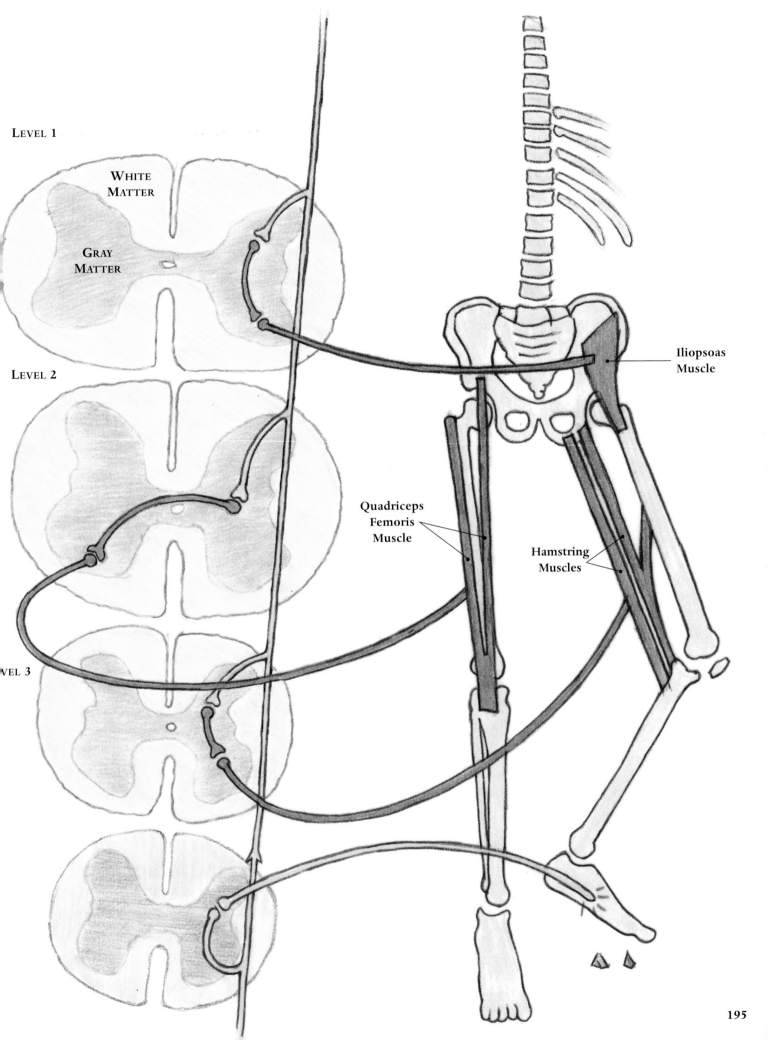

LEVEL 1

WHITE
MATTER

GRAY
MATTER

LEVEL 2

VEL 3

Iliopsoas
Muscle

Quadriceps
Femoris
Muscle

Hamstring
Muscles

195

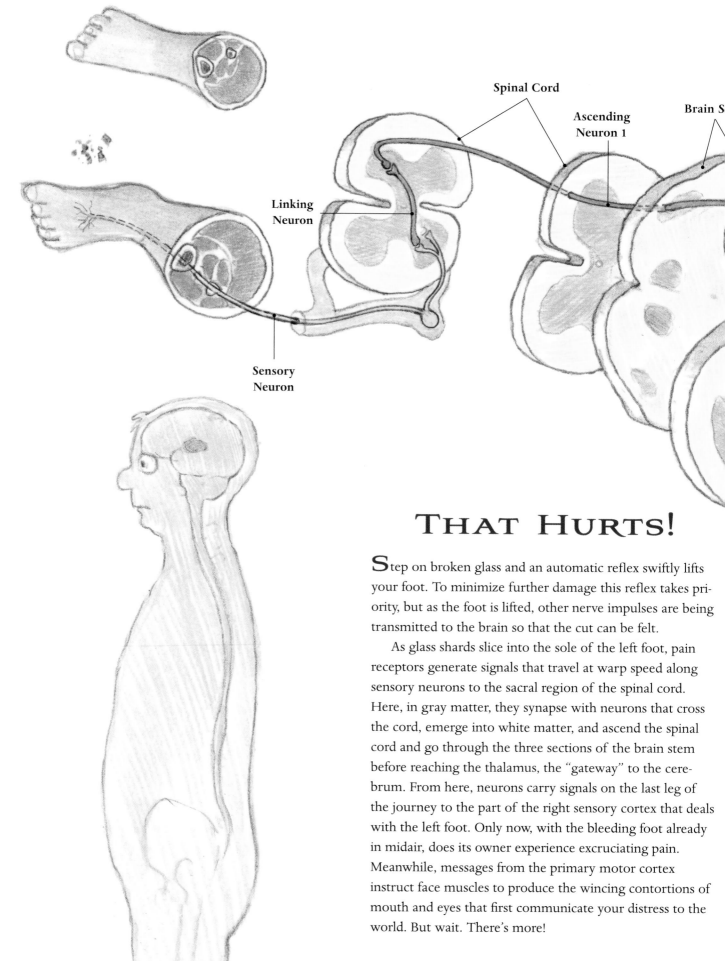

Spinal Cord

Ascending Neuron 1

Brain S

Linking Neuron

Sensory Neuron

THAT HURTS!

Step on broken glass and an automatic reflex swiftly lifts your foot. To minimize further damage this reflex takes priority, but as the foot is lifted, other nerve impulses are being transmitted to the brain so that the cut can be felt.

As glass shards slice into the sole of the left foot, pain receptors generate signals that travel at warp speed along sensory neurons to the sacral region of the spinal cord. Here, in gray matter, they synapse with neurons that cross the cord, emerge into white matter, and ascend the spinal cord and go through the three sections of the brain stem before reaching the thalamus, the "gateway" to the cerebrum. From here, neurons carry signals on the last leg of the journey to the part of the right sensory cortex that deals with the left foot. Only now, with the bleeding foot already in midair, does its owner experience excruciating pain. Meanwhile, messages from the primary motor cortex instruct face muscles to produce the wincing contortions of mouth and eyes that first communicate your distress to the world. But wait. There's more!

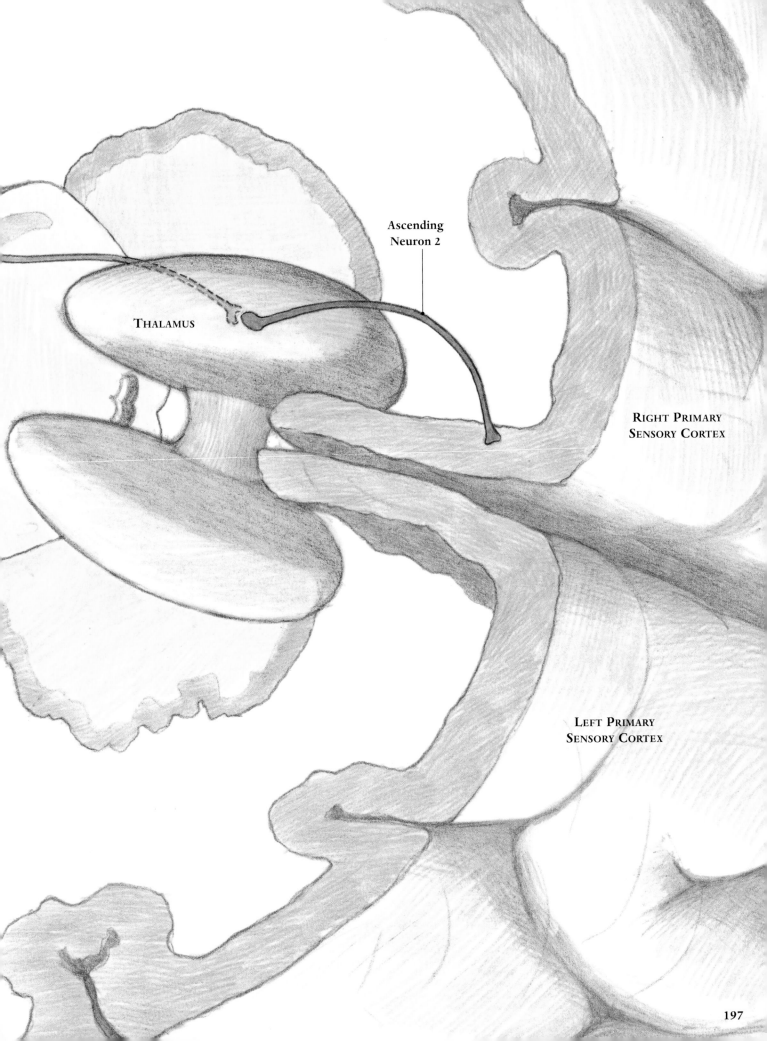

Ascending
Neuron 2

THALAMUS

RIGHT PRIMARY
SENSORY CORTEX

LEFT PRIMARY
SENSORY CORTEX

Bump!

In the middle of the night a strange sound can provoke fear and with it a pounding heart. A charging bull would evoke the same response. In both cases our body is simply doing what comes naturally by marshaling its resources to either confront a threat or run away from it.

Inside each cerebral hemisphere is a group of structures that form the limbic system or "emotional brain." When we hear or see something scary, the amygdala—the limbic system's fear coordinator—is activated and alerts the hypothalamus. The hypothalamus in turn revs up the body-rousing sympathetic division of the autonomic nervous system. Nerve signals carried by sympathetic motor neurons rapidly bring about a number of simultaneous changes to routine body operations.

In a frenzy of activity, tiny airways inside the lungs widen to get more oxygen into the bloodstream as the heart rate increases to pump more oxygen-rich blood to the muscles. Capillary beds in the skin and digestive system are shut down to divert blood to where it is needed: in the heart, brain, and muscles. Arterioles inside muscles widen to increase blood flow to hungry muscle cells. Extra glucose is released from liver cells to increase the amount of fuel in the blood. Mental alertness and metabolic rate increase, while the eyes' pupils widen to improve the view of the outside world. And last but not least, the adrenal glands release the hormone epinephrine into the bloodstream to reinforce the actions of the autonomic nervous system.

Strong and alert, the body is now ready to fight or flee. The prefrontal cortex, made aware of the threat by the seeing and hearing parts of the brain and by the hypothalamus, now has to decide what action to take.

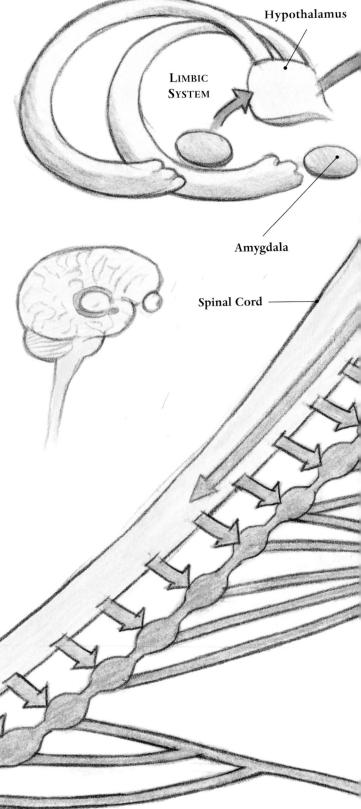

Hypothalamus

Limbic System

Amygdala

Spinal Cord

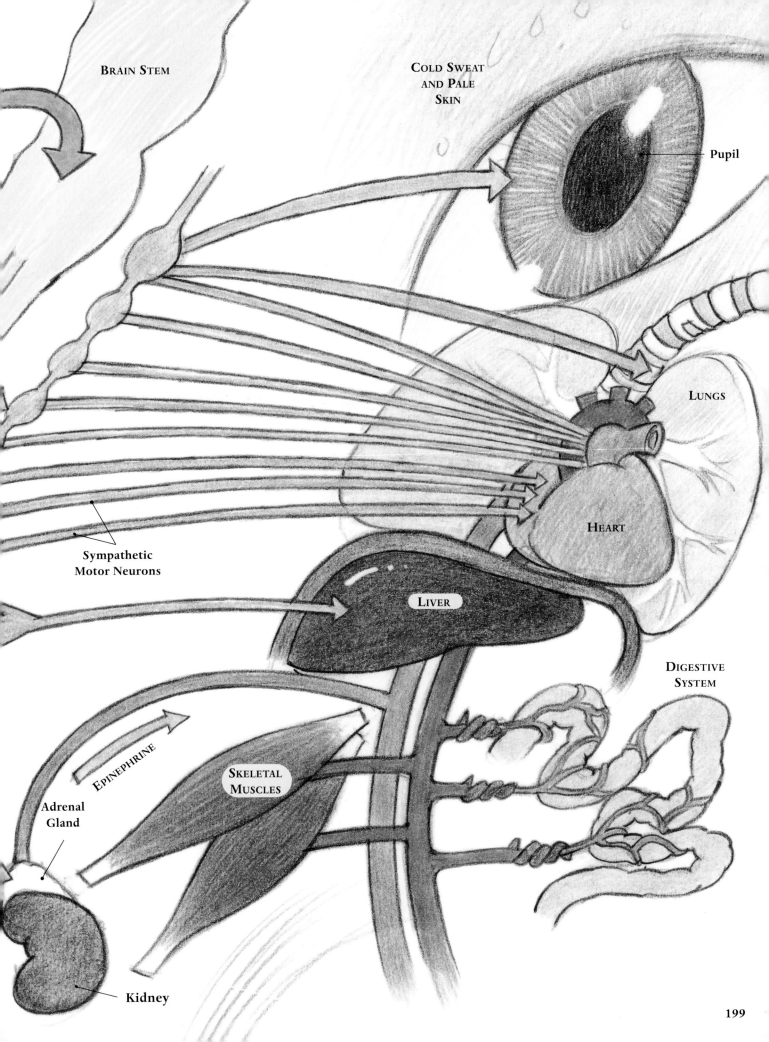

BRAIN STEM

COLD SWEAT
AND PALE
SKIN

Pupil

LUNGS

Sympathetic
Motor Neurons

HEART

LIVER

DIGESTIVE
SYSTEM

EPINEPHRINE

SKELETAL
MUSCLES

Adrenal
Gland

Kidney

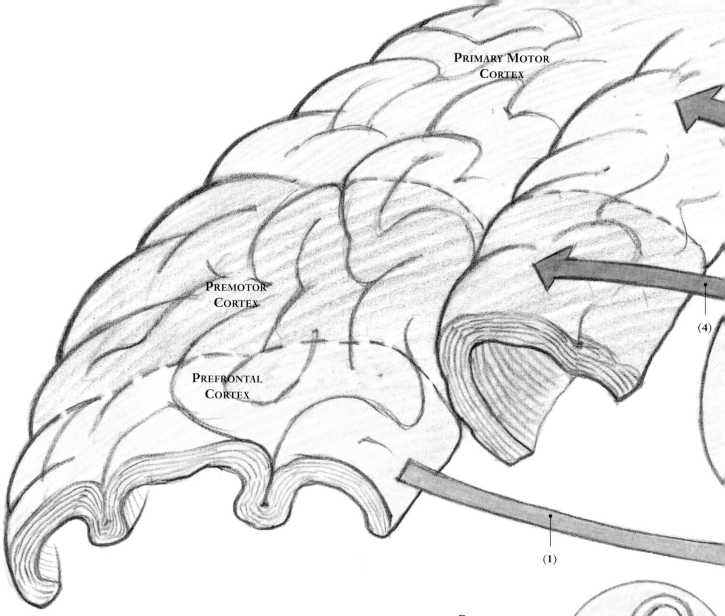

PRIMARY MOTOR
CORTEX

PREMOTOR
CORTEX

PREFRONTAL
CORTEX

(4)

(1)

GOTTA RUN

Imagine if when ordering groceries online, you simply
typed in "FOOD." Sometime later you'd find a disorganized
pile of mostly unwanted items on your doorstep. Now
imagine if your brain simply issued the instruction
"MOVE." Chaos would ensue as your limbs thrashed
around randomly and you ended up in a confused heap. In
reality, the brain's planning and execution of movement are
both tightly controlled.

The prefrontal cortex, the thinking part of the cerebral
cortex, has received word of imminent danger from the limbic system. Putting prudence over pride, it decides the body
should run away, and sends messages (1) to the cerebellum
and to the basal nuclei—masses of gray matter deep within
the cerebrum's white matter—requesting the best strategy
for a hasty retreat.

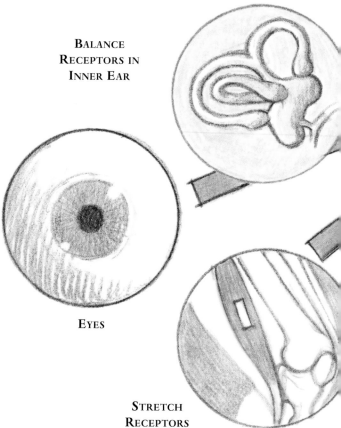

BALANCE
RECEPTORS IN
INNER EAR

EYES

STRETCH
RECEPTORS

(3)

(5)

(4)

(3)

BASAL NUCLEI

(2)

(2)

CEREBELLUM

Brain Stem

Spinal Cord

(6)

SKELETAL MUSCLES

the premotor cortex—the repository of skilled movements—which has a big influence over the primary motor cortex.

Once equipped with a plan of action, the primary motor cortex initiates movement. Long axons projecting from its neurons (5) carry impulses down the spinal cord, where they synapse with motor neurons (6). These trigger the precisely timed muscle contractions needed for running while constant feedback to the cerebellum fine tunes movement every step of the way.

The cerebellum continuously receives a stream of input (2) about the body's current position and movement from stretch receptors in muscles, tendons, and joints, from the eyes, and from balance receptors in the ears. Having collated this information, the cerebellum calculates the extent and sequence of muscle contraction that will be required for running. This part of the plan is sent promptly (3) to the primary motor cortex by way of the thalamus. Meanwhile the basal nuclei have been working on "stopping" and "starting" as well as detailed patterns of movement. Their ideas go (4) via the thalamus to

ON AUTOPILOT

You don't have to think about boosting your heart rate every time you run, or sweating whenever it is hot. These and a host of other body processes are controlled by your body's unseen and unsung autopilot, the autonomic nervous system. Through motor neurons arising from the brain stem and spinal cord, it controls smooth muscles in internal organs and cardiac muscle in the heart, and stimulates certain glands. It has two opposing divisions—parasympathetic and sympathetic—that balance each other by acting respectively as "brake" and "accelerator" to maintain near constant conditions inside the body.

Control of blood pressure shows the autonomic nervous system in action. When the heart pumps blood, it creates pressure inside arteries. Although blood pressure varies naturally depending on how active we are, the two autonomic divisions keep it within safe levels, prohibiting it from becoming dangerously high or low. Blood pressure is monitored by pressure receptors in the walls of the aorta and carotid arteries that send signals along sensory neurons to a cardiovascular center in the medulla. This sends signals through autonomic motor neurons to regulate heart rate and control blood flow along arterioles in the tissues.

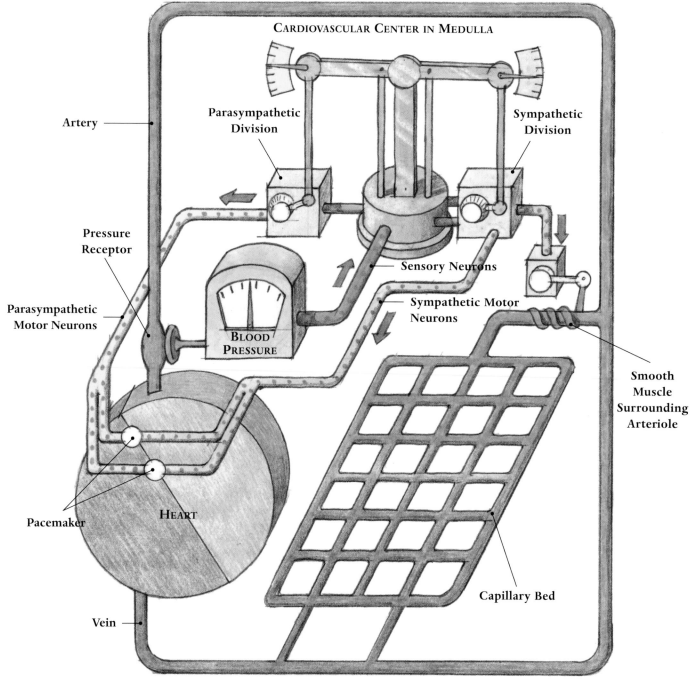

CARDIOVASCULAR CENTER IN MEDULLA

Artery

Parasympathetic Division

Sympathetic Division

Sensory Neurons

Pressure Receptor

Sympathetic Motor Neurons

Parasympathetic Motor Neurons

BLOOD PRESSURE

Smooth Muscle Surrounding Arteriole

Pacemaker

HEART

Capillary Bed

Vein

Normal Blood Pressure (opposite)

When we're resting, parasympathetic output to the heart from the cardiovascular center dominates sympathetic output so that the pacemaker sets the heart rate at around seventy beats per minute. Sympathetic output to arteriole muscles keeps them slightly contracted so there's some resistance to blood flow.

High Blood Pressure

High blood pressure stretches pressure receptors so they fire signals faster to the cardiovascular center. In response, the center increases the rate at which signals pass down parasympathetic motor neurons—and decreases the firing rate of sympathetic motor neurons—to the heart's natural pacemaker so that heart rate drops. The cardiovascular center also sends fewer impulses along sympathetic motor neurons to smooth muscles surrounding arterioles, which relax and widen, reducing resistance to blood flow. This, as well as the slowing of the heart rate, reduces blood pressure.

Low Blood Pressure

A fall in blood pressure is matched by a sharp decrease in the firing of signals from pressure receptors to the cardiovascular center. This drop cuts parasympathetic output to the heart but increases sympathetic output. A barrage of signals is sent along sympathetic motor neurons to the pacemaker, which increases the rate and force of heart contraction. The cardiovascular center also increases sympathetic output to arteriole smooth muscles, which narrow arterioles and offer greater resistance to blood flow. This, as well as increased heart rate, raises blood pressure.

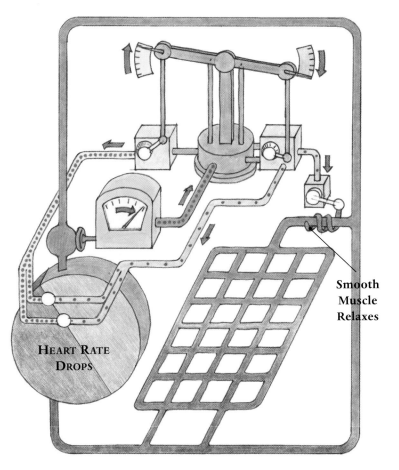

Heart Rate Drops

Smooth Muscle Relaxes

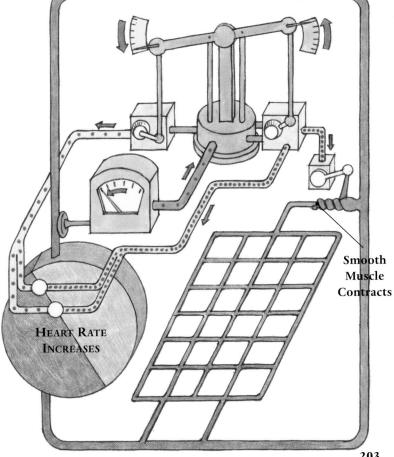

Heart Rate Increases

Smooth Muscle Contracts

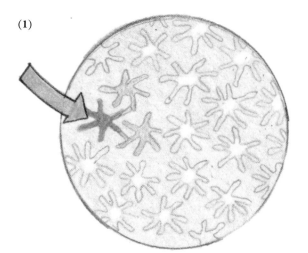

(1)

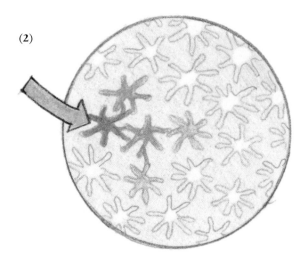

(2)

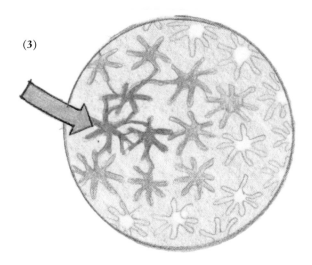

(3)

REMEMBER THIS

Memory is our life's logbook. Without it we would have no sense of time, no means of learning anything, no possibility of social interaction, and no ability to find our way from A to B. Most memories are short-term, lasting a matter of seconds or minutes. But more significant events are stored for longer periods.

Different sensory components—sights, sounds, smells, and so on—are interpreted by specific sensory regions of the cerebral cortex. These experiences are then bounced back and forth between each region and the hippocampus—part of the limbic system. Over time this cerebral game of Ping-Pong firmly establishes memories in the cortex, and the representations in the hippocampus fade away. Remembering words, ideas, and concepts happens in much the same way. However, unconscious long-term memories, such as remembering how to ride a bike, are stored in the cerebellum, basal nuclei, and motor cortex.

Most of our experiences are soon forgotten, but the more significant ones make it from short-term to long-term memory. For this to happen, the temporary pattern of neuron firing established in short-term memory must be repeated again and again to build a network that makes the arrangement permanent. When a neuron sends signals to two neighbors (1), they become more responsive to the first neuron so that in future all three are more likely to fire together. Nerve signals then sent by the neighbors to their neighbors link more neurons, and the network grows (2). With each repetition, synapses between network neurons become more efficient and their connections stronger (3), eventually creating a unified web that represents a single long-term memory (4).

Memories related to the same event are stored in different parts of the cortex and interconnected. For this reason, triggering just one such memory will often conjure up many others.

(4)

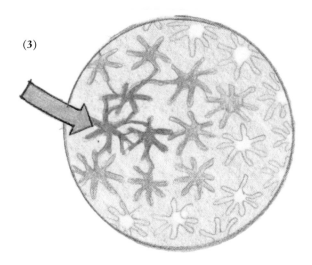

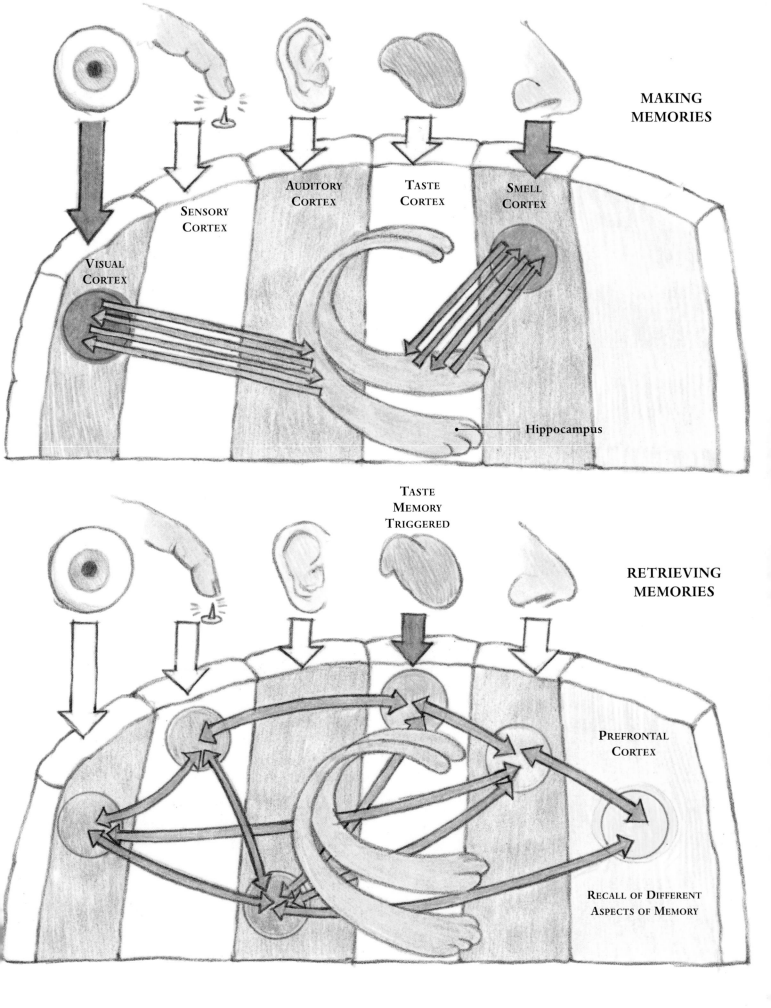

MAKING
MEMORIES

SENSORY
CORTEX

AUDITORY
CORTEX

TASTE
CORTEX

SMELL
CORTEX

VISUAL
CORTEX

Hippocampus

TASTE
MEMORY
TRIGGERED

RETRIEVING
MEMORIES

PREFRONTAL
CORTEX

RECALL OF DIFFERENT
ASPECTS OF MEMORY

GOOD NIGHT

At the end of a long day, under orders from its brain stem and hypothalamus, our brain switches from being awake to a state of reduced activity and we feel it's time to nod off. Sleep is essential for good health. It gives the body a break and the brain a chance to sort and store the avalanche of information it has picked up during waking hours. But sleep doesn't interfere with the routine processes that keep the body's internal conditions in balance. The control of breathing and heart rates, the monitoring of blood glucose levels, and myriad other regulatory chores go on uninterrupted whether it's night or day.

Through the night two types of sleep—deep and REM (rapid eye movement) sleep—follow each other repeatedly. As we descend into deep sleep our brain activity, blood pressure, and body temperature all decrease, but we're still able to toss and turn in bed. We then ascend to a near-waking state by moving into REM sleep, when the brain is more active but the body becomes immobile. The switch between deep and REM sleep happens several more times until it's time to wake up.

SWEET DREAMS

Despite being deprived of sensory input when asleep, we still have experiences in the form of dreams. Most occur during REM sleep, when our muscles are paralyzed so we cannot act out whatever scenarios the brain is creating. Only the eyeball muscles function, rapidly moving the eyes to scan imaginary visual scenes.

Dreams are evidently spinoffs from the processing of the sensations, thoughts, events, and decisions of the preceding day. They seem to draw particular fuel from the endless replaying of sensory experiences on their way to long-term memory. It is probably the simultaneous replaying of disparate experiences that stirs up the heady mix of perceived images, sounds, and emotions that is the stuff not only of dreams but also of nightmares.

CHEMICAL CONTROL

The nervous system does not hold a monopoly when it comes to body management and communication. A second network, the endocrine system, wields control by releasing into the bloodstream chemical messengers called hormones that alter the inner workings of specific target cells. By so doing it regulates many important processes, including cell metabolism, growth, puberty and reproduction, and the body's reaction to stress.

Although the two control systems are linked and do interact, they could not be more different. The nervous system's tight-knit neuron network carries electrical signals at lightning speed and has short-term results. Hormones, on the other hand, work much more slowly and have longer-lasting effects. And far from being tight knit, the endocrine system consists of a disparate array of organs scattered through the head, neck, and trunk. Some are dedicated endocrine glands, while others—including the hypothalamus, pancreas, ovaries, and testes—have only part of their structure devoted to releasing hormones.

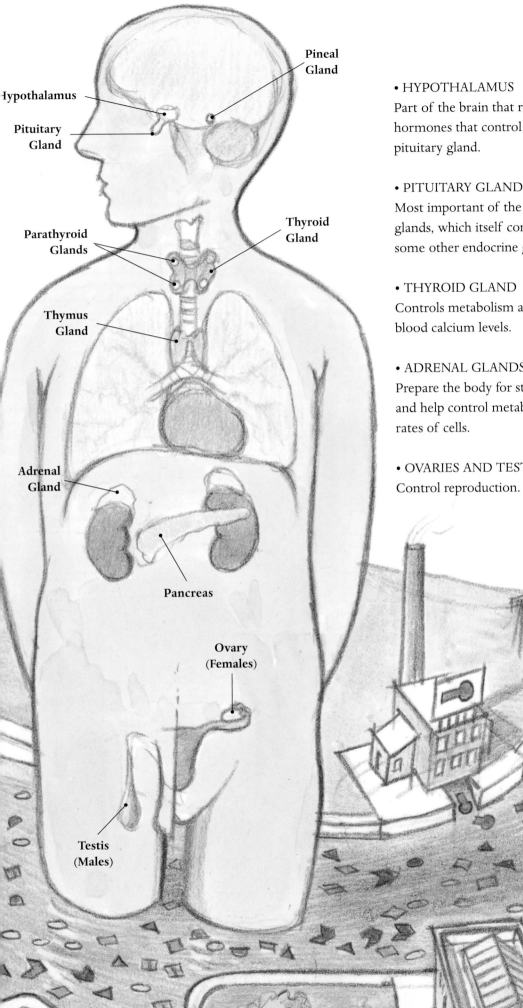

- **HYPOTHALAMUS**
Part of the brain that releases hormones that control the pituitary gland.

- **PITUITARY GLAND**
Most important of the glands, which itself controls some other endocrine glands.

- **THYROID GLAND**
Controls metabolism and blood calcium levels.

- **ADRENAL GLANDS**
Prepare the body for stress and help control metabolic rates of cells.

- **OVARIES AND TESTES**
Control reproduction.

- **PINEAL GLAND**
Controls the internal body clock.

- **PARATHYROID GLANDS**
With the thyroid gland, regulate blood calcium levels.

- **THYMUS GLAND**
Most important in childhood (after which it shrinks) in activating parts of the immune system.

- **PANCREAS**
Controls levels of glucose in the blood.

209

DELIVERING THE MESSAGE

Although every cell in the body is exposed to any hormone circulating in the blood, only certain target cells get the message. That's because these target cells possess receptors to which their specific hormone can bind. Once in contact with its target, the hormone triggers changes in one or more of that cell's activities, such as cell division, protein synthesis, or enzyme activation.

How a hormone interacts with its customers' receptors depends on one thing—its molecular structure. Most hormones, including insulin and epinephrine, are derived from amino acids. They cannot penetrate a cell membrane, so they stay outside their target cell. The remaining hormones—secreted by the ovaries, testes, and outer part of the adrenal glands—are steroids, derived from cholesterol. They readily pass through lipids in the cell membranes of their targets and go right in.

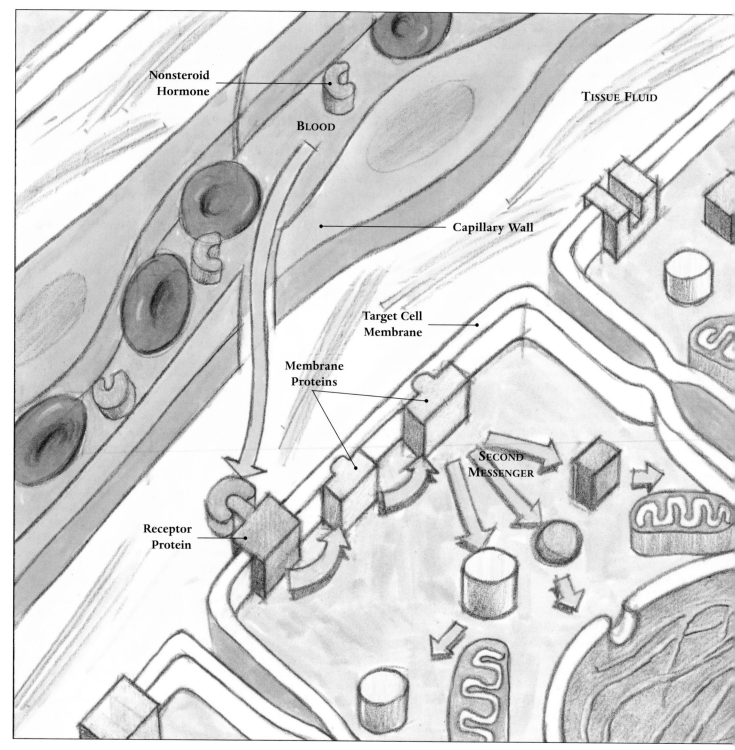

When a nonsteroid hormone arrives at its target cell (opposite), it binds to a receptor protein projecting from the cell's surface. Binding activates the receptor and alters its shape, a change that resonates through a chain of other membrane proteins that generate, in the cell's cytoplasm, a second messenger. This messenger then activates—or deactivates—the enzymes that trigger the desired change to the cell's activities.

Steroid hormones (below) don't stand on ceremony. They pass straight through the target cell's membrane and cytoplasm and into its nucleus. Here the hormone binds to a receptor protein that brings it into contact with the cell's chief executive officer—its DNA. Interaction between the hormone and DNA switches on a gene, an instruction for making a particular protein that, as required, changes some aspect of the target cell's routines.

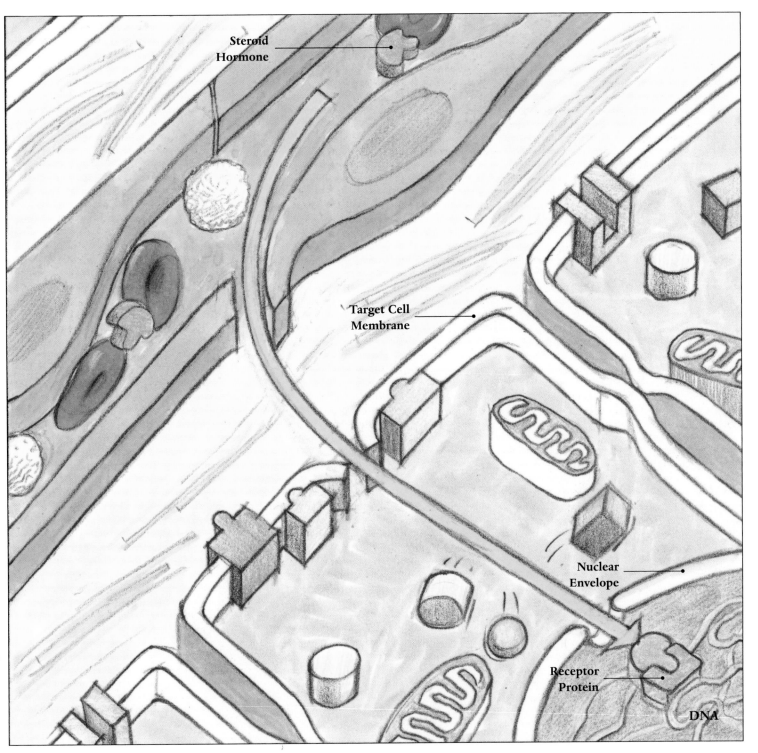

Steroid
Hormone

Target Cell
Membrane

Nuclear
Envelope

Receptor
Protein

DNA

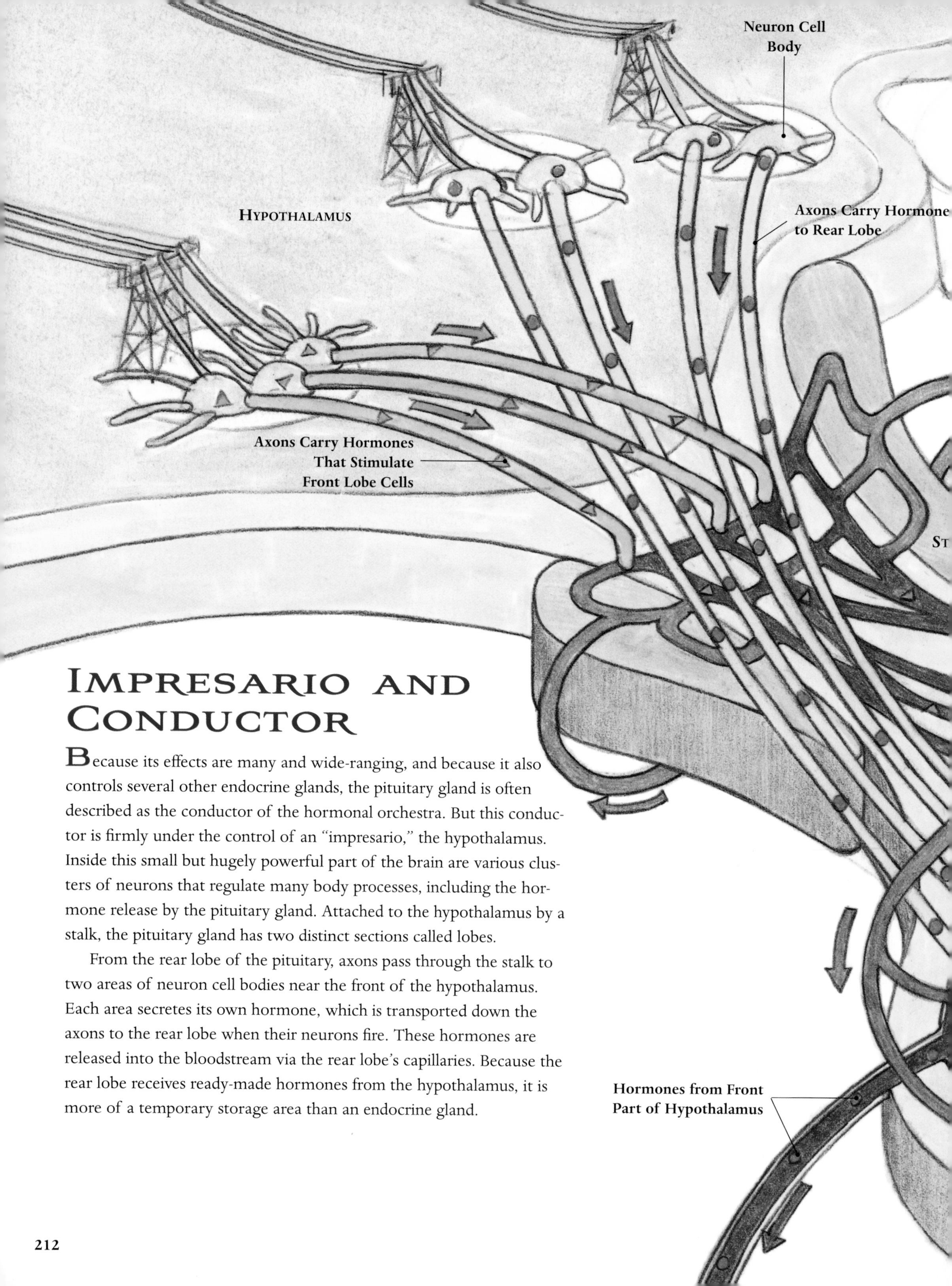

HYPOTHALAMUS

Axons Carry Hormone
to Rear Lobe

Axons Carry Hormones
That Stimulate
Front Lobe Cells

IMPRESARIO AND CONDUCTOR

Because its effects are many and wide-ranging, and because it also controls several other endocrine glands, the pituitary gland is often described as the conductor of the hormonal orchestra. But this conductor is firmly under the control of an "impresario," the hypothalamus. Inside this small but hugely powerful part of the brain are various clusters of neurons that regulate many body processes, including the hormone release by the pituitary gland. Attached to the hypothalamus by a stalk, the pituitary gland has two distinct sections called lobes.

From the rear lobe of the pituitary, axons pass through the stalk to two areas of neuron cell bodies near the front of the hypothalamus. Each area secretes its own hormone, which is transported down the axons to the rear lobe when their neurons fire. These hormones are released into the bloodstream via the rear lobe's capillaries. Because the rear lobe receives ready-made hormones from the hypothalamus, it is more of a temporary storage area than an endocrine gland.

Hormones from Front
Part of Hypothalamus

ST

Communication between the hypothalamus and the front lobe of the pituitary is through the bloodstream. Neurons near the back of the hypothalamus secrete hormones that travel down axons and are deposited into the capillary network in the stalk. These hormones are then carried by portal veins to a second capillary network that supplies the front lobe's hormone-making cells. Newly arrived hypothalamus hormones stimulate front lobe cells to release their own hormones into the bloodstream.

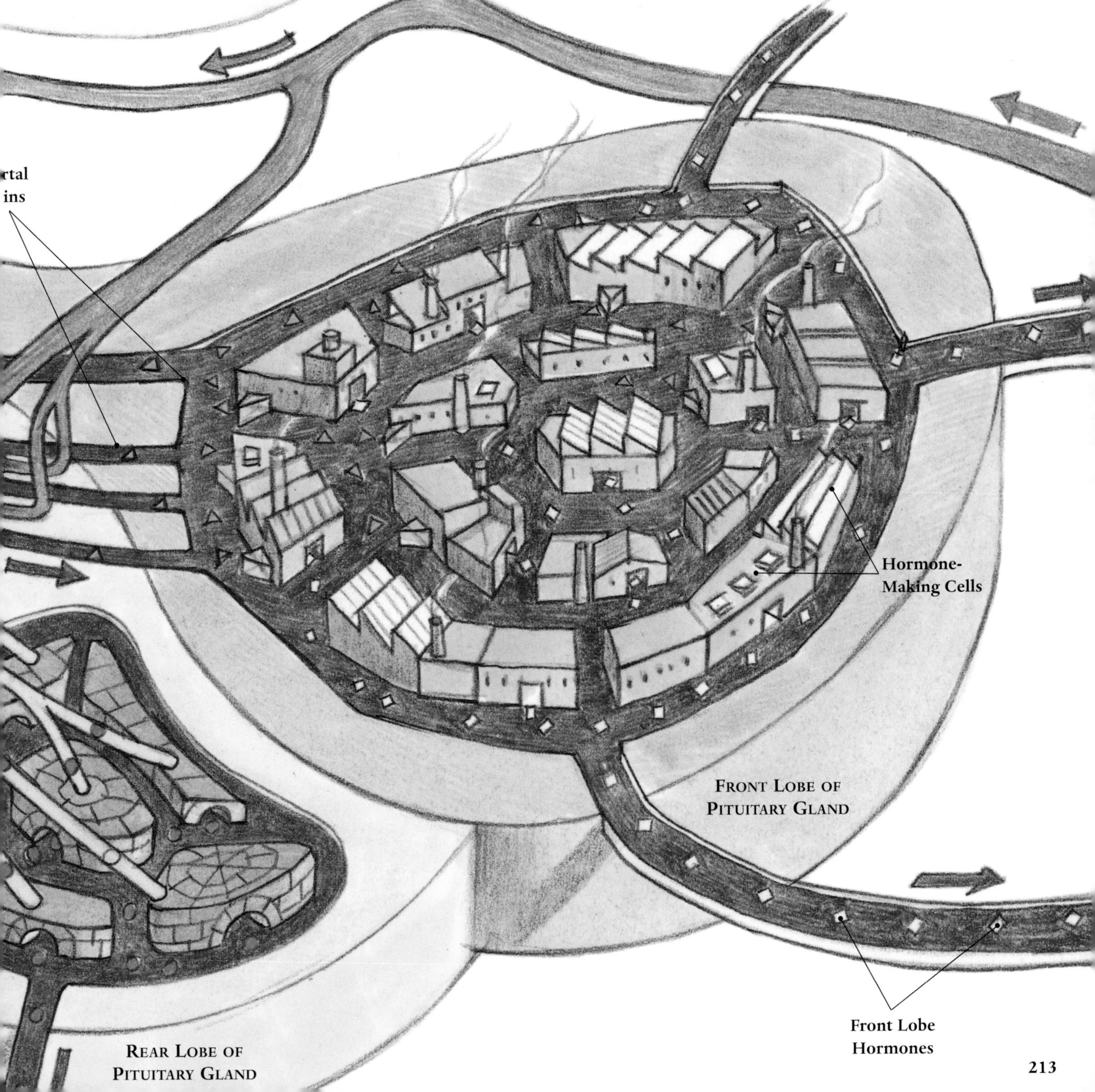

rtal
ins

Hormone-
Making Cells

Front Lobe of
Pituitary Gland

Front Lobe
Hormones

Rear Lobe of
Pituitary Gland

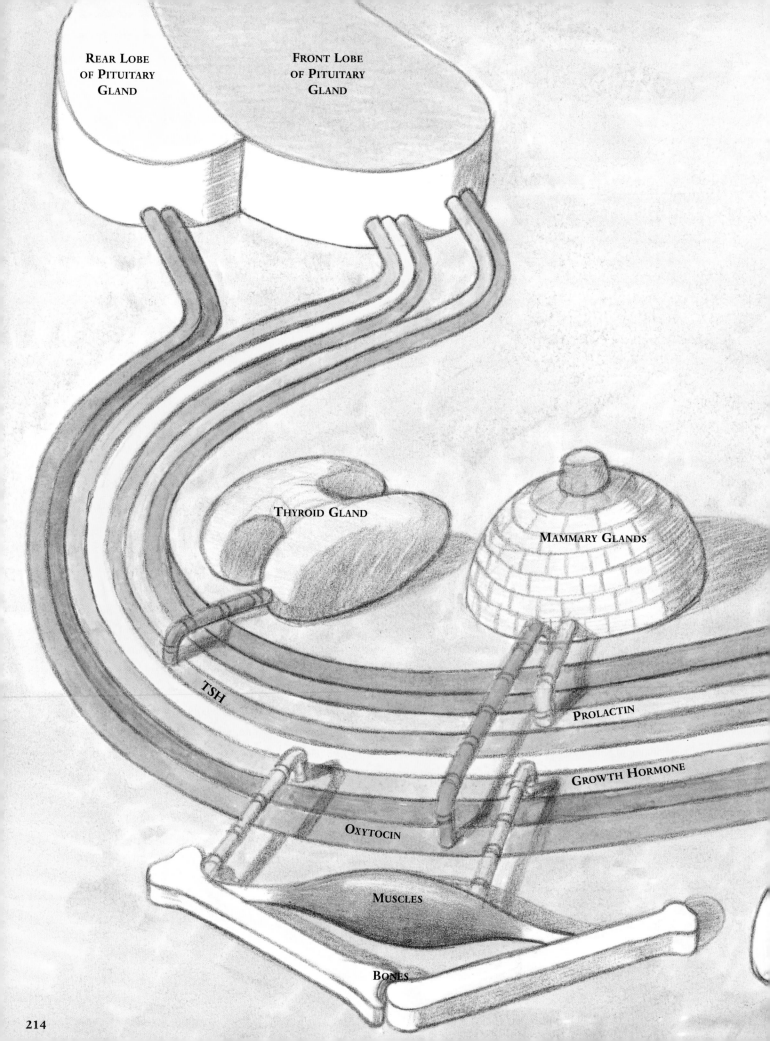

REAR LOBE
OF PITUITARY
GLAND

FRONT LOBE
OF PITUITARY
GLAND

THYROID GLAND

MAMMARY GLANDS

TSH

PROLACTIN

GROWTH HORMONE

OXYTOCIN

MUSCLES

BONES

PROLIFIC PITUITARY

No bigger than a small raisin, the pituitary gland dominates the endocrine system. It releases eight key hormones that control growth, reproduction, and much more.

Two of these hormones, oxytocin and antidiuretic hormone (ADH), are made by the hypothalamus, then stored and released on demand by the rear lobe of the pituitary. At the end of pregnancy, oxytocin triggers the contractions of the uterus that make birth happen and then releases milk from mammary glands to feed the new arrival. Antidiuretic hormone (ADH) helps the body hold on to precious water by increasing the concentration of urine from the kidneys when water levels in the blood fall.

Growth hormone, one of the pituitary's front lobe hormones, encourages body growth by stimulating both cell division and the manufacture of proteins in most tissues but especially in bones and muscles. Another hormone, prolactin, stimulates milk production by the mammary glands during and after pregnancy.

The four remaining front lobe hormones stimulate other endocrine organs to release their own hormones. Thyroid-stimulating hormone (TSH) tells the thyroid gland to release thyroxine in order to regulate the metabolic rate of the body's cells. Adrenocorticotropic hormone (ACTH) instructs the adrenal glands to release several steroid hormones to help regulate metabolism and combat stress. In women, follicle stimulating hormone (FSH) and luteinizing hormone (LH) target the ovaries, causing the maturation and release of an egg, as well as secretion of the female sex hormone estrogen. In men, FSH and LH target the testes, stimulating sperm production and release of testosterone, the male sex hormone.

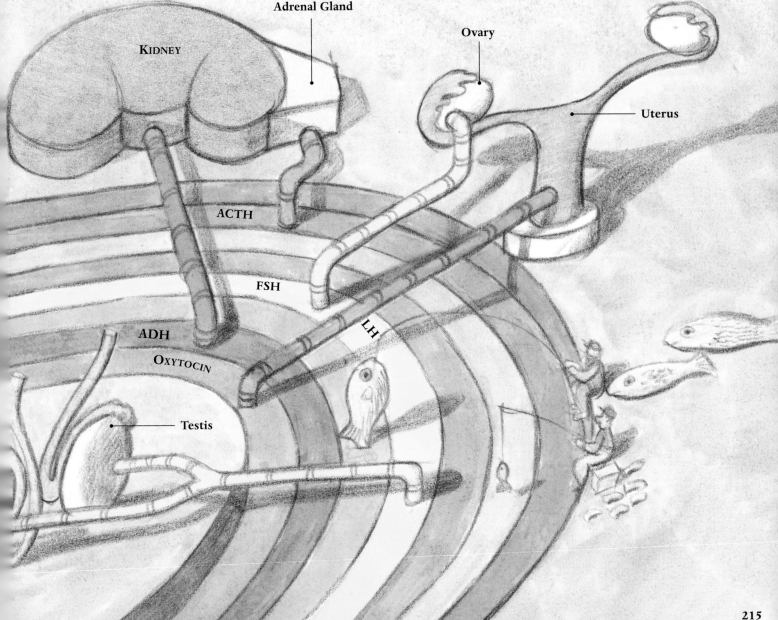

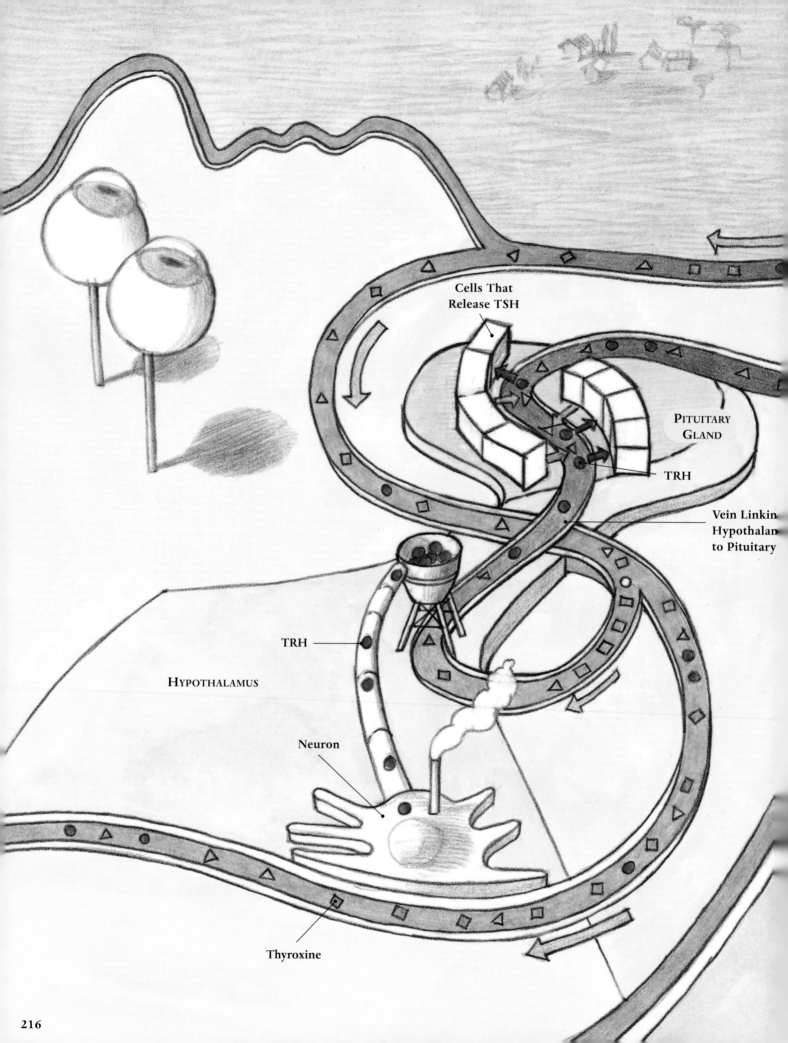

Cells That
Release TSH

PITUITARY
GLAND

TRH

Vein Linkin
Hypothalam
to Pituitary

TRH

HYPOTHALAMUS

Neuron

Thyroxine

LARYNX

HEART
AND LUNGS

TRACHEA

THYROID GLAND

Thyroxine

TSH

A LITTLE FEEDBACK

Imagine being inside a heated room with its "ideal" temperature set at 65°F (18°C). When room temperature rises above this set point, a thermostat turns off the furnace that heats the room's radiator. As the room cools and its temperature falls below the set point, the thermostat switches on the furnace and the temperature rises. This is negative feedback—a change in one direction that triggers a correction in the opposite direction.

In exactly the same way, negative feedback controls the levels of individual hormones circulating in the blood so they exert neither too little nor too great an effect on their target cells. Here's an example.

Located on the trachea, just below the larynx, the thyroid gland releases thyroxine. Targeting most body cells, this hormone peps up their metabolic rate, encouraging them to "burn" energy-releasing glucose. Too little thyroxine leaves

a person lethargic, while too much makes his or her heart pound and metabolism overheat.

To maintain the desired balance, levels of thyroxine in the blood are monitored by the hypothalamus. If they fall below "normal," neurons secrete thyrotropin-releasing hormone (TRH) into the veins, which carry it to the front lobe of the pituitary gland. TRH then targets and stimulates cells inside the pituitary gland that secrete thyroid-stimulating hormone (TSH). Blood carries TSH, via the heart and lungs, to the thyroid gland, where it triggers the release of thyroxine.

If the concentration of thyroxine in the blood rises above required levels, it is detected by the hypothalamus, which immediately cuts secretion of TRH. As a consequence, secretion of TSH and thyroxine fall as well.

CHAPTER 5

BATTLE STATIONS

WE SHARE PLANET EARTH with millions of different species, including bacteria, viruses, and other microorganisms. Although invisible to the naked eye, a select band of these tiny creatures called pathogens are capable of causing us harm should they invade the body. Because pathogens may be lurking in the air we breathe, the food we eat, and the fluid we drink, as well as on anything we touch—or as in the case of certain bugs, on things that touch us—that threat is present every second of the day.

Fortunately, each of us is protected by varying levels of homeland security. Outer barriers—the most familiar being the skin—keep most pathogens at bay. Should these barriers be breached, an inbuilt repair mechanism fixes the damage as germ-killing cells seek out and destroy the invaders. Internal record keepers take note of those invaders for future reference and even more rapid destruction.

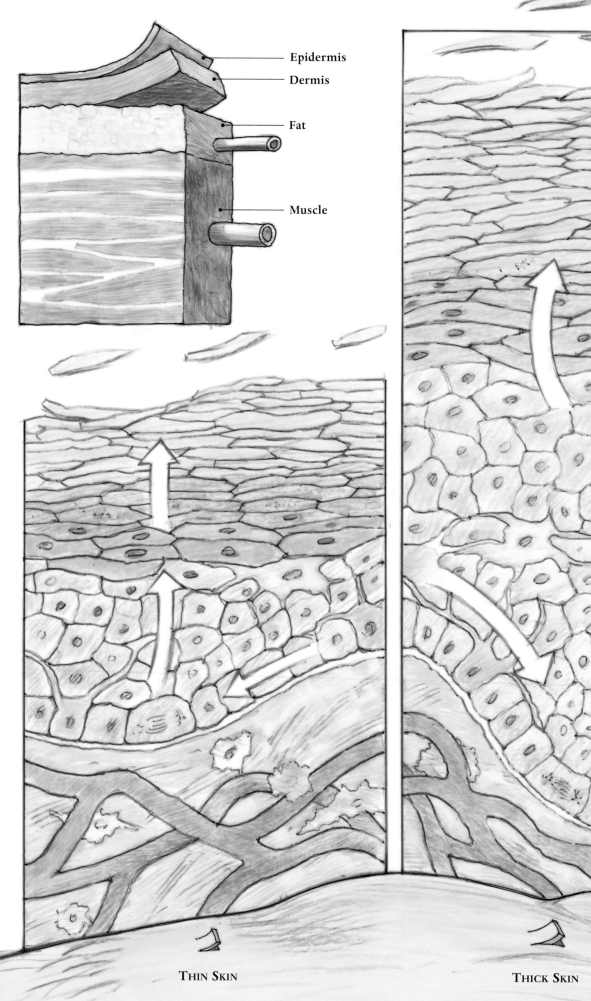

Epidermis

Dermis

Fat

Muscle

THIN SKIN

THICK SKIN

WEAR AND TEAR

Washable, waterproof, germproof, and self-repairing, skin, the heaviest of body organs, is literally the frontline of defense, protecting our delicate insides from the harsh world outside. Skin has two layers that are firmly "glued" together—the epidermis on top and the thicker dermis below. The epidermis is thickest on the hard-working palms and fingers, as well as on the soles of our feet. With no direct blood supply, the cells of the epidermis depend on deliveries from the dermis, a tough but stretchable connective tissue equipped not just with blood vessels but also with nerve endings and sweat glands.

The surface of the epidermis is continually being worn away. But its cells are constantly replaced by a nonstop production line manned by unspecialized stem cells in the deepest part of the epidermis. When these cells divide by mitosis, some of their offspring remain in place to divide again; the rest are pushed upward toward the skin's surface. Along the way they manufacture a tough, resilient protein called keratin, which is also found in hair, nails, hooves, and rhino horns. As these cells migrate they gradually flatten and fill with keratin fibers, their nuclei and other internal structures disappearing along the way. Once too distant from any blood supply, they die, but remain bonded together by a waterproof adhesive until they are lost as some of the millions of skin flakes that fall from our bodies daily. Their sacrifice is our protection.

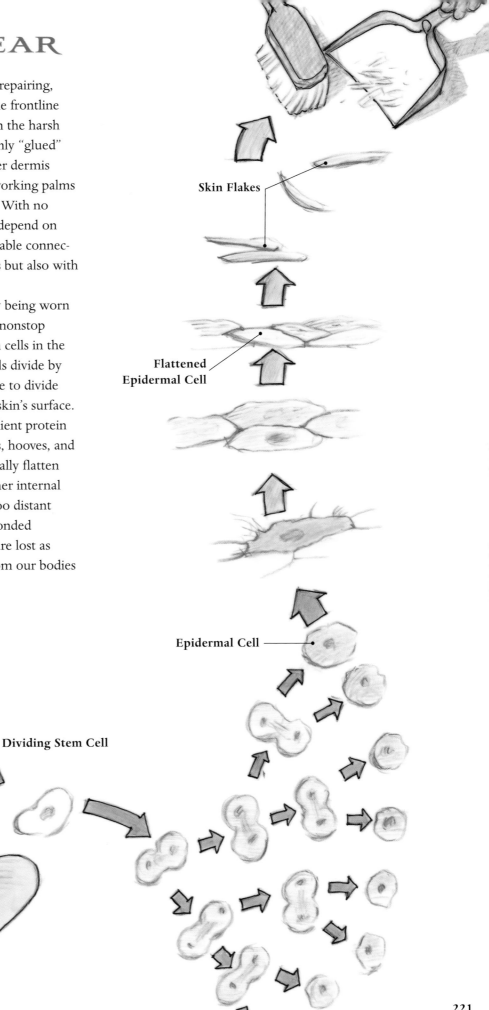

Skin Flakes

Flattened Epidermal Cell

Epidermal Cell

Stem Cell

Dividing Stem Cell

Blood, Sweat, and Hairs

Skin helps the body maintain a steady internal temperature of 98.6°F (37°C). Working with the brain's hypothalamus, which serves as a thermostat, blood vessels in the skin act as radiators. When the weather is hot or we heat up during exercise, the vessels that loop through the dermis are instructed to widen. The increased flow of warm blood releases excess body heat into the surrounding air.

As another temperature-controlling mechanism, coiled sweat glands in the dermis filter blood plasma to produce salty sweat. When it is released through pores and onto the skin's surface, the sweat evaporates, drawing heat from the body and cooling it down. If it is cold outside, blood vessels in the skin narrow and sweat glands decrease production. Heat loss is cut and the body warms up.

While many mammals have fur to keep them warm, most of the hairs that sprout from our skin are too fine and short to offer much insulation. Linked to touch sensors in the dermis, these hairs are more useful as tripwires that detect newly landed insects before they can bite or sting us.

Hairs grow from follicles that extend from the epidermis down into the dermis. At the bottom of the follicle, epithelial cells divide repeatedly by mitosis. As their offspring move upward, fill with keratin, and eventually die, they fuse

Sweat Pore

Sweat Duct

Sweat Gland

222

together and are shaped by the walls of the follicle to form a strand of hair. Glands that open into the upper follicle release oils that lubricate hairs and skin and make them waterproof.

In cold conditions our hairs often spring to attention, their follicles pulled by tiny muscles. In hairier mammals this action forms an insulating layer of air to trap heat. We humans just get goose bumps.

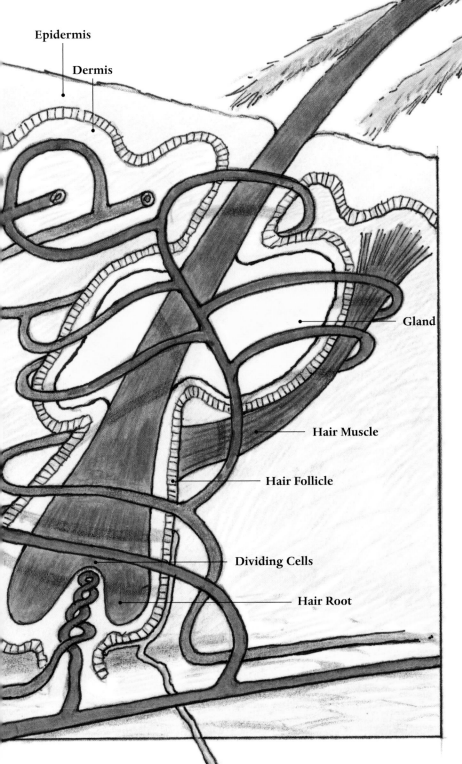

Epidermis

Dermis

Gland

Hair Muscle

Hair Follicle

Dividing Cells

Hair Root

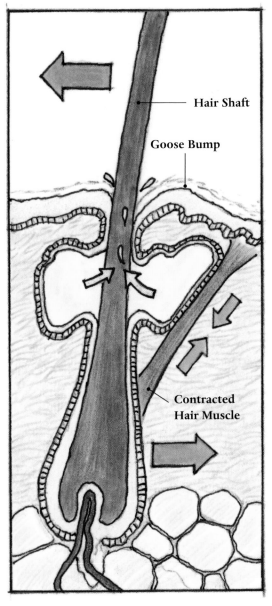

IN COLD AIR

Hair Shaft

Goose Bump

Contracted Hair Muscle

UNEASY PEACE

Seen close up, the skin is far from being flat and featureless. Undulating and littered with loose skin flakes, the epidermal surface is pierced by sweat pores and hair follicles, from which tree trunk–like shafts thrust upward. Billions of bacteria feed, grow, and reproduce here, seemingly at peace with their human host. They are particularly drawn to moist areas such as the armpits, groin, and between the toes. Also appealing are the areas around sweat pores and hair follicles, the secretions of which provide nutrients.

But skin is not an ideal environment for bacteria. Constant shedding of skin flakes makes it unstable. Its dryness discourages colonization. Secretions such as oil and sweat are acidic, and sweat also contains chemicals that kill bacteria or at least retard their multiplication. So rather than passively accepting all bacteria, skin has the ability to limit the growth of bacterial colonies and even to select one type over another. "Good" bacteria are encouraged to occupy space that might otherwise be populated by dangerous pathogens. But this principle of "my enemy's enemy is my friend" breaks down when the skin barrier is damaged.

STICK TOGETHER, KIDS.
HERE COMES OUR BIG BREAK.

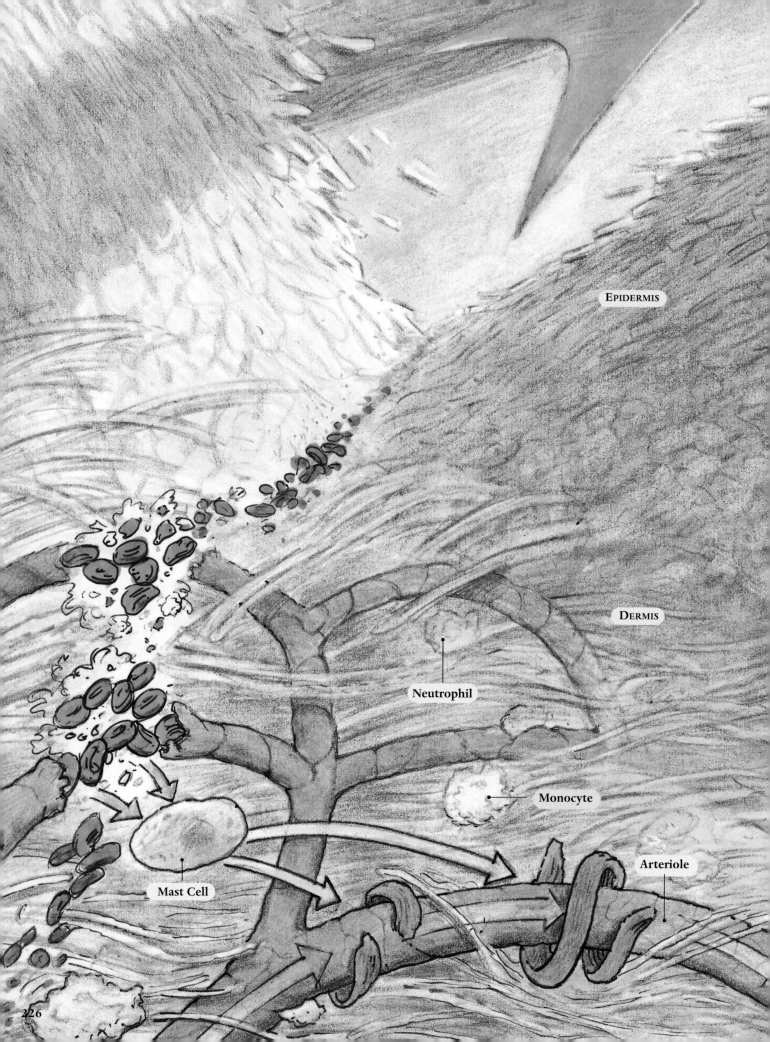

EPIDERMIS

DERMIS

Neutrophil

Monocyte

Mast Cell

Arteriole

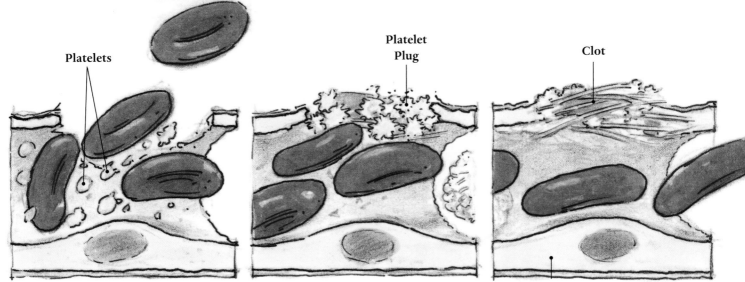

Platelets

Platelet Plug

Clot

Blood Vessel Wall

ONLY A SCRATCH

Any breach in the skin barrier that results in torn blood vessels requires immediate attention from the body's defenses. The first item of business is to stop the leak. At the wound site, passing blood platelets swell and become spiky. They stick to each other and create a plug that quickly stems some of the flow. Damaged tissues and clumped platelets trigger the conversion of a protein in the plasma into a tangle of fibers that traps blood cells and forms a clot. As the clot tightens, the edges of the wound are pulled together, after which repair cells move in to fix the damage. When its job is done, the clot is dismantled or, if it is at the skin's surface, it dries to form a scab that eventually falls off.

While blood is clotting, specialized white blood cells called neutrophils and monocytes seek out and destroy bacteria that have infiltrated the defenses during the confusion. As the ground troops of the body's immune system, these cells circulate continuously in the bloodstream, awaiting just such an encounter. They are summoned to the damage site when body cells such as mast cells release chemicals that cause a number of local changes. Arterioles widen to increase blood flow and deliver extra supplies to the site. Capillaries become super leaky, allowing fluid carrying oxygen and food to ooze into the damage zone.

Attracted by the chemical alarm, white blood cells in the area first cling to the insides of capillaries long enough to squeeze through gaps in the capillary wall. Once behind enemy lines, they begin their search-and-destroy missions. Monocytes are transformed into even bigger and hungrier cells called macrophages. This whole process, called the inflammatory response, causes the redness, heat, swelling, and pain at the site of the scratch. While it may feel uncomfortable, inflammation is essential for pathogen destruction and tissue repair.

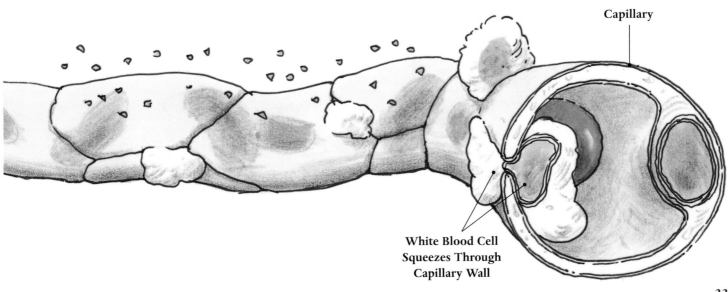

Capillary

White Blood Cell Squeezes Through Capillary Wall

KNOW YOUR
ENEMY

The smallest and most abundant of all living things on the planet are bacteria, and they are found everywhere, from clouds to colons. Most are harmless, some are beneficial, but a few, given half a chance, will invade our tissues and make us sick. These are called pathogens.

Whether rod-shaped, like this one, spherical, or spiral, bacteria share a structure that is quite unlike that of body cells. Though they have a cell membrane and contain cytoplasm, ribosomes, and a single loop of DNA, bacteria lack a nucleus and any other internal structures. The cell membrane is encased within a rigid wall that shapes the bacterium. Projecting "hairs" called pili allow pathogenic bacteria to anchor to cells. Such unique features are studied keenly by scientists who search for "weak spots" to be attacked by bacteria-killing drugs that won't affect our cells.

Most pathogenic bacteria cause damage by releasing poisonous toxins that disrupt or destroy our cells. Once ensconced in the warm, nutrient-rich conditions of the tissues, bacteria divide rapidly by doubling up their DNA and splitting in two. If unchallenged by the body's defenses—an unlikely event—a single bacterium could potentially divide once every twenty minutes, producing five billion trillion (5,000,000,000,000,000,000,000) offspring in just twenty-four hours.

Luckily this particular invader has yet to reproduce, and there's a rather large and very hungry macrophage creeping up behind it.

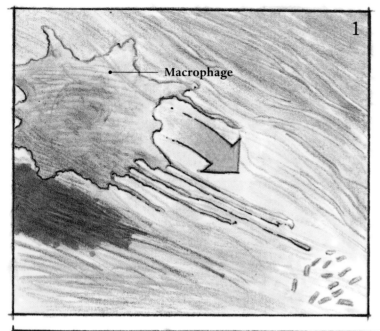

Macrophage

FOREIGN FOOD

To a macrophage anything foreign is there to be eaten. When bacteria enter the body and find their way into the tissues, they leave a chemical trail that is detected by receptors on a patrolling macrophage's cell membrane. In response, the intrepid hunter reorganizes its cytoskeleton and sends out tentacle-like extensions that home in on its prey.

If receptors on these extensions recognize incriminating markers on the bacterial surface, they bind to them. This attachment is even stronger if the bacterium has already been coated with proteins called antibodies. These make the pathogen not only "tastier" to macrophages but also easier to grip.

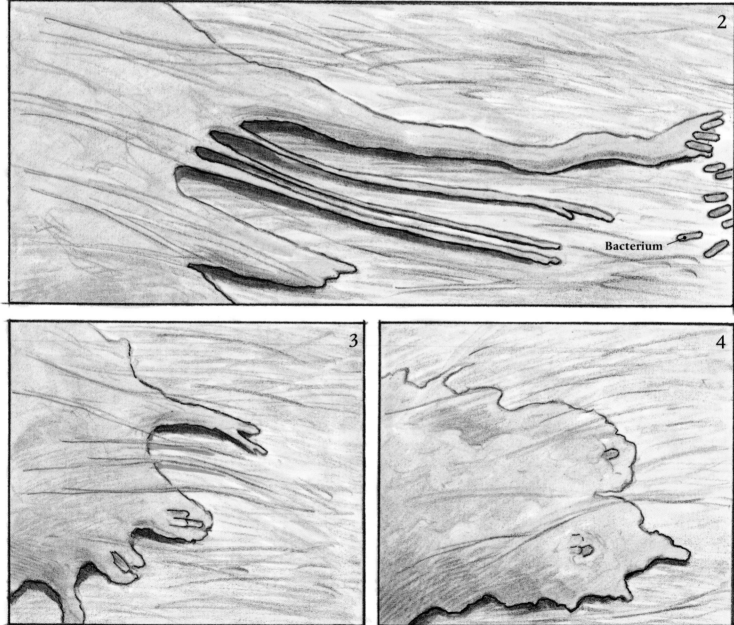

Bacterium

Once captured, the bacterium is drawn into the macrophage and packaged in a sac pinched off from the cell membrane. As it moves through the cytoplasm, the sac fuses with a lysosome—a membrane-enclosed sac filled with digestive enzymes. These enzymes safely dismantle the bacterium without digesting the macrophage itself. Any indigestible components are ejected from the macrophage as, with a flourish of economy, the piece of cell membrane pinched off earlier is restored to its rightful place.

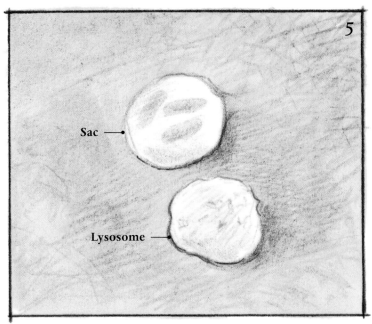

Sac

Lysosome

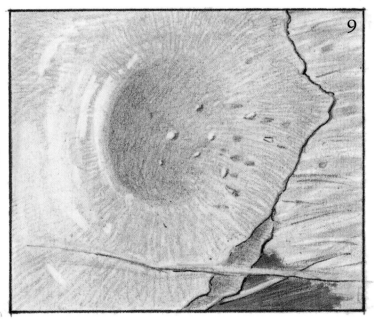

Drain and Defend

Every day some 50 pints (24 liters) of fluid leaves the blood as it flows along capillaries delivering essentials to tissue cells and removing their wastes. All of this fluid eventually returns to the bloodstream and most of it does so through the capillaries, but some 6 to 8 pints (3–4 liters) escapes along the way. The vital job of draining this excess tissue fluid and returning it to the bloodstream to restore normal blood volume and concentration is performed by the body's second, lesser-known transport network, the lymphatic system.

The finest branches of this network, called lymph capillaries, weave their way between blood capillaries and tissue cells. The ends of the capillaries farthest from the heart are sealed off while tiny flaps in their walls act as one-way swinging doors, allowing tissue fluid in but not out. Once trapped inside, the excess fluid becomes lymph, a watery mixture of plasma proteins, white blood cells, and debris. Lymph is pushed along the network of increasingly larger vessels by the squeezing action of surrounding skeletal muscles. Valves, like those in veins, prevent backflow. Eventually the vessels join together to form trunks, which flow into two large ducts that empty the lymph into left and right subclavian veins.

Drainage is not the only role of the lymphatic system. Defense is also a priority. Dotted along lymph vessels, like beads on a string, are small swellings called lymph nodes. These serve two primary purposes. They filter lymph on its way from tissues to bloodstream to remove bacteria and any other dangerous cargo that may have escaped destruction in the tissues. And they give one type of immune system cells, called lymphocytes, a place to proliferate and to launch an attack should they be stirred into action by the presence of pathogens.

Lymph Capillary

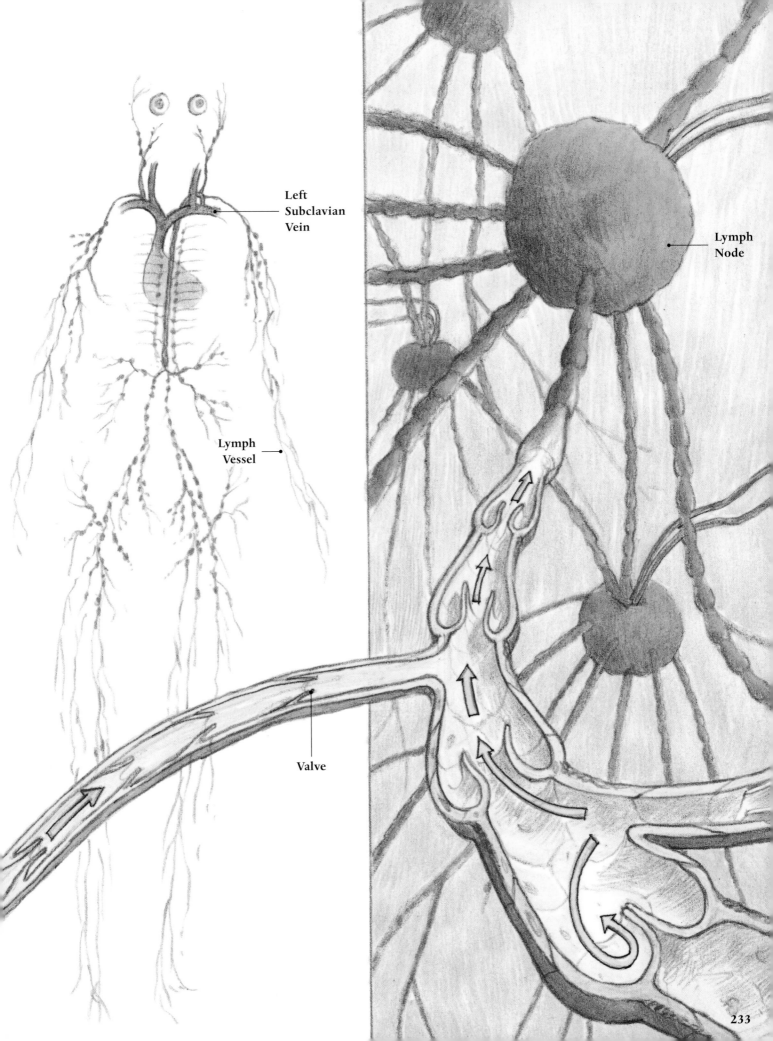

Left
Subclavian
Vein

Lymph
Node

Lymph
Vessel

Valve

CLEAN AND CLONE

As lymph flows through a lymph node it is "cleaned" to remove pathogens. At the same time, lymphocytes exposed to pathogens clone themselves, making identical copies to fight their enemies. Lymph enters each node at the cortex and departs from the medulla. The cortex is divided into compartments by extensions off the tough outer capsule. Within each compartment, mobile lymphocytes and other immune system cells are supported by a honeycomb of fibers.

While as a group lymphocytes can respond to millions of antigens, individually they react—via cell surface receptors—to just one specific pathogen antigen. This is a skill they develop as they mature either in bone marrow (B cells) or the thymus gland (T cells). B cells and T cells arrive at the node via the bloodstream and eventually leave through a lymph vessel.

During its stay—be it long or short—a lymphocyte may be activated to launch an attack by contact, either direct or indirect, with a specific pathogen. The outer portion of the cortex contains areas of densely packed lymphocytes, the centers of which are populated by activated and proliferating B cells. The deeper cortex contains multiplying T cells. The medulla houses strands of mature B cells that release pathogen-immobilizing antibodies.

Between arrival and departure, lymph flows in one direction along broad channels called sinuses. Fibers crisscrossing the sinuses support macrophages that engulf passing pathogens. The number of lymph vessels entering a node is greater than the number of those leaving. This clever tactic slows down the lymph traveling through the node, giving immune cells time to do their job.

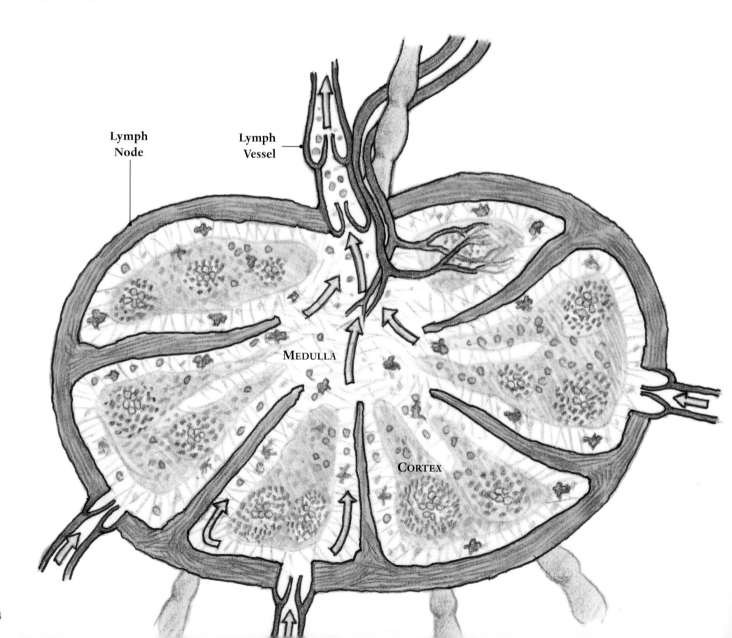

Lymph Node

Lymph Vessel

MEDULLA

CORTEX

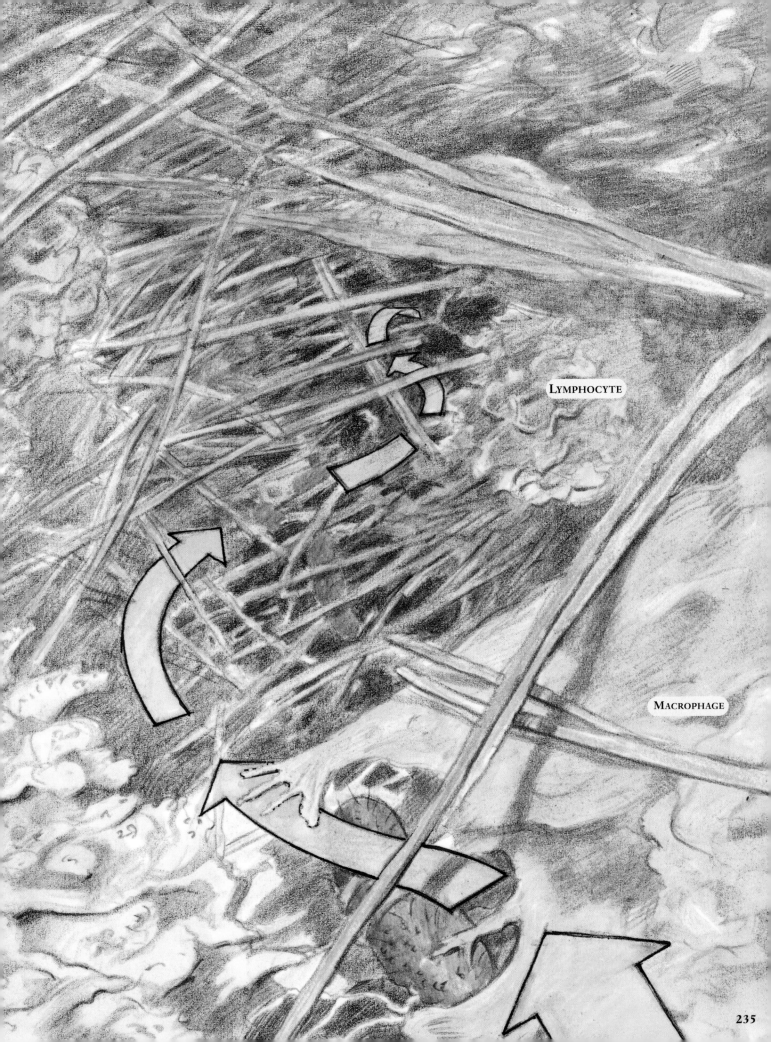

LYMPHOCYTE

MACROPHAGE

ANTIBODY ATTACK

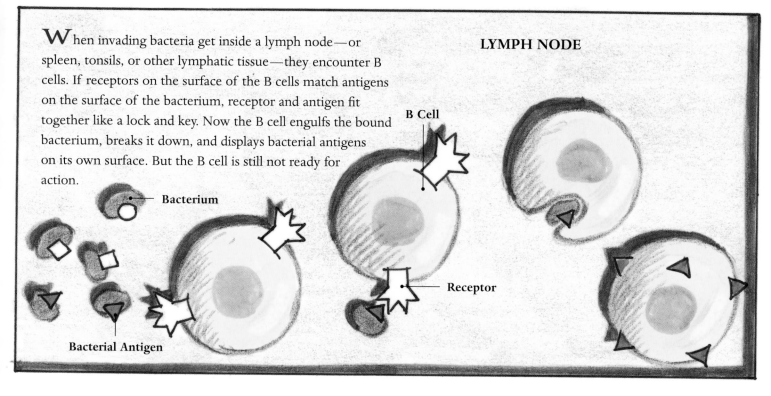

When invading bacteria get inside a lymph node—or spleen, tonsils, or other lymphatic tissue—they encounter B cells. If receptors on the surface of the B cells match antigens on the surface of the bacterium, receptor and antigen fit together like a lock and key. Now the B cell engulfs the bound bacterium, breaks it down, and displays bacterial antigens on its own surface. But the B cell is still not ready for action.

LYMPH NODE

B Cell

Receptor

Bacterium

Bacterial Antigen

Meanwhile, in the skin, a dendritic cell has tracked down and engulfed the same type of bacterium, and it too displays the invader's antigens on its surface. Upon entering a lymph node, this cell presents those antigens to a helper T cell—a type of lymphocyte that helps coordinate the entire immune response. Once activated by the encounter, the helper T cell promptly clones itself.

SKIN

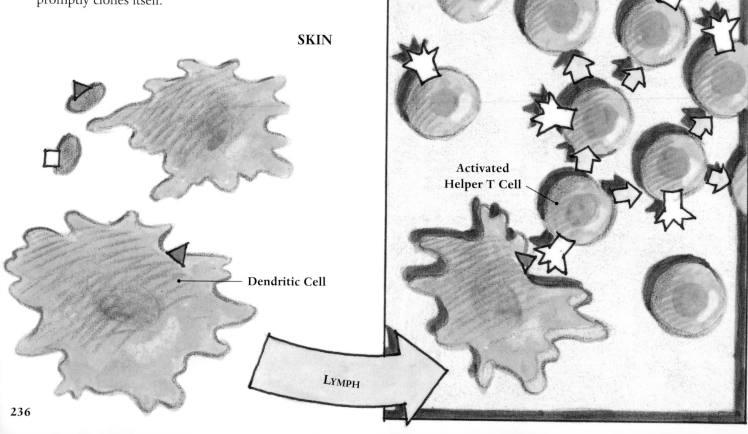

Activated Helper T Cell

Dendritic Cell

LYMPH

An activated helper T cell then binds with and stimulates one of the B cells originally activated by the same antigen. Prodded into action, this B cell divides rapidly and produces big plasma cells that each churn out up to two thousand antibody molecules a second. In a blanket attack these antibodies are shipped out of the node in both blood and lymph and bind to their chosen bacteria, marking them for destruction by germ-eating macrophages.

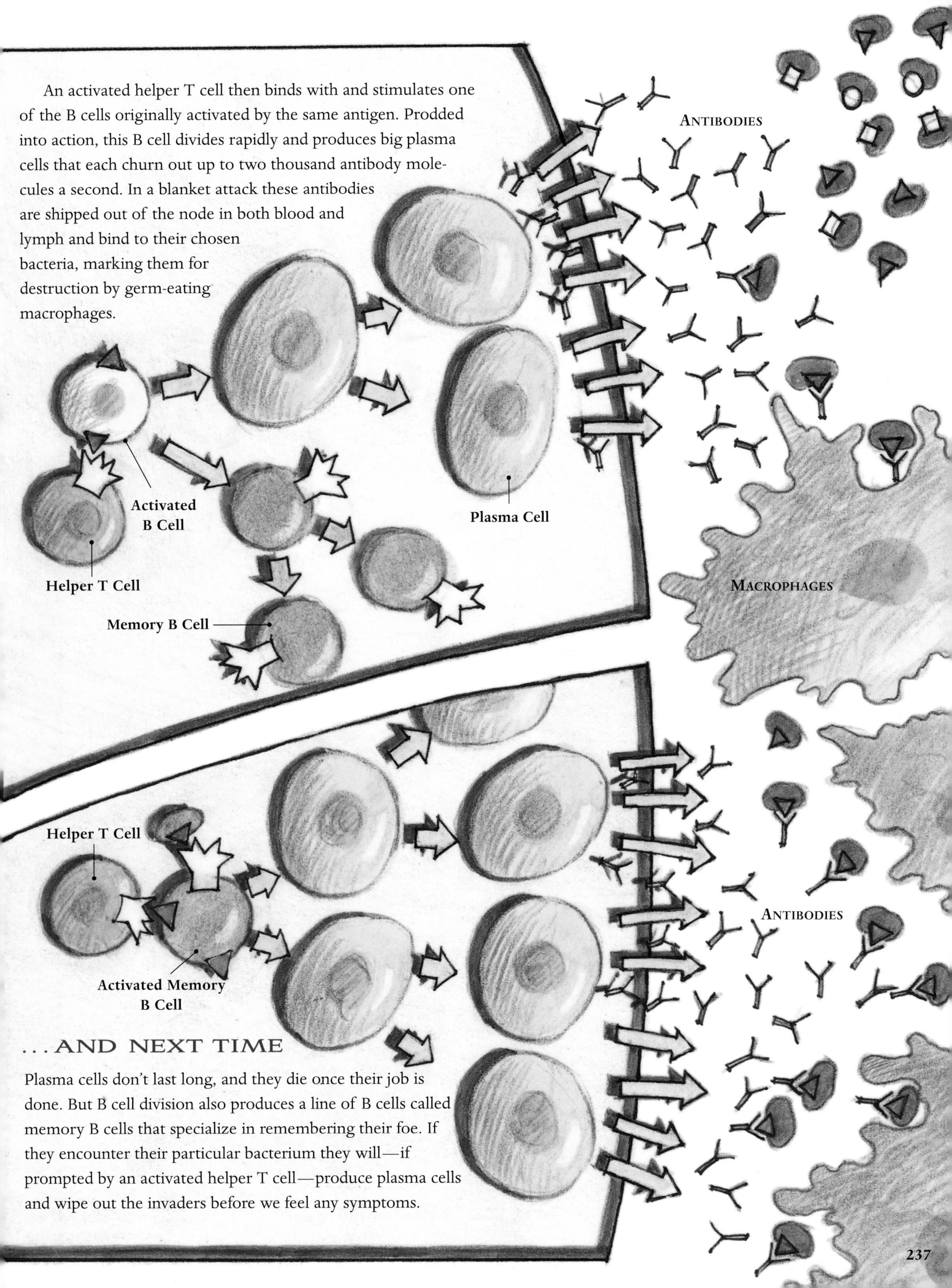

ANTIBODIES

**Activated
B Cell**

Helper T Cell

Plasma Cell

Memory B Cell

MACROPHAGES

Helper T Cell

ANTIBODIES

**Activated Memory
B Cell**

. . . AND NEXT TIME

Plasma cells don't last long, and they die once their job is done. But B cell division also produces a line of B cells called memory B cells that specialize in remembering their foe. If they encounter their particular bacterium they will—if prompted by an activated helper T cell—produce plasma cells and wipe out the invaders before we feel any symptoms.

FLU ALERT

Consider the insidious sneeze. A tickling inside the nose triggers a sudden, reflex expulsion of air from the lungs that blasts the irritation out through the nostrils. Thousands of tiny droplets are immediately propelled our way, some of which may very well be home to a platoon of flu (influenza) viruses.

Unlike bacteria, viruses are not cells. They are more chemical packages than living organisms. They don't feed, breathe, or excrete, and they lack mitochondria, ribosomes, and ATP. But they are pathogens nonetheless. In order to replicate, viruses must not only invade a living cell but also hijack its inner workings, a process that usually ends with the destruction of the unfortunate host cell. This, along with the effects of the immune system's response, produces the symptoms of the disease, be it flu, a cold, measles, mumps, or any of the viral infections that prey on us humans.

Although virus shapes vary, they share the same basic structure. The flu virus shown here is around one hundred times smaller than a red blood cell. At its core is its genetic material, in this case eight strands of RNA carrying the ten genes needed to build a new virus. Some viruses use DNA instead. Around the core is a protective protein coat called a capsid. Flu viruses, along with many other types of virus, are also enclosed by a membrane envelope "stolen" from the host cell to aid in cell invasion and to help avoid detection. Projecting through the outer membrane—like an orange studded with cloves—are two types of surface proteins (called H and N) that act as antigens. There are several versions of both H and N; these are numbered and used to identify the particular kind of flu, such as H5N1, a form of bird flu that may infect humans.

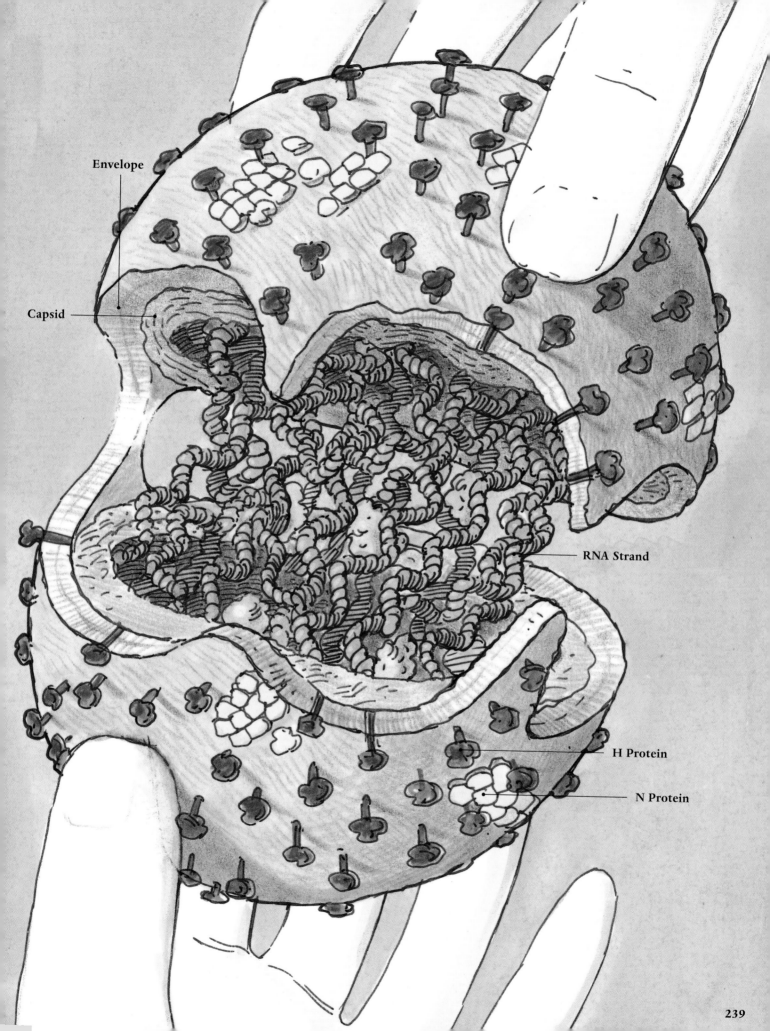

Envelope

Capsid

RNA Strand

H Protein

N Protein

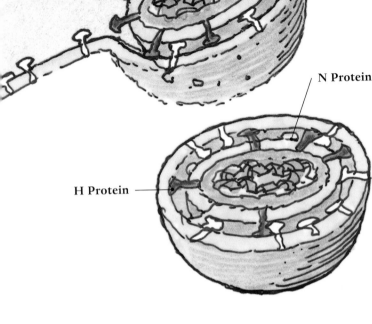

Flu Virus

Host Cell Membrane

N Protein

H Protein

Acid Bath

POPULATION EXPLOSION

If we are unlucky enough to breathe in a flu virus, it will probably settle on the lining of our nose, throat, or trachea, where its protruding H proteins will then bind to a cell membrane. Doing what comes naturally, the cell will enclose the virus in a membrane sac and treat it to an acid bath. Instead of being destroyed, however, the wily virus responds by dumping its cargo of RNA and proteins into the cytoplasm of its host.

The viral RNA strands are now free to enter the cell's nucleus along with the virus's own RNA-copying enzymes. Using host cell nucleotides as raw materials, both strands and enzymes go to work making multiple messenger RNA copies of the ten viral genes. These messenger RNA strands then migrate into the cytoplasm, where they employ host ribosomes to manufacture thousands of copies of the viral proteins.

The new H and N proteins move to and embed themselves in the host cell membrane. The other proteins head into the nucleus, where multiple copies of the viral RNA strands are being made. The new capsid proteins build packages, each of which will enclose a set of eight newly made viral RNA strands.

The loaded capsids then travel from the nucleus toward the cell surface, where each is surrounded by a piece of host membrane studded with surface proteins. N proteins eventually "cut" the virus free to set off in search of a new target. This sequence is repeated thousands of times, puncturing the membrane and destroying the host cell in the process.

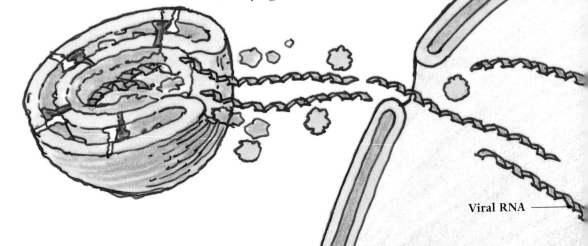

Viral RNA

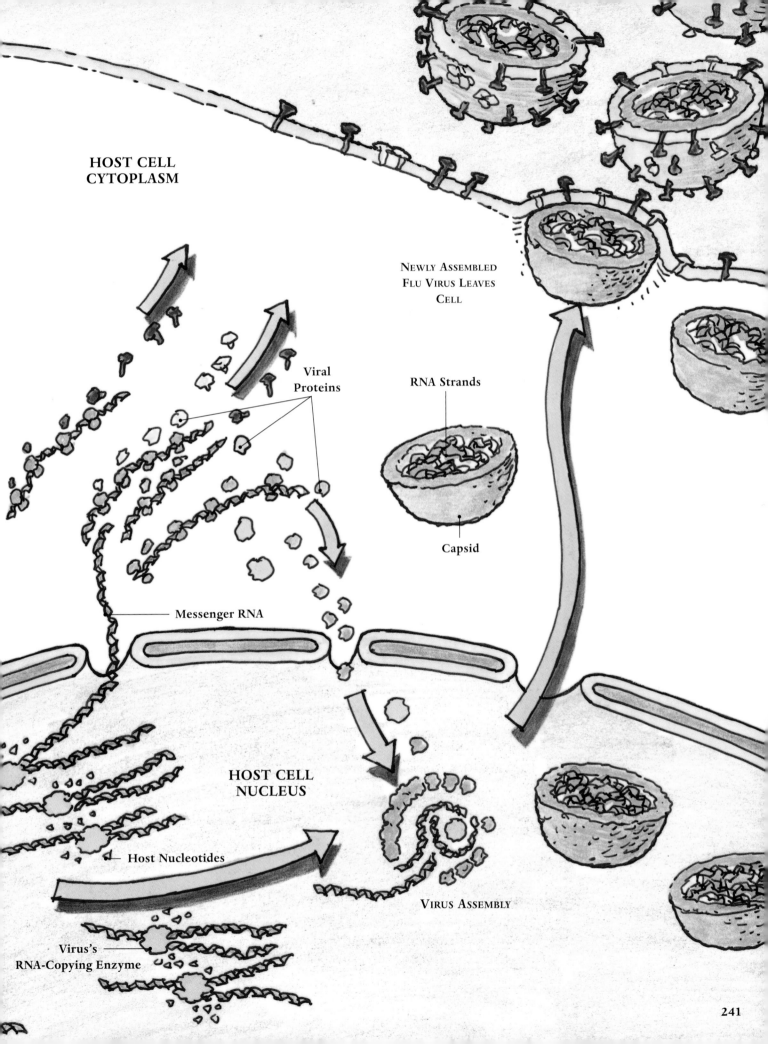

HOST CELL
CYTOPLASM

Viral
Proteins

NEWLY ASSEMBLED
FLU VIRUS LEAVES
CELL

RNA Strands

Messenger RNA

Capsid

HOST CELL
NUCLEUS

Host Nucleotides

VIRUS ASSEMBLY

Virus's
RNA-Copying Enzyme

KILLER CELLS

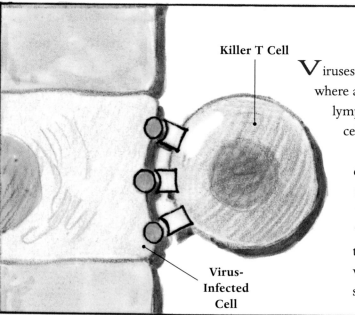

Killer T Cell

Virus-Infected Cell

Viruses make multiple copies of themselves while hiding inside cells, where antibodies can't touch them. It takes the special ops force of the T lymphocytes called killer T cells to seek out and destroy infected bod cells and put their virus factories out of business.

Always on the lookout for trouble, killer and helper T cells are constantly traveling around the body in blood and lymph, infiltrat ing tissues where there are signs of infection. If a body cell is hos to viruses, it displays some of their antigens on its cell membrane This identifies it as being abnormal to any passing killer T cells that might be carrying matching receptors. Although a killer T ce will bind to an infected cell, it can't take any action until it gets th signal from a helper T cell.

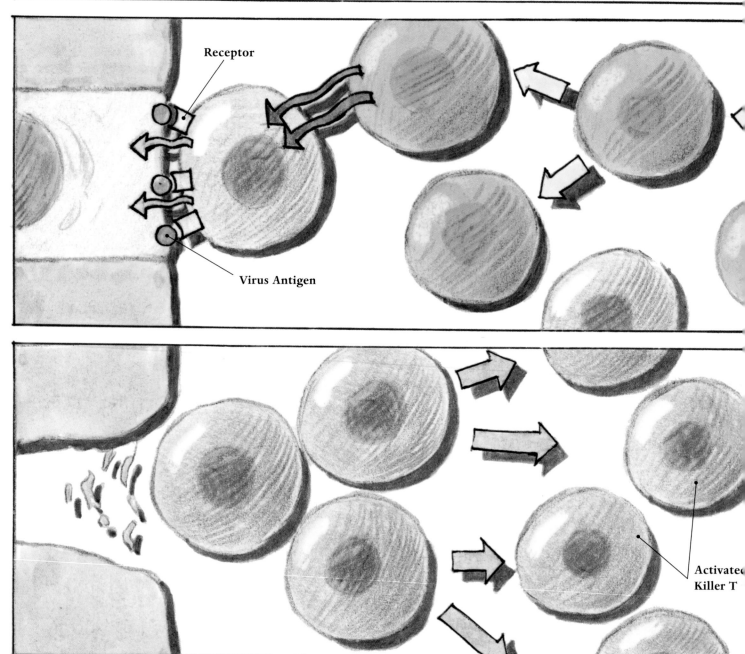

Receptor

Virus Antigen

Activated Killer T

242

Macrophage

Activated Helper T Cell

Elsewhere, a macrophage has consumed some free viruses identical to the ones multiplying inside the host cell and now displays their antigens on its surface. A helper T cell with membrane receptors specific for those antigens binds to the macrophage and is "switched on." It divides repeatedly and its clones release chemicals that energize the bound killer T cell. After first killing the infected cell by making holes in its cell membrane, the killer T cell divides rapidly, producing offspring that will seek out and destroy all of the body cells infected with that same virus. As with B cells, some of the clones of both helper and killer cells are long-lived memory T cells that will spring into action should the virus return.

Other lymphocytes called NK cells are also stimulated by helper T cells. They kill in the same way as their killer T cousins, but they're not so picky and will destroy any infected body cell.

Natural Killer (NK) Cell

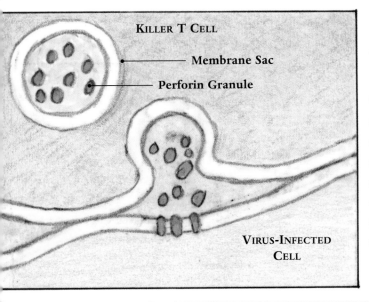

KILLER T CELL

Membrane Sac

Perforin Granule

VIRUS-INFECTED CELL

CHEMICAL WARFARE

Once killer T cells and their prey are tightly bound to one another, membrane sacs containing granules of a substance called perforin fuse with the T cell's membrane, thereby emptying their contents into the space between the two cells. As the killer T cell detaches to find more virus-laden cells, the perforin bores channels through the infected cell's membrane. This allows water to rush in, causing the cell to swell, break apart, and die.

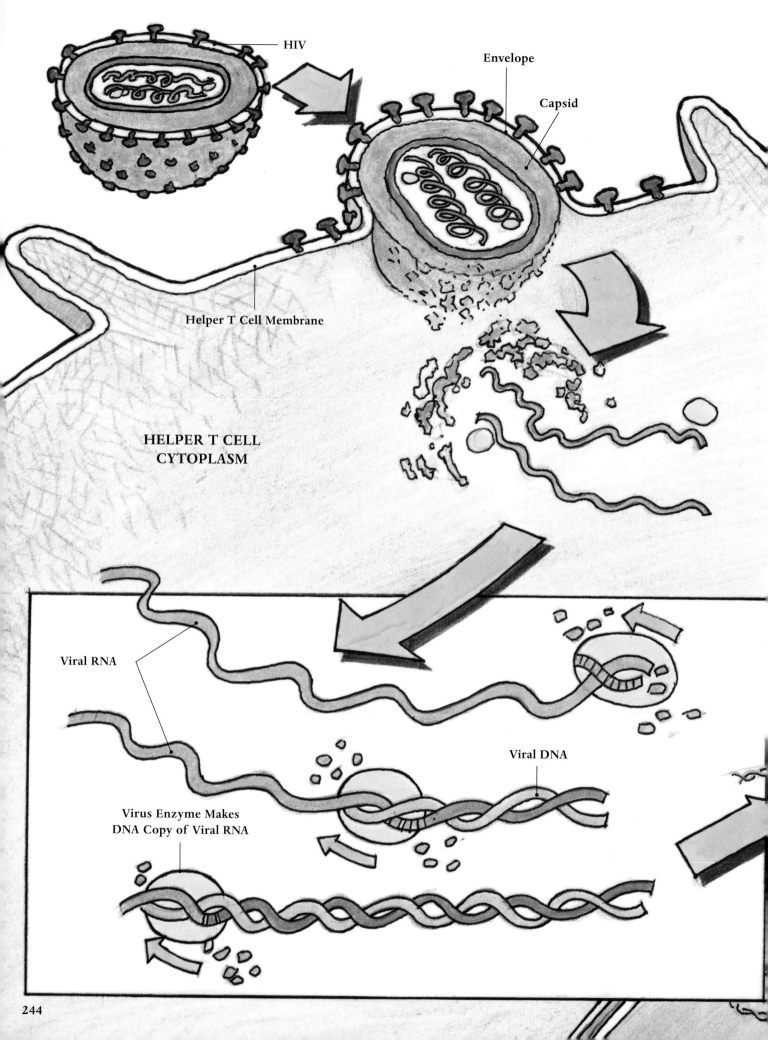

HIV

Envelope

Capsid

Helper T Cell Membrane

HELPER T CELL
CYTOPLASM

Viral RNA

Viral DNA

Virus Enzyme Makes
DNA Copy of Viral RNA

WEAKENED DEFENSES

As activators of B cells and killer T cells, helper T cells are the fixers of the immune system. Unfortunately, they are not invincible. Their primary foe is human immunodeficiency virus, or HIV. Having gained access to the body via blood, semen, vaginal fluids, or breast milk, HIV attaches to a helper T cell, fuses with its cell membrane, and releases its RNA and proteins into the host cell's cytoplasm.

Here the RNA is quickly converted into double-stranded DNA that migrates to the nucleus, where it is spliced into the helper T cell's own DNA. The genes in the "implanted" DNA are copied as strands of messenger RNA that move back out to the cytoplasm to be translated into viral proteins. The implanted DNA is then used as a template to make multiple copies of the virus's RNA. These along with the newly made proteins are now packaged into thousands of new viruses. As they bud off to infect other helper T cells, the new viruses destroy their host.

The body's initial response to HIV is to step up production of helper T cells. But after years of assault, helper T cells start dying more quickly than they can be replaced. When their numbers drop below a certain level, the immune system can no longer fend off attacks and the person falls prey to a range of infections known as acquired immunodeficiency syndrome (AIDS) that eventually kill him or her.

While a cure for HIV infection remains elusive, there are now drugs that can target different stages of HIV replication, preventing the virus from gaining the upper hand and giving sufferers hope of a reasonable life span.

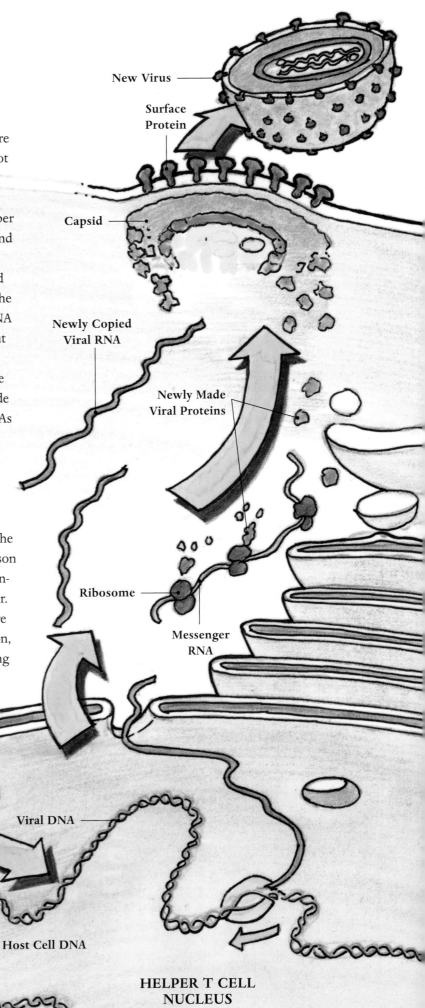

New Virus

Surface Protein

Capsid

Newly Copied Viral RNA

Newly Made Viral Proteins

Ribosome

Messenger RNA

Viral DNA

Host Cell DNA

HELPER T CELL NUCLEUS

Harmful Rays

Pathogens are not the only threat to our well-being. Among numerous environmental hazards are the invisible ultraviolet (UV) rays in sunlight. Although epidermal cells can protect us from routine wear and tear, they are also nearly transparent. UV rays penetrating these cells can potentially damage DNA in the nuclei of cells deep inside the skin. Naturally, the body has taken certain precautions to reduce the danger.

Spider-shaped melanocytes at the base of the epidermis make a brown-black pigment called melanin that, with a dash of pink from the blood, colors the skin. More important, however, melanin absorbs UV rays.

Melanin is made in membrane-enclosed sacs that migrate up the "legs" of the melanocyte. Once released, melanin is absorbed by surrounding epidermal cells and accumulates in the upper part of each one. This creates a "sunshade" that stops UV rays from getting to the precious nucleus below. As epidermal cells flatten and move toward the skin's surface, they carry their melanin with them.

The more we expose ourselves to UV rays, the harder our melanocytes have to work to protect us. The number of melanocytes can't increase, only the quantity of melanin—and the depth of suntan—they produce. But while a tan is short-lived, overexposure to the sun can provide a more enduring souvenir of a leisurely vacation—damage to DNA with its possible serious consequences.

VACATIONER

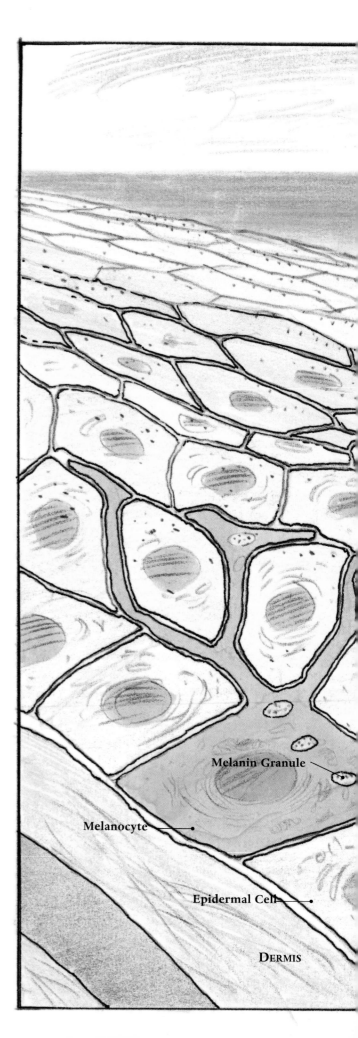

Melanin Granule

Melanocyte

Epidermal Cell

DERMIS

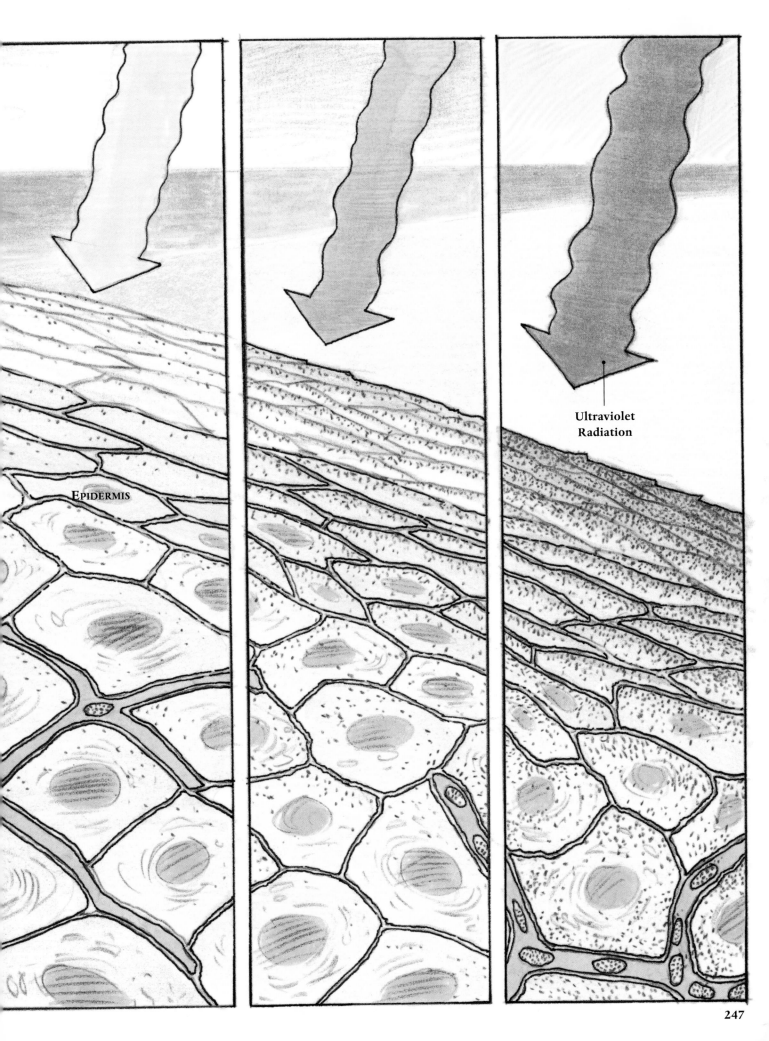

EPIDERMIS

Ultraviolet
Radiation

ENEMY WITHIN

Twenty percent of us human beings are done in by cancer. While there are several different kinds of cancer, some more sinister than others, they all begin with the transformation of a normal body cell into a deviant one. This Jekyll-to-Hyde conversion is the result of several changes, called mutations, in the cell's DNA. These mutations usually accumulate over time, having been triggered by a range of factors that might include sunlight, certain viruses, or cancer-causing chemicals. Because cancer cells have abnormal markers on their surface, they are usually identified as "foreign" and destroyed either by killer T or NK cells before they cause trouble. But some manage to avoid the immune system's attention.

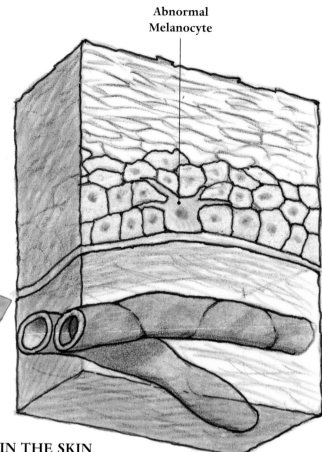

Abnormal Melanocyte

IN THE SKIN

GROWING TUMOR

Whether the result of prolonged exposure to sunlight or because of spontaneous changes, one of the melanocytes shown here has stopped playing by the rules. Genes that once controlled its division and growth have mutated into versions that allow uninhibited multiplication. The result is the growth of a malignant tumor—in this case called a melanoma. As the tumor elbows its way into the dermis, some malignant cells break away and are carried off in lymph capillaries and blood vessels. Those that reach lymph nodes will hide out and proliferate.

ELSEWHERE IN THE BODY

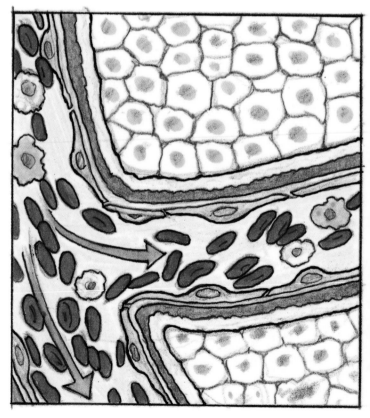

NEW LOCATIONS

These and other escapees from the original skin tumor are then carried by blood to unsuspecting tissues, where the melanoma cells squeeze through capillary walls. Once in the tissue, they divide rapidly to build up a secondary tumor. Before long this deadly intruder is consuming disproportionate amounts of the body's resources.

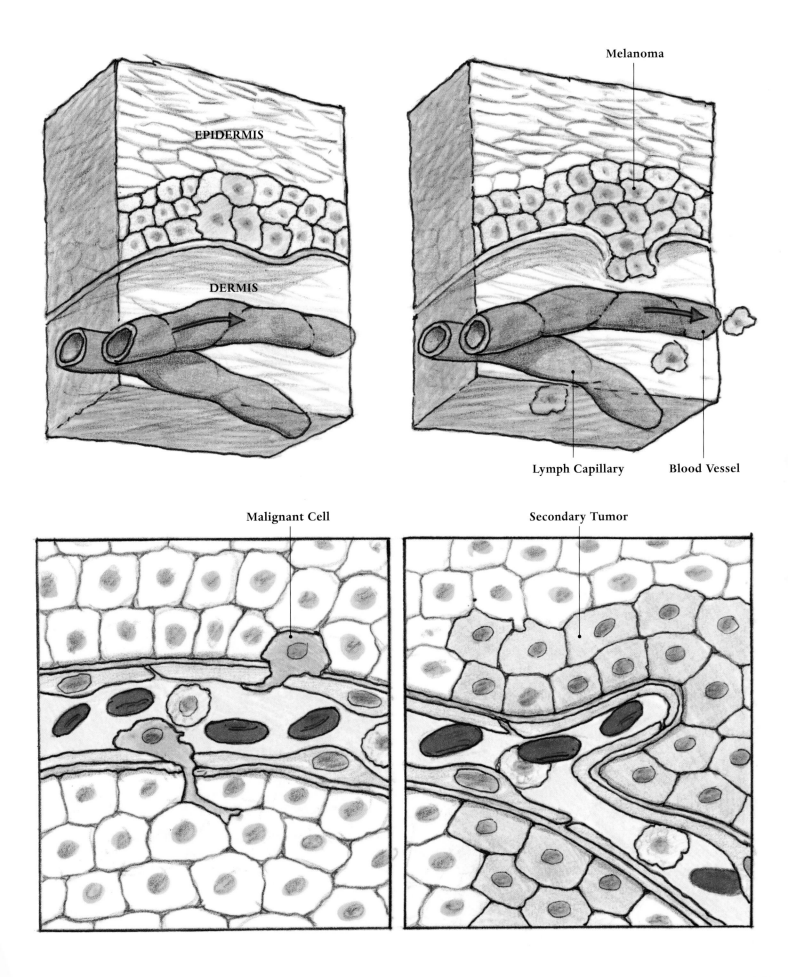

EPIDERMIS

DERMIS

Melanoma

Lymph Capillary

Blood Vessel

Malignant Cell

Secondary Tumor

249

OVERREACTION

The immune system is our great defender, but sometimes it goes too far. In some people it can launch an attack against foreign substances that are perfectly harmless. This overreaction, called an allergy, is uncomfortable and can be dangerous.

Asthma is an increasingly common problem that may be triggered by an allergic response to airborne particles. Any breathed-in pollen, mold spores, a pet's skin flakes, or other particles that bypass the respiratory system's filters are engulfed by macrophages in airway tissues, displayed on their cell membranes, and presented as antigens to helper T cells. In most people the helper T cells "ignore" the antigens as small and insignificant. But for those with asthma, the antigens act as allergens, substances that trigger an allergic response. An activated helper T cell stimulates a B cell to proliferate into plasma cells that release antibodies. These antibodies attach to the surface of mast cells in the walls of bronchi and bronchioles. Their owner is now sensitized to the allergen and primed to react.

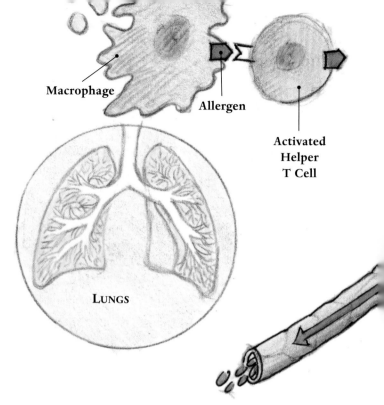

Macrophage

Allergen

Activated Helper T Cell

LUNGS

OPEN BRONCHUS

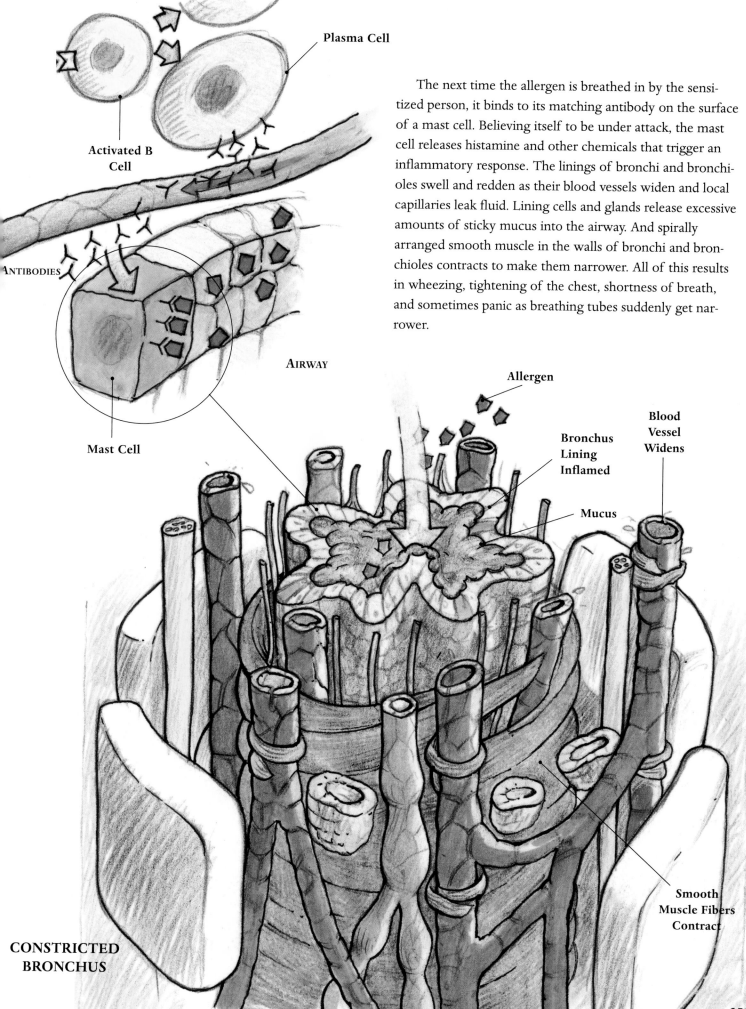

Plasma Cell

Activated B Cell

ANTIBODIES

Mast Cell

AIRWAY

The next time the allergen is breathed in by the sensitized person, it binds to its matching antibody on the surface of a mast cell. Believing itself to be under attack, the mast cell releases histamine and other chemicals that trigger an inflammatory response. The linings of bronchi and bronchioles swell and redden as their blood vessels widen and local capillaries leak fluid. Lining cells and glands release excessive amounts of sticky mucus into the airway. And spirally arranged smooth muscle in the walls of bronchi and bronchioles contracts to make them narrower. All of this results in wheezing, tightening of the chest, shortness of breath, and sometimes panic as breathing tubes suddenly get narrower.

Allergen

Bronchus Lining Inflamed

Blood Vessel Widens

Mucus

Smooth Muscle Fibers Contract

CONSTRICTED BRONCHUS

MUSCLE

DERMIS

EPIDERMIS

A Little Backup

The first time pathogens invade the body, they catch the immune system by surprise. It takes naïve—previously unchallenged—B Cells days to mount a primary response and release antibodies against the enemy. During that time we will probably experience the symptoms of infection. But, should that pathogen return, the immune system—equipped with a clear memory of its foe—is primed and ready for action. Its secondary response is a rapid knockout punch that leaves the pathogen reeling and us symptom-free.

But things don't always work out this way. Some particularly virulent pathogens establish themselves with such speed and ferocity that the immune system's primary response is just too little too late, especially in the most vulnerable—children and teens. Just decades ago, infectious diseases such as measles and whooping cough were killing children in the developed world. Today, thanks to vaccination, that threat is gone.

Vaccination craftily exploits the fact that the immune system's response to a second exposure to pathogens is much faster and more vigorous than it is the first time around. The trick then is to engineer a controlled first exposure that will not harm the child. This is done using a vaccine, a liquid that contains weakened or dead versions of a pathogen that still display those all-important antigens but do not cause the disease.

The vaccine is injected either just under the dermis or into skeletal muscle. Conveyed by lymph to a lymph node, the weakened pathogen is identified by and binds to its matching naïve B cell. Once activated by helper T cells, the B cell proliferates into plasma cells that produce antibodies. Activation of B cells also produces those all-important memory B cells, thereby priming the immune system for when, or if, the "real" version of the pathogen invades the body. Forewarned is forearmed.

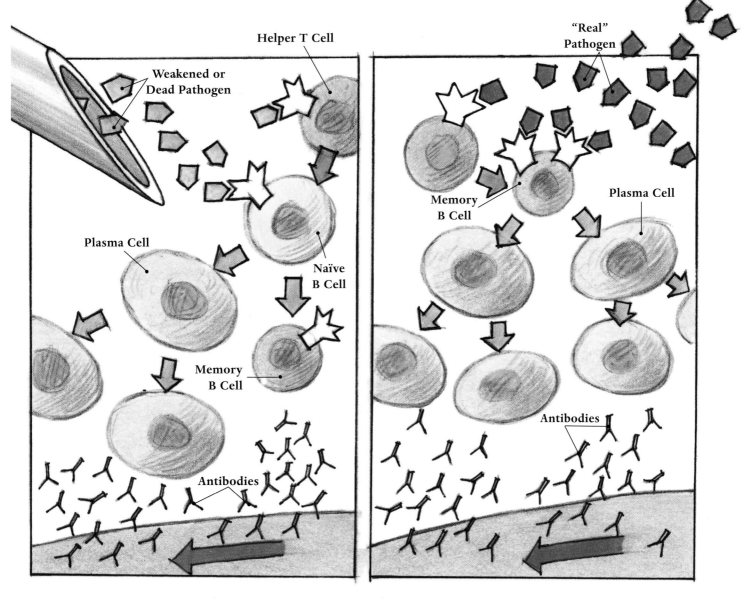

CHAPTER 6
MOVING ON

ASIDE FROM EVERYDAY WALKING AND RUNNING, we humans can crawl, leap, climb, dive, and even pirouette. We can also exploit the flexibility and dexterity of our hands and fingers to wield chopsticks, thread a needle, play the piano, or, when everything else is just too much effort, press buttons on a TV remote.

All our movements require orchestrated interaction between the two primary parts of our structural system— our bony skeleton and our muscles. With a signal from the nervous system, muscles shorten, pulling on and thereby changing the position of one or more bones. This basic sequence is behind every move we make and is often accomplished without a thought. Thanks to split-second timing and razor-sharp coordination, we can move around the dance floor with reasonable confidence or simply turn the page.

Pillars and Struts

Because of the way we usually see bones, it is easy to think of them as dry and lifeless. The fact is, they are neither. Moist, supplied with both blood and lymph vessels as well as nerves, bones are as much organs as the heart and brain.

A third of the material of which bone is built is collagen fibers. These provide flexibility and resistance to stretch. The other two-thirds are the mineral salts, mainly calcium phosphate, that make bones hard. As bones grow, both materials are woven together and arranged in such a way as to provide maximum strength while keeping the overall weight down. The result is a dense outer layer of compact bone surrounding a much lighter core of spongy bone.

Protected by a blood vessel–rich outer membrane called the periosteum, compact bone is the second-hardest tissue in the body after tooth enamel. It is made of microscopic, parallel weight-bearing pillars called osteons. Looking a little

like tiny tree trunks, osteons are constructed of concentric layers. Collagen fibers run diagonally through the layers, alternating in direction from one to the next, a feature that resists twisting forces. In the center of each osteon is a canal that carries the vessels and nerves. Between the concentric layers are cells called osteocytes that maintain the bone. Each osteocyte inhabits its own little space and communicates with other osteocytes through fine extensions to transfer oxygen, food, and wastes through gap junctions.

While osteons generally follow the length of the bone, the honeycomb of struts and plates that makes up the spongy bone is oriented along lines of stress. This arrangement reinforces the overall strength of a bone without adding much to its weight. The spaces within spongy bone are filled with either fat-storing yellow bone marrow or blood cell–manufacturing red marrow. In a long bone, marrow also fills an open cavity that runs down the center of its shaft.

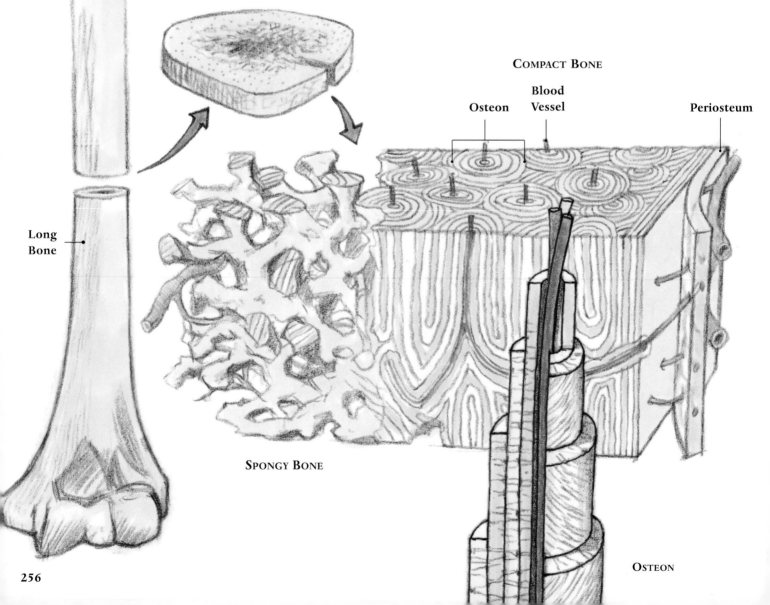

Long Bone

Spongy Bone

Compact Bone

Osteon

Blood Vessel

Periosteum

Osteon

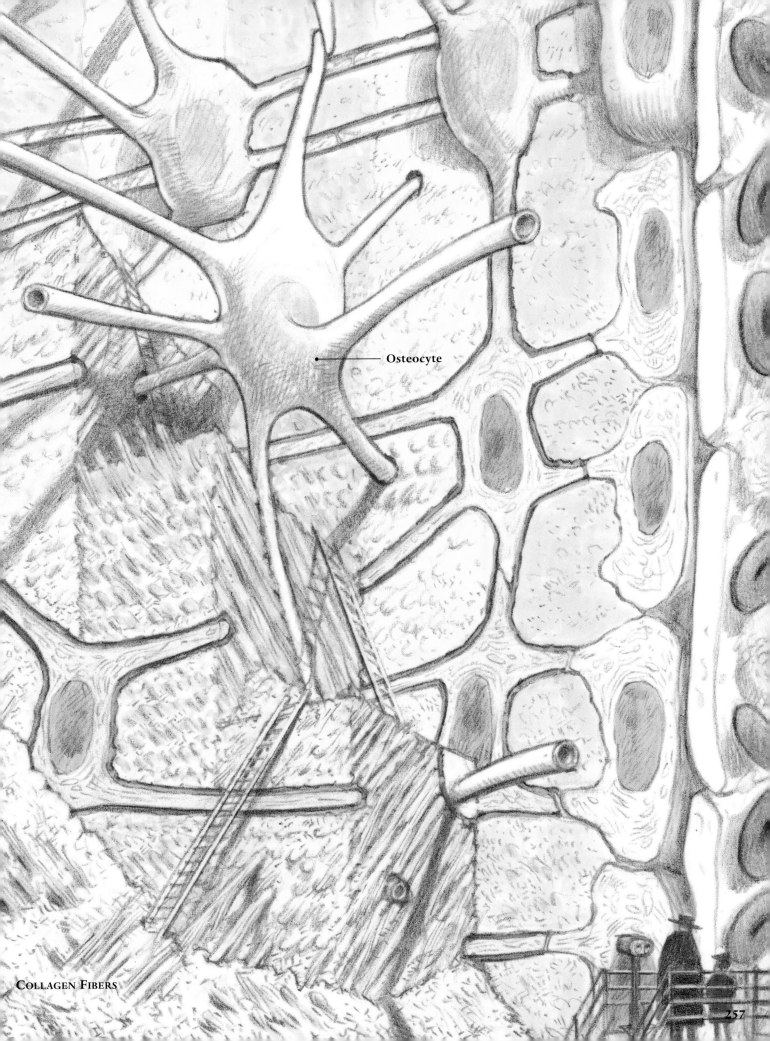

Osteocyte

COLLAGEN FIBERS

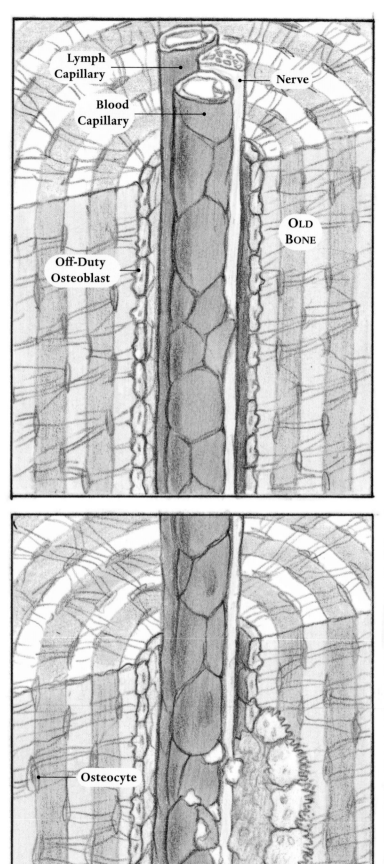

Lymph
Capillary

Nerve

Blood
Capillary

OLD
BONE

Off-Duty
Osteoblast

LET'S REMODEL

By our early twenties our bones have stopped growing, just like the rest of the body. But that doesn't mean they will remain the same forever. In fact, they are constantly being adjusted in response to the loads imposed on them when we stand or move. This process is called remodeling, and it began when we were toddlers. Stresses and strains change the shape and structure of bone where needed by galvanizing two types of bone cells into action. There are the osteoclasts, which dismantle old bone, and the osteoblasts, which form new bone. Both work together in an exercise of balanced teamwork.

Osteoclasts cling to the surface of bone and secrete enzymes that digest collagen and acids that break down calcium salts. As they burrow deep into bone, the tunnels they create are invaded by other cells, including activated osteoblasts. Working behind the osteoclast front line, these smaller bone builders deposit new bone tissue. Those that get buried in the process become the osteocytes that will maintain the new bone tissue. As work progresses, branches of blood capillaries grow down the tunnels to supply oxygen and nutrients to both the demolition and the construction crews.

Osteocyte

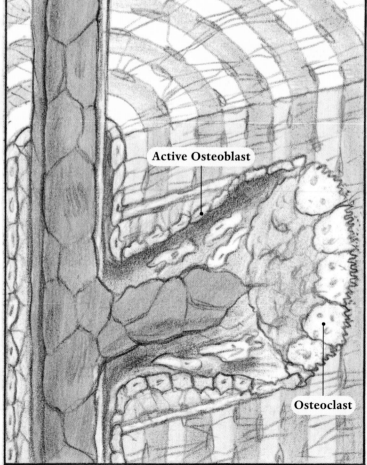

Active Osteoblast

Osteoclast

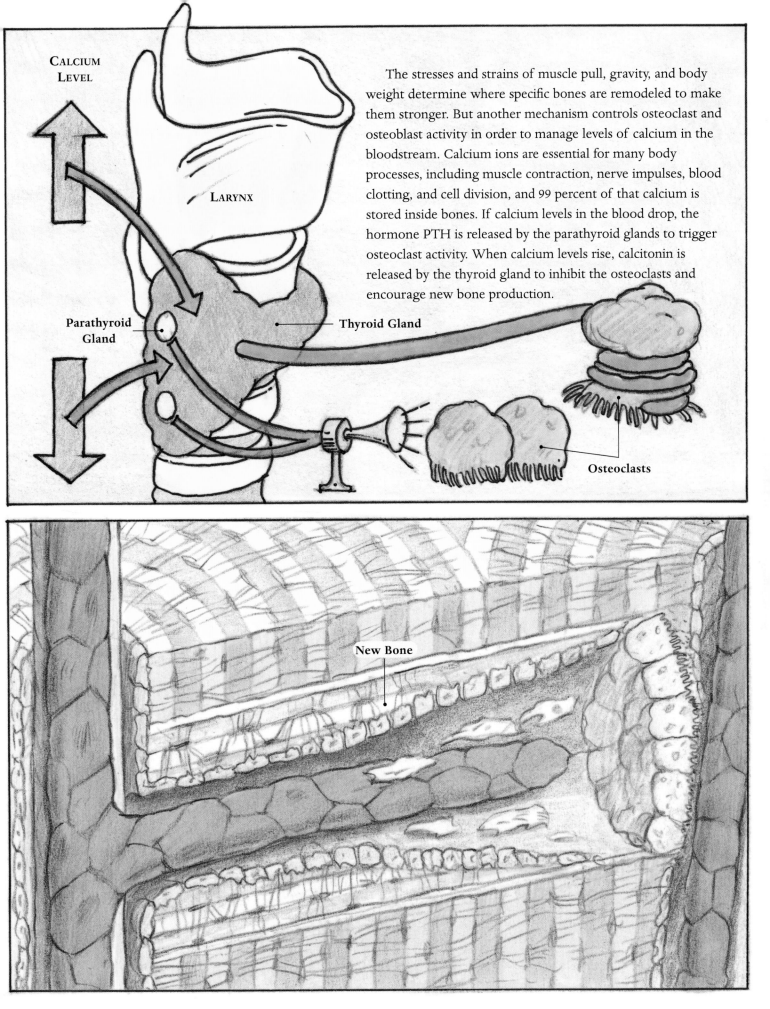

CALCIUM
LEVEL

LARYNX

Parathyroid
Gland

Thyroid Gland

Osteoclasts

The stresses and strains of muscle pull, gravity, and body weight determine where specific bones are remodeled to make them stronger. But another mechanism controls osteoclast and osteoblast activity in order to manage levels of calcium in the bloodstream. Calcium ions are essential for many body processes, including muscle contraction, nerve impulses, blood clotting, and cell division, and 99 percent of that calcium is stored inside bones. If calcium levels in the blood drop, the hormone PTH is released by the parathyroid glands to trigger osteoclast activity. When calcium levels rise, calcitonin is released by the thyroid gland to inhibit the osteoclasts and encourage new bone production.

New Bone

FIBER TO FILAMENT

Myofibril

Fiber

Nerve-Muscle
Junction

Actin Filament

Myosin
Filament

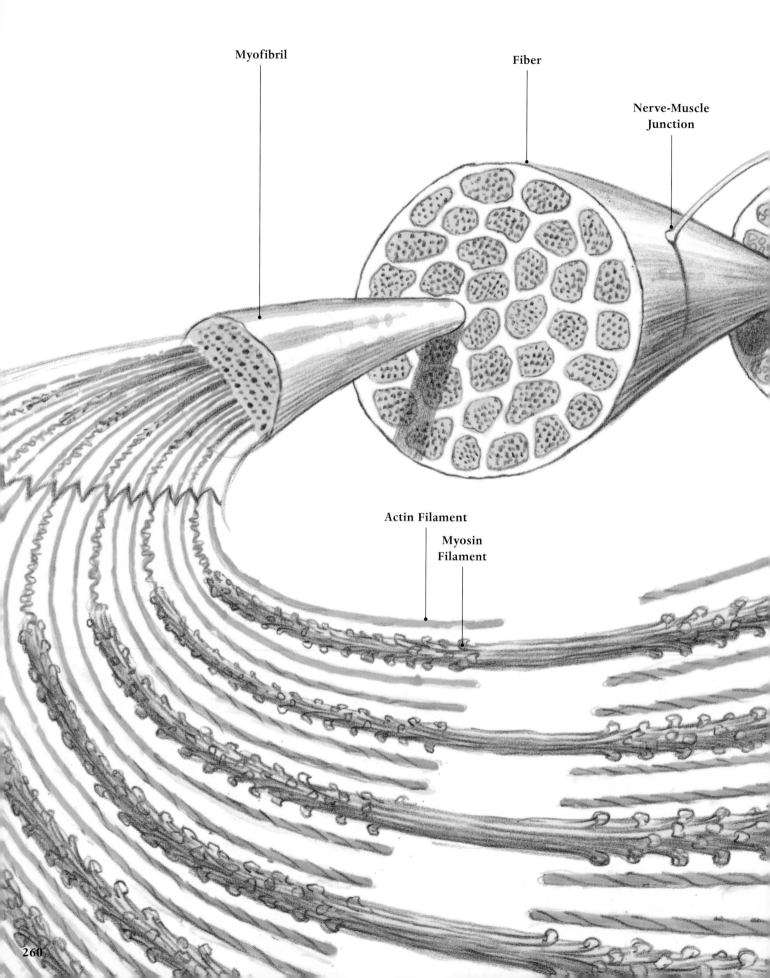

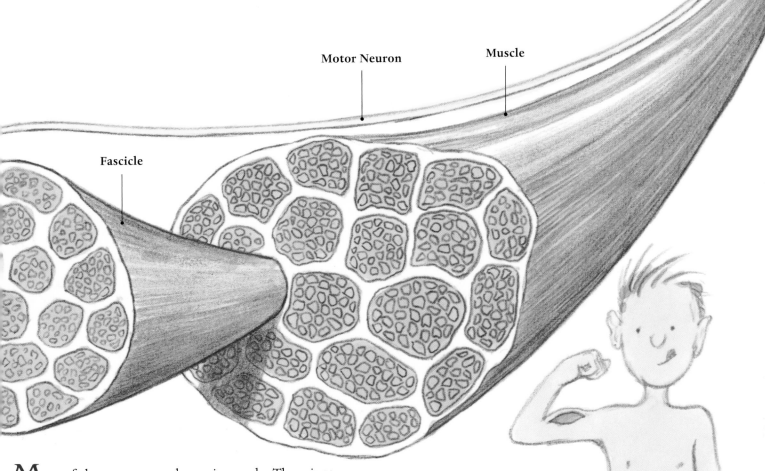

Motor Neuron

Muscle

Fascicle

Most of the meat on our bones is muscle. There is so much of it, in fact, that it can account for up to half of our body weight. Available in all shapes and sizes, muscles shorten on command, stretch when necessary, and then bounce back to their normal resting length.

Each skeletal muscle is a bundle of fascicles, and each fascicle is a bundle of specialized cells called fibers with a sophisticated internal organization that ensures maximum pulling power. Every muscle fiber is packed with parallel rods called myofibrils, and every one of these contains a parallel arrangement of filaments. The thicker filaments are built from the "motor" protein myosin, while the thinner ones are made of actin. The filaments within each myofibril are organized into short segments called sarcomeres.

It is the interaction between myosin and actin that makes muscles contract, but they don't do it spontaneously. Each fiber is "wired up" to a motor neuron through a synapse-like nerve-muscle junction. When a nerve impulse arrives from the brain or spinal cord, it makes the axon terminal release neurotransmitter molecules that trigger an electrical change in the membrane of the muscle fiber—just like a nerve impulse. Transmitted through inward folds of the membrane, this electrical change causes the interaction between actin and myosin.

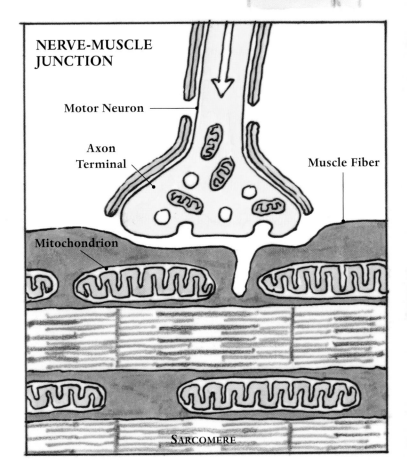

NERVE-MUSCLE JUNCTION

Motor Neuron

Axon Terminal

Muscle Fiber

Mitochondrion

SARCOMERE

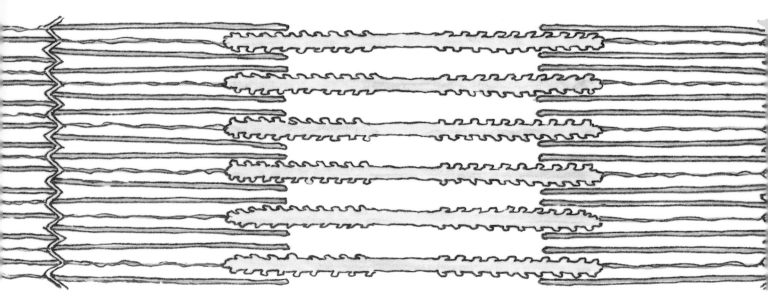

PULLING POWER

A single myosin molecule resembles two entwined golf clubs, and it takes roughly two hundred of these molecules to form a thick filament. The twin heads of each molecule are capable of attaching to special binding sites on a thin actin filament, but only if they aren't blocked by tropomyosin, a spiraling stringlike protein.

Even when a muscle is relaxed, each myosin head is already activated by the breakdown of ATP into ADP and phosphate. The energy released by this action sets the myosin head into an upright "cocked" position (1).

When a nerve impulse tells a muscle fiber to contract, calcium ions are released. These attach to special sites on the tropomyosin, moving the whole strand to one side and exposing the binding sites. Now each activated myosin head can form a cross bridge to the actin filament (2).

This action changes the shape of the heads, causing them to bend toward the center of the sarcomere, pulling the attached actin filaments with them. As this is happening, the ADP and phosphate are released from the myosin head for recycling (3).

Once this entire sequence is complete, a new ATP molecule binds to the myosin heads, causing them to loosen their grip on the actin-binding sites so that the cross bridges detach (4). Once again, the ATP is broken down into ADP and phosphate, and the myosin head is reactivated. It is now ready to bind to the next site and continue its "walk" along the actin filament (5).

It is the repeated making and breaking of cross bridges that shortens the sarcomeres and causes the muscle to contract. When nerve impulses cease, calcium ions are removed, tropomyosin once again blocks the binding sites, and the muscle relaxes.

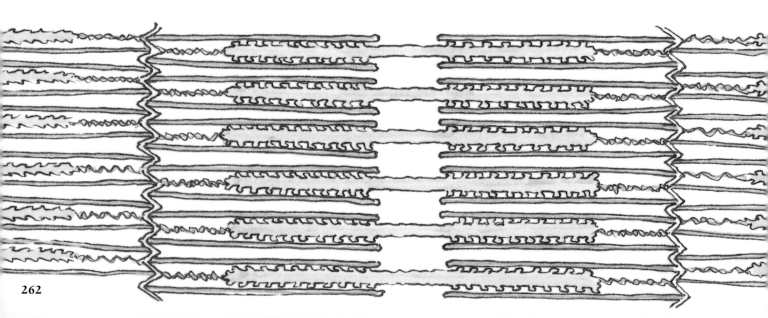

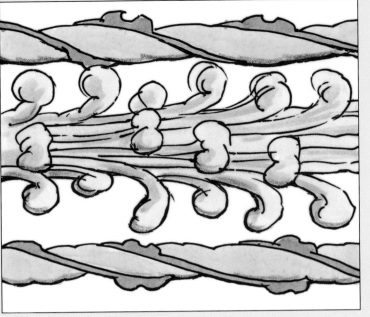

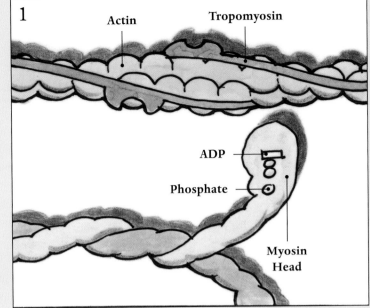

1 — Actin, Tropomyosin, ADP, Phosphate, Myosin Head

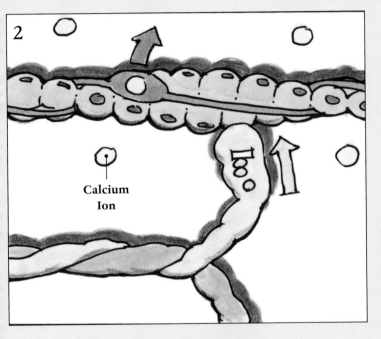

2 — Calcium Ion

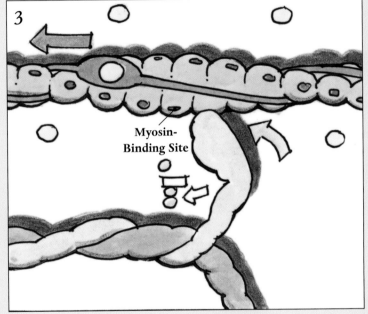

3 — Myosin-Binding Site

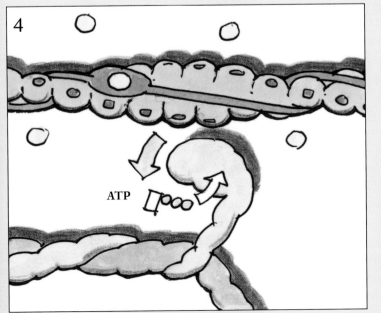

4 — ATP

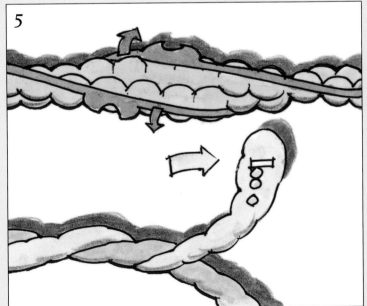

5

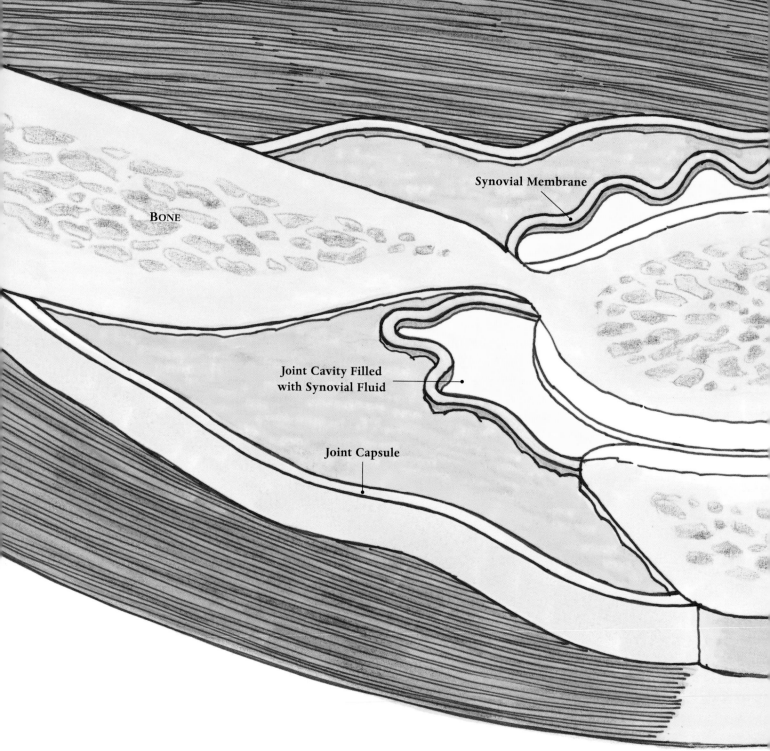

Synovial Membrane

BONE

**Joint Cavity Filled
with Synovial Fluid**

Joint Capsule

SMOOTH MOVES

Joints are formed where two or more bones meet. As well as providing varying amounts of stability, most joints are built to resist crushing and tearing by allowing one bone to move against another with less friction than two ice cubes sliding over each other. Stability depends in part on a tough, fibrous capsule that encloses each joint and holds the bones together. Most joint capsules are reinforced by collagen-rich connective tissue straps called ligaments.

Inside the joint, the ends of the bone are capped with a special glassy cartilage and separated by a narrow space. The surrounding capsule is lined with a membrane that secretes oily synovial fluid into this cavity. As thick as raw egg white, this fluid makes cartilage even more slippery than it is already. Between movements the fluid soaks into the cartilage. During movements, it is forced out, like water squeezed from a sponge, to lubricate the smooth cartilage surface.

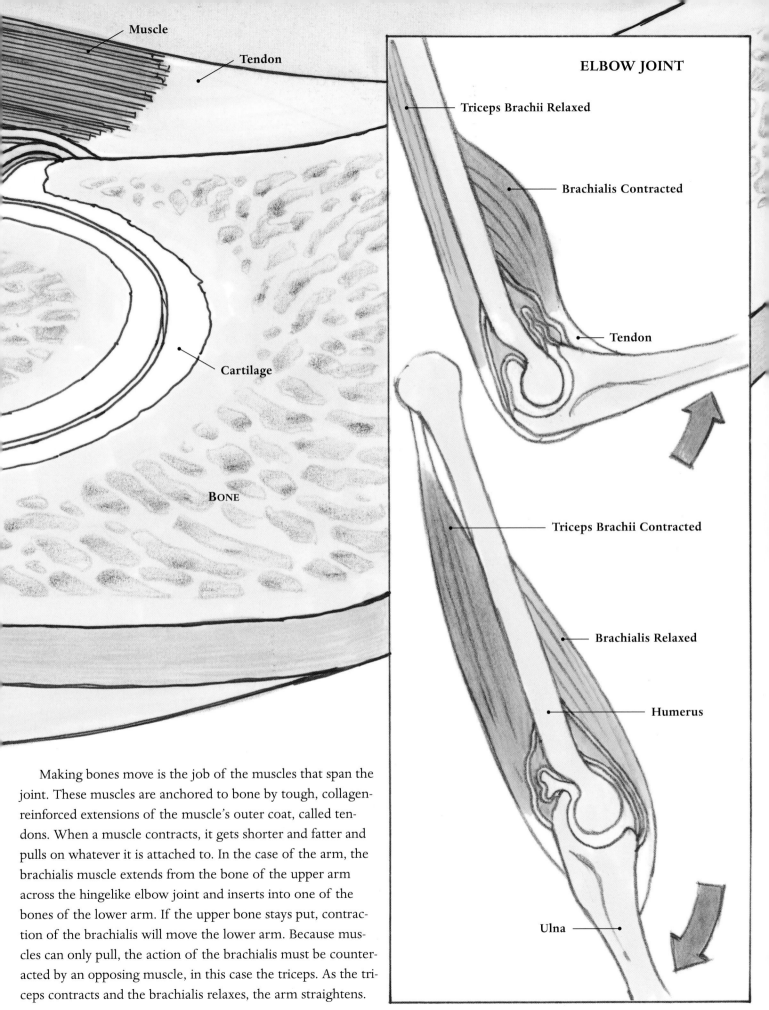

Muscle

Tendon

Cartilage

BONE

ELBOW JOINT

Triceps Brachii Relaxed

Brachialis Contracted

Tendon

Triceps Brachii Contracted

Brachialis Relaxed

Humerus

Ulna

Making bones move is the job of the muscles that span the joint. These muscles are anchored to bone by tough, collagen-reinforced extensions of the muscle's outer coat, called tendons. When a muscle contracts, it gets shorter and fatter and pulls on whatever it is attached to. In the case of the arm, the brachialis muscle extends from the bone of the upper arm across the hingelike elbow joint and inserts into one of the bones of the lower arm. If the upper bone stays put, contraction of the brachialis will move the lower arm. Because muscles can only pull, the action of the brachialis must be counteracted by an opposing muscle, in this case the triceps. As the triceps contracts and the brachialis relaxes, the arm straightens.

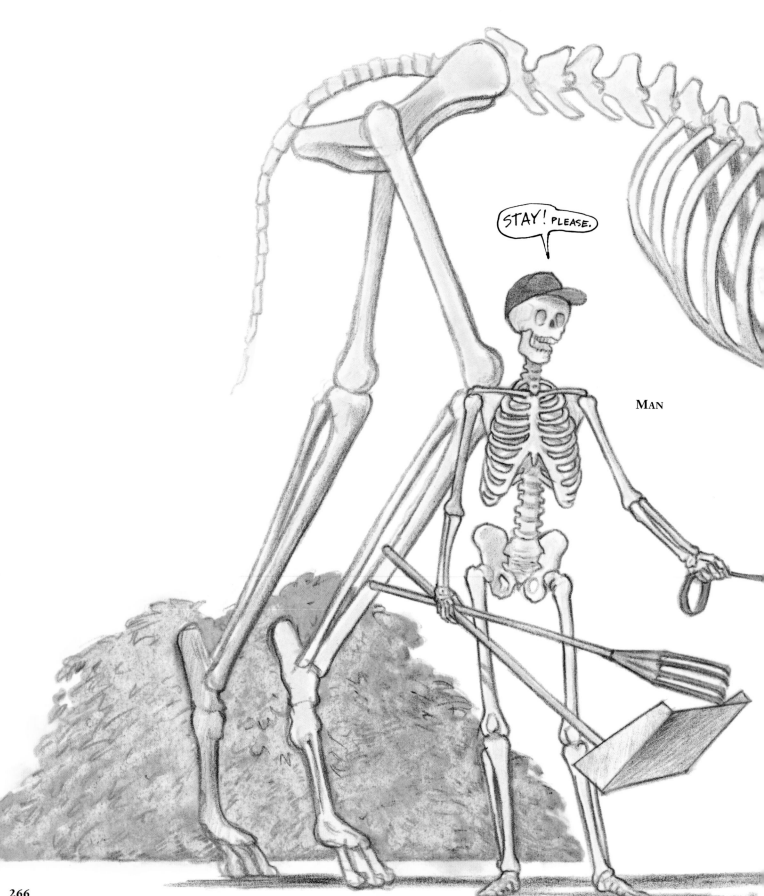

BEAST

UPRIGHT CITIZEN

Most mammals, including man's best friend, share the same basic type of supportive skeletal framework. A more or less horizontal backbone, tail at one end, head at the other, is attached by hip and shoulder girdles to four movable supporting limbs, two behind and two in front. Slung from the backbone are the body's main organs—some within a protective rib cage. But we humans stand out from and in fact stand above much of the rest of the mammalian crowd.

At some point in time our ancient ancestors took to walking on two legs rather than four. Being upright introduced new forces and postures to which the tinkering hand of evolution responded with many changes to the skeleton. No longer horizontal, the backbone became a curved, weight-bearing column topped by the skull. To provide better support when standing and pushing off when walking, platform feet developed at the ends of our strong legs. Our former front limbs gave up some of their sturdiness to become more flexible arms, hands, and fingers, allowing us to reach out and grasp objects and to pick up after our pets.

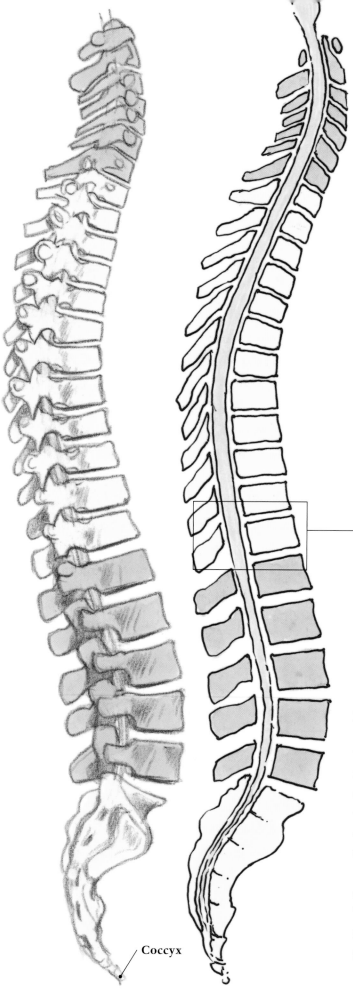

Coccyx

CURVY COLUMN

A precarious-looking stack of twenty-six oddly shaped bones called vertebrae supports the head and trunk. But unlike your average column, the vertebral column, or spine, is neither solid nor inflexible. It isn't even straight. The vertebrae form four slightly curved sections, each with its own job to do. Cervical vertebrae support the head and neck, while the thoracic vertebrae connect with the ribs. The heavy-duty lumbar vertebrae of the lower back bear most of the body's weight, while the fused vertebrae of the sacrum attach the backbone to the pelvis. The tiny coccyx is just a reminder of the time when our ancestors had tails.

Working together, the four curves confer strength as well as a natural springiness to the backbone as it positions and balances the weight of the head and trunk directly over the legs.

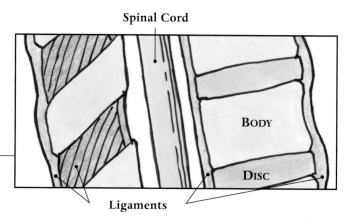

Spinal Cord

BODY

DISC

Ligaments

Although each vertebra has slightly different proportions, all but one have a chunky, weight-bearing body and a vertebral arch that surrounds and protects the delicate spinal cord. Limited movement between one vertebra and the next is made possible by the insertion of a cartilage disc that is tough around the outside but squishy in the center. Added together these small movements allow us to bend, twist, or even perform a back flip. Intervertebral discs also act as shock absorbers when we walk, run, or jump. Interlocking projections off the vertebral arches control movement between adjacent vertebrae. Cartilage-covered facets between these projections are bathed in synovial fluid to reduce friction.

Holding all the pieces together and preventing too much movement in any one direction are a variety of ligaments. They run up the front and back of the column and between the projections. Back muscles also attached to these projections reinforce the ligaments and provide movement.

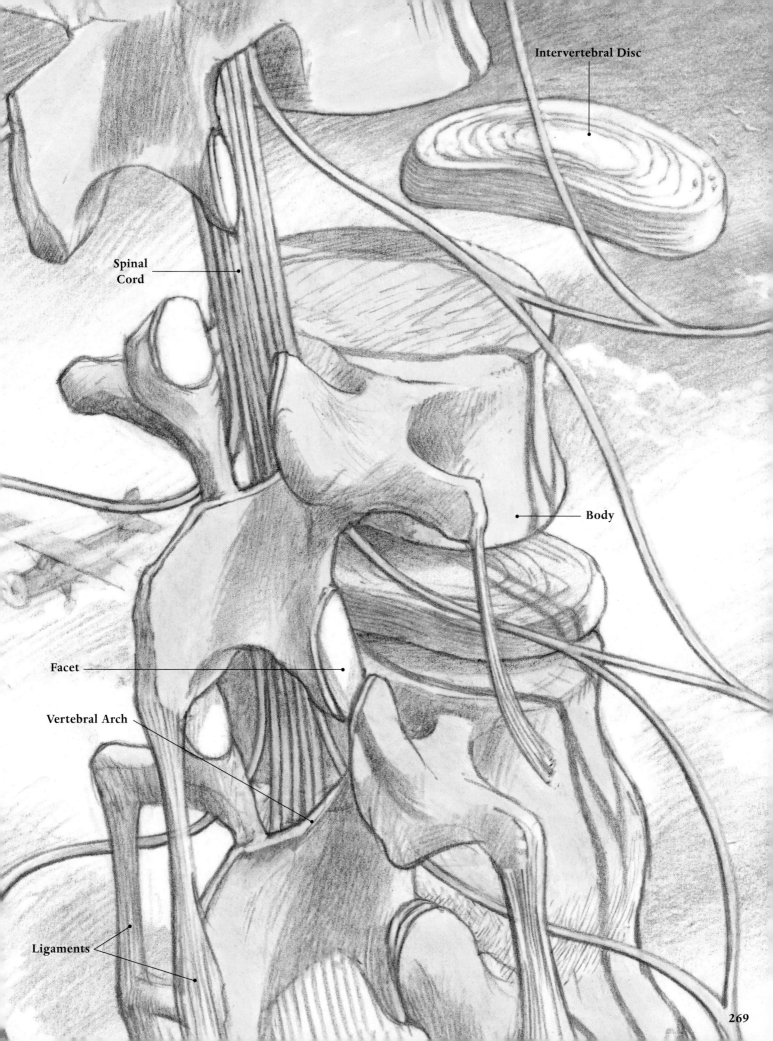

Intervertebral Disc

Spinal
Cord

Body

Facet

Vertebral Arch

Ligaments

269

Occipital Bone

Opening for Spinal Cord

Left Parietal Bone

Left Temporal Bone

Atlas

HEADQUARTERS

Cradled by the atlas on top of the spine are the twenty-two bones that make up the skull. Except for the lower jaw or mandible, which has to move when we eat, drink, or speak, they are all locked together in early childhood and become completely fused by the time we are adults, giving the entire skull great strength. Tiny openings for nerves and blood vessels pepper the structure, but the largest opening, found at the base of the skull, allows the connection between the brain and spinal cord.

The skull has two main parts. The first is the cranium, which is constructed from eight bones and which surrounds, supports, and protects the brain. Its "dome" is made from four thin, curved plates and two temporal bones, which also contain the organs of hearing and balance. The frontal bone forms the forehead; two parietal bones, along with the temporal bones, make up the sides and top of the cranium; and the occipital bone provides the back and base. The spinal cord enters the skull through an opening in the occipital bone. The remaining pieces of the cranium are the butterfly-shaped sphenoid bone, which connects with all the other cranial bones, and the equally complex ethmoid bone, which forms part of the nasal cavity.

The second part of the skull consists of the fourteen bones that form the face and jaws. Two zygomatic bones contour the cheek, while two fused maxillae form the upper jaw, which, like the mandible, sports a row of teeth. The remaining facial bones combine with cranial bones to build the nasal cavity and eye sockets. Small muscles anchored to both facial and cranial bones pull the skin to produce the tiny yet precise movements that can turn a happy smile into a gloomy grimace.

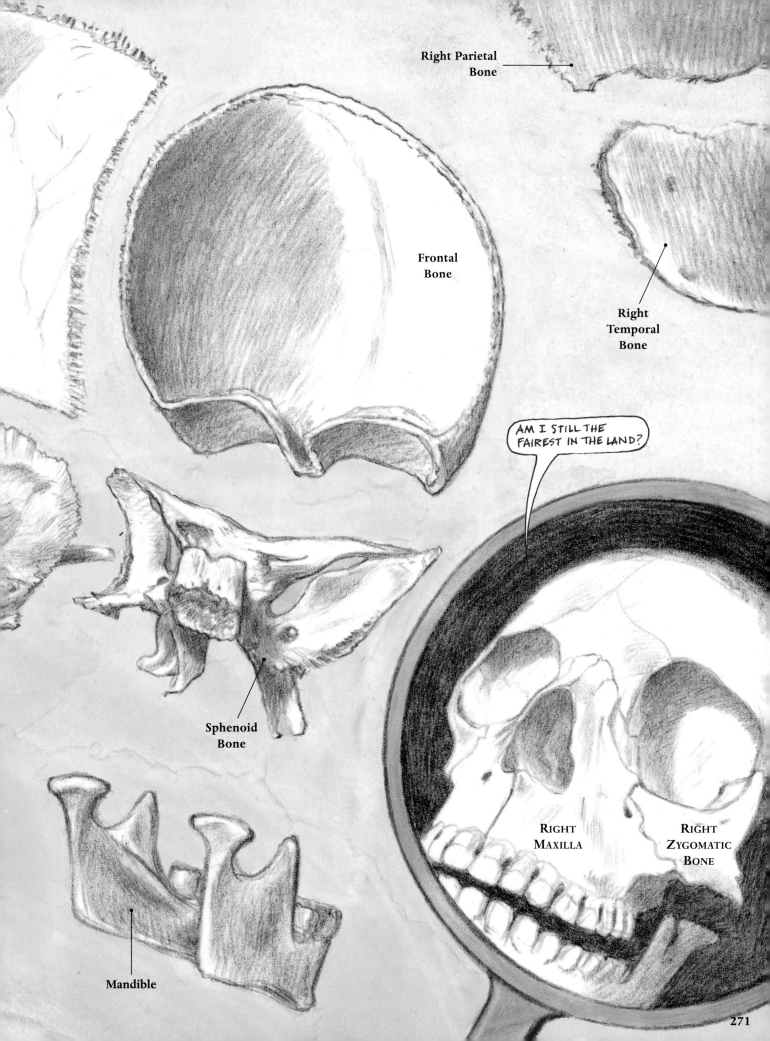

271

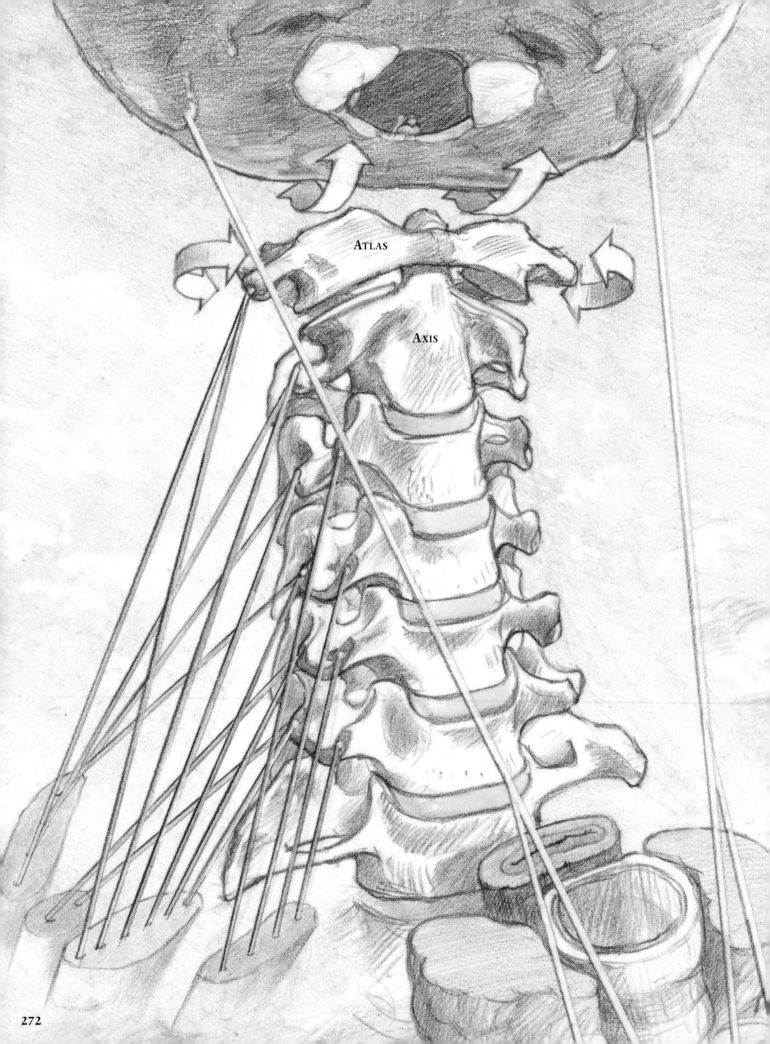

ATLAS

AXIS

Yes and No

The average head is a tad smaller than a soccer ball but weighs ten times as much. It's supported by and perched squarely on top of the cervical vertebrae. To keep the head more or less balanced above the hips and feet, both it and the neck rely on various ligaments and muscles for stability. At the same time, however, the head must be free to make controlled movements so that our eyes can survey the world around us and we can indicate yes or no with a mere nod or shake of the head.

These simple movements are made possible by the two uppermost cervical vertebrae. The atlas, which stands at the very top of the backbone, cradles the skull and allows it to tilt backwards and forward. Next in line is the axis. It supports the atlas and permits it to rotate from side to side. Both atlas and axis are different from each other and from all the other vertebrae. The atlas is a ring of bone without a vertebral body, while the small body of the axis extends into a vertical projection against which the atlas moves. There is also no intervertebral disc between them. Below the axis, normal bending and twisting movements are possible.

Making these movements happen are a number of overlapping muscles. They originate either from the spine or from the shoulder bones and pull either on the skull or on the cervical vertebrae.

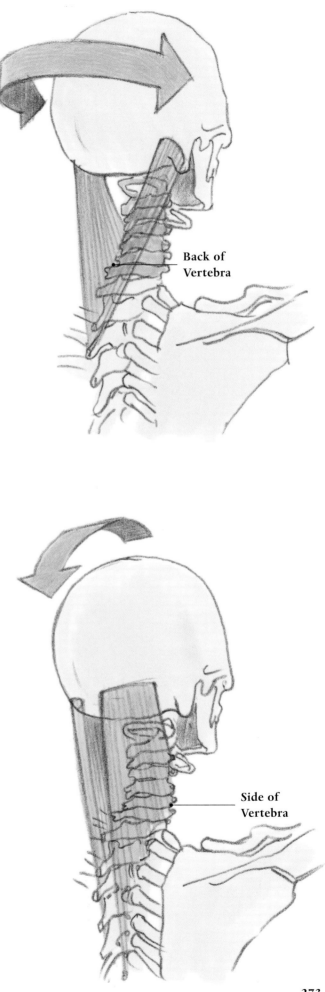

Back of Vertebra

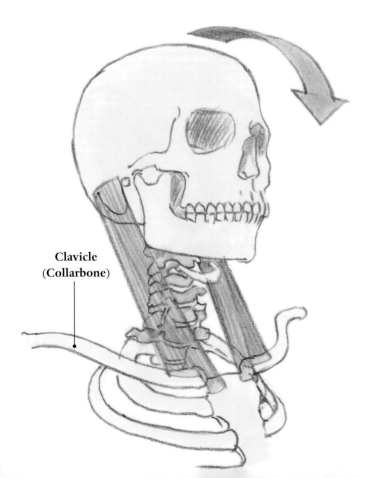

Clavicle (Collarbone)

Side of Vertebra

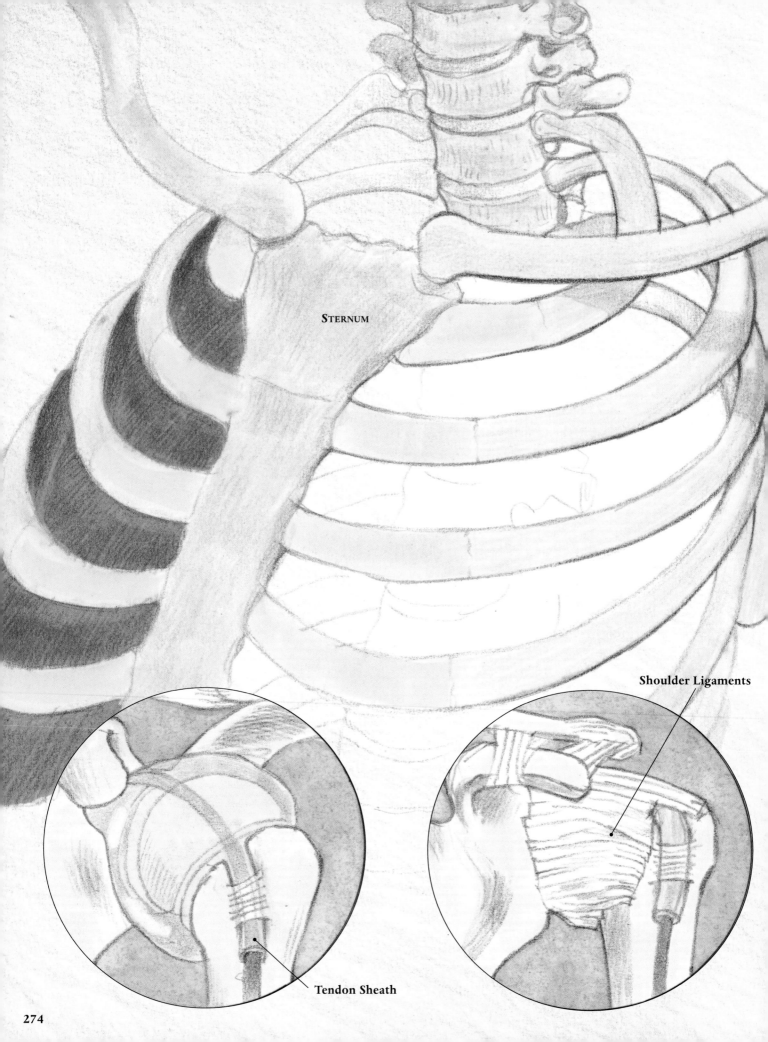

STERNUM

Shoulder Ligaments

Tendon Sheath

A Shoulder to Hang From

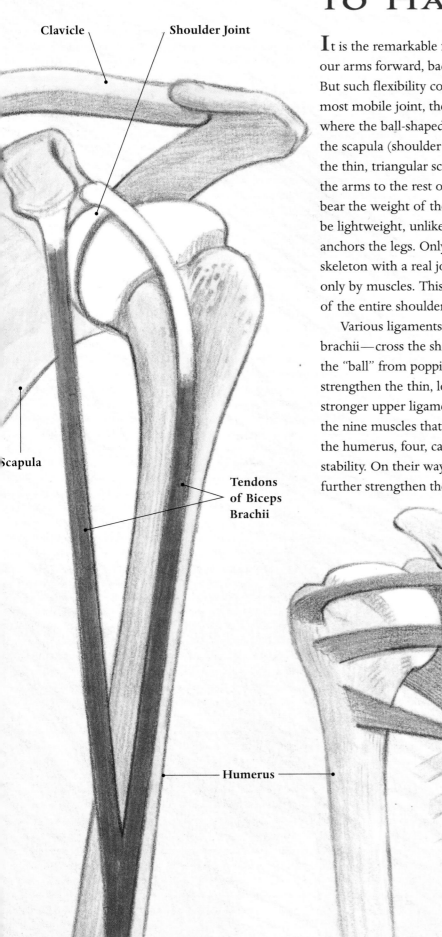

Clavicle

Shoulder Joint

Scapula

Tendons of Biceps Brachii

Humerus

It is the remarkable freedom of the shoulder that allows us to swing our arms forward, backwards, out to the side, or around in a circle. But such flexibility comes with a price. In addition to being the body's most mobile joint, the shoulder is also its least stable. It is formed where the ball-shaped end of the humerus fits into a shallow cup of the scapula (shoulder blade). Along with the clavicles (collarbones), the thin, triangular scapulae form the two pectoral girdles that attach the arms to the rest of the body. Because they don't usually have to bear the weight of the body when we move, the pectoral girdles can be lightweight, unlike the solid, unyielding pelvic girdle, which anchors the legs. Only the clavicle is attached to the main axis of the skeleton with a real joint. Both scapulae move freely, held in place only by muscles. This permits great mobility not just of the arm but of the entire shoulder.

Various ligaments and tendons—including a tendon of the biceps brachii—cross the shoulder joint to make it more stable and prevent the "ball" from popping out of its "socket." Three weak ligaments strengthen the thin, loose capsule surrounding the joint, while stronger upper ligaments carry some of the weight of the arm. Of the nine muscles that originate on the pectoral girdle and insert on the humerus, four, called the rotator cuff muscles, specialize in joint stability. On their way to the humerus, their tendons merge with and further strengthen the capsule.

ROTATOR CUFF

Scapula

275

NEWTON'S APPLE

The arm is made up of three long bones. The humerus, which runs from shoulder to elbow, serves the upper arm. The radius and ulna, which run from elbow to hand, serve the forearm. The all-round suppleness of the shoulder combined with the various degrees of motion allowed by the thirty or so joints of the arm and hand allows the upper limb to perform an incredible range of movements. But because the muscles of the upper limb (like all muscles)

Humerus

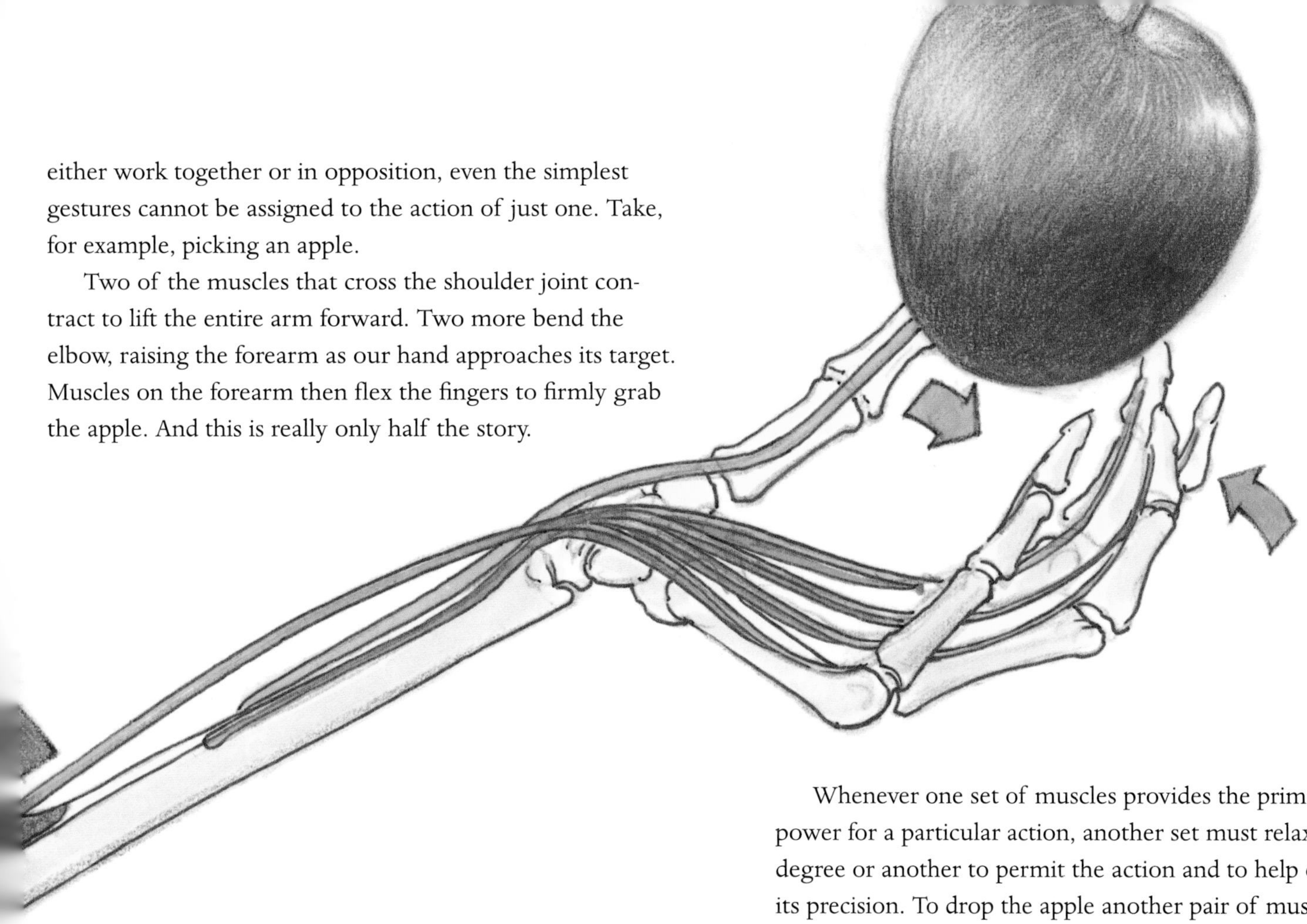

either work together or in opposition, even the simplest gestures cannot be assigned to the action of just one. Take, for example, picking an apple.

Two of the muscles that cross the shoulder joint contract to lift the entire arm forward. Two more bend the elbow, raising the forearm as our hand approaches its target. Muscles on the forearm then flex the fingers to firmly grab the apple. And this is really only half the story.

Whenever one set of muscles provides the primary power for a particular action, another set must relax to one degree or another to permit the action and to help ensure its precision. To drop the apple another pair of muscles rotates the radius around the ulna so that our hand is facing downward. Muscles on the back of the forearm now take over, extending our fingers and allowing the apple to fall.

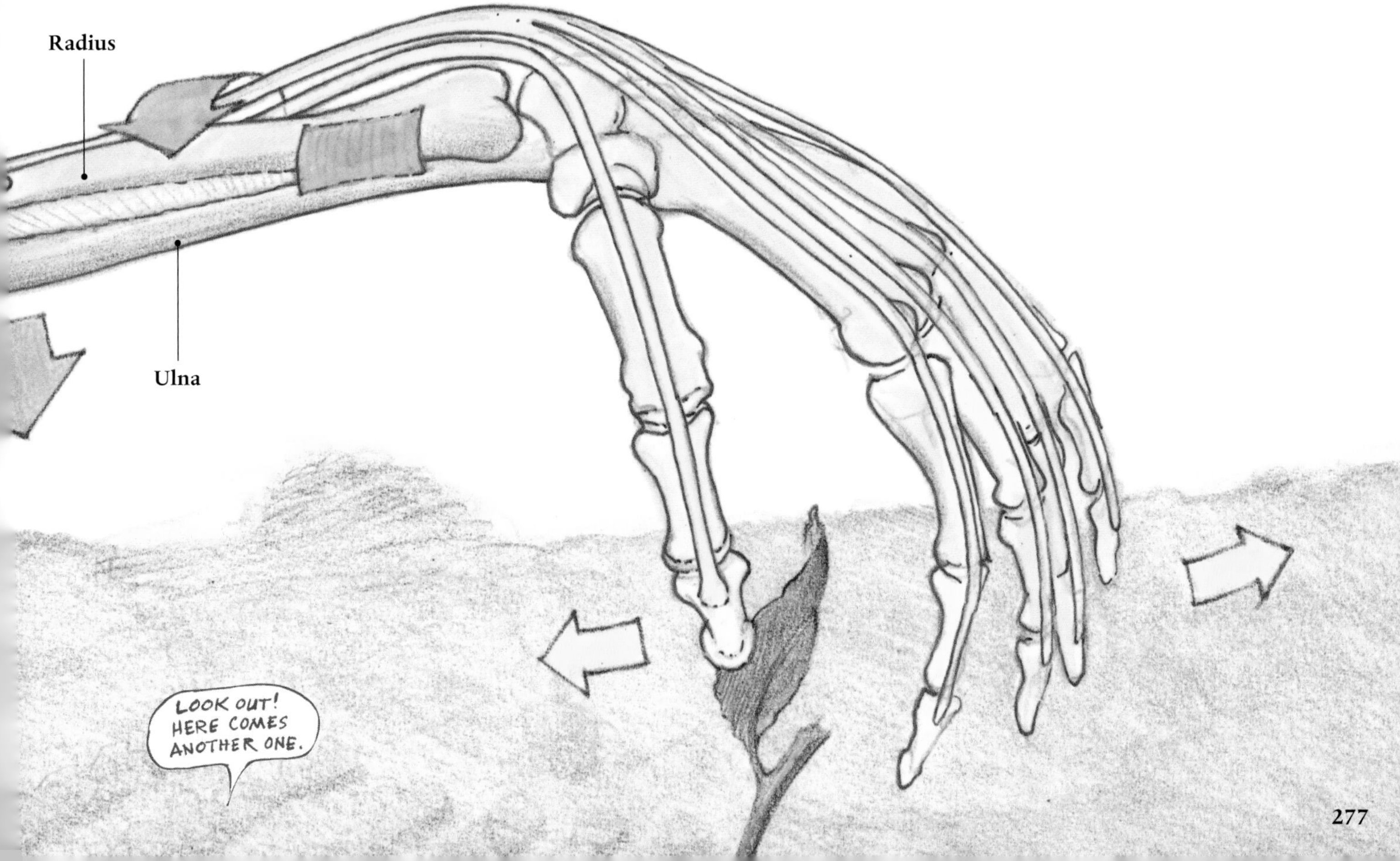

Radius

Ulna

LOOK OUT! HERE COMES ANOTHER ONE.

Radius

Saddle
Joint

Carpal

Ulna

FLEXING FINGERS

The hand begins with the wrist, a collection of eight closely fitting bones called carpals, and the palm, comprising five metacarpals. The synovial joints between these bones allow some flexibility. Greater but still limited freedom is permitted by the hinge joints between the phalanges that make up the fingers and thumb. Most of the dexterity of the fingers can be attributed to the movement in the knuckle joints between phalanges and metacarpals. It is the combination of all the joints that allows fingers to curl into the palm or to extend fully, or to splay outward. But whether threading a needle or gripping a rope, hands owe their greatest versatility to the orientation and operation of the opposable thumb. A flexible saddle joint at its base allows it to cross in front of the palm, and to touch, or oppose, the tips of the other fingers.

Metacarpal

If most of the muscles that operate the fingers were located in the hands themselves, we'd be wearing "mittens" year round instead of sporting the remarkable implements that are such a trademark of the human species. To eliminate the unwieldy bulkiness, muscles that flex the wrist and fingers are located primarily in the front of the forearm, while extensors are located at the back. Both sets of muscles taper into long, thin tendons that extend across the wrist to the various finger bones. They pass over the wrist through a tunnel with sides defined by carpal bones and with a roof formed by a ligament band that prevents the tendons from bulging out during contraction. There are some small muscles in the palm to control more precise actions, including those all-important movements of the thumb. The forearm muscles are responsible for more powerful operations such as gripping.

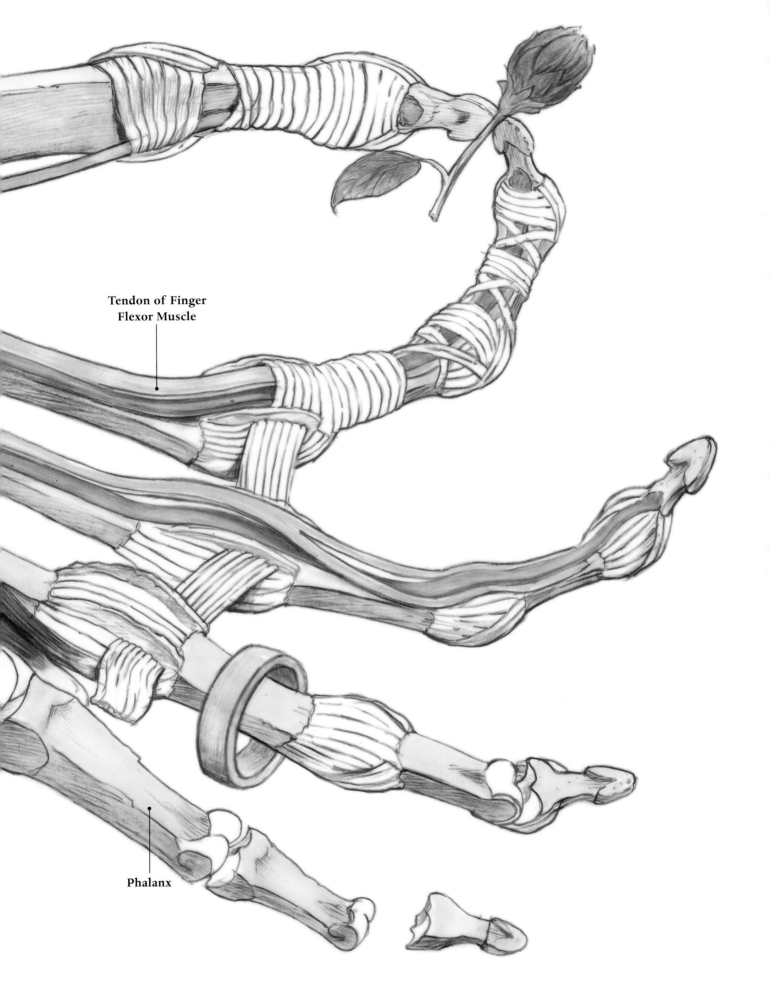

Tendon of Finger Flexor Muscle

Phalanx

A STURDY BASE

Put your hands on your hips and you'll feel the "wings" of your pelvic girdle. As might be expected, with the job of transmitting the upper body's weight to the legs and keeping them far enough apart so we can balance that weight, this part of our skeleton is big, strong, and rigid.

The complete girdle, commonly known as the bony pelvis, is built from two hip bones—each made up of three bones that have become fused together—and the sacrum. The hip bones are connected at the front by a cartilage joint that allows very little movement. At the back, they interlock with the upper portion of the sacrum through synovial joints, the gliding movements of which are inhibited by some of the strongest ligaments in the body.

In addition to serving as the critical link between backbone and legs, this basin-shaped ring of bones provides anchorage for various muscles, including those that keep us upright. It also surrounds, supports, and protects organs such as the bladder. The thick muscular floor that spans the lower opening of the pelvis prevents the organs from being pushed down and out by everyday contractions and gravity.

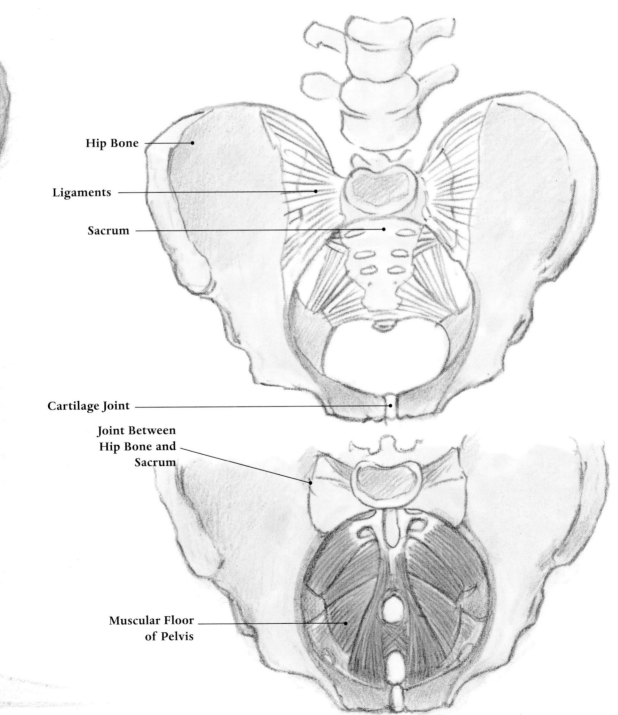

Hip Bone

Ligaments

Sacrum

Cartilage Joint

Joint Between
Hip Bone and
Sacrum

Muscular Floor
of Pelvis

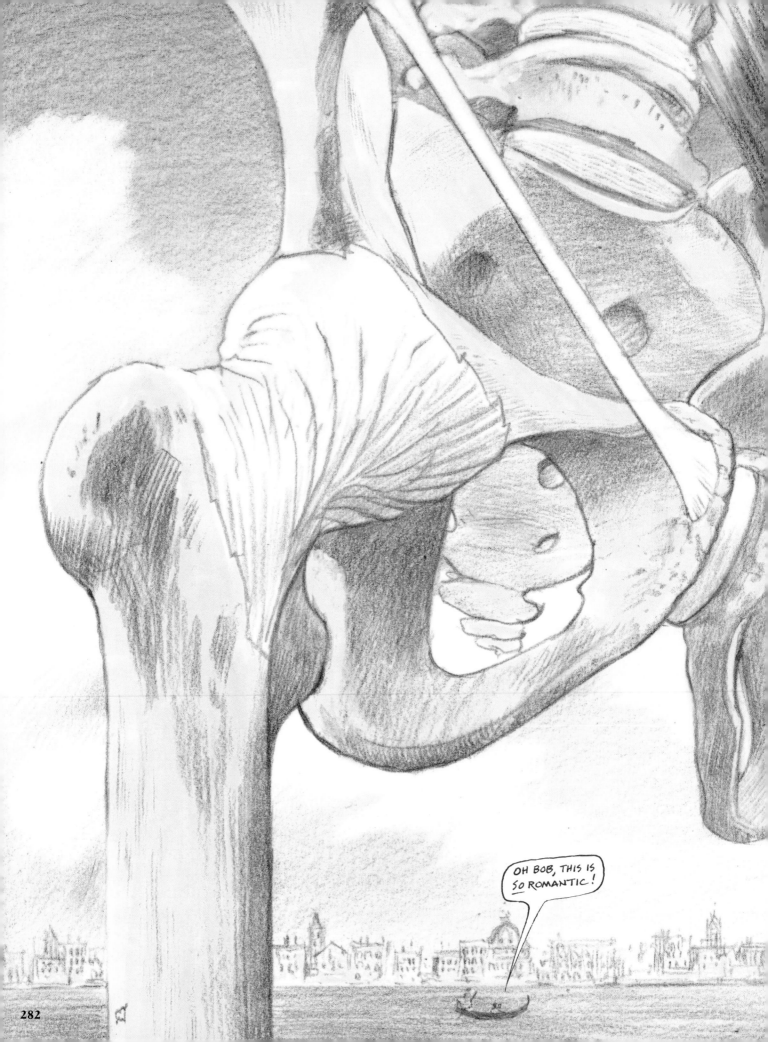

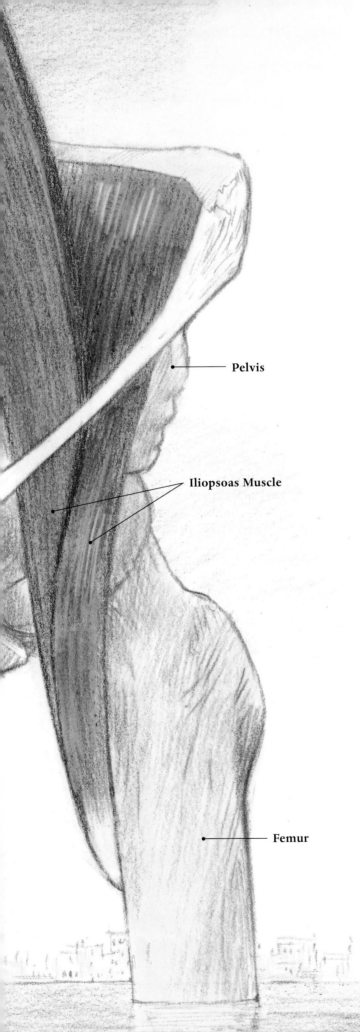

Pelvis

Iliopsoas Muscle

Femur

BRIDGE OF THIGHS

To support and move the body takes strength and power. The pelvis and thighbones, along with the muscles, tendons, and ligaments that connect them, have plenty of both. Deep sockets scooped into the outer sides of both hip bones enclose the ball-shaped heads of the thighbones. Both joints are reinforced by ligaments as well as by the tendons and muscles that pass across them. While the hip joint obviously has less freedom of movement than the shoulder joint, fortunately for us when we stand, walk, run, or jump, it has much more stability.

The head of the thighbone, or femur, and the angled neck that attaches it to the shaft consist largely of spongy bone. The struts that make up this bone are aligned to carry forces from the joint downward into the femur's shaft, which through its surrounding compact bone resists vertical compression.

Some of the body's mightiest muscles are anchored to the pelvis and reach down to the femurs and beyond. In front the iliopsoas flexes the leg at the hip, while the quadriceps femoris tugs on the tibia to straighten the leg. At the rear the buttock muscles—the body's biggest—launch us upward when we rise from sitting or go climbing, while the hamstrings both straighten the leg at the hip and bend it at the knee.

The other essential function of hips arises during childbirth. To accommodate the passage of a wide-shouldered, big-brained baby, a woman's pelvis, though not as strong as a man's, is broader and shallower and offers a bigger central opening.

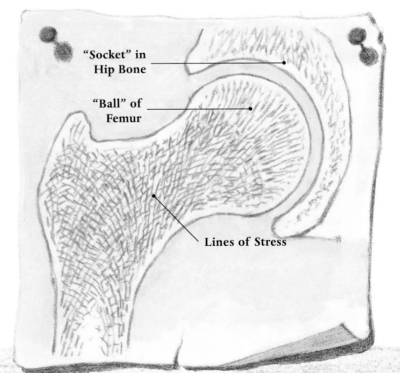

"Socket" in Hip Bone

"Ball" of Femur

Lines of Stress

BEND AND LOCK

When we stand, walk, or run, our knees have to withstand the full downward force of the body's weight. At the same time, this joint between the femur (thighbone) and tibia (shinbone) has to flex and extend—and rotate a little—to allow us to move. It is hardly surprising then that the knee is the largest and most complex joint in the body.

The convex projections at the end of the femur form hingelike joints with the slightly concave surfaces on top of the tibia. A C-shaped cartilage gives greater depth to each concave surface to prevent side-to-side slippage by the femur. Another joint exists between the femur and the kneecap bone. This small bone glides across the femur's head during movement and helps protect the knee joint.

Extra strength and stability are gained by an array of ligaments, including the patellar ligament, which is a continuation of the tendon of the powerful thigh muscle that straightens the knees. Other external ligaments "fill the gaps" in the patchy joint capsule and prevent the knee from bending forward in the "wrong" direction. Inside the joint, the X-shaped cruciate ligaments stop the surfaces of the femur and tibia from slipping backwards and forward. The tendons of muscles that cross the knee joint also provide reinforcement.

The knee joint has an extra feature—a built-in energy-saving device. As we stand up, putting all our weight on our knees, the femurs twist inward on the tibias, tightening the ligaments and compressing the C-shaped cartilages. This locks the knee into a rigid structure and provides steady support. Now we can stand without having to waste much energy on muscle contraction. To test how useful and effective this feature is, see how long you can stand with your knees bent.

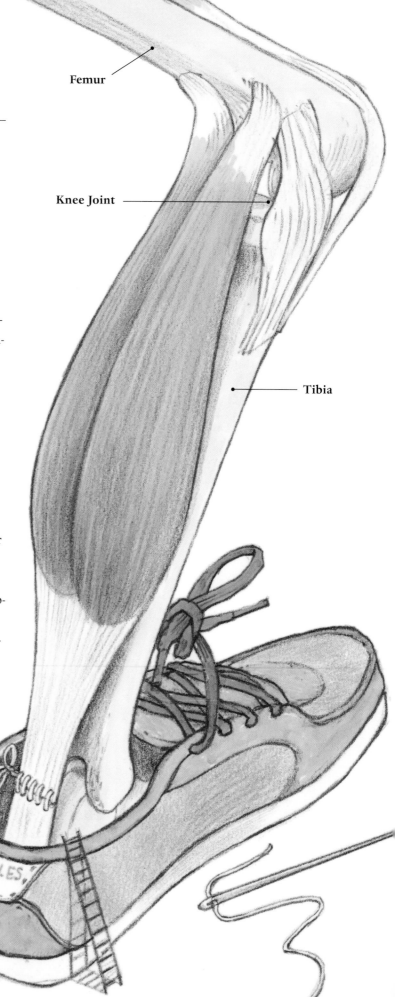

Femur

Knee Joint

Tibia

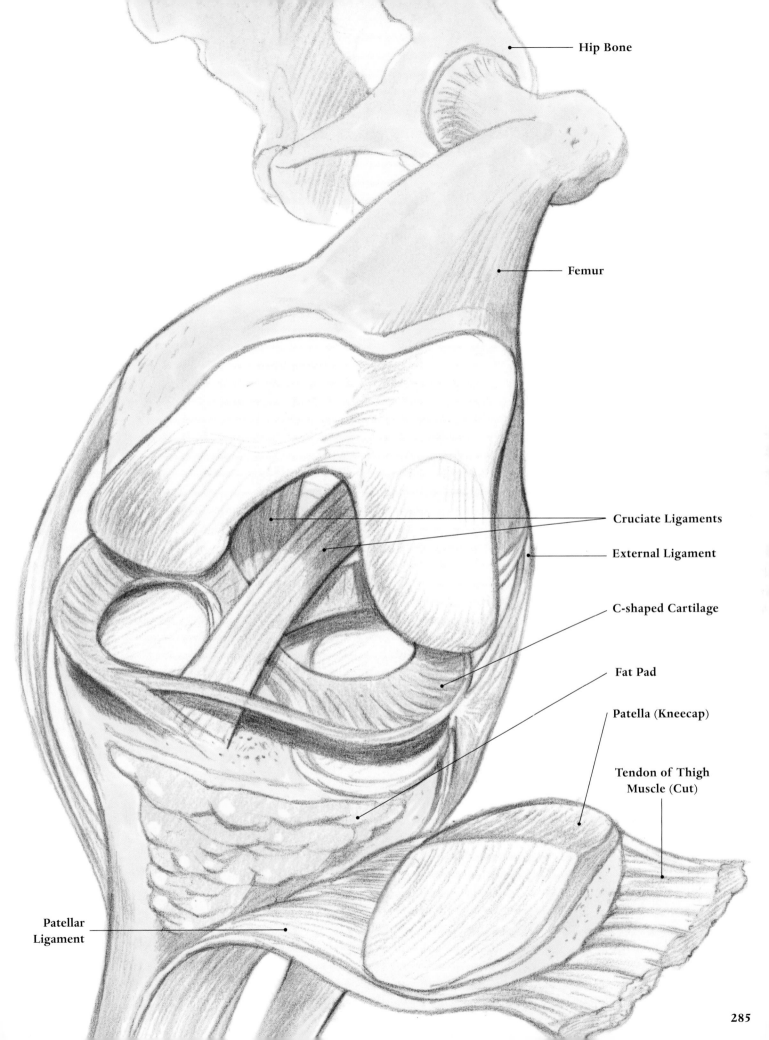

Hip Bone

Femur

Cruciate Ligaments

External Ligament

C-shaped Cartilage

Fat Pad

Patella (Kneecap)

Tendon of Thigh
Muscle (Cut)

Patellar
Ligament

Spread the Weight

Unlike our versatile chimp relatives, we can't use both hands and feet to easily grasp objects. Our feet are primarily for walking or running, or, if absolutely necessary, dancing. These two mobile platforms are hinged from the ends of the two bones of the lower leg, the tibia and fibula. Muscles attached to the back and front of the lower leg pull on these platforms to support our weight, stop us from falling over, propel the body forward when we move, and absorb the shocks along the way.

Superficially, the bony infrastructures of feet and hands look very similar, with twenty-six bones in the former and twenty-seven in the latter. The most obvious differences are found between the heel end of the foot and the wrist. In the foot, seven tarsal bones (as opposed to eight carpals in the wrist) include the chunky talus, which forms a hinge joint with the shinbones, and beneath it the even bigger heel bone, through which body weight is thrust earthward. The five long metatarsal (sole) bones, more parallel than the diverging metacarpals of the hand, are restrained and stabilized by ligaments that stop them from splaying outward. The phalanges of the foot are far shorter than those of the hands, making grasping just about impossible but allowing the toes to play a vital role in walking.

FIBULA

TIBIA

Heel Bone

Metatarsals (Green)

Metacarpals (Purple)

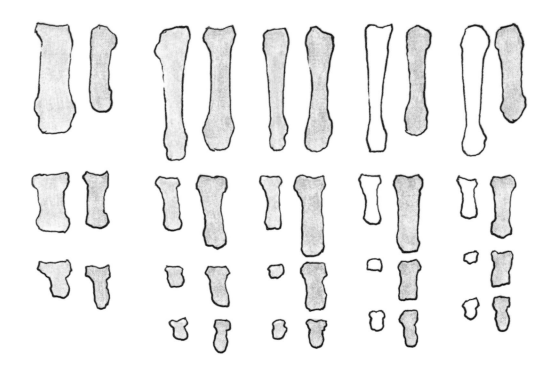

Foot Phalanges (Green)

Hand Phalanges (Purple)

Thanks to their arches, feet have an intrinsic springiness that spreads the body's weight. Three arches—two lengthwise and one crosswise—are created by the interlocking shapes of foot bones, along with the pull of tendons and ligaments. They keep the sole of the foot off the ground so that when we push downward they can give a little and then bounce back when we lift off. This remarkable piece of pliable engineering not only puts a spring in our step and makes us more energy efficient, but also enables us to negotiate uneven terrain without stumbling.

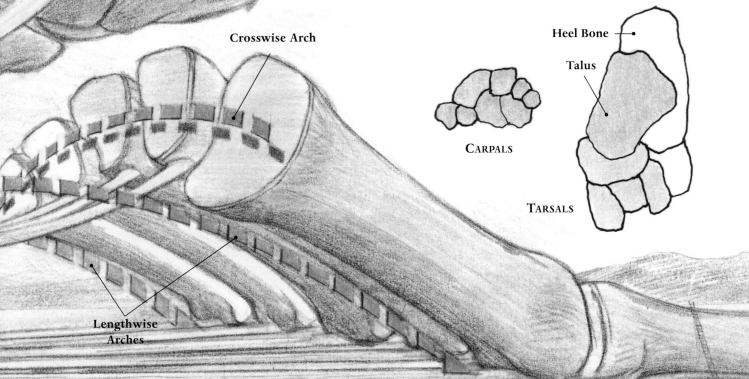

Crosswise Arch

Lengthwise Arches

Heel Bone

Talus

CARPALS

TARSALS

STEP BY STEP

When we stand we naturally position our weight directly above our hips. If we start to fall forward, we instinctively stick out a leg to catch ourselves. This is the first step in walking, something we learn at a young age and then quickly take for granted, relying on our brain to precisely coordinate the sequence and timing of muscle contractions that ensure we don't fall flat on our face.

Walking has two phases. The swing phase happens when one foot is on the ground and the other swings past it, and the double support phase is when both feet are briefly on the ground at the same time. And that's where we start (1).

As hip flexors pull the first leg forward like a pendulum, the second leg is made stiff and its firmly planted foot becomes the new back foot (2). The first leg's quadriceps

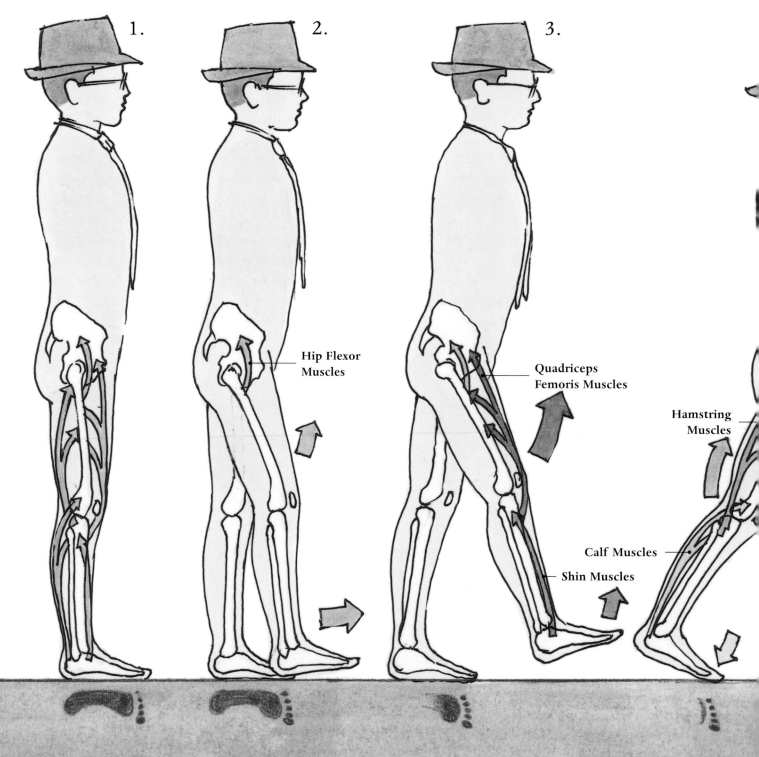

1.

2.

Hip Flexor Muscles

3.

Quadriceps Femoris Muscles

Hamstring Muscles

Calf Muscles

Shin Muscles

femoris muscles contract and straighten that leg as it swings, while shin muscles at the front of the lower leg lift the foot and toes upward to prevent them from dragging along the ground (3).

As one foot lands after swinging, the second, which is temporarily the back foot, is about to undergo liftoff (4). While the hamstrings pull the thigh backward and bend the knee, powerful calf muscles turn this foot downward, putting us on tiptoes and lifting the heel off the ground. Muscle power is then transmitted through the ball of the foot, pushing it off the ground. Its last points of contact are those bent-down toes.

A walk turns into a run when the swing of the pendulum speeds up. Both feet spend part of the process off the ground at the same time, sending the legs into a bouncy pogo-stick mode that relies on the springiness of tendons.

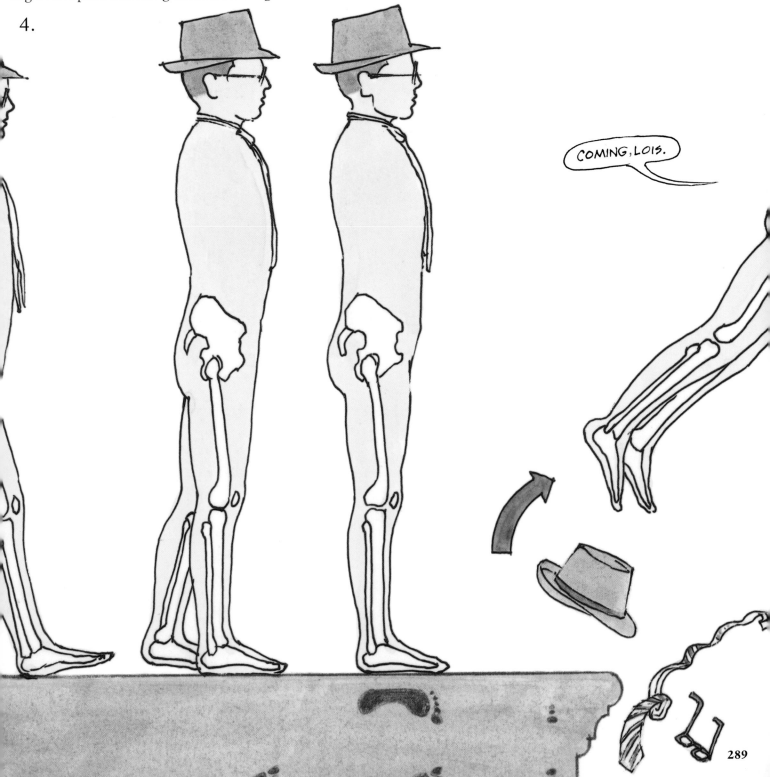

CHAPTER 7

EXTENDING THE LINE

HUMANS TRAVEL A FIXED PATH THROUGH LIFE, from childhood to teen, young adult to middle age to elderly, and inevitably face death—but not extinction. Reproduction is the insurance policy that guarantees we continue as a species despite the limits of a normal life span. Two cells—one from each parent—fuse together to generate a unique, never-before-seen, multitrillion-celled offspring. And so, as one generation takes the final curtain call, another is waiting in the wings.

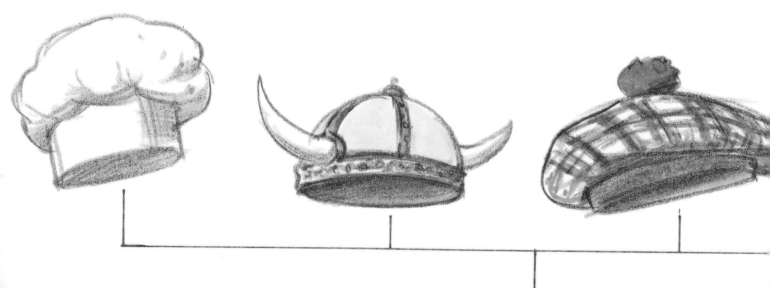

HERS

'N'

The reproductive system has two distinctive features: it comes in two models—female and male—and it remains dormant in both sexes from birth until spurred into action in the early teens by the hormonal storm of puberty. Despite their differences, both female and male systems make and release specialized sex cells that unite to produce babies. A woman's system releases eggs until she reaches menopause in her fifties; a man's sperm production can carry on for life.

Located mainly inside the body, the female reproductive organs include two ovaries and fallopian tubes, a uterus, and a vagina. The outside part of the reproductive system, the vulva, includes protective folds of skin called labia.

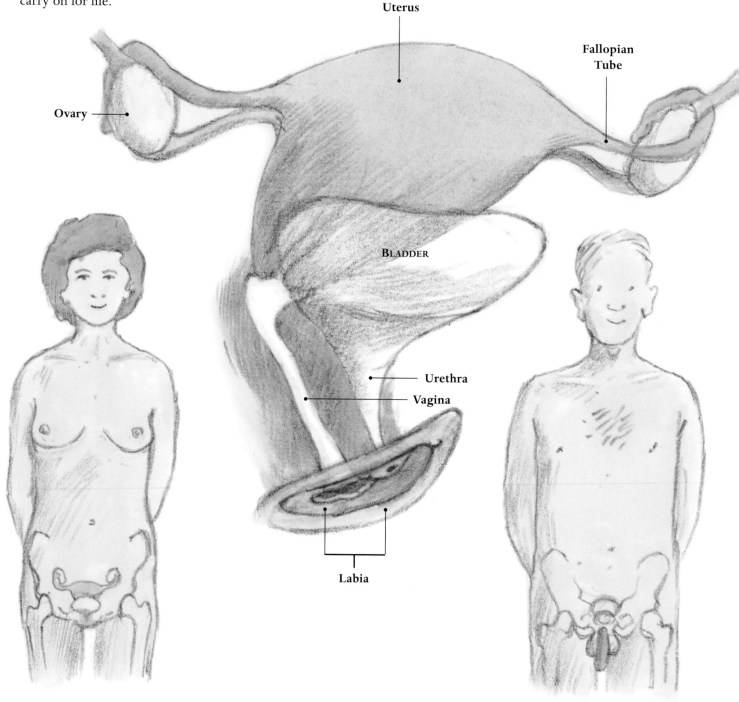

Uterus

Fallopian Tube

Ovary

BLADDER

Urethra

Vagina

Labia

HIS

There's no mistaking the outside bits of the male reproductive system—a baglike scrotum containing two sperm-making testes, and the penis. Connecting the testes and penis internally is a system of tubes and glands. The final exit for sperm, the urethra, runs along the center of the penis and is shared with the urinary system.

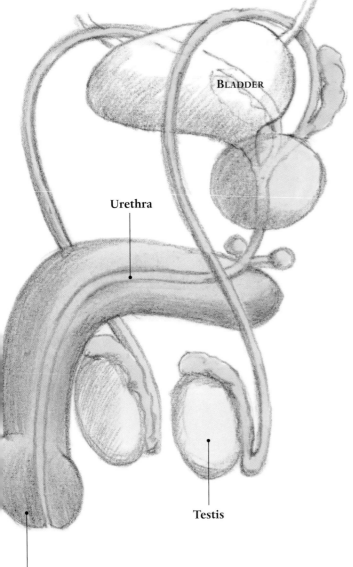

BLADDER

Urethra

Testis

Penis

HALF AND HALF

Every body cell has in its nucleus forty-six chromosomes. Half of them came from Mom and half from Dad. The twenty-three maternal chromosomes each have a look-alike paternal partner. These partners—called homologous chromosomes—carry genes that control the same body features but not always the same versions of those features. For example, while members of one homologous pair both carry the gene that determines eye color, one partner might favor blue, the other brown, or both the same color.

When producing sex cells the body mixes up the chromosome ingredients, tweaking the genetic makeup to improve the odds of survival. This process requires a special kind of cell division called meiosis that happens only in the ovaries and testes. While mitosis produces two identical offspring cells, meiosis yields four sex cells that are not identical and have only half the number of chromosomes as their "parent."

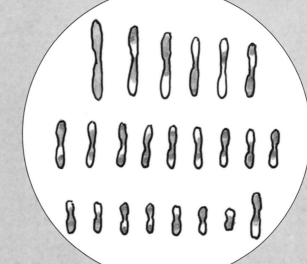

MEIOTIC MIXER

Meiosis makes sex cells. It requires two separate divisions—termed I and II—and, as in mitosis, both are accomplished in a number of stages. In this illustration one pair of homologous chromosomes is used to represent all twenty-three pairs. Each chromosome consists of two identical linked strands called chromatids.

DIVISION I

1. and 2. Prophase I
When the music starts, the maternal and paternal chromosome partners snuggle up and wrap their chromatid ends around each other.

(1) Pieces of chromatid break off and are swapped between partners in a process called crossing over. Finally a microtubule spindle is assembled (2).

3. Metaphase I
With no particular order or orientation, paired homologous chromosomes then gather at the center of the cell.

4. Anaphase I
Partners are then pulled apart by the spindle to opposite ends of the cell. The cell now divides to produce two new cells, each with twenty-three randomly selected maternal and paternal chromosomes, and with added variations produced by crossing over.

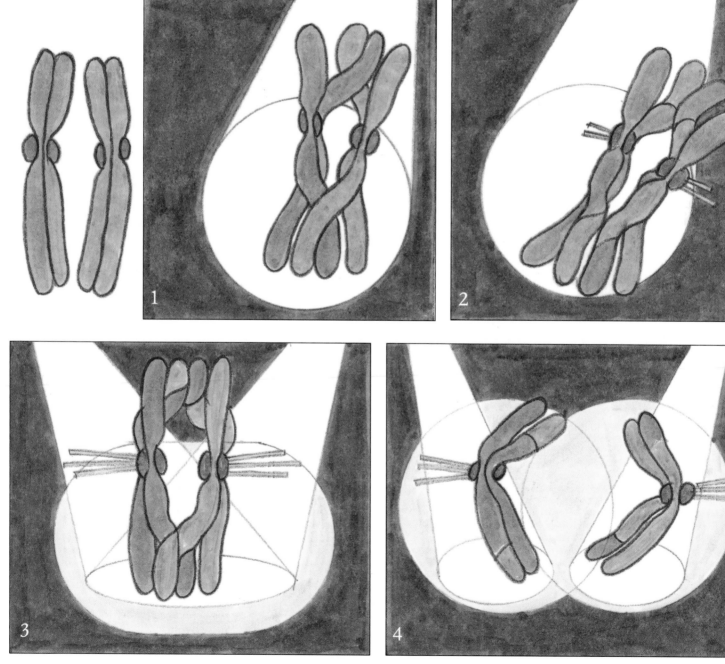

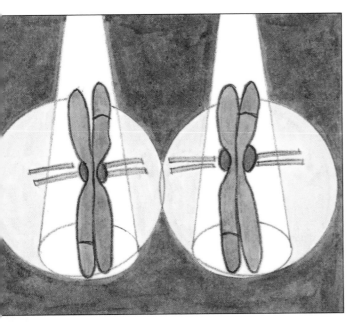

DIVISION II

5. Metaphase II

Chromosomes in both cells line up on the equator of a new spindle.

6. Anaphase II

Chromosomes are pulled apart and each of their chromatids is dragged to opposite ends of its cell. Each chromatid now becomes a chromosome in its own right.

7. Sex Cells

Division of the cytoplasm produces four cells, each with its own set of twenty-three chromosomes carrying a mix of different versions of particular genes. One of those chromosomes will help determine the sex of a child at fertilization. In the egg it is an X chromosome, and in the sperm it can be either an X or a Y chromosome.

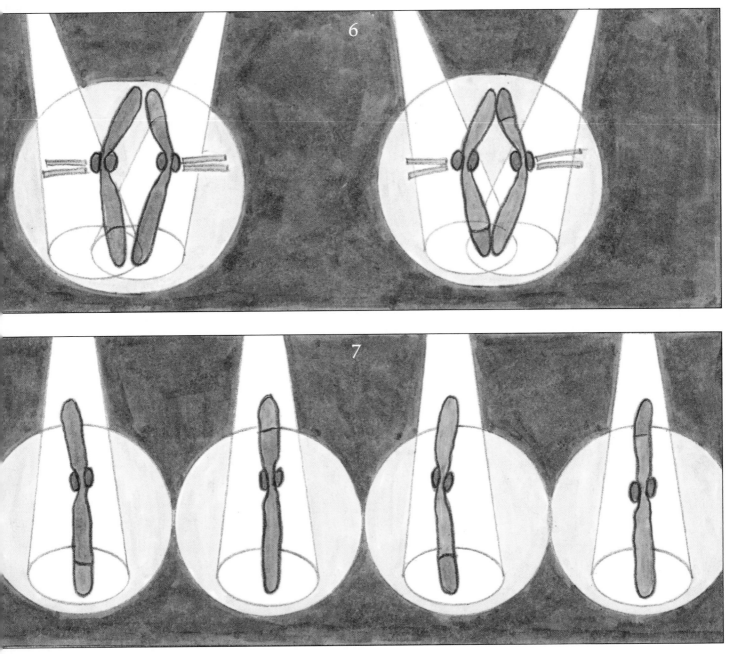

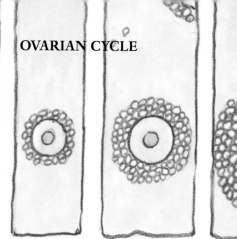

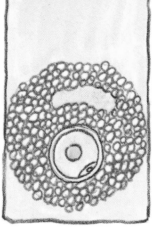

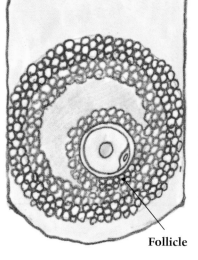

Follicle

OVULATION

LH

FSH

Egg

Fimbria —

ESTROGEN

TWENTY-EIGHT DAYS

Approximately every twenty-eight days a woman's reproductive system experiences two linked sequences of events, called cycles, to prepare itself for possible fertilization. Controlling these cycles are two hormones from the pituitary gland—FSH and LH—and estrogen and progesterone from the ovaries.

OVARIAN CYCLE

At birth, a girl's ovaries are filled with thousands of immature but aspiring eggs packaged inside tiny bags of cells called follicles. Once a month, one of the pituitary hormones (FSH) stimulates some of these follicles to enlarge and mature. Gradually, all but one fall by the wayside, leaving a single large, fluid-filled follicle that forms a bulge on the side of the ovary. Estrogen, secreted by follicle cells, stimulates the release of the second pituitary hormone (LH). This triggers ovulation around day fourteen. Having released its egg, the ruptured follicle then seals itself and releases progesterone (see opposite). If there is no fertilization, as is usually the case, the sealed follicle disappears and the cycle starts up again.

MENSTRUATION

MENSTRUAL CYCLE

| 1 | 2 | 3 | 4 | 5 | 6 | 7 | 8 | 9 | 10 | 11 | 12 | 13 | 14 | 15 |

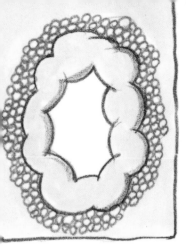
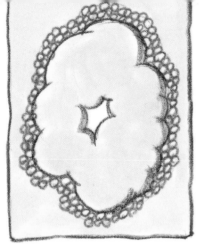

MENSTRUAL CYCLE

Ovary

Uterus

Endometrium

PROGESTERONE

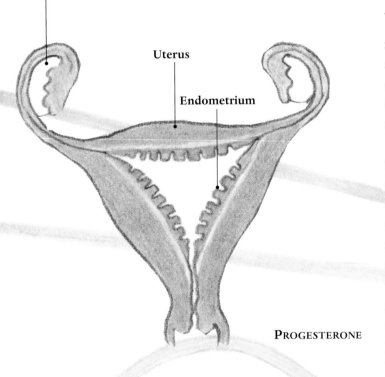

While the ovarian cycle prepares an egg for release, the menstrual cycle gets the uterus ready to receive the egg should it be fertilized. Estrogen and progesterone released during the ovarian cycle control the timing of the menstrual cycle, thus ensuring close cooperation between the two cycles.

Changes during the menstrual cycle affect the lining of the uterus. In the first five days of the cycle this lining, or endometrium, disintegrates. As a result, blood and tissue cells pass out through the vagina during what is called menstruation. Stimulated by estrogen, the endometrium then rebuilds itself, getting thicker and generating a richer blood supply. After ovulation, progesterone makes the endometrium even more velvety, with more blood vessels as well as glands that release nutrient fluids to pamper the new arrival, expected around day twenty-one. If fertilization doesn't happen, preparations grind to a halt. As estrogen and progesterone levels plummet, one reproductive cycle ends and the next begins.

MENSTRUATION

18   19   20   21   22   23   24   25   26   27   28   1   2   3   4

THE LONELY EGG

Once a mature egg has burst out of its ovary, it must enter the fallopian tube if it is to reach the uterus. To help guide the egg, the opening of the fallopian tube is funnel shaped and fringed with fingerlike extensions called fimbriae. Though these surround the ovary, they don't make a secure connection. A newly released egg could escape into the space between abdominal organs and be lost forever.

To minimize this risk, the muscular walls of the fallopian tube contract, causing the fimbriae to drape over and "explore" the ovarian surface. At the same time, beating cilia from epithelial cells lining the funnel create a current that draws the egg toward safety.

Cilia continue to move the egg toward the uterus, aided by squeezing movements of the fallopian tube wall, like those that move food down the esophagus. Cells in the lining not involved in movement release nutrients that nourish the egg.

If, as is usually the case, fertilization has not happened within twenty-four hours after ovulation, the egg passes through the final narrow section of the fallopian tube. Its window of opportunity now closed, the lonely egg enters the uterus, where it breaks down and its parts are absorbed.

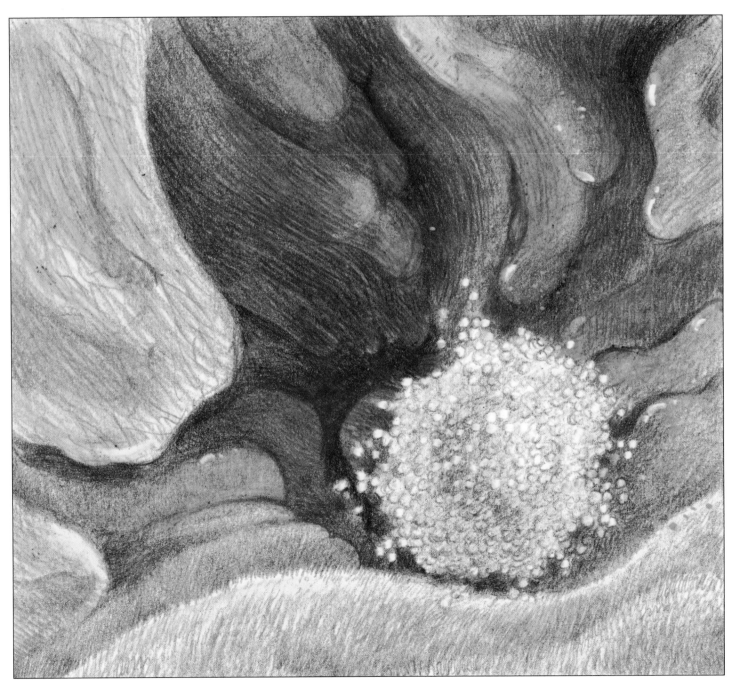

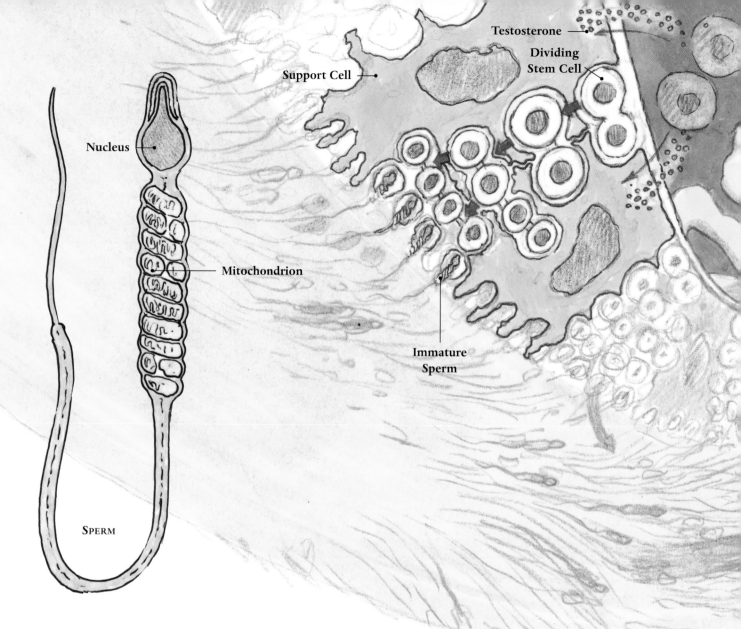

Nucleus

Mitochondrion

SPERM

Support Cell

Testosterone

Dividing Stem Cell

Immature Sperm

BIOGRAPHY OF A SPERM

Sleek and streamlined, the eager sperm cell is perfectly formed to do its job. A flattened "head" contains the nucleus, into which its twenty-three chromosomes are crammed. A long, beating "tail" is the sperm's driving force. And in between, a coil of mitochondria provides the energy.

From puberty onward, millions of sperm are produced every day by the testes. Both testes are divided into more than 250 wedge-shaped chambers, each one containing up to four tightly coiled seminiferous tubules. The walls of these tubules are the sperm factories. Stem cells adjacent to a tubule's outer covering divide by mitosis. Some of their offspring move inward, where they divide by meiosis to produce rounded cells that, in time, shed their cytoplasm and gain a tail to become the immature sperm that are released into the tubule's central cavity. During the two to three

months this process takes, support cells nurture and protect the sperm-to-be.

Free, but unable to propel themselves along the seminiferous tubules, immature sperm are pushed in fluid to the epididymis, a comma-shaped mass of tubules that hug the top and back of each testis. Over the next month, sperm mature and finally become mobile before moving into the ductus deferens.

The same pituitary hormones involved in the ovarian cycle—FSH and LH—here stimulate release of the male hormone testosterone from cells surrounding the seminiferous tubules. In addition to encouraging sperm production, testosterone maintains male sexual characteristics such as facial hair and a deep voice.

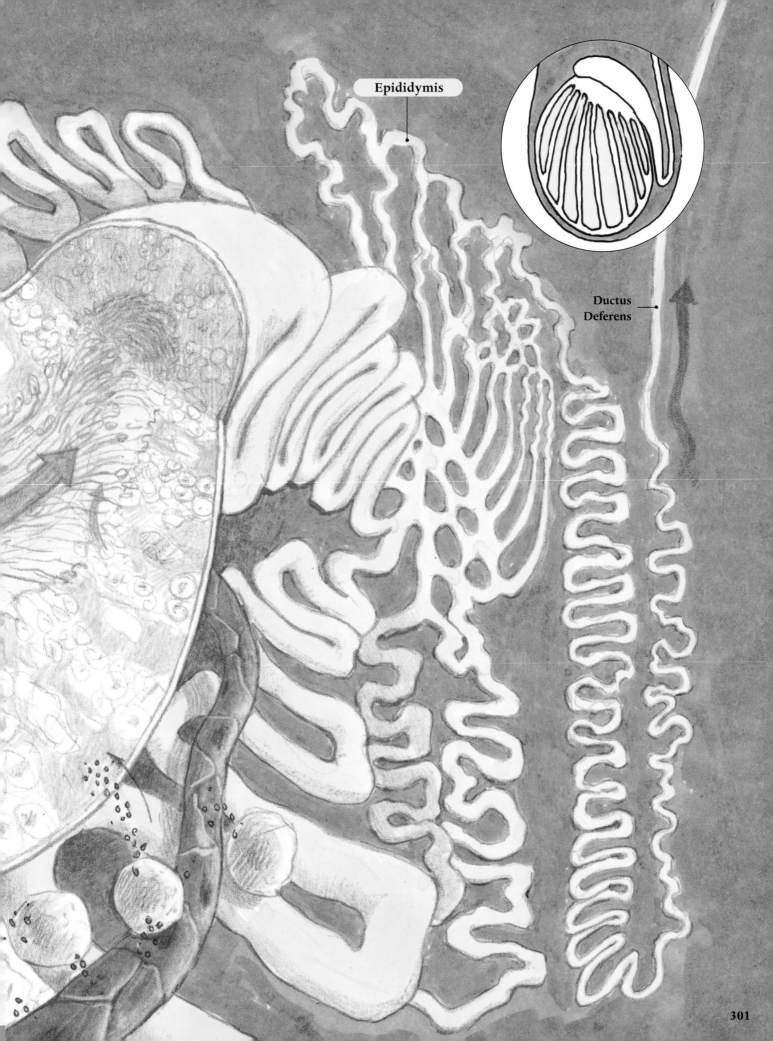

Epididymis

Ductus
Deferens

DELIVERY DEVICE

Making and maturing sperm is the first step in the male contribution to the reproductive process. The next is for sperm to get to the penis, a journey they will undertake only just prior to being squirted from the tip of the penis in a process called ejaculation.

When required, smooth muscles within the walls of each long ductus deferens push sperm on their way. Both looping pathways travel upward from the testes, downward along each side of the bladder, and finally into the prostate gland, where they empty into the urethra. The urethra passes through the root of the penis and into a spongy body, one of three "cylinders" that run along the shaft of the penis. The spongy and cavernous bodies are filled with empty spaces and have a rich blood supply.

The seminal vesicles release fluid that energizes the passing sperm. They also supply fructose, a sugar that acts like rocket fuel. Just before ejaculation, the prostate gland releases a milky liquid, which also activates sperm, into the urethra through tiny trapdoors. The mixture of fluids and sperm is called semen. Since the urethra is used primarily to carry acidic urine—and sperm don't "like" acid conditions—an alkaline pre-ejaculation fluid is released by the bulbourethral glands to make the passage "sperm-friendly."

The first section of each ductus deferens is where sperm are stored for weeks or months. If not ejaculated, older sperm are broken down and their parts recycled. This first section is also surrounded by a cremaster muscle that either pulls the testes up closer to the body or relaxes to lower them. This keeps the sperm factory at a steady 5°F (3°C) below body temperature—the optimum for sperm production.

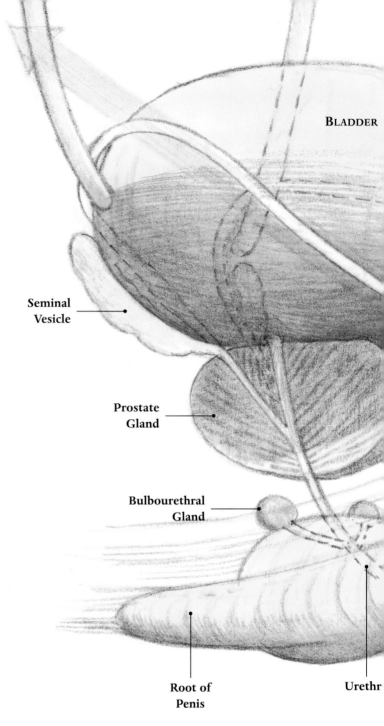

BLADDER

Seminal
Vesicle

Prostate
Gland

Bulbourethral
Gland

Root of
Penis

Urethr

Cremaster Muscle

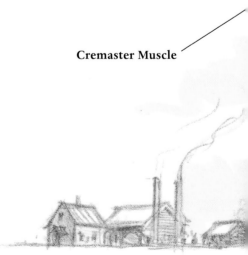

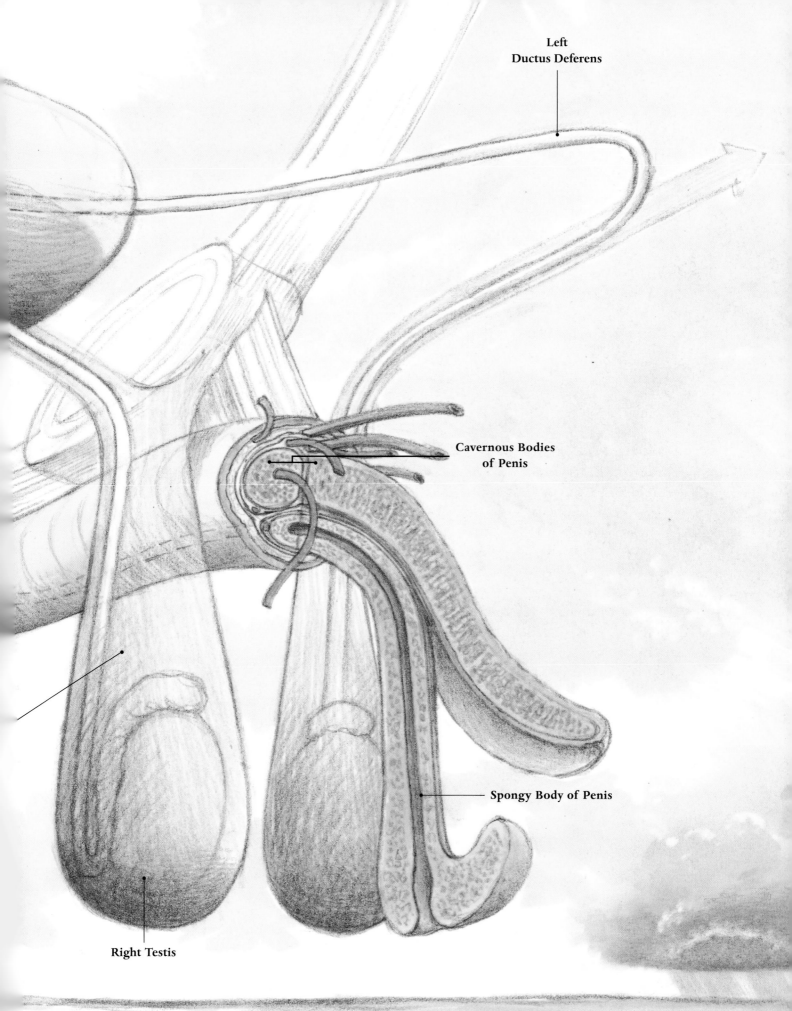

Left
Ductus Deferens

Cavernous Bodies
of Penis

Spongy Body of Penis

Right Testis

303

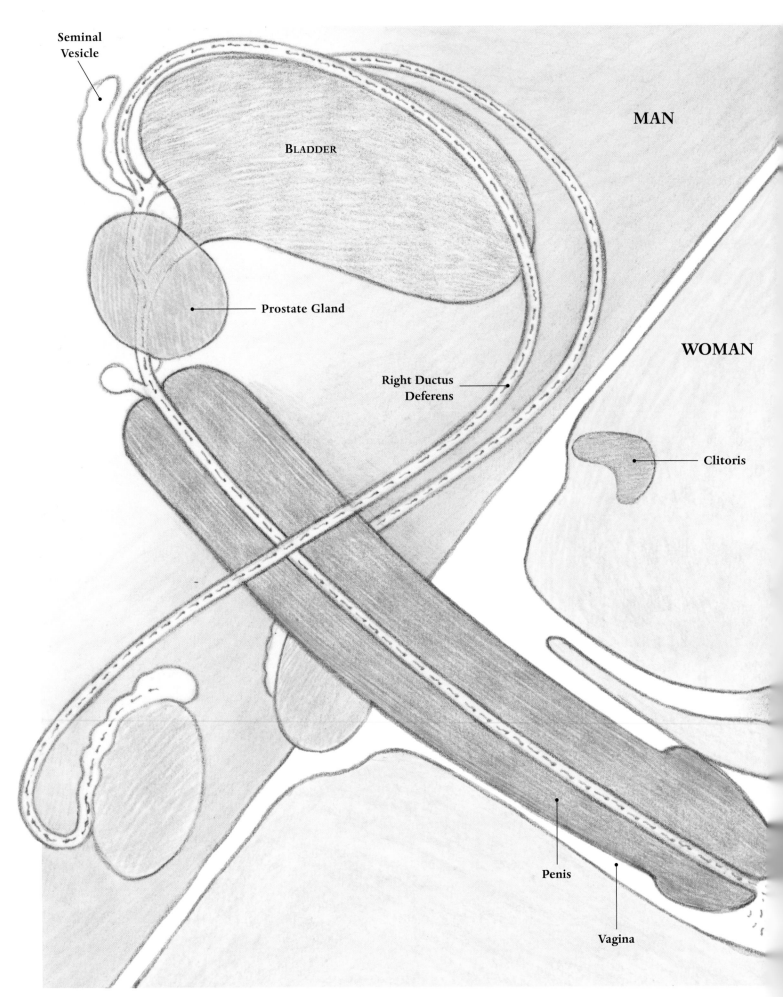

Seminal
Vesicle

BLADDER

MAN

Prostate Gland

WOMAN

Right Ductus
Deferens

Clitoris

Penis

Vagina

304

CONTACT!

In order to get sperm within swimming distance of an egg so that fertilization can happen, the penis must first be inserted into the vagina. This is made possible by a process orchestrated by the brain and spinal cord. Touch, sights, sounds, and other stimuli result in a flood of nerve messages that relax smooth muscles surrounding arterioles in the penis, increasing its blood supply. As its cavernous and spongy bodies fill with blood, they temporarily pinch off the veins, preventing any escape of blood. This makes the penis larger and stiffer so it can be pushed into the vagina. In a woman, similar stimuli cause erection of the sensory clitoris and lubrication of the vagina, which is now ready to receive the erect penis.

Back-and-forth movements of the penis inside the vagina send a barrage of impulses to the man's spinal cord and brain. When these reach a critical level, they cause both ductus deferens and seminal vesicles as well as the prostate gland to contract, forcing sperm-containing semen into the urethra. Then, in a process called ejaculation, muscles at the base of the penis contract forcefully and repeatedly to propel millions of sperm along the urethra, out through the tip of the penis, and into the vagina and cervix. Now the hazardous journey to the fallopian tubes can begin.

Immediately after ejaculation, stimulation of the penis declines, smooth muscles constrict arterioles, and blood spaces empty. The penis returns to its normal limp state.

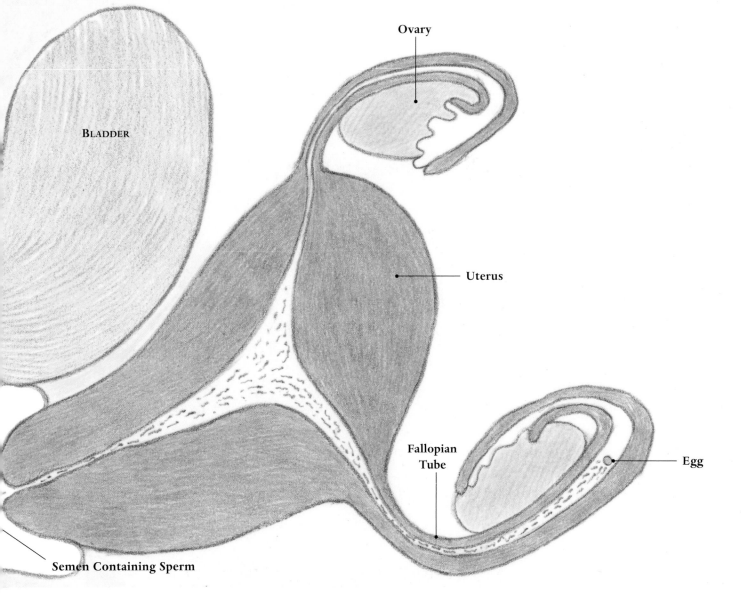

Ovary

Bladder

Uterus

Fallopian Tube

Egg

Semen Containing Sperm

INCREDIBLE JOURNEY

Millions of ejaculated sperm trade the comfort of a man's reproductive ducts for the harsher environs of a woman's vagina. Many spill back out through its entrance. Others survive only a short time in the vagina's acidic secretions. Nevertheless, some sperm reach the cervix of the uterus and swim into the mucus that fills its canal. Most of the time this mucus is thick, acidic, and all but impenetrable. For a few days around the time of ovulation, however, the mucus barrier becomes thinner and more alkaline—in short, more welcoming. Those sperm that aren't weak, tailless, two-headed, bent, or otherwise encumbered have a fighting chance of surviving long enough to embark on the five-inch (thirteen-centimeter) trip through the uterus and fallopian tube to the egg. But the clock is ticking. Sperm only live for twenty-four to seventy-two hours. And more problems lie ahead as they swim through the uterus.

Of the sperm that get through the cervical mucus, a few thousand or perhaps only several hundred of the most robust swimmers will make it into the egg-containing fallopian tube. The legion of the lost include sperm that either swam in circles, ran out of energy, went up the "wrong" fallopian tube toward the ovary that didn't release an egg that particular month, or got eaten by neutrophils and macrophages.

At some point on their trip, successful sperm are transformed from mere hopefuls into potential fertilizers. The enzyme-containing "cap" that sits on a sperm's head becomes so fragile that on impact it will easily rupture to release its egg-penetrating contents. These sperm also become hyperactive, a useful condition if you're fighting against the great tide of cilia that is wafting the egg toward you and all your competitors.

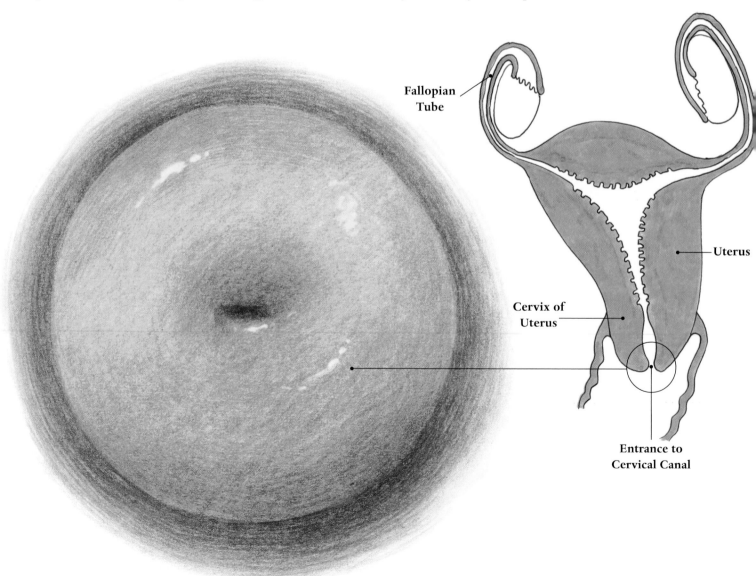

Fallopian Tube

Uterus

Cervix of Uterus

Entrance to Cervical Canal

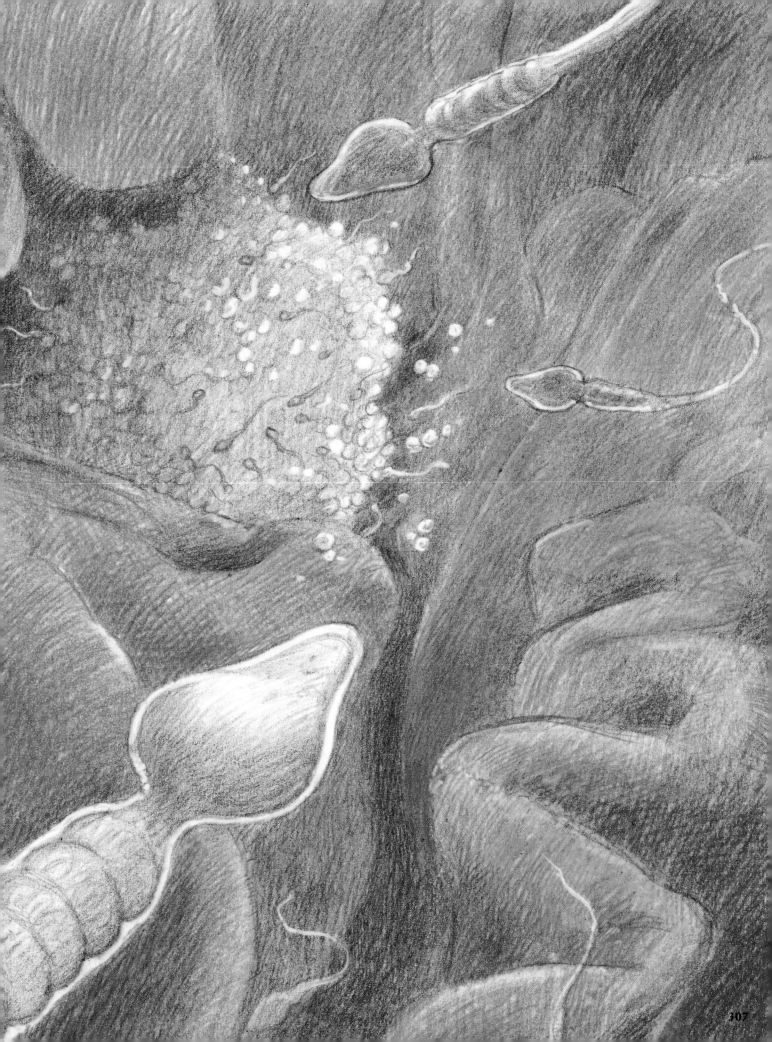

WINNER TAKES ALL

At the end of a grueling journey comes the opportunity for fertilization—fulfillment for one sperm, disappointment and doom for the rest.

1. Inside the wide middle section of the fallopian tube, a mass of wriggling sperm bind to a rotating egg, all intent on being the one to penetrate its defenses. The outer barrier is one of follicle cells. The inner barrier is a thick, clear zone laid down outside the egg's cell membrane as it matured in the ovary.

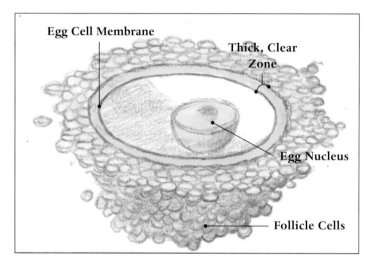

2. A sperm pushes its way between follicle cells. On making contact with the inner layer, its cap ruptures, releasing digestive enzymes.

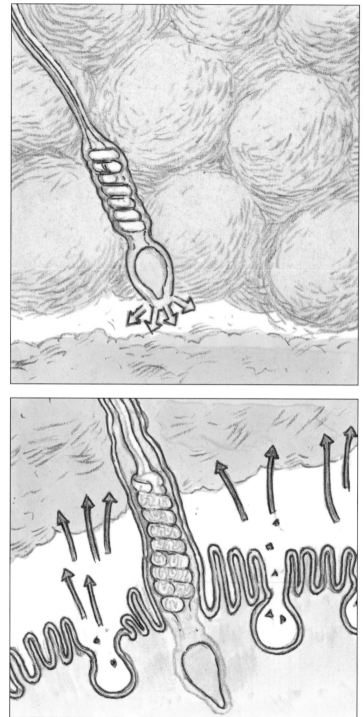

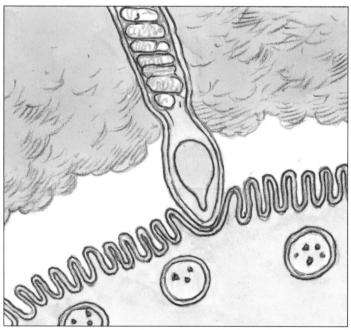

3. With the inner layer already weakened by enzymes released by hundreds of unsuccessful sperm, this Johnny-come-lately easily eats its way through to the egg's cell membrane.

4. When sperm and egg make contact, their membranes fuse and open and the sperm's nucleus and tail are pulled inside the egg. At the same time, chemicals just under the egg cell's membrane are released to prevent any further sperm from attaching. The drawbridge is up.

The "winning" sperm's tail disintegrates and its nucleus edges closer to that of the egg. Their respective nuclear membranes break down, each liberating twenty-three chromosomes that mingle to form the "full set" of forty-six chromosomes needed to make a new human being. If both the egg and sperm contribute X sex chromosomes, this human will be female. But if the sperm supplies a Y chromosome, resulting in an XY combination, it will be male.

The forty-six chromosomes divide by mitosis and the fertilized egg splits into two identical cells. As this tiny embryo-to-be travels along the fallopian tube toward the waiting uterus, cell division is repeated again and again. Within days those two cells will become four, then eight, then sixteen, and eventually . . . just too many to count.

FERTILE GROUND

Six days after fertilization, the embryo-to-be, still no bigger than the period at the end of this sentence, is floating in the uterus and about to embed itself in the endometrium and become a full-fledged embryo.

Everything's ready for the new arrival. The lining of the uterus has—under orders from hormones estrogen and progesterone released by the ovaries—reached maximum thickness. Long, branching glands extend from the endometrium's surface deep into the tissue below. The number of spiral arteries arising from deeper vessels running parallel to the surface has greatly increased. Secretions from the glands and essential supplies delivered by the spiral arteries will nurture the embryo until more permanent arrangements can be made.

But if the egg is not fertilized, or the embryo-to-be doesn't embed itself, the ovary stops secreting progesterone, the hormone responsible for keeping the endometrium thick and well supplied. Its spiral arteries go into spasm, closing off the blood supply and causing the newly built layer to be shed from the wall of the uterus and pass out through the vagina during menstruation.

EMBRYO-TO-BE

ENDOMETRIUM

GLAND

SPIRAL ARTERY

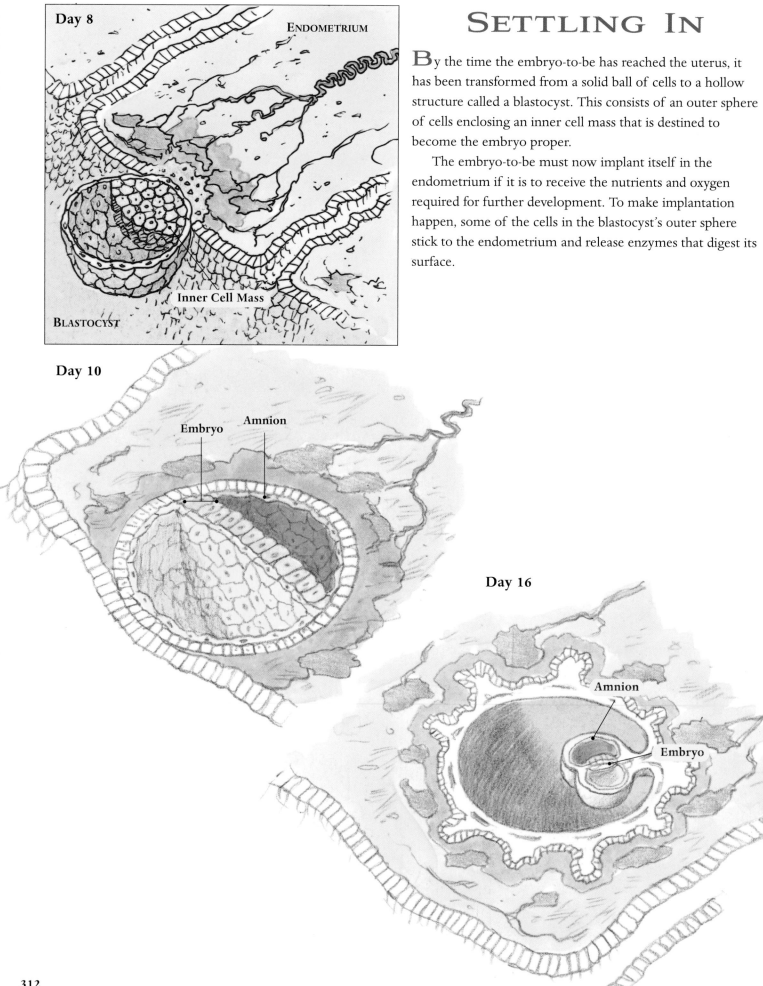

Day 8

ENDOMETRIUM

Inner Cell Mass

BLASTOCYST

SETTLING IN

By the time the embryo-to-be has reached the uterus, it has been transformed from a solid ball of cells to a hollow structure called a blastocyst. This consists of an outer sphere of cells enclosing an inner cell mass that is destined to become the embryo proper.

The embryo-to-be must now implant itself in the endometrium if it is to receive the nutrients and oxygen required for further development. To make implantation happen, some of the cells in the blastocyst's outer sphere stick to the endometrium and release enzymes that digest its surface.

Day 10

Embryo   Amnion

Day 16

Amnion

Embryo

Eight days after fertilization, the endometrium has been eaten away sufficiently for the blastocyst to burrow into it. The damaged endometrium then repairs itself to encase and protect its solitary lodger. The blastocyst's outer sphere also releases a hormone that "tells" the sealed follicle in the ovary to stay intact and continue producing the progesterone needed to prevent menstruation, which would end the pregnancy before it has a chance to begin. Meanwhile, the blastocyst's inner mass of cells—now the embryo—not only continue to multiply but also move around and become specialized as they build tissues and organs. Outside the embryo, a protective fluid-filled bag called the amnion starts to develop.

Thirty-two days after fertilization, the embryo—now the size of a small pea—has a head, trunk, tiny tail, paddlelike limbs, and, internally, developing organs and systems. The blastocyst's outer layer pushes fingerlike villi into the endometrium. Embryonic blood vessels in these villi pick up oxygen and food that diffuse from nearby maternal blood vessels and transport them back to the embryo through a sturdy lifeline.

Day 32

Maternal Blood Vessel

Villi

EMBRYO

Amnion

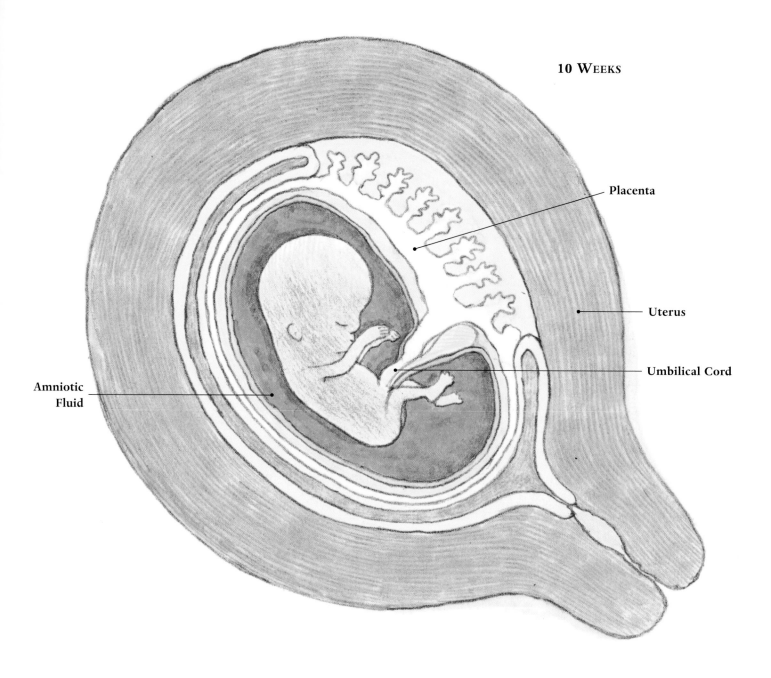

Placenta

Uterus

Umbilical Cord

Amniotic
Fluid

A Work in Progress

Once an embryo enters its ninth week after fertilization it is called a fetus. Ten weeks beyond fertilization and floating in a sea of protective amniotic fluid, this fetus is two and a half inches (sixty millimeters) long. It consists of billions of cells and is six hundred times bigger than the fertilized egg from which it arose.

Since their implantation, the cells have been growing and specializing and the tiny individual they have molded is now recognizably human. It has facial features and it can squint, swallow, and wrinkle its forehead. Fingers and toes have separated and nails are starting to grow. The internal organs

are in place, and the heart has been beating for several weeks.

The villi that first absorbed nutrients for the embryo from its mother's circulatory system have now, in combination with the endometrium, developed into a highly effective food supply and waste removal system called the placenta. Inside the placenta, fetal and maternal blood supplies come close but never mix. Diffusion ensures that food and oxygen pass from her to him and wastes travel in the opposite direction. A two-way flow of blood through vessels in the umbilical cord links the placenta to the fetus.

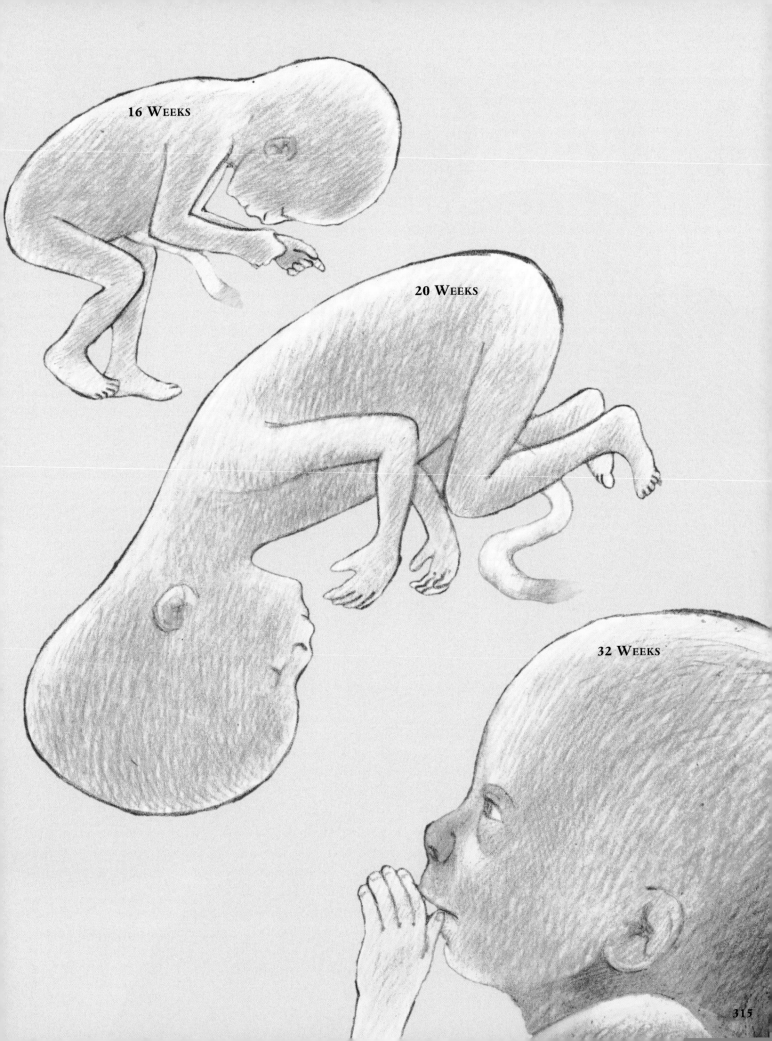

16 Weeks

20 Weeks

32 Weeks

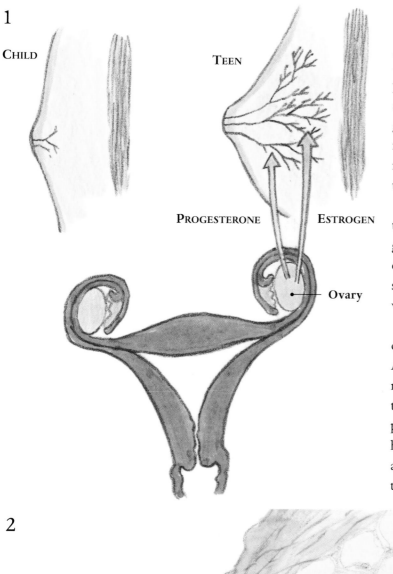

1

CHILD

TEEN

PROGESTERONE

ESTROGEN

Ovary

HOME COOKING

Like other mammals, human females feed, or have the potential to feed, their babies with natural, nutritionally balanced milk. It is produced within each breast by a mammary gland that consists of milk glands and their ducts, the latter radiating around and opening into the nipple. When not required to provide meals on demand, which is most of the time, the breasts are filled primarily with fat.

Preparations begin during puberty as increasing levels of the hormones estrogen and progesterone stimulate the growth of breasts in girls (1). During pregnancy higher levels of those same hormones, produced primarily by the placenta, stimulate the proliferation of the milk-making glands along with the ducts that will deliver the milk when needed (2).

Toward the end of pregnancy a pituitary gland hormone called prolactin stimulates the milk glands to produce milk. After birth the physical stimulus of a baby sucking on the nipples directly triggers—via the nervous system and hypothalamus—the release of more prolactin to keep milk supplies coming. It also causes the pituitary to release another hormone called oxytocin. This contracts smooth muscle around the milk glands in order to push milk along toward the nipple (3).

2

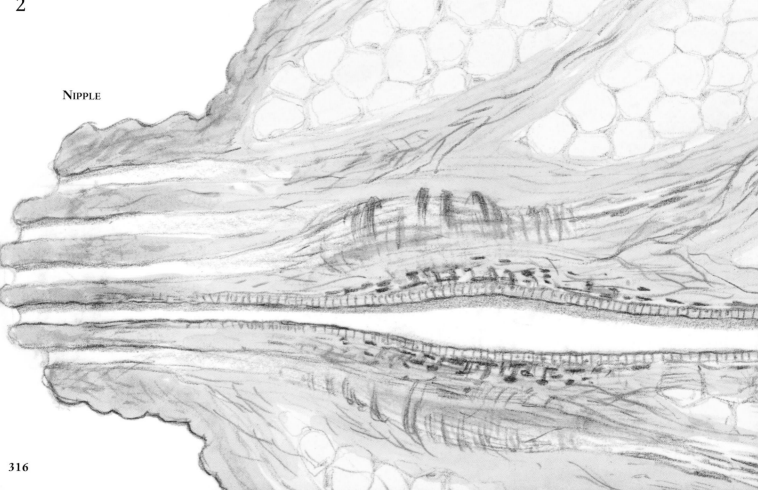

NIPPLE

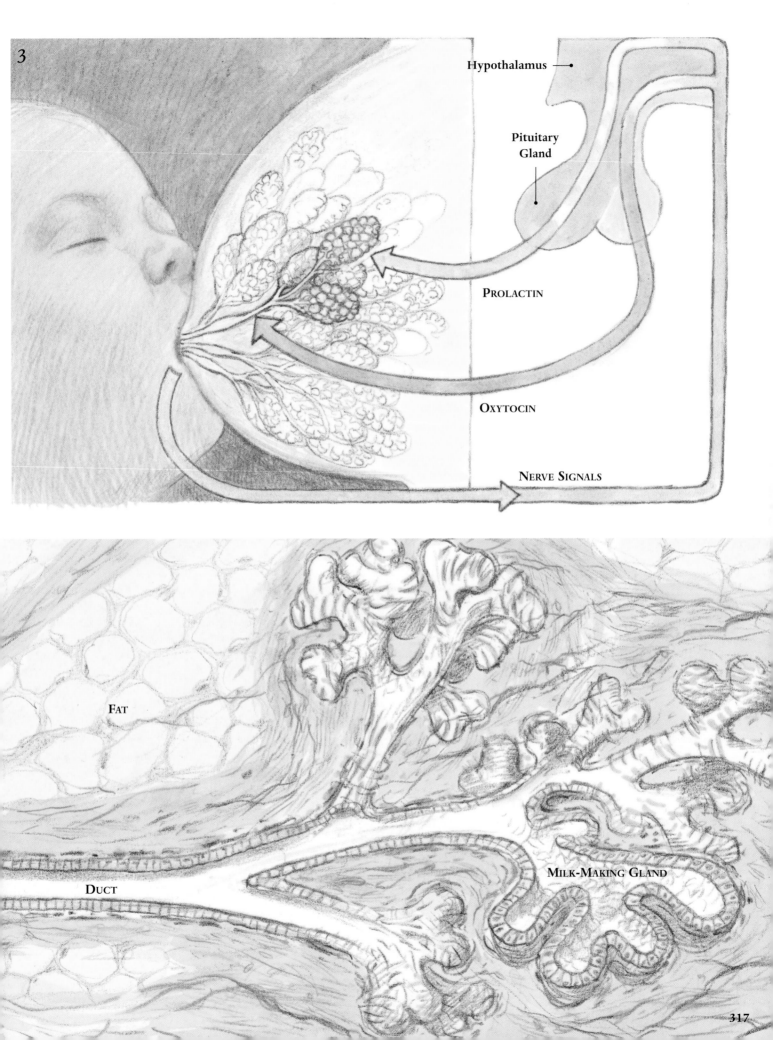

3

Hypothalamus

Pituitary Gland

PROLACTIN

OXYTOCIN

NERVE SIGNALS

FAT

DUCT

MILK-MAKING GLAND

TIME'S UP

For much of the last 270 days, the fetus has lolled about in pitch darkness—warm, serenaded by the reassuring beat of its mother's heart, and completely cared for. In short, bliss. But now the fetus is plump and ready and all signals are go for launch. Home for so long, the uterus will contract repeatedly and with such force that the baby will be pushed unceremoniously into the bright, noisy, and unpredictable world outside.

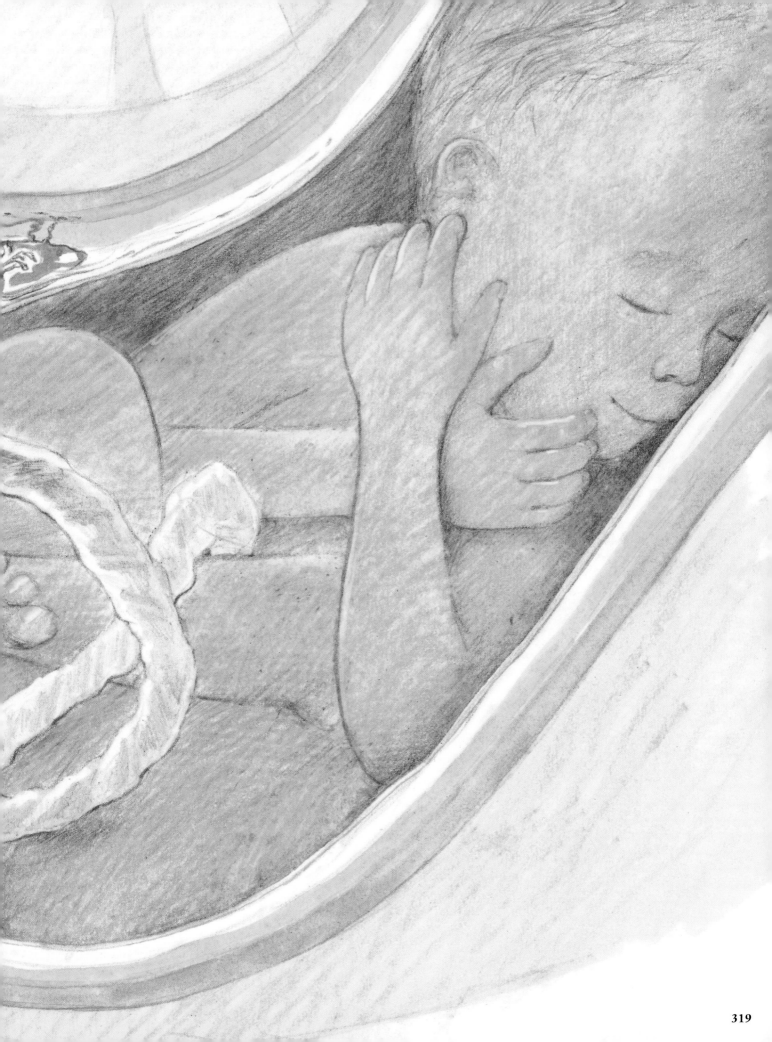

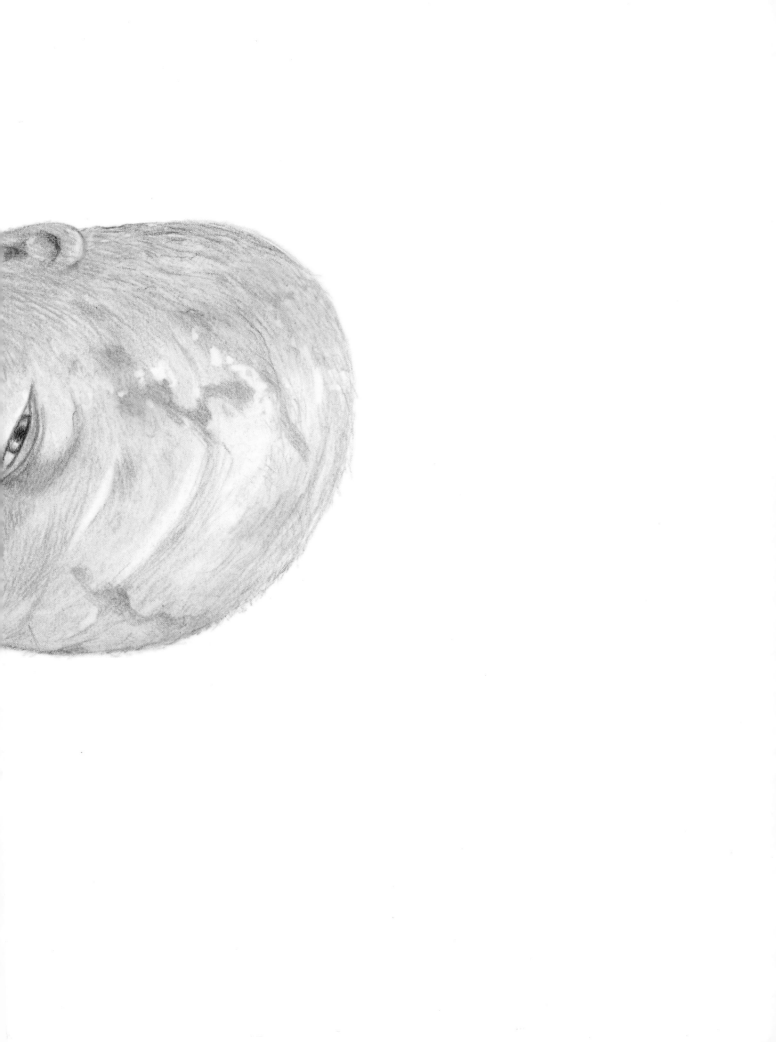

GLOSSARY

A word in *italics* indicates a cross-reference to another entry in the glossary.

A

ABDOMEN The lower half of the trunk—the central part of the body—which contains most of the digestive *system*, along with the urinary and reproductive *organs*.

ACIDIC Describes a liquid such as *gastric juice* that has the properties of an acid—sour-tasting and corrosive.

ACTIN A *protein* that is the building block of the thin filaments that provide one of the three components of a *cell's cytoskeleton* and also plays a key role in *muscle* contraction.

AIR PRESSURE The "weight" of air in the atmosphere that produces a downward-pushing force.

ALIMENTARY CANAL The tube extending from the lips to the anus that forms the main part of the digestive *system*, consisting of the mouth, throat, *esophagus*, and small and large intestines.

ALKALINE Describes a liquid such as pancreatic juice that can neutralize (make neutral) an *acidic* liquid so that it no longer has the properties of an acid.

ALLERGEN Any substance that triggers an *allergic response* in a person.

ALLERGIC RESPONSE An excessive and inappropriate response by the *immune system* to a substance, termed an *allergen*, that is normally harmless, and which can cause, for example, inflammation or skin rashes.

ALVEOLUS (plural: ALVEOLI) One of the 150 million microscopic air sacs in each lung through which *gas exchange* occurs.

AMINO ACID One of a group of twenty different substances that are the building blocks of *proteins*.

AMYLASE A digestive system *enzyme* that breaks down *starch* in food into simpler *sugars*.

ANTIBODY A type of *protein* released by *B cells* of the *immune system* that binds to a specific *pathogen* and marks it for destruction.

ANTIGEN A substance attached, for example, to the surface of bacteria and other *pathogens* that is recognized as foreign by the *immune system* and therefore activates it; antigens on *red blood cells* are recognized as foreign when transfused from a donor to a recipient who has a different *blood group*.

AORTA The large *artery* through which *oxygen*-rich blood leaves the heart.

APPENDIX A fingerlike projection from the first part of the large intestine that, in humans, plays no part in digestion but which assists the *immune system*.

ARTERIOLE A very small *artery*.

ARTERY A *blood vessel* that carries blood away from the heart; most arteries carry *oxygen*-rich blood.

ATOM A minute particle that is the smallest part of an element—a pure substance such as *carbon* or *oxygen* that cannot be broken down into a simpler substance—that can exist on its own. Atoms are built from particles called *protons*, *neutrons*, and *electrons*.

ATP (ADENOSINE TRIPHOSPHATE) A substance found inside *cells* that stores and transports *energy* and releases it where required.

ATRIUM (plural: ATRIA) One of the two smaller chambers of the heart that receive blood from either the lungs (left atrium) or the body (right atrium).

AUTONOMIC NERVOUS SYSTEM The section of the nervous *system* that automatically regulates many body processes, including heart rate and pupil size.

AV NODE (ATRIOVENTRICULAR NODE) A small region of the heart that forms the sole electrical connection between the *atria* and *ventricles*.

AXON The long, thin process that extends from a *neuron's* cell body and carries signals to another neuron or a *muscle fiber*.

B

BACTERIA (singular: BACTERIUM) A group of single-celled *microorganisms*, some of which cause disease in humans.

BASAL LAMINA A supporting, adhesive "sheet" that is secreted by, and which underlies, *epithelial cells*.

BASAL NUCLEI Areas of *gray matter* located within the *white matter* of the *cerebrum* that play a part in controlling movement.

BASE One of a small group of substances that form the "letters" of the coded instructions carried by the *nucleic acids DNA* and *RNA*.

B CELL (B LYMPHOCYTE) A type of *white blood cell* that plays a key part in the *immune system* by releasing *antibodies* that target specific *pathogens*.

BILE A greenish-yellow liquid that is produced by liver *cells* and is released into the small intestine, where it aids the *digestion* of *fat*.

BILLION A number equivalent to one thousand *million* (1,000,000,000).

BLOOD GROUP One of four possible types of blood found in humans—A, B, AB, or O—each of which is determined by the presence or absence of *antigens* on the surface of *red blood cells*.

BLOOD TRANSFUSION The transfer of blood from one person (the donor) to another (the recipient).

BLOOD VESSEL A tube—such as an *artery*, *vein*, or *capillary*—that carries blood.

BOLUS A rounded mass of chewed food that can be swallowed.

BOND The force of attraction that holds *atoms*, *ions*, or *molecules* together.

BRAIN STEM The part of the brain that connects it to the *spinal cord* and controls vital functions such as breathing and heart rate.

BRONCHIOLE Inside the lungs, a small branch of a *bronchus* that leads to *alveoli*.

BRONCHUS (plural: BRONCHI) An airway that leads from the *trachea* into each lung and which branches into smaller bronchi.

C

CANCER One of a group of diseases, such as skin cancer, caused by *cells* dividing out of control.

CAPILLARY A microscopic *blood vessel* that supplies individual body cells as it carries blood between *arterioles* and *venules*.

CAPILLARY BED An interweaving network of *capillaries* that carries blood through the *tissues*.

CAPSID The *protein* coat of a *virus*.

CARBOHYDRATE One of a group of substances, including *complex carbohydrates*, such as *glycogen*, and *sugars*, such as *glucose*, the *molecules* of which consist of *carbon*, hydrogen, and *oxygen atoms*.

CARBON A substance, the *atoms* of which bond with each other to form the "backbone" of *carbohydrates*, *proteins*, *lipids*, and most other *molecules* that build and operate the body.

CARBON DIOXIDE A gas breathed out from the lungs that is the waste product of *energy* released by *cells*.

CARDIAC MUSCLE A type of *muscle* found only in the heart.

CAROTID ARTERY An *artery* that carries *oxygen*-rich blood to the head and brain.

CARTILAGE A tough, flexible type of *connective tissue* that helps support certain body parts and covers the ends of bones in *joints*.

CELL One of the *trillions* of microscopic living units from which the body is constructed.

CELL BODY The part of a *neuron* that contains its *nucleus*.

CELL DIVISION The process by which *cells* multiply by dividing into two.

CELL MEMBRANE The thin *membrane* that surrounds a *cell*, separates it from its surroundings, and controls the entry and exit of most substances to and from the cell's *cytoplasm*.

CENTRAL NERVOUS SYSTEM The part of the nervous *system* that consists of the brain and the *spinal cord*.

CEREBELLUM Part of the brain that ensures that the body is balanced and moves in a coordinated way.

CEREBRAL CORTEX The thin surface layer of each of the brain's *cerebral hemispheres* that is made up of *gray matter* and processes information relating to movement, the senses, thought, and memory.

CEREBRAL HEMISPHERE One of two halves, left or right, of the *cerebrum*.

CEREBROSPINAL FLUID A clear liquid that circulates inside and around the *central nervous system* and helps to nourish and protect the brain and *spinal cord*.

CEREBRUM The largest part of the brain, which controls sensation, conscious thought, and movement.

CHEMICAL REACTION A process that, through the rearrangement of *atoms*, changes one substance into another.

CHOLESTEROL A type of *lipid* that forms part of *cell membranes* and is used to make *steroid hormones*.

CHROMATID One of two identical linked strands formed when a *chromosome* copies itself just before *cell division*.

CHROMOSOME One of forty-six strands of *DNA* found inside the *nucleus* of most body *cells*. Chromosomes, which contain *genes*, coil up and shorten during *cell division* into structures visible under a *light microscope*.

CHYME A souplike liquid consisting of semidigested food that passes into the small intestine from the stomach during *digestion*.

CILIA (singular: CILIUM) Microscopic, hairlike projections from certain body *cells* that sweep backwards and forward to move materials, such as *mucus*, over the cells' surface.

CIRCULATORY SYSTEM The *system*, consisting of the heart, blood, and *blood vessels*, that supplies *oxygen* and nutrients to body *cells* and removes their wastes.

CLONE One of the genetically identical descendants of a single *cell* produced by *mitosis*, or the act of producing such descendants.

COCHLEA The coiled structure inside the inner ear that houses sound *receptors*.

COLLAGEN A tough, fibrous structural *protein* that strengthens *connective tissues* such as *cartilage*.

COMPLEX CARBOHYDRATE A *carbohydrate*, such as *glycogen* or *starch*, that is made from chains of *glucose* subunits and used as an *energy* store.

CONE A type of *photoreceptor* found in the *retina* of the eye that provides color vision and works best in bright light.

CONNECTIVE TISSUE A type of *tissue*, such as *cartilage*, bone, or *fat*, that holds the body together and supports and protects its *organs*.

CRANIAL NERVE One of twelve pairs of *nerves* that originate from the brain.

CUSP One of the raised edges found on premolar and molar teeth.

CYTOKINESIS The division of the *cytoplasm* following *mitosis* or *meiosis* to produce two new *cells*.

CYTOPLASM The gel-like fluid that occupies a *cell* between its *cell membrane* and *nucleus*.

CYTOSKELETON The network of *rods* and filaments inside a *cell* that supports it, moves its internal structures, and plays a part in *cell division*.

D

DENDRITE A short, branched process that extends from a *neuron's cell body* and receives signals from other neurons.

DENDRITIC CELL A type of *cell*, found mainly in the skin, that plays a part in the *immune system* by engulfing a *pathogen* and identifying it by "presenting" its *antigens* to a *lymphocyte*.

DENTIN Hard, bonelike *tissue* that gives a tooth its basic shape by forming a layer under the *enamel* that extends downward into the tooth's root.

DERMIS The lower, thicker layer of the skin that lies beneath the *epidermis* and contains *blood vessels*, sweat *glands*, and sensory receptors.

DIAPHRAGM The dome-shaped sheet of *muscle* that separates the chest cavity from the *abdomen*, and which plays a key role in breathing.

DIFFUSION The random movement of *molecules* in a gas or liquid from an area of high concentration to one of low concentration until they are evenly spread out.

DIGESTION The process by which complex substances in food are broken down into simpler ones that can be absorbed into the bloodstream and used by *cells*.

DNA (DEOXYRIBONUCLEIC ACID) A substance that stores instructions in the form of *genes* inside the *nucleus* of body *cells*. A DNA *molecule* consists of two long, intertwined *nucleic acid* strands.

E

ELASTIN A fibrous, structural *protein* that can stretch and recoil and gives elasticity to *connective tissues*.

ELECTRON A tiny particle with a negative electrical charge that is found inside an *atom* and moves around its *nucleus* at high speed.

ELECTRON MICROSCOPE An instrument, more powerful than a *light microscope*, that uses an *electron* beam focused by magnetic lenses to produce highly magnified images of very small objects, such as the components of body *cells*.

EMBRYO The name given to a developing baby between the time of its implantation in the *uterus* and the end of the eighth week after *fertilization*.

ENAMEL The hardest material inside the body that covers the crown, the exposed part of a tooth above the gum.

ENDOCRINE GLAND A type of *gland*, such as the thyroid gland, that releases *hormones* into the bloodstream.

ENDOMETRIUM The lining of the *uterus*.

ENERGY The capacity for performing work. Energy may be stored, such as in *glucose* or *ATP*, or released to enable a *chemical reaction* inside a *cell* to take place or to move the body.

ENZYME A type of *protein* that greatly speeds up the rate of *chemical reactions* inside and outside *cells* without itself being changed in the process.

EPIDERMIS The upper, thinner layer of the skin that protects the *dermis* beneath it, and from which the topmost layer of dead *cells* is constantly being worn away and replaced.

EPIGLOTTIS A movable flap of *cartilage* at the root of the tongue that, during swallowing and to prevent choking, covers the entrance to the *larynx* until food or drink enters the *esophagus*.

EPITHELIAL TISSUE (EPITHELIUM) A *tissue* that consists of one or more layers of closely packed *cells*, and covers the body's surface, lines tubes and cavities such as the *alimentary canal*, and forms *glands*.

ESOPHAGUS A muscular tube that propels food from the throat to the stomach by *peristalsis*.

EXTENSOR A *skeletal muscle* that increases the angle of a *joint*—such as straightening the leg at the knee—by making bones move farther apart.

F

FALLOPIAN TUBE A narrow tube through which a newly released egg is transported from an *ovary* to the *uterus*.

FAT A type of *lipid* that is normally solid at room temperature (an oil, such as olive oil, is a lipid that is liquid at room temperature); both fats and oils are *energy* rich, made from *fatty acids*, and found in many foods. Also the name given to a *connective tissue*, made of fat *cells*, that stores energy and insulates and protects.

FATTY ACID A *molecule*, consisting almost entirely of a long chain of *carbon* and hydrogen *atoms*, that is one of the building blocks of *fats*, oils, and *phospholipids*.

FECES Semisolid masses of waste consisting of undigested food and *bacteria* that are formed in the large intestine and eliminated through the anus.

FERTILIZATION The fusion of a female egg and male sperm that occurs in a *fallopian tube*.

FETUS The name given to a baby developing in the *uterus* from the ninth week after *fertilization* to birth.

FIBER [DIET] Material in plant foods that cannot be digested but which adds bulk to food, giving *muscles* in the intestine wall something to push against, so improving their efficiency.

FIBER [MUSCLE] The name given to a *muscle* cell.

FLEXOR A *skeletal muscle* that decreases the angle of a *joint*—such as bending the arm at the elbow—by making its bones move closer together.

G

GANGLION CELL A type of *neuron* found in the *retina* of the eye that relays signals from *photoreceptors* to the brain.

GAP JUNCTION A channel between two neighboring *cells* that allows the passage of substances between them.

GAS EXCHANGE The movement by *diffusion* of *oxygen molecules* from the air to the bloodstream and of *carbon dioxide* molecules in the opposite direction, which takes place inside the lungs.

GASTRIC Describes something relating to the stomach.

GENE One of the 25,000 instructions controlling production of the *proteins* that construct and operate *cells* and are contained within the *DNA molecules* that make up a *cell's chromosomes*.

GEODESIC DOME A curved structure constructed using short, interconnected struts to support its surface.

GLAND A collection of *cells* that produce substances that are released into or onto the body; *endocrine glands* release their products into the bloodstream, while other types of glands, such as salivary glands and sweat glands, release their products through ducts (tubes).

GLOBULAR PROTEIN A type of *protein*, such as an *enzyme* or *antibody*, that is folded into a compact structure, as opposed to fibrous, structural proteins such as *collagen* or *elastin.*

GLUCOSE The main *sugar* circulating in the bloodstream that is the primary source of *energy* for the body's *cells.*

GLYCOGEN A *complex carbohydrate* that consists of linked *glucose molecules,* is used by the body as an *energy* store, and is stockpiled in liver and *muscle* cells.

GOLGI APPARATUS A set of flattened *membrane* sacs inside a *cell* that package *proteins* for both export and use inside the cell.

GRAVITY A natural force of attraction between two bodies; for example, between Planet Earth and an object on its surface, such as a human being, with the larger mass exerting the stronger pull, keeping our feet on the ground.

GRAY MATTER A *tissue* found in the *central nervous system* that consists mainly of the *cell bodies* and branching *dendrites* of *neurons* and which forms the surface layer of the *cerebrum* and the inner part of the *spinal cord.*

H

HEMOGLOBIN A complex iron-containing *protein* that is found inside *red blood cells* and carries *oxygen.*

HEPATOCYTE A liver *cell.*

HISTAMINE A substance released by *cells* in *tissues* that are damaged or reacting to the presence of *allergens,* and that triggers an *inflammatory response.*

HOMOLOGOUS Describes a matching pair of *chromosomes* that are the same size and share the same pattern of *genes* but may, individually, contain different versions of those genes.

HORMONE A substance, released into the bloodstream by an *endocrine gland,* that acts as a chemical messenger by changing *cell* activities to regulate a body process.

HYDROCHLORIC ACID A strong acid— a liquid capable of dissolving metals—that in the body is produced by *gastric glands* and aids the digestion of *proteins* in the stomach.

HYPOTHALAMUS A small but impor-tant region of the brain that monitors many body processes and regulates them by way of the *autonomic nervous system* and through *hormones* released by the pituitary *gland.*

I

IMMUNE SYSTEM The collection of defense *cells*—notably *lymphocytes* and *macrophages*—in the *circulatory* and *lymphatic systems* and other tissues that detect, destroy, and, in some cases, retain a memory of invading *pathogens.*

IMPRESARIO A person who is in charge of organizing events such as concerts, plays, or operas.

INFLAMMATORY RESPONSE An auto-matic defensive reaction by a body *tissue* to injury and/or *pathogen* invasion that involves increased blood flow and leakage of fluid to the affected area, which makes it red, swollen, hot, and painful.

INTERCOSTAL MUSCLE One of a team of *skeletal muscles* that connect adjacent ribs and move the rib cage during breathing.

INTERVERTEBRAL DISC A pad of *cartilage* with a gel-like core that is found between adjacent *vertebrae* in the backbone and allows limited movement between those vertebrae and cushions them against sudden jolts.

ION An *atom* that has lost or gained an *electron* to give it, respectively, either a posi-tive or a negative electrical charge.

J

JOINT A part of the skeleton where two or more bones meet.

K

KERATIN A structural *protein* found in the *epidermis,* hair, and nails that makes those structures tough and waterproof.

L

LARYNX Also called the voice box, a fun-nel-like *organ* constructed from *cartilage* plates that links the throat to the *trachea* and houses the *vocal cords.*

LIGAMENT A band of tough *connective tissue* that holds bones together where they meet at *joints.*

LIGHT MICROSCOPE An instrument that uses light rays focused by glass lenses to produce magnified images of very small objects, such as body *cells.*

LIMBIC SYSTEM A group of structures located within the brain that is involved with memory and emotions.

LIPID One of a group of substances, made primarily from *carbon,* hydrogen, and a few *oxygen atoms,* that are building materials and *energy* stores, and which include *fats,* oils, *phospholipids,* and *steroids,* such as *cholesterol.*

LYMPH The excess *tissue fluid* that is drained from the *tissues,* passes along *lymph vessels,* is filtered by *lymph nodes,* and then is returned to the bloodstream.

LYMPHATIC SYSTEM A one-way system of vessels that extends to all parts of the body, removes excess fluid called *lymph* from the *tissues,* and houses *immune system* cells.

LYMPH NODE A bean-shaped swelling in a *lymph vessel* that contains *immune system cells* and removes *pathogens* and debris from *lymph.*

LYMPHOCYTE One of a group of *white blood cells* found in the *circulatory* and *lymphatic systems* that play a key part in the *immune system* by releasing *antibodies* or by destroying *pathogens.*

LYMPH VESSEL One of the channels that make up the *lymphatic system* and collect and transport *lymph.*

LYSOSOME A *membrane* sac in a *cell's cytoplasm* that is filled with digestive *enzymes* used to break down worn-out cell compo-nents for recycling or foreign substances.

LYSOZYME A substance contained in sweat, tears, and *saliva* that kills some types of harmful *bacteria.*

M

MACROPHAGE One of a group of large *white blood cells,* derived from *monocytes,* that are found in many body *tissues* and which engulf *pathogens* and debris.

MACULA An oval region in the center of the *retina* that contains mostly *cones* and produces detailed color images in the brain.

MARROW A soft *tissue* found within bones; yellow marrow stores *fat,* and red marrow manufactures blood *cells.*

MAST CELL A type of defense *cell* found in *connective tissues*, such as in the *dermis*, that detects damage, *pathogens*, or foreign substances and triggers an *inflammatory response* by releasing *histamine* and other substances.

MATERNAL Describes something associated with a mother.

MEDULLA OBLONGATA Also called the medulla, the lowest section of the *brain stem*, which controls heart rate, breathing rate, and blood pressure.

MEIOSIS A type of *cell division* that occurs only in the *ovaries* and *testes* and produces sex *cells* that are not identical to each other and contain just one set of *chromosomes*.

MELANIN A brown-black pigment that colors skin and hair.

MELANOCYTE A type of *cell* in the skin's *epidermis* that produces and releases *melanin*.

MEMBRANE [CELL] A microscopically thin film consisting of a double layer of *phospholipid molecules* that surrounds a *cell* and many of the structures inside it.

MEMBRANE [TISSUES] A thin layer consisting of *epithelial tissue* underpinned by *connective tissue* that covers or lines an internal or external body surface.

MENSTRUAL CYCLE A sequence of changes to the lining of a woman's *uterus* that is repeated around every twenty-eight days, and which prepares the lining to receive a fertilized egg.

MENSTRUATION Also called a period, the monthly shedding of blood and the lining of the *uterus* through the vagina if an egg is not fertilized.

METABOLIC RATE The rate at which *energy* is utilized by *metabolism*.

METABOLISM The sum total of all the *chemical reactions* that take place inside the body, especially inside *cells*.

MICROORGANISM A tiny living thing, such as a *bacterium*, that can be seen only by using a microscope.

MICROVILLI (singular: MICROVILLUS) Tiny projections from the free surface of *epithelial cells*, such as those covering *villi* in the small intestine, that increase the surface area for absorption.

MIDBRAIN The upper section of the *brain stem*, which is involved with hearing and visual *reflexes*.

MILLION A number equivalent to one thousand thousand (1,000,000).

MILLISECOND A very short period of time equal to one-thousandth of a second.

MINERAL One of more than twenty substances, such as calcium and iron, that are essential for good health and must be present in the diet.

MITOCHONDRION (plural: MITOCHONDRIA) One of several *membrane*-bound structures inside a *cell* that use *oxygen* to release *energy* from *glucose* and other fuels.

MITOSIS A type of *cell division* used for growth and repair that results in the production of two new *cells*, each with identical *chromosomes*.

MOLECULE A particle consisting of two or more *atoms* held together by *bonds*.

MONOCHROME Describes an image in black and white.

MONOCYTE A type of *white blood cell* that is attracted to areas of *tissue* invaded by *pathogens* and becomes transformed into a *macrophage*.

MOTOR NEURON A type of *neuron* that carries signals from the *central nervous system* to a *muscle* or *gland*.

mRNA (MESSENGER RNA) A type of *RNA* that copies part of the information stored in *DNA* and carries it to the *cytoplasm*, where it is used to make a specific *protein*.

MUCUS A thick, sticky fluid that lubricates and protects the surfaces of certain *membranes* and, in the *respiratory system*, traps dust and *pathogens*.

MUSCLE A type of *tissue* that contracts—gets shorter—to produce movement.

MYELIN A fatty material that forms an insulating sheath around the *axons* of certain *neurons* and which increases their transmission speeds.

MYOFIBRIL One of thousands of parallel, rodlike bundles of *myosin* and *actin* filaments found inside a *muscle fiber*.

MYOSIN A "motor" protein consisting of thick filaments that interact with thin *actin* filaments to shorten a *myofibril* and make a *muscle* contract.

N

NASAL CAVITY The air-filled space behind the nose that is divided into two halves—left and right—and connects the nostrils to the upper part of the throat.

NEPHRON One of around a million microscopic filtration units inside each kidney that produce *urine*.

NERVE A cable-like bundle of *neurons* that relay signals between the *central nervous system* and the body.

NERVE-MUSCLE JUNCTION A place where the end of a *neuron* and a *muscle fiber* meet but do not touch (see SYNAPSE), and through which the muscle fiber receives instructions to contract.

NEURON A nervous *system cell* that generates and transmits electrical signals.

NEUROTRANSMITTER A substance released when a nerve signal reaches the end of a *neuron*, crosses the gap between that neuron and its neighbor (see SYNAPSE), and triggers a nerve signal in the neighboring neuron; it is also released at a *nerve-muscle junction*.

NEUTRON A tiny particle that lacks any electrical charge and is found inside the *nucleus* of an *atom*.

NEUTROPHIL A type of *white blood cell* that engulfs and digests *pathogens*.

NITROGEN A gas found in the air; its *atoms* are found in *amino acids*, *proteins*, *nucleic acids*, and some other *molecules* that make up the body.

NK CELL Or natural killer *cell*; a type of *lymphocyte* that plays a part in body defense by recognizing and destroying *virus*-infected cells and *tumor* cells.

NUCLEIC ACID One of a group of complex substances that include *DNA* and *RNA*, and which is built from millions of *carbon*, hydrogen, *oxygen*, *nitrogen*, and phosphorus atoms organized into subunits called *nucleotides*.

NUCLEOTIDE One of a group of building blocks used to construct *DNA* and *RNA molecules*, consisting of a *base*, a *sugar*, and a phosphorus-containing group.

NUCLEUS [ATOM] The small central core of an *atom* that contains *protons* and *neutrons*.

NUCLEUS [CELL] The control center of a *cell* that is surrounded by a double *membrane*, or envelope, and which contains the cell's *DNA*.

NUTRIENT A substance—such as a *carbohydrate, protein, fat, vitamin,* or *mineral*—that is taken into the body in food and which is required for *energy* and building *cells*.

O

OPTIC TRACT A continuation of the optic *nerve* that runs from the point where the two optic nerves cross over to the visual part of the *thalamus*.

ORGAN A body part, such as a kidney or lung, that has a specific function or functions and consists of two or more types of *tissues*.

OSTEOCYTE A type of *cell* that is found in bone *tissue*.

OVARIAN CYCLE A sequence of changes inside a woman's *ovary* that is repeated around every twenty-eight days, and during which an egg matures and is released.

OVARY One of two reproductive *organs* in a woman's body that release eggs and the *hormones* that prepare the body for pregnancy.

OXYGEN A gas found in the air that is breathed into the lungs and used by *cells* to release *energy;* its *atoms* are found in *carbohydrates, proteins,* and many other substances found inside the body.

P

PACEMAKER Alternative name for the heart's SA node; also the name given to an artificial device surgically implanted into the chest to control heart rate when the natural pacemaker is defective.

PAPILLA One of the small projections on the tongue, some of which house taste buds.

PATERNAL Describes something associated with a father.

PATHOGEN A *bacterium, virus,* or other type of *microorganism* that causes disease in humans.

PELVIS The basinlike girdle formed by the two hip bones and the sacrum that attaches the legs to the skeleton.

PEPSIN A digestive *enzyme* released into the stomach that breaks down *proteins* and works best in *acidic* conditions.

PERICYTE A spider-shaped *cell* that helps to stabilize the wall of a *capillary*.

PERISTALSIS A progressive wave of contractions of *smooth muscle* in the walls of hollow *organs* that moves material, for example, the movement of food along the *alimentary canal*.

PHOSPHOLIPID A type of *lipid,* the *molecules* of which organize themselves into double layers that form *membranes* around and inside *cells*.

PHOTORECEPTOR A type of sensory *receptor* found in the eye that responds to light by generating nerve signals.

PHOTOSYNTHESIS The process by which plants utilize the *energy* in sunlight to combine *carbon dioxide* and water to make *sugars* and *complex carbohydrates* such as *starch*.

PLACENTA A temporary *organ* that is formed in the *uterus* during pregnancy from the *tissues* of both mother and *fetus,* within which maternal and fetal blood supplies come into close contact, and through which the fetus receives *oxygen* and *nutrients*.

PLASMA The liquid part of blood that contains dissolved substances, such as food and wastes, and in which *red* and *white blood cells* and *platelets* are suspended.

PLATELET A *cell* fragment found in blood that plugs breaks in *blood vessels* and helps blood form clots.

PLEURAL MEMBRANE One of two membranes that, respectively, line the inside of the chest cavity and cover the lung, the narrow space between which is filled with fluid that enables them to slide over each other during breathing.

POLAR MOLECULE A type of *molecule,* such as water, one part of which has a slight negative electrical charge and one part has a slight positive electrical charge.

PONS The central section of the *brain stem,* which relays signals between brain and *spinal cord* and between the *cerebrum* and *cerebellum*.

PORTAL VEIN A *vein* that carries blood from one *organ* to another, such as the portal vein that carries food-rich blood from the small intestine to the liver.

PREFRONTAL CORTEX The complex region of the *cerebral cortex* at the front of the brain that is involved with intelligence, learning, reasoning, memory, judgment, and personality.

PROTEIN One of a group of varied and versatile substances, made mainly from *carbon,* hydrogen, *oxygen,* and *nitrogen atoms* and built from subunits called *amino acids* that perform a wide range of functions as, for example, *enzymes, antibodies,* or structural proteins.

PROTON A tiny particle with a positive electrical charge that is found inside the *nucleus* of an *atom*.

PTERYGOID Pronounced "terry-goid"; one of four *muscles* that contribute to movements of the lower jaw.

PUBERTY A period of rapid growth in the early teens during which the reproductive system matures and the body takes on an adult appearance.

PYRUVATE A substance produced by the breakdown of *glucose* and which is then broken down, with the help of *oxygen,* inside a *mitochondrion* to release *energy, carbon dioxide,* and water.

Q

QUADRICEPS FEMORIS A set of four thigh *muscles* that contract, pulling on *tendons* that cross the knee, to straighten the leg.

R

RECEPTOR [CELL MEMBRANE] A *protein molecule* that projects from a *cell membrane* and which binds specifically to another molecule such as a *hormone* or a *neurotransmitter*.

RECEPTOR [SENSORY] A specialized nerve *cell* or the ending of a *sensory neuron* that responds to a specific *stimulus* by sending signals to the *central nervous system*.

RED BLOOD CELL A type of blood *cell* that lacks a *nucleus*, is filled with *hemoglobin*, and transports *oxygen*.

REFLEX An automatic, split-second, unconscious response to a *stimulus* that often protects the body from danger.

REPLICATION The process by which a *DNA molecule* makes a precise copy of itself.

RESPIRATORY SYSTEM The *system*, consisting of the *nasal cavity*, throat, *larynx*, *trachea*, *bronchi*, and lungs, by which *oxygen* is taken into the body and waste *carbon dioxide* is removed.

RETINA The thin, light-sensitive *membrane* that lines the inside of the rear half of the eye and contains millions of *photoreceptors*.

RIBOSOME One of many small structures inside a *cell*—either free in the *cytoplasm* or attached to *rough endoplasmic reticulum*—in which the assembly of *proteins* from *amino acids* takes place.

RNA (RIBONUCLEIC ACID) A substance that consists of a single strand of *nucleic acid* and which copies and translates the instructions stored in *DNA* to make *proteins*.

ROD A type of *photoreceptor* found in the *retina* of the eye that provides black-and-white vision and works best in dim light.

ROUGH ENDOPLASMIC RETICULUM A network of interconnected, flattened *membrane* sacs studded with *ribosomes* inside a *cell's cytoplasm* that makes *proteins* and other substances and provides channels for their transport and storage.

S

SALIVA Watery liquid released into the mouth by the salivary *glands*, especially during chewing, which moistens and lubricates food to aid swallowing.

SA NODE (SINOATRIAL NODE) A small region of the wall of the right *atrium* that acts as the heart's natural *pacemaker* by triggering and controlling the rate of heartbeats.

SARCOMERE One of many units of highly arranged *actin* and *myosin* filaments that are repeated along the length of a *muscle fiber's myofibril*.

SELF-BRACING Describes how skull bones reinforce each other when locked together by immovable *sutures*.

SENSORY NEURON A type of *neuron* that carries signals from sensory *receptors* to the *central nervous system*.

SEX CHROMOSOMES One of the twenty-three pairs of *chromosomes* found in the *nucleus* of most body *cells* and that determine whether an individual is male or female.

SKELETAL MUSCLE A type of *muscle* that is attached by *tendons* to the bones of the skeleton, moves the body, and is under conscious control.

SMOOTH MUSCLE A type of *muscle* that is lo-cated in and produces movement in the walls of hollow *organs*, such as the stomach and bladder, and which is not under conscious control.

SOLUTION A mixture consisting of one substance that is dissolved in another, such as salt dissolved in water.

SOUND WAVE A vibration that spreads through the air and is detected by the ears.

SPHINCTER A ring of *muscle* that surrounds an opening and which opens or closes to control the flow of liquid through that opening.

SPINAL CORD The bundle of nervous *tissue* that extends down the back from the brain and relays signals between the brain and the body, processes information, and controls many *reflexes*.

SPINAL NERVE One of thirty-one pairs of *nerves* that arise from the *spinal cord*.

STARCH A *complex carbohydrate* produced by plants that, when eaten, is broken down to *glucose* by digestive *enzymes*.

STEM CELL An unspecialized *cell* that divides by *mitosis* to produce multiple identical copies, some of which give rise to a range of specialized cells.

STEREOSCOPIC Describes the three-dimensional vision produced when the brain compares the slightly different, overlapping views "seen" by left and right eyes.

STERNUM Or breastbone; the flat bone at the front of the chest that is attached to the ribs by strips of *cartilage*.

STEROID One of a group of *lipids* that have rings of *carbon atoms* in their *molecules*, including *cholesterol* and some *hormones* such as estrogen.

STIMULUS (plural: STIMULI) Any change in the body's external or internal environment that causes a response by the nervous *system*, such as the smell of food causing a feeling of hunger and the release of *saliva*.

STRETCH RECEPTOR A sensory *receptor* found in *muscles* and *tendons* that responds to the stretching of those *tissues* and sends signals to the brain that aid in the coordination of posture, balance, and movement.

SUBCLAVIAN VEIN One of two *veins*, left and right, that carry blood from the arms toward the heart.

SUGAR A simple, sweet-tasting *carbohydrate* such as *glucose*.

SURFACTANT A substance that reduces the surface tension—the "skin"—on the surface of water.

SUTURE An immovable *joint* between two bones in the skull.

SYNAPSE The junction between two *neurons*—or between a neuron and a *muscle fiber*—in which they do not touch but are separated by a narrow gap.

SYNOVIAL FLUID An oily liquid that is secreted by the *membrane* within a *synovial joint*, and which lubricates that joint.

SYNOVIAL JOINT A freely movable *joint* in which the bone ends are covered by *cartilage* and separated by a fluid-filled space.

SYSTEM A group of linked *organs* that work together to perform specific functions.

T

T CELL (T LYMPHOCYTE) A type of *white blood cell* that plays a key part in the *immune system* by destroying *pathogen*-infected cells and *cancer* cells or by activating other immune system cells.

TENDON A cord or sheet of strong *connective tissue* that attaches a *skeletal muscle* to a bone.

TESTIS (plural: TESTES) One of two reproductive *organs* in a man's body that produce sperm and the *hormones* that prepare the body for reproduction.

THALAMUS Twin egg-shaped masses of *gray matter* located between the *cerebral hemispheres* that relay incoming sensory signals to areas of the *cerebral cortex*.

TISSUE An organized group of one type of *cell*, or similar types of cells, that work together to perform a specific function or functions.

TISSUE FLUID A fluid derived from the liquid that seeps out of *capillaries*, is found in the small spaces between *cells*, and transfers substances between blood and cells and provides a constant environment around cells.

TOXIN A poison, specifically one released inside the body by a *pathogenic bacterium*.

TRACHEA Or windpipe; the tube located in the chest that carries air between the *larynx* and *bronchi*, and which is reinforced with *cartilage* rings.

TRILLION A number equivalent to one thousand *billion* (1,000,000,000,000).

tRNA (TRANSFER RNA) A type of *RNA* that collects a specific *amino acid* and delivers it to a *ribosome* during *protein* manufacture.

TUMOR An abnormal *growth of cells* that may be the result of *cancer*.

U

UMAMI A savory taste, one of five tastes in food that are detected by the tongue.

UREA A *nitrogen*-containing waste substance that is produced by the liver from excess *amino acids* and which is removed from the body in *urine*.

URETER A tube that carries *urine* from a kidney to the bladder.

URETHRA A tube that carries *urine* from the bladder to the outside of the body.

URINE A liquid produced by the kidneys that contains water and salts that are excess to the body's requirements, as well as dissolved wastes, such as *urea*.

UTERUS A hollow *organ* with a thick, muscular wall that is part of the female reproductive system, and which is where a fertilized egg settles to develop into a baby.

V

VEIN A *blood vessel* that carries blood toward the heart. Most veins carry *oxygen*-poor blood.

VENTRICLE [BRAIN] One of the interconnected, fluid-filled cavities in the brain through which *cerebrospinal fluid* circulates.

VENTRICLE [HEART] One of the two larger chambers of the heart that pump blood to either the body (left ventricle) or the lungs (right ventricle).

VENULE A very small *vein*.

VERTEBRA (plural: VERTEBRAE) One of the irregular-shaped bones that make up the vertebral column, or backbone.

VESTIGIAL Describes a structure that may once have had a role but is now apparently functionless.

VILLUS (plural: VILLI) One of the millions of fingerlike projections from the lining of the small intestine that increase the surface area for the *digestion* and absorption of *nutrients*.

VIRUS One of a group of nonliving packages of *proteins* and *nucleic acids* that invade *cells* in order to reproduce and which cause diseases such as flu.

VISUAL CORTEX The area of the *cerebral cortex* that receives and interprets signals from the eyes, producing "images" of the outside world.

VISUAL FIELD The entire area in front of a person that he or she is able to see when the head is still.

VITAMIN One of more than thirteen *nutri-ents*, including vitamins A and C, that are needed in minute amounts in the diet to maintain normal body functioning.

VOCAL CORDS One of two *membrane* folds that are stretched across the *larynx* and produce sounds when air passes between them.

W

WATER VAPOR A form of water present in the air, produced when *molecules* evaporate from liquid water.

WHITE BLOOD CELL One of a group of blood *cells*, including *lymphocytes*, *macrophages*, *monocytes*, and *neutrophils*, that as part of the *immune system* form a defense force that fights infection.

WHITE MATTER A *tissue* found in the *central nervous system* that consists of *axons* surrounded by insulating *myelin* and which forms the inner part of the *cerebrum* and the outer part of the *spinal cord*.

INDEX

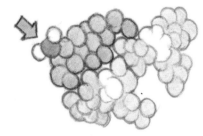

24, 26–27; of egg and sperm during fertilization, 308–9; migration of ions and molecules through, 26, 34, 39, 42–43, 133–35, 151–52

cells: communication between, 26, 52, 150–51; description, 14–15; nutrients from blood, 54; sex (*see* egg; sperm); size, 16, 50; support structure, 28–30, 52; types, 50–51; wastes, 14, 39, 54

cerebellum, 160, 161, 162, 200–201, 204

cerebrospinal fluid, 162–63, 164

cervix, 305, 306, 307

chewing, 106–7, 109, 110–11

childbirth, 215, 283, 318

cholesterol, 26, 131

chromosomes: contribution by both parents, 293, 294, 295, 309; description, 45; during meiosis, 293, 294–95; during mitosis, 46–49; number in cell nucleus, 293, 294, 300, 309; X and Y, 295, 309

chyme, 115, 120, 122

cilia. *See under* "hair"

circulatory system: carbon dioxide gathered by, 57, 58–59, 67, 69, 88–89; description, 76–77 (*see also specific parts of the body*); location in the body, 54; network (*see* arteries; capillaries; veins); oxygen delivery, 57, 58–59; pump (*see* heart); response to danger, 198; response to heat and cold, 222

clitoris, 304, 305

cochlea, 169, 170, 171

collagen, 54, 80, 256, 257, 258, 264

colon, 142–43, 144

communication: body–brain, 158, 159, 160, 161, 188–89; between cells, 26, 52, 150–51; between people (*see* language; sounds, making; speech); *see also* nerves

connective tissue, 54–55, 66, 72, 75, 264

cornea, 174, 175, 177, 185

corpus callosum, 157

cortex: auditory, 171, 173, 205; description, 155, 157, 158–59; "language" (*see* Broca's area; Wernicke's area); location in the body, 157, 162–63; motor and premotor, 158, 172, 173, 200–201, 204; prefrontal, 198, 200, 205; premotor, 200; sensory, 161, 192, 193, 197, 204, 205; smell, 205; taste, 205; visual, 180, 181, 182, 183, 187, 205

crying, 185

cytoplasm, 12, 40, 42, 240, 245, 295

cytoskeleton, 28–30, 230

D

defecation, 146–47

dendrite, 150, 151, 153, 154, 155, 236

dermis, 192, 220, 221, 222, 223, 249, 252

diaphragm, 64, 92, 96, 127, 147

diffusion, 23, 69, 89, 314

digestion of food, 114–25

digestive system, 54, 127

diseases, 238, 244–45, 248–51, 253

DNA (deoxyribonucleic acid): during cell division, 46–49; damage or mutation, 246, 248; description, 32, 33, 44; instructions copied onto RNA, 34–35; in mitochondria, 42; replication, 44–45; total length in nucleus, 22; in viruses, 238, 244, 245

drugs and medications, 131, 228, 245

ducts: bile, 120, 128; in cochlea, 170; in kidney, 137, 139; pancreatic, 121; sweat, 222; that empty the lymph, 232

ductus deferens, 300, 302, 303, 304, 305

duodenum, 114, 115, 120–21, 126

dura mater, 164, 165

dust. *See* particles from the outside world

E

eardrum, 168, 169

ears, 168–69. *See also* hearing

eating. *See* food; tasting

egg: born with lifetime supply, 296; chromosomes in, 293, 295; description, 50; during fertilization, 308–9; journey to the uterus, 298–99; release, 215, 292, 296

ejaculation, 302, 304–5

elbow, 265, 277

electrons, 17, 18–19, 21, 22, 42–43

embryo-to-be and embryo, 309–13

endocrine system, 54, 208–9, 210–11

endometrium, 297, 310, 311, 312–13, 314

endoplasmic reticulum, 14, 38, 39

energy for cells: from glucose, 23, 39, 40–41, 132; regulated by mitochondria, 14, 42, 78; storage and release from ATP, 42–43, 262

energy for muscles and tissues, 39, 40

enzymes: in blastocysts, 312; in bone to break down collagen, 258; in cells (*see* enzymes in cells); for food digestion, 119, 120, 121, 122, 125, 132, 231; proteins accelerate action, 31; in saliva, 111; in

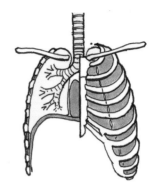

sperm, 306

enzymes in cells: activation by hormones, 210, 211; to break down ATP and glucose, 40–41; to break down cell waste, 39, 231; to break down pyruvate, 42; for DNA copying or replication, 35, 44, 45, 240, 241, 244

epidermis, 192, 220–21, 222–23, 224, 246–47, 252

epididymis, 300, 301

epiglottis, 63, 112, 113

epinephrine, 198, 199, 210

epithelial cells, 51, 103, 104, 125, 222

epithelial tissue, 52–53, 55

erection, 305

esophagus, 63, 112, 113, 114

estrogen, 215, 296, 297, 310, 316

eyeball, 175, 176–77, 180, 181, 184–85

eyelid, 174, 175, 184, 185

eyes, 159, 161, 166, 174–79, 180, 184–85. *See also* seeing

F

fallopian tube, 292, 298–99, 305, 306, 308, 309

fat cells, 50, 316, 317

fats, in food, 101

fatty acids, 24, 39, 40, 119, 121, 125, 131

fear, 198–99

feces, 144–47

females: childbirth by, 215, 283, 318; making milk, 214, 215, 316–17; menopause, 292; menstrual cycle, 296–97, 310; ovarian cycle, 296; pelvis shape, 283; reproductive system, 292; sex cells (*see* egg)

fertilization, 297, 299, 308–9, 310

fetus, 314–19

fibroblasts, 51, 54, 55

fingers, 277, 278–79, 286, 287

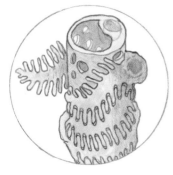

body, 64, 97, 217; response to danger, 198, 199

luteinizing hormone (LH), 215, 296, 300

lymph, 232, 234

lymphatic system, 55, 232–33. *See also* nodes, lymph

lymphocytes, 51, 72, 73, 232, 234, 235. *See also* T cells

lymph vessels, 122, 124, 125, 232–33, 234, 256, 258

lysosomes, 14, 38, 39, 231

M

macrophages: bacteria killed by, 131, 230–31, 235, 237, 243; description, 51, 130; foreign debris destroyed by, 131, 250; sperm killed by, 306

males, 292, 293, 300, 302–3. *See also* sperm

marrow, 71, 73, 234, 256

mast cells, 226, 250, 251

medulla: brain stem, 160, 161, 171, 202, 234; kidney, 136, 137

meiosis, 293, 294–95, 300

melanocytes, 246, 248, 249

membranes: cell (*see* cell membrane); in the cochlea, 170, 171; eardrum, 168, 169; envelope of a virus, 238, 239, 244; in the lungs, 64, 65, 67, 69, 93; mitochondrion, 42, 43; mucus-lined in the nasal cavity, 61; nuclear envelope, 26, 34, 46, 49; in the retina, 178, 179; in the small intestine, 122; synovial, 264; which protect the brain, 164, 165

membrane sacs, 39, 153, 231, 240, 243, 246

memory, 103, 158, 204–5

men. *See* males

menopause, 292

menstrual cycle, 296–97, 310

mental abilities, 157, 158–59, 198. *See also* memory

microscopes, 10, 12, 14

microtubules, 29, 30, 39, 46–49, 294, 295

midbrain, 160, 161, 171, 180

minerals. *See* vitamins and minerals

mitochondria: energy supplied to the cell by, 14, 41, 42–43, 300; in muscle cells, 78, 79, 261; recycling of worn-out, 39; in sperm, 300

mitosis, 46–49, 221, 300

molecules, 20–21, 23, 24

monocytes, 72, 73, 226, 227

motions. *See* movements

motor neurons: connection with muscle, 260–61; signals carried by, 188, 190–91, 194, 198–99, 201–2

mouth, 94, 107, 109

movements: bending and twisting, 268; controlled by the brain, 158, 161, 172, 173, 200–201, 261; coordination of, 83, 157, 161, 200–201, 255, 288–89; flexing the fingers, 278–79; grasping objects, 267, 277, 278–79; head, 161, 272–73; impulses for (*see* motor neurons; nerves, connection with muscles); lifting the foot, 194, 195, 289; rising from sitting, or climbing, 283; shoulder and arm, 275, 276–77; walking or running, 267, 284, 286, 287, 288–89

mucus, 61, 103, 111, 113, 116–17, 251, 306

muscles: connection with nerves, 260, 261, 262; contraction and relaxation, 49, 259, 261, 262–63, 265, 277; description, 51, 260–61; energy used by, 39, 40, 96; nerves (*see* motor neurons; nerves, connection with muscles); skeletal, 90, 190, 199, 201, 232; smooth, 190, 202, 203, 251, 302, 305, 316; timing of contractions, 201, 288; *see also specific parts of the body*

muscular system, 55

myelin sheath, 188, 189

myofibril, 260, 261. *See also* actin; myosin

myosin, 49, 260–61, 262–63

N

nails, 221

nasal cavity, 60–63, 94, 103, 113, 166, 185, 270

nephron, 136, 137, 138

nerves: bone, 258; cells (*see* neurons); connection with muscles, 260, 261, 262; cranial, 188; description, 188–89; in the nipple, 316, 317; optic, 178, 180, 181; in the small intestine, 122; in the spine, 188, 190

nervous system: autonomic, 161, 175, 177, 190, 198, 202–3; cells (*see* neurons); communication, 150–51; description, 188–89; location in the body, 54; and movement (*see* motor neurons; nerves, connection

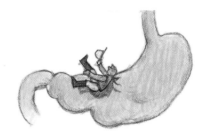

with muscles); sending signals, 152–53. *See also* brain; brain stem; spinal cord

neurons: brain network, 154–55, 204, 212; description, 50, 150, 151; linking, 191, 194, 196; motor (*see* motor neurons); sensory (*see* sensory neurons); signals sent between, 152–53, 188, 204

neurotransmitters, 153, 170, 261

neutrons, 17, 18, 19

neutrophils, 51, 72, 73, 226, 227, 306

nitrogen, 19, 24

NK (natural killer) cells, 242, 243, 248

nodes: AV and SA, 82, 83, 96; axon, 188; lymph, 232, 233, 234–37, 248

nose. *See* nasal cavity; smelling

nucleic acids, 24. *See also* DNA; RNA

nucleotides, 32, 33, 34, 36, 240, 241

nucleus, 14, 17, 21, 70, 71, 300, 308–9

nutrients, 100–101, 127, 131, 299, 310, 313, 314

O

optic nerve, 178, 180, 181

organs, 54, 64, 166, 202, 256, 267, 281

osteoblasts, 51, 258

osteoclasts, 51, 258, 259

osteocytes, 51, 256, 257, 258

ovarian cycle, 296

ovaries, 209, 215, 292, 296, 297, 316

ovulation, 296, 306

oxygen: body's demand for, 96, 198; carried by red blood cells, 50, 58–59, 67, 71, 88–89; cell energy cycle, 42–43, 57, 78; exchange with carbon dioxide, 58, 59, 67, 68–69, 76, 88–89; made by plants, 58, 59; molecule description, 18, 19, 20–21, 24; supply for the fetus, 314

oxytocin, 214, 215, 316, 317